COMBAT EFFECTIVENESS IN THE PACIFIC WAR

COMBAT EFFECTIVENESS IN THE PACIFIC WAR

HOW AMERICAN AND JAPANESE FORCES FOUGHT THEIR CAMPAIGNS IN WW2

RICHARD ALLAN BURKLUND
LIEUTENANT COLONEL,
UNITED STATES ARMY (RETIRED)
PH.D., UNIVERSITY OF GLASGOW,
UNITED KINGDOM

FRONTLINE
BOOKS

COMBAT EFFECTIVENESS IN THE PACIFIC WAR
How American and Japanese Forces Fought Their Campaigns in WW2

First published in Great Britain in 2026
by Frontline Books
An imprint of
Pen & Sword Books Ltd
Yorkshire - Philadelphia

ISBN 9781036181901

A CIP catalogue record for this book is available from the British Library

Typeset by Lapiz Digital
Printed and bound in the UK by CPI Group (UK) Ltd,
Croydon, CR0 4YY.

Printed on paper from a sustainable source by
CPI Group (UK) Ltd, Croydon, CR0 4YY

The Publisher's authorised representative in the EU for product safety is
Authorised Rep Compliance Ltd., Ground Floor, 71 Lower Baggot Street,
Dublin D02 P593, Ireland.
www.arccompliance.com

For a complete list of Pen & Sword titles please contact
PEN & SWORD BOOKS LTD
47 Church Street, Barnsley, South Yorkshire, S70 2AS, England
E-mail: enquiries@pen-and-sword.co.uk
Website: www.pen-and-sword.co.uk
or
PEN & SWORD BOOKS
1950 Lawrence Rd, Havertown, PA 19083, USA
E-mail: uspen-and-sword@casematepublishers.com

To the United States Army:

'I have eaten your bread and salt.

I have drunk your water and wine.

The deaths ye died I have watched beside

And the lives ye led were mine.'

Rudyard Kipling, *Prelude*, Stanza 1

With love, admiration, and gratitude to W5, LKV, RCB, TP and AM (U of G!), my mother and father, my sister and brother, and especially VSB and KLB!

CONTENTS

LIST OF FIGURES

MILITARY MAP SYMBOLOGY

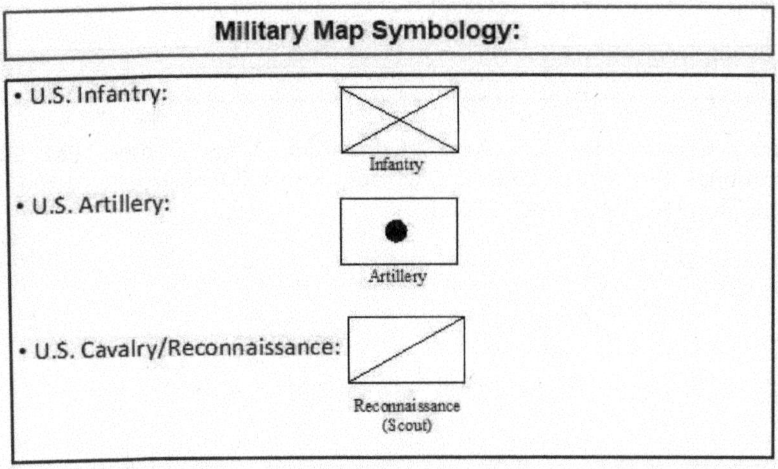

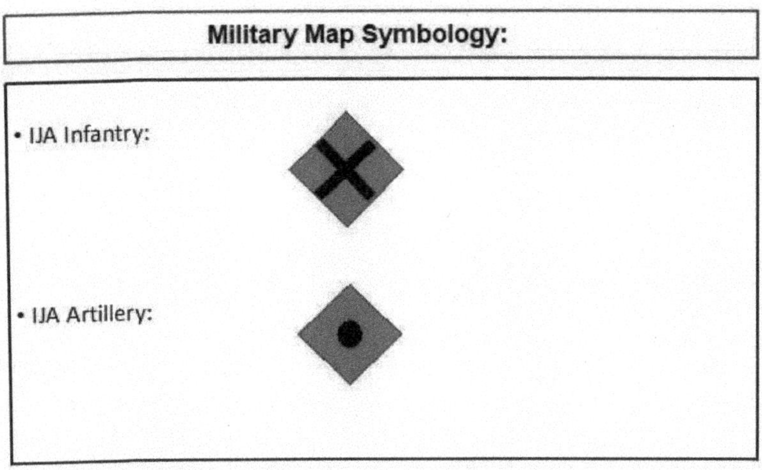

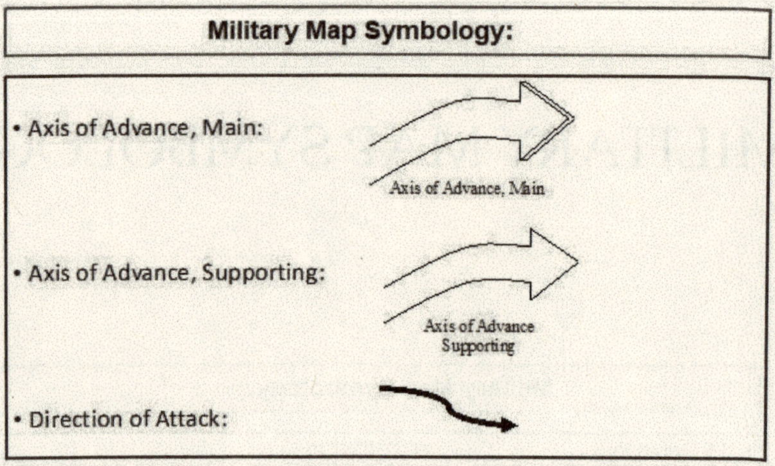

(Source: Commander, US Army Combined Arms Center, FM 101-5-1, Operational Terms and Graphics, Headquarters, Department of the Army, Washington DC, 1985/1997/2004.)

INTRODUCTION

One of the most popular historical debates about the Second World War has concerned the relative combat effectiveness of the adversaries in the European theatre. Some historians have promoted the tactical superiority of the Axis forces (particularly the German Wehrmacht) over the United States Army. Their contention was that the Axis forces were much more competent and combat effective than their adversaries and that the Allies eventually won only because of their overwhelming resources and superior firepower. Other historians countered that the US Army was successful in the Second World War because of its mastery of combined arms warfare and its ability to quickly adapt to new and unanticipated conditions and environments.[1] Surprisingly, a similar comparative analysis of combat effectiveness has not been conducted for the Pacific War. This Eurocentric bias has been attributed to the influence of the 'Germany first' strategy, the maritime nature of the Pacific theatre (which lends itself to a predominantly naval-centric narrative), that the greater weight of press coverage went to the easier to reach and more hospitable European theatre, and the avoidance of the troubling issue of the racially inspired atrocities committed by both sides in the war.[2]

Chapter One

STRATEGIC CULTURE AND THE WILL TO FIGHT IN THE PACIFIC WAR

> 'In all matters which pertain to an army, organization [*sic*], discipline and tactics, the human heart in the supreme moment of battle is the basic factor. It is rarely taken into account; and often strange errors are the result. We must consider it!'[3]

Introduction

Like the two-faced Roman god, Janus, we look to the past to see what we can learn while simultaneously gazing toward the future to see how we might use this knowledge. Over eighty years have passed since the Second World War, but it remains relevant as probably the most significant event of the twentieth century. As such, it continues to resonate into the twenty-first century. While contemporary adversaries and allies formulate goals and objectives to address the twenty-first century strategic environment, particularly in the Indo-Pacific area the study of the Second World War offers significant insights in the competitive arenas of diplomacy, information, the military and economics. Unfortunately, the US Army's official history seems to have neglected its many campaigns in the Pacific theatre. The focus on the conflict in Europe overlooked not only the global scope of army operations in the war (which continues to this day) but also the army's demonstrated adaptability to fight and win in the diverse conditions of the Indo-Pacific theatre.[4]

In the fight against Japan, pre-war American hubris quickly gave way to alarm and embarrassment as the highly effective Japanese land, air and naval forces won decisive victories in Singapore, the Philippines and Burma.[5] The shock and awe of these defeats earned the Japanese a grudging respect from their American opponents, however this seems to have been forgotten in the eighty years since the war. The prevailing attitude now is that the American victory was inevitable, and that the Japanese were always doomed to failure because they could never match the industrial might of the US.[6] While the Americans did eventually enjoy superiority in firepower and logistics, this view unfairly dismisses the fighting abilities of the Japanese forces and ignores the fact that over three and half years of vicious fighting were required to earn this victory.[7] In contrast to this belief in the inevitability of American victory we are presented with the epic saga of the US Marine Corps in the Pacific. This narrative enshrines the courage and sacrifice of the Marines in their gallant struggle against their implacable Japanese foes forgetting the seeming ineluctable defeat that awaited them. As one army commander remarked at the time, 'Out here, mention is seldom seen of the achievements of the Army ground troops whereas the Marines are blown up to the skies.'[8] Despite the fact that the army contributed 3 field armies and 21 divisions to the Pacific theatre and suffered 41,592 ground troops killed or missing in action and 145,706 wounded (not counting the additional 24,230 casualties suffered by the US Army Air Force (USAAF), appreciation of the army's contribution was diminished by unbalanced press coverage that favored the depiction of the US Marine Corps as a glamorous and elite force, propagandising their epic feats of arms.[9] Paradoxically, in this telling, American victory is not assured or assumed, and success is not attributed to mere numerical superiority but instead to American valour and fighting spirit.[10]

During the Second World War, no other army or marine division saw more combat in the Pacific than the 7th Infantry Division. The division displayed great *esprit de corps* and it serves as an excellent model of the will to fight at both the unit and individual levels.[11] The 7th Infantry Division's experience in the Pacific provides a unique opportunity for a combat case study of the Second World War. This book offers a tactical-level perspective of combat performance and mission accomplishment over an extended period and across changing battlefield conditions and environments, derived from official unit histories, participants' war diaries, doctrinal manuals and reference works, including an analysis of the operational environment, the weather, the effects of weapons, unit organisation and the condition of the units involved. While no single unit can exemplify an entire army, by studying the 7th Infantry Division as it fought from the North

Pacific to the Central Pacific, to the Philippines, and finally to Okinawa, it serves as an excellent point of reference to examine both American and Japanese combat effectiveness and their relative strategic/tactical cultures. This approach allows for the examination of the various parts to better understand the whole.[12]

Rather than accepting the premise that American industrial capacity and the sheer numerical superiority that it produced were the only reasons that the US was able to prevail over its allegedly qualitatively superior foes, I believe that American victory in the Pacific War owed as much to the decisive importance of willpower and strategic culture as it did to numerical superiority.

This study is composed of two principal elements: first, an analysis of the battles of the US 7th Infantry Division in the Pacific theatre during the Second World War and second, a comparison of the strategic cultures of Japan and the United States as a backdrop to those battles. In following the campaigns of a single division, we explore the ways in which American strategic and tactical culture allowed US forces to overcome the challenges of adverse weather, terrain and a tenacious enemy, and the decisive importance of willpower and the less explored influence of strategic culture on the outcome of the war.[13] Operating at times without the support of their usual combat multipliers of close air support, armour and artillery, the 7th Infantry Division's successes in battle illustrate the importance of understanding both quantifiable, technical combat force factors and the intangible cultural elements that also influence combat effectiveness, like the will to fight. We acknowledge the American superiority in some technologies and weapons, but we find that the Japanese also held distinct advantages and that American victory was due as much to the combination of good leadership and sound combined arms doctrine and tactics and not merely to overwhelming mass.

Strategic culture was of equal importance to the outcomes of the Pacific War as the often cited imbalance of power calculus. In Japan's case, its martial culture contributed to both its initial successes and its eventual failure. I explore the questions of relative combat effectiveness by examining the influence of strategic culture and the power of elusive concepts like the 'will to fight' and the 'will to sacrifice'. Recent research has identified many variables that can help us to understand the complex and amorphous nature of the human will to fight. The simplified model that I use to measure the will to fight includes political, economic and military factors, such as technology, industrial capacity, political-military relations and popular support; relevant contexts like government type, national identity and conflict duration;

and mechanisms that influence will to fight such as indoctrination, social pressures and casualties.[14] Also drawn from recent research are the metrics that populate a simplified model of the disposition to fight from the individual soldier to the society. These factors that influence the soldier, the organisation and the society include, but are not limited to identity, leadership, training, support, doctrine, strategy, motivations and expectations.[15]

This cultural approach to military history also examines the personal perspectives of American and Japanese veterans to explore the intangible factors that are so essential to understanding psychology, identity and morale, and thus gain an appreciation of both American and Japanese strategic culture and its effects on combat. I compare Japanese and American leadership, discipline, unit cohesion, operations, logistics, fire support and intelligence, and the strengths and weaknesses of their respective approaches to doctrine, organisation and training for their impact on morale and will to fight.[16]

We see that the American will to win at any cost (even if it meant committing genocide), contrasted with the Japanese will to sacrifice (even if that meant complete self-extermination), and the related themes of the ideologies represented by *gyokusai*, *bushidō*, the *Senjinkun* and *yamato damashii*. This synthetic approach takes us beyond a surface analysis of battle events (the measures of performance) to a 'deep dive' into the linkages between strategic culture and its influence and consequences (the measures of effectiveness).

Military History and Strategic Culture

Scholars have taken a cultural approach to the interpretation of military history for as long as history has been studied. In his *History of the Peloponnesian War*, Thucydides describes the political and cultural differences between the warring city-states as a way of explaining their relative behaviours.[17] I contend that historical analysis of the strategic and tactical culture of the American and Japanese forces in the Second World War, comparing their respective beliefs and modes of behaviour illustrates how it shaped their objectives, means, organisation and actions.[18] I further contend that the causes of success and/or failure were deeply rooted in intrinsic American and Japanese values. What then are the body of attitudes and beliefs that guided and circumscribed Japanese and American thought on strategic questions? What influenced the way strategic issues were formulated? How were the vocabulary and the perceptual parameters of their respective strategic debates established?[19]

Strategy, Tactics and Doctrine

Before launching into a discussion of strategic culture and the importance of the human factor of the will to win we must first define and describe the overarching framework of the field. When referring to a general plan of action, a concept or an organisational 'vision' many people use the term strategy to describe what is no more than an outline of current ideas that may become future actions. This is inappropriate because it fails to recognise the complexity of true strategy and strategic thinking.[20] This section will provide an examination of strategic theory and its applicability and relationship to strategic culture.

Military theorists have categorised warfare into three broad levels: strategic, operational and tactical. These divisions were first developed during the Napoleonic Wars and were further refined during the American Civil War and the Franco-Prussian War. Although many use these terms, few really understand their distinct meanings and proper applications. They will have an important influence on the rest of the study therefore it is essential to recognise that there are differences between tactics and strategy.

Carl von Clausewitz distinguished the levels by their relationships to one another in time, space and mass. He developed the traditional view that tactics concerned what happened on the battlefield while strategy involved the events that led to and from the battlefield.[21] Von Clausewitz further concluded that tactical victories were meaningless if they were not the means to obtain a political end that would result in peace.[22] He theorised a link (*Verbindung*) between strategy and tactics along a continuum of effort for the purposes of achieving political objectives.[23] The proper tactical objective to be attained could only be determined by a study of national strategy. 'To bring a war, or any one of its campaigns to a successful close requires a thorough grasp of national policy. On that level strategy and policy coalesce.'[24]

It is thus a premise that political goals guide strategic objectives to provide the purpose, focus and justification for strategic and tactical actions.[25] It has been said that 'strategy is the art of the possible' but it is difficult to know what really is possible.[26] It is nevertheless assumed that the future can be studied and anticipated, and that current choices can influence the future environment. Strategists study the environment and develop a strategy that identifies possibilities and then provides direction for future action.[27] In seeking to create both synergy and symmetry of the political, economic and military power available, strategy follows a linear process considering objectives (ends), ways (concepts) and means (resources), expressing a calculated and logical relationship between the concepts, capabilities and resources that will create desired outcomes with acceptable levels of risk.

Tactics and strategy both consider the ends, ways and means as courses of action are developed, and they are both bounded by the criteria of suitability, feasibility and acceptability; however, they differ in their scope, assumptions and premises.[28] Strategy is constrained by the environment within which it operates, bounded and defined by the physical geography, the international and domestic political system, and by the cultures and beliefs of the many actors who live in the environment. This environment is a complex interactive system, where institutions, organisations and differing beliefs and worldviews challenge, contradict and collide. Finally, as an inherently human process, strategy is influenced by human passions, values and cultural perceptions.[29]

As modern military theory evolved the operational level was seen as a link between the strategic and tactical levels of war. The development of the operational level of war has been attributed to Helmuth von Moltke, as demonstrated by the 'operational art' that he employed in leading Prussian forces in the 1860s and 1870s.[30] In actual practice these three levels of war tend to be blurred, each involving planning, analysis, preparation and execution functions.

Throughout the twentieth century these concepts matured into a paradigm that depicts national strategy along a horizontal plane of political, economic, psychological, and military elements and military strategy in a vertical continuum of strategic, operational and tactical levels. In this continuum, military strategy occupies the top tier of a hierarchical structure that includes tactics and operations. They are distinguished from one another by differing functional, temporal and geographic aspects. Functionally and temporally, tactics is the domain of battles, which can range from a firefight between two platoons or involve a battle between two corps and is measured in minutes, days or weeks. The operational level resides between the vertical hierarchy of strategy and tactics and is designed to achieve the optimal mix of ends, ways and means. Operational art encompasses the spectrum of the campaign, a series of battles linked together in task and purpose, taking place over a longer period. Strategy occupies the domain of conflict between nations and other international actors with an even greater time horizon. Tactics plays out on a narrow geography, operations occur on a broader regional playing field and strategy can be theatre-wide, intercontinental or global.[31] This then represents the modern continuum of strategy to tactics.

Let's now examine the relationship between doctrine, strategy and tactics. Doctrine is essential to military organisations both as the method whereby timeless principles of combat and lessons learned are disseminated to the force as well as the expression of how that force conceptualises warfare. Doctrine is both a process and a method that encompasses organising, manning, equipping, modernising, training, deploying and employing the force. Doctrine reflects a military institutions' preparations for combat and represents its understanding of the strategic and tactical realities that it faces.[32] Finally, doctrine represents a military's institutional belief system about its duties, roles and relationships within society. This belief system determines the way the military fights, the relationship it has with the state and society and its military culture. These are the products of the broader cultural, political, social and environmental domains in which this belief system and military culture developed. Military doctrinal ontology follows a hierarchy of technical manuals, tactical manuals, operational treatises and strategic policies. The full spectrum of strategic and operational concepts is delineated in doctrine. Doctrine is thus a tangible expression of strategic and tactical culture.[33] Furthermore, there is a relationship to be explored between doctrine, strategic culture and tactical culture.

The Cultural Roots of Warfare

In 1937, Alfred Vagts began to explore the cultural roots of warfare in his *A History of Militarism*.[34] The concept that there are national 'ways of war' was further advanced in the early twentieth century by military theorists like Julian Corbett.[35] He made a distinction between the continental national strategy of Germany and the maritime national strategy of Great Britain that was based on the differing geographic influences on the respective national characters, the Germans being influenced by their central European location to focus on land warfare and the British as an island nation focusing on sea power.[36] This argument was refined by Sir Basil H. Liddell Hart when he advocated the 'indirect approach' as the proper, traditional 'British Way in Warfare'; avoiding large-scale land warfare and leveraging sea power for economic gain.[37]

However, it can be exceedingly difficult to define and understand strategic culture. Any definition of culture is liable to suffer from vague boundaries owing to the complexity involved with deciding what elements to include and what to exclude.[38] The primary difference rests on whether to include human behaviour within the definition or whether to exclude it.[39] Thus, scholars do not agree on how to define strategic culture or on a precise methodology to study it. There is also a great deal of confusion over what strategic culture can explain, how it is supposed to explain it, and how much it will explain.[40] Nevertheless, some analysts have said that while culture 'may be vague ... it is not mysterious', and that it is possible to identify its fundamental characteristics.[41]

Clifford Geertz defined culture as

> an historically transmitted pattern of meanings embodied in symbols, a system of inherited conceptions expressed in symbolic form by means of which men communicate, perpetuate, and develop their knowledge about and attitudes towards life.[42]

This has provided a useful model to historians to use in understanding how patterns of meanings could lead to distinct behaviours.[43] One prominent theory on strategic culture was first developed during the Second World War and then was further defined during the Cold War by sociologists and anthropologists. It posited that distinctive cultural patterns could be detected and that they shaped both individual personalities and the society. This school produced a wide range of 'national character studies' of both Germany and Japan. Particularly revelatory were the insights into the contradictory national character of Japan and the duality of Japanese culture.[44] These studies explored national culture in terms of its language, religion and customs as a way of finding connections between a nation's character or culture and its patterns of behaviour and actions. They revealed links between Japan's strategic choices and their important underlying cultural factors.[45]

Drawing on the work of Ruth Benedict and others, the current concept of strategic culture is a direct descendant of political culture and of the idea that a particular national character or style can be discerned which drives strategic thought and action.[46] It seems obvious that culture clearly influenced the outcomes of the Second World War in part by conditioning American and Japanese perceptions, strategic preferences and governmental processes. Despite criticisms about the potential for stereotyping and the reification of culture other anthropologists and sociologists have continued with this approach to strategic culture.

From Strategy to Strategic Culture

The analytic construct of strategic culture emerged during the Cold War to assess the differences American and Soviet nuclear weapons strategy and arms control negotiations. Theories arose that were based on the belief that culture influences the ways that nation states view and respond to the strategic environment.[47]

The genesis of this approach was the concern among analysts and policymakers that the 'mirror-imaging' of Western values and ideas were not allowed to creep into assessments of Soviet strategies and intentions.[48] Jack Snyder, who coined the term strategic culture, was attempting to answer the question, 'Can cultural analysis tell us anything significant about strategic outcomes?' Snyder described it as a 'body of attitudes and beliefs that guides ... thoughts on strategic questions and influences the way strategic issues are formulated ...' He believed that over time certain ideas, beliefs, historical legacies and attitudes about military power and the use of force, were socialised until they, 'achieve[d] a state of semi-permanence.'[49] Another pioneer in the field of using strategic culture to analyse an opponent was Colin Gray who asserted that the differences in strategic cultures stemmed from differences in history and geography, providing the background to strategy and policy choices and were strategic predispositions that were always influential on decision making and international behaviours.[50] He felt that strategic culture represents a history of ideas; a 'nation's way of war flows from its geography and society and reflects its competitive advantage. It represents an approach that a given state has found successful in the past.'[51] These scholars led an approach that described broad historical patterns of strategic behaviour that were attributed to cultural causes. It suffered from the tendency to stereotype behaviours and from the expectation that an adversary would always behave in the same way.

A more analytical approach was subsequently offered that used narrower definitions of what was meant by culture and that sought more rigorous testing methods. One example of this approach was that of Elizabeth Kier, who contended that organisational culture rather than shared cultural values has a greater effect on strategic behaviour due to the bias in the decision-making process that resulted from the way that the organisation was structured.[52]

There is a third generation of work on strategic culture, with Alastair Iain Johnston's, *Cultural Realism: Strategic Culture and Grand Strategy in Chinese History* often being cited as the best example of this methodological approach. Johnston investigated the character of Chinese strategic culture and possible causal links to Chinese military actions during the Ming dynasty (1368–1644 CE) and concluded that strategic culture exists as an 'ideational milieu that limits behavioural choices', and from which 'one could derive specific predictions about strategic choice.'[53] He defined strategic culture as

> an integrated system of symbols (i.e. argumentation structures, languages, analogies, metaphors, etc.) that acts to establish pervasive and long lasting grand strategic preferences by formulating concepts of the role and efficacy of military force in interstate political affairs, and by clothing these conceptions with such an aura of factuality that the strategic preferences seem uniquely realistic and efficacious.[54]

Rather than defining strategic culture as a pattern of behaviour, Johnston described it as the pervasive and long-lasting attitudes exhibited by a nation and that culture shapes behaviour but does not cause it.[55]

Cultural interpretations of history and the concept of strategic culture experienced a revitalisation with the rise of constructivism in the 1990s. This concept proposes that shared norms and identities shape behaviour in ways that contradict other paradigms. With the argument that 'national identities are social-structural phenomena' the constructivist paradigm offers an approach that shows connections between the formation of national identity and national traditions, culture and history.[56] The foundations of these beliefs and values rest on shared language and common values. This social identity shapes both short term and long-term strategic culture and resulting national strategic actions.[57]

Most scholars nevertheless agree that all strategy unfolds within a cultural context and that strategic culture is a social construct that includes key assumptions, preferred methods of operation, traditions and habits of thinking and behaviour.[58] Strategic culture is developed through an internal process wherein significant issues concerning doctrine, strategy and operational art are debated, refined and eventually executed.[59] This conceptualisation of a national way of war is influenced by the existing perception of national martial traditions, the interpretation of lessons learned from recent military conflicts, an understanding of current threats and a vision of future conflicts.[60] This vision of the future combat environment is often assumed to be consistent and predictable, and in accordance with national hopes, plans and preconceived ideas.[61] Additionally, developing a successful strategic culture requires a thorough analysis and understanding of anthropology and sociology in order for the belligerents to approach these clashes of culture with confidence in their cultural supremacy and therefore in their military culture.[62] Once established, a strategic culture tends to remain fixed unless forced to change by 'dramatic events or traumatic experiences' that invalidate these core values and beliefs.[63]

The historiography of strategic culture has moved from describing the history of ideas on warfare to an amorphous cultural analysis and thus the definitions of national ways of war have expanded from military patterns to customs and practices, and then on to beliefs.[64] Some scholars feel that strategic culture is better defined as belief in the efficacy of experience and experience-based intuition, taken together with improvisation, material strength and technology. Others feel that a way of war is merely a set of practices, rather than a history of ideas. Thus, while the cultural approach to interpreting military history and in particular, the debate over strategic culture has experienced a dialectic of thesis, antithesis and synthesis, the question remains yet unresolved.[65]

Taking a cultural approach to the history of war runs the risk of criticism for its seeming lack of theoretical and methodological rigour or for the possibility of reductionism and determinism that lurk in a cultural account of war. It has been said that current theoretical approaches should include the scope and content, the objects under analysis, and the historical circumstances that existed to identify the relationship between strategic culture and its historical effects. The approaches that have been used have been unable to offer a convincing research design because it is not clear how strong a deterministic effect strategic culture has on behaviour and because of the wide range of variables that can contribute to or compete with it.[66] I will attempt to gauge this through discourse analysis of a range of different sources.

For the purposes of my study, I used Miriam Becker's definition of strategic culture: 'a nation's traditions, values, attitudes, patterns of behaviour, habits, symbols, achievements and particular ways of adapting to the environment and solving problems with respect to the threat or use of force.'[67] I find this definition appealingly succinct and concise. Its relative simplicity offers a good foundation for exploration of the meaning and importance of many of the relevant factors.

A specific premise that I will follow in this case study is that strategic culture exists as an integrated system of shared symbols, values, behaviours and traditions that works through commonly understood decision-making processes that are shaped or influenced by societal perceptions and preferences, which thereby inform and influence how decision makers envision and respond to the strategic environment.[68]

From Strategic Culture to Tactical Culture

There is a joke about the national characteristics of the adversaries in the Second World War. I have not researched its provenance, but I use it to introduce the concept of 'tactical culture'. It goes roughly as follows: If you encounter a unit you can't identify, fire a shot above their heads so it won't hit anyone. If they respond to with precise rifle shots, they're British. If they respond with a torrent of machine gun fire, they're German. If they retreat, they're French. If they switch to your side, they're Italian. If they shoot back but apologise, they're Canadians. If nothing happens for five minutes and then your position is suddenly and absolutely obliterated by field artillery and air strikes, they're American.[69]

In a non-serious way this describes the popular perceptions of each nations' military. I think that it also represents the concept of 'tactical culture'. Just as there is a hierarchy that extends from strategy to tactics, I believe that there is a supporting concept to strategic culture which is that of tactical culture, which really represents the place where military doctrine and military organisational culture combine. I propose this term as a foil to strategic culture to explain the interplay between the echelons.

There is a relationship between a nation's 'way of war' and its 'way of warfare'.[70] Strategic culture (the way of war) is implemented through a tactical culture (the way of warfare) that expresses prevailing military attitudes and beliefs through actions taken on the battlefield. There is an intersectionality between tactical culture and military organisational culture and the way that they define and shape how an organisation functions as expressed through the 'habitual practices, default programs, hidden assumptions, and unreflected cognitive frames' that support its actions.[71] Many studies of cultural, behavioural and identity science have shown how culture can influence individual and organisational performance.[72] Every unit; every squad, platoon, company and battalion, has a unique personality and a distinctive character. Edgar Schein explains organisational culture as,

> A pattern of shared basic assumptions learned by a group as it solved its problems of external adaptation and internal integration, which has worked well enough to be considered valid and, therefore, to be taught to new members as the correct way to perceive, think, and feel in relation to those problems.[73]

Schein's 'Model of Organizational Culture' posits that any group has a surface level of visible structures and behaviours, a middle level consisting of shared beliefs, values and rules, and finally a deeper level of shared assumptions that shape perceptions and guide behaviour.[74] Each unit has a collective set of beliefs, values and customs that are the result of that cohort's training and experiences. These distinctive traits and this persistent, pattern of thought, attitudes, actions or set of practices becomes the tactical culture. This is itself a synthesis of a unit's past experiences, lessons learned and group beliefs that influence each unit's collective belief in themselves and is the foundation of their methods of warfighting and their confidence in their success on the battlefield.[75]

Tactical culture specifically reflects the preferred military techniques and operational style used by a force. Just as strategic culture flows from a nations' geography, history and competitive advantages so too does tactical culture derive from the choice of technologies and weapons used, how they have been employed in the past, with what effect and with what expectations.[76] This tactical culture is more likely to influence how a unit performs on the battlefield than higher policies or directives.[77]

The characteristics of tactical culture include elements like esprit de corps, pride, cohesion, loyalty and will power. It also includes capabilities like leadership and individual and collective training. Doctrine also represents part of tactical culture by expressing an organisation's beliefs about the best methods to conduct military operations. As the military's institutional belief system about its duties, roles and relationships, and the guide for how it will fight, doctrine combined with military organisational culture forms the tactical culture that guides unit actions. Tactical culture is thus rooted in the traditions and customs of the service and the unit, and it reflects the goals, objectives, beliefs, values and behaviours of that unit. It is an expression of how the unit views itself and the battlefield and how they intend to meet current and future challenges. For example, the tactical culture of Germans in the Second World War, could be characterised by a pattern of vigorous tactical movement, a preference to attack despite the odds, and a flexible system of command that gave officers the freedom to act in the absence of orders from higher authorities.[78] The keystone of tactical culture is the will to fight. It is an essential element of combat effectiveness because this willpower determines how well a unit fights and whether it succeeds in the fight.[79]

No theory of strategic culture is without flaws, but the use of this concept as an interpretive lens to explain historical events remains compelling. All previous attempts to determine the effect of culture on strategic behaviour suffered from the methodological shortcoming of treating strategic culture as an independent variable. This is flawed because culture does not act of its own accord. It may influence human behaviour but it does not motivate it.[80] Culture cannot cause anything to happen, however, if one knows the culture of a society, one can understand much about the possibilities, probabilities and variations of action within that society.[81] A culture-based analysis of historical events offers richer sources of explanation for an adversary's behaviours if one can ascertain how cultural values, symbols and beliefs influence the decision-making process.[82]

To examine the strategic culture of the American and Japanese forces in the Pacific War, I will also consider the following overarching elements: ideas, symbols, values and behaviours. Within a given culture, the symbolic experiences, ritual practices, patterns of behaviour and cultural meanings are the cultural products that influence and provide the resources for the construction of strategies of action. Culture influences strategies and tactics by providing values, habits, skills and ideologies towards which actions are oriented.[83] I drew from the deductive analytical framework developed by Forrest Morgan, which develops a conceptual model of strategic culture by linking the fundamental elements of strategic decision making – perception, preference and process – to the cultural factors of symbols, values and behaviours.[84]

American strategic culture developed similarly to its European contemporaries as a response to the Industrial Revolution by emphasising tactics that massed firepower and manoeuvre to achieve superiority at the decisive point. It is *sui generis,* however, in its expression of beliefs and habits found in American culture such as showing respect for human life and individual political rights, equal opportunity and equal burden sharing, the defence of free market capitalism, isolationism and unilateralism. American strategic culture also exhibits almost naive optimism, strategic impatience, deep faith in technology and a tendency to view every conflict as an existential crusade in defence of democracy, motivated by the will to win to overthrow tyranny.[85]

These unique cultural determinants have influenced American strategy and military operations. Russell Weigley interpreted American strategic thought as following two basic types of strategy: annihilation and attrition.[86] Weigley characterised American strategy as using overwhelming force to 'grind down opponents with firepower and mass.'[87] His *American Way of War* was considered the definitive work on the subject for thirty years however, there have been newer interpretations that challenge his conclusions.

His definitions of attrition and annihilation have been objected to as confusing and simplistic (for example: at what point does continual attrition result in inevitable annihilation?). It has also been pointed out that the crucial period from the American Civil War to the Second World War was less strategically ambivalent that he had portrayed it and that this interpretation gives too little attention to alternative strategies that arose in American thought.[88] Brian Linn has instead discovered several schools of strategic thought woven through over 200 years of American military history. He summarised them and their most famous American exponents as: attrition (Washington), Napoleonic (Lee), annihilation (Grant), partisan war (Greene), sea-power (Mahan) and air power (Mitchell).[89] Another suggested historical pattern of American strategic culture is that of punishment, pacification, protection and profit as traditional goals.[90] The continuing study of American strategic culture may yield further insights. If we can say anything with certainty it may be that the American strategic culture and the American way of war has been as subject to change as the new weapons and tactics that were introduced to the fight.

Japan too, has a very distinctive culture and one can see the effects of cultural conditioning in many aspects of Japanese society. Throughout its history, Japanese society has experienced tremendous transformation in religion and social systems ranging from feudalism, to nationalism, modernisation and militarism. Yet throughout these vicissitudes Japan developed a unique cultural identity which adapted to these changes and emerged intact. By being physically separated from the rest of Asia and through its deliberate isolation from Western influences for almost 300 years, Japan developed an unusually homogenous society and culture. One of the most distinctive elements of Japanese society is its strategic culture.

Japan has been viewed as a 'warrior nation' with an ancient martial culture. The *bakufu* military government that ruled the country from 1185 CE to 1868 CE set a martial tone by its very name, meaning a 'field headquarters'. Ruled by the *Sei-i-tai Shogun*, the 'great general who subdues the eastern barbarians', the country developed a social caste system wherein the military became a hereditary nobility. Eventually, as Japan moved towards becoming a modern nation-state it came to be guided by a warrior ethic called *bushidō*. We shall explore this in greater detail later. For now, we will only note that a specific feature of Japanese culture is its proud tradition of military virtue that extolled the preference for death in battle over the humiliation of surrender or defeat.[91]

During the Second World War the Japanese government mounted a concerted effort to motivate the Japanese public to endure extraordinary sacrifice throughout the imperial era by elevating, intensifying, and in some cases, distorting or reinterpreting several traditional values and symbols.[92] Did this deliberate manipulation of the culture reveal a hidden, fatal flaw in their strategic and tactical approaches? Did the Japanese fail to win the Second World War *because* of their strategic culture? If so, why?

Some have attributed Japan's defeat to being 'out-gunned' and 'out-produced' by the Americans and their allies. This imbalance of power was widely acknowledged before the war, yet the Japanese appear to have ignored it. While they understood that the US had the potential for massive firepower because of its material resources the Japanese felt that the Americans lacked fighting spirit, tactical finesse and operational skill; a *cultural* assessment of enemy weakness. Japanese strategic culture conditioned the way Imperial Japan viewed conflict with the Americans. Their belief in Japan's unique martial culture, its proud tradition of military virtue and preference for death over humiliation or defeat led them to war and eventual defeat.[93]

This tendency to glorify idealised warrior virtues has been cited by many historians to explain Japanese fanaticism, but less remarked upon is how Japanese strategic and tactical culture were affected by this cultural conditioning that also inculcated the belief that Japan was a unique and special nation with a divine mission to rule the world.[94] Arguably, this strategic culture drove Japan as it modernised and militarised in the early twentieth century. This culture produced a proficient imperial army and navy that burst onto the world stage, ready to compete with other great powers. Eventually, the Imperial Japanese Army (IJA) seized control of the state and the nation went to war with America. Japan's strategic culture had led it to victory previously, but it was flawed, unable to deal with defeats, valuing its reputation and judgment over public honesty, and was deeply imbued with the glorification of ritualised death.[95]

My hypothesis is that certain relevant Japanese cultural traits such as the symbolism of the emperor, the core values like *Wa* (Harmony), with its ingrained social behaviours such as the seeking of consensus contributed to the creation of an idiosyncratic Japanese strategic culture that in turn had the unintended but consequential outcome of adhering to stoicism, conformity, conservatism and blind obedience to the point of defeat. Japanese warrior virtues glorified courage, loyalty and sacrifice, and made any other course of action seem dishonourable. The Japanese veneration of stoicism further strengthened their belief in their ability to triumph through sacrifice.[96]

The Will to Fight

'In war the chief incalculable is the human will.'[97] The will to fight represents the ineffably human nature of combat. Every element from strategic culture to leadership to doctrine and training combine to influence the will to fight. Without it, any technological advantage is useless if soldiers lack the determination to use it.[98] Integral to a successful tactical culture is the inherent desire to close with and destroy the enemy. Individual soldiers and small units are the intrinsic agents of tactical culture and the critical nodes for 'will to fight'.[99] This is because at the unit level small group cohesion, organisational capabilities and unit leadership come together.[100] Willpower gives a force a capability to succeed in combat that is greater than just materiel superiority or overwhelming firepower.[101]

American doctrine has alternatively embraced and ignored the concept of the will to fight for over a century. Current US Army and US Marine Corps doctrine state that the will to fight is the single most important factor in war.[102] However, it has had no stable, central place in American doctrine or practice, and it is often defined in vague and impractical terms. Perhaps, this is because it is so poorly understood as an emotional / psychological human condition.[103] The pattern amongst Western militaries has been that after a major war some aspects of the will to fight are incorporated into doctrine but the lessons fade, emphasis shifts again to a focus on employing materiel capabilities and achieving physical effects. The importance of viewing war as the clash of opposing and irreconcilable wills must then be hastily relearned.[104]

Exploring tactical culture and the will to fight are important to improving our understanding of the outcome of the Pacific War as a contrast to the linear, deterministic view that 'superior technology plus economic power' yielded American victory. I believe that Japanese strategic and tactical culture was based on the *will to sacrifice* in contrast to the American strategic and tactical culture of the *will to win*, and that this difference strongly determined the outcome.[105] In subsequent chapters I will compare the nature and power of the respective Japanese and American motivations, capabilities, perseverance, determination, sacrifice and passion.

A Model of the Will to Fight

In 2018, RAND published two reports that defined the will to fight as,

> the determination to conduct sustained military and other operations for some objective even when the expectation of success decreases or the need for significant political, economic, and military sacrifices increases.[106]

It declared that breaking the enemy's will to fight while sustaining one's own will to fight is the key to success in battle and went on to ask:

- Why does an individual soldier, a military unit, a military organisation, a national leader or an entire nation fight or not fight?
- What is the value of will in comparison to the quantity and quality of military equipment, or the application of tactics or strategy?[107]
- Why do some units have greater combat effectiveness?
- How do strategic culture and the elusive concepts of the 'will to fight'/'will to sacrifice', contribute to combat effectiveness?
- What role does tactical culture play?

Currently most military historians treat war and the analysis of combat effectiveness primarily as a contest of opposing equipment and methods. War is a fundamentally human endeavor; thus, we should focus as much on the human elements. Because war is not a mechanical process that can be controlled precisely by laws, statistics, or machines we should also avoid assumptions about controlled and predictable environments and outcomes.[108]

The key findings of their 'National Will-to-Fight Model' that relate to strategic culture are that will to fight is the least understood aspect of war; fully totalitarian or democratic governments often show the strongest will to fight and national identity can have strong influence but can also be manipulated; and the effective use of engagement and indoctrination/messaging improves chances of victory.[109]

The key findings of the 'Unit Will-to-Fight Model' were that, although much of the discussion focuses on terms like morale, cohesion and discipline there are no commonly accepted definitions or explanations of these key terms.[110] This study concluded that will to fight can be assessed but not measured: there is no way to accurately quantify will to fight or delineate its precise value. At the tactical level will to fight it is a fundamental of warfare, yet it defies accurate and precise quantification.[111]

According to the 2018 RAND study, 'Will to Fight: Returning to the Human Fundamentals of War', there are several influential variables.[112] These include:

- Identity, which is multi-faceted, culturally obtained, unique and dynamic. Desperation, involving fear of death, the need for self-preservation and when no other options exist.
- Revenge, which can have historical roots or more immediate, personal motivations.

- Economical, arising from fulfilling the basic need for subsistence to the desire for socioeconomic advancement.
- Ideological, reflecting commitment to a cause or belief system.
- Cohesion, when as a member of a group one adheres to the vertical and horizontal bonds of association and to the tasks and social structures of the group.[113]
- Leadership, which involves directing and encouraging combative behaviour.
- Morale, which is a transient, partial indicator of will to fight, expressing the individual and collective feelings about the current situation.[114] (The Oxford English Dictionary defines 'morale' as 'the confidence, enthusiasm, and discipline of an individual or group of people.').[115]

Their findings declared that when 'will to fight' is evenly matched the side with superior capabilities and which inflicts greater casualties on the other should win … except when it doesn't. They also found that a nation with high will to fight can nevertheless overcome capability shortfalls and high casualties to outlast their opponent (for example, North Vietnam) and that a nation's high will to fight could fade as their opponent's will grows while attrition degrades their previously greater capabilities and resolve (for example, Nazi Germany).[116]

The unit will to fight model contains analytical factors that influence the will to fight, categorised as:

- Motivations, the drivers of will to fight that help form individual disposition.
- Capabilities, the competencies and physical assets available to soldiers and the support they receive from the unit level through the societal level of assessment.
- Culture, which includes behavioural norms, control measures and influences that affect individual and unit disposition and decisions to fight.[117]

RAND's findings suggest that when will to fight is evenly matched, differing capabilities and heavy casualties may weaken or strengthen an adversary's national will to fight, but this does not account for every instance and thus is not predictive.[118]

Strategic culture was as important to the outcomes of the Pacific War as the imbalance of power. Japanese strategic culture caused them to believe that they were unique in their fighting spirit. Their hope of victory was based on their faith that spiritual superiority would neutralise materiel superiority. The Japanese believed that they would win because their unique fighting spirit would overcome the forces and technology arrayed against them.

Dramatis Personae

When human voices are overlaid onto history we may find links between perceptions, decisions and actions and gain new understanding of war through the explanatory power of culture. Here are brief biographical sketches of some of the soldiers who we will meet: Ralph Eyde, Dr Paul Nobuo Tatsuguchi, Dean E. Galles, Albert V. Hartl, Wayne C. Zimmerman, Francis T. Pachler, Dick Laird and Yahara Hiromichi.

Ralph Eyde

Ralph Eyde provides an insightful personal perspective to these events in the collection of the hand-written letters of the Eyde family of Rockford, Illinois. This collection, only recently discovered in a storage facility in Arizona, was written by three brothers who served in the war; one in the US Marine Corps, one in the US Army Air Force, and Ralph Eyde who fought on Attu and Kwajalein with the 7th Infantry Division. Through their letters to their family and each other they captured the horrors of combat across four years of war and beyond.[119]

Dr Paul Nobuo Tatsuguchi

Dr Paul Nobuo Tatsuguchi was an American-educated Japanese doctor who served in the Imperial Japanese Army in the Second World War and was subsequently killed during the Battle of Attu. In his diary, which was captured by the 7th Infantry Division at the end of the battle, he carefully recorded his observations and experiences throughout the battle. He documents the preparations for the Japanese counterattack, which was the most notorious '*banzai* charge' executed by Japanese troops during the war.[120]

Dean E. Galles

Dean E. Galles was commissioned as an officer in the US Army in June 1941, and served in the 7th Infantry Division, 32nd Infantry Regiment. He was awarded the Silver Star, the nation's third highest honour; two Bronze Stars, one for valour; three Purple Hearts for wounds in battle and the Combat Infantry Badge for his service on Attu, Kwajalein, the Philippines and Okinawa.[121]

Albert V. Hartl

Albert V. Hartl was a reserve officer who rose from the rank of lieutenant to colonel and commanded at both Battalion and Regimental levels. He was twice awarded the Silver Star and three Bronze Stars in actions from Attu to Okinawa.[122]

Wayne C. Zimmerman

Wayne C. Zimmerman graduated from the US Military Academy at West Point in 1919. He retired as a major general. He was awarded the Distinguished Service Cross for extraordinary heroism on Attu Island while commanding a regiment.[123]

Francis T. Pachler

Francis T. Pachler was also a graduate of the US Military Academy who retired as a major general. He rose from second lieutenant to colonel while in the 7th Infantry Division and served successively as a company, battalion and regimental commander at Attu, Kwajalein, Leyte and Okinawa.[124]

Dick Laird

Dick Laird was a company first sergeant who fought on Attu, Kwajalein, Leyte and Okinawa. He was awarded the Silver Star and Bronze Star Medal but suffered nightmares for years after the war, thinking that that he had killed Dr Tatsuguchi on Attu, 'a guy that should not have been there.'[125]

Yahara Hiromichi

Yahara Hiromichi was a colonel in the IJA, who espoused the tactics of attrition rather than the usual IJA hand-to-hand frontal attack. As chief planner for the Thirty-Second Army staff on Okinawa he was the architect of their defensive plan.[126]

Chapter Two

THE BATTLE OF ATTU: TACTICAL CULTURE AND *GYOKUSAI*

> 'I will become a deity with a smile in the heavy fog. I am only waiting for the day of death.'[127]

Introduction

When one imagines the Pacific War of 1941–1945, the images that come to mind are of azure waters, sparkling beaches and lush rain forests. We do not envision a climate of freezing temperatures, snow, rain, fog and gale force winds lashing rocky coastlines and barren snow-capped mountains. Yet these were the battlefield conditions that confronted the Japanese and American adversaries who fought on the Aleutian Islands in May 1943. The Battle of Attu was the only ground offensive battle fought on US territory during the Second World War. It was planned to be a three-day operation, but it turned into a bloody three-week ordeal in the jagged mountains of the Aleutian Island that could have been won by either side.[128]

This chapter will explore the tactical culture of the two adversaries. Tactical culture is the nexus of a units' preferred methods of warfighting and operational style. In this case the comparison of Japanese and American tactical culture throws into stark relief the differing principles, techniques and procedures, institutionalised as the overarching framework for action that the two adversaries felt would result in combat effectiveness and mission accomplishment.[129] American tactical culture demonstrated a will to win; to overcome obstacles, kill the enemy and fight as a team of teams to victory, whereas Japanese tactical culture demonstrated the will to sacrifice; to kill the enemy and if that was not possible then to die instead.

The Japanese had identified the Russians as their primary hypothetical enemy since 1907 and considered the Bering Sea and the Aleutians part of their sphere of influence.[130] American strategic planners had identified Japan as a likely enemy in the Pacific several years before the attack on Pearl Harbor, and they took the threat most seriously. General Mitchell had considered a northern war with Japan as early as 1923, as he stated in his official testimony to Congress:

> I am thinking of Alaska. In an air war, if we were unprepared Japan could take it away from us, first by dominating the sky and creeping up the Aleutians ... Japan might well seize enough of Alaska to creep down the western coast of Canada. Then we would be in for it.[131]

The Japanese had specifically demonstrated their interest in the Aleutians as early as 1931 when their fishing ships visited the area. Both the Americans and the Japanese viewed the Aleutians as a strategic avenue of approach to attack the other from the north across the Bering Sea and Japanese advance parties were sent to the area to conduct surveys of the area before Pearl Harbor.[132]

The Operational Environment: The Battle of Komandorski Islands

Deeply indoctrinated with the Mahanian doctrine of winning a decisive sea battle that would destroy the US Pacific Fleet and quickly end the conflict, in May 1942 the Japanese Imperial General Headquarters ordered an attack on the Midway Islands.[133] Simultaneous with their attack on Midway, the Japanese launched air and amphibious attacks on the Aleutian Islands. This was intended to divert American forces from the main effort at Midway, protect the Imperial Japanese Navy from an attack from the north, and obstruct communications between the US and the Soviet Union. They also intended to construct advanced airbases for future offensive action.[134] In concert with an air attack on Dutch Harbor the Japanese conducted landings on Kiska and Attu on 7 June 1942. Although they had only planned to hold the islands until December 1942, the Japanese later decided to remain, and they reinforced and repositioned their forces to defend against anticipated American attacks.[135] The continuing occupation of the islands prompted an American counterattack to retake the lost territory.

The American's first step was to interrupt the Japanese resupply efforts to their Aleutians garrisons. On 26 March 1943, a naval task force, led by the heavy cruiser USS *Salt Lake City*, patrolling off the Komandorski Islands west of Attu, detected a force of eight Japanese warships escorting two transports bound for Attu with supplies and troops. A confused and chaotic four hour long naval battle ensued which was characterised as 'an old-fashioned long-range ship-to-ship duel.'[136] Each side jousted in the fog, scoring hits on one another, but the battle was inconclusive; no ships were sunk and both forces withdrew. Nevertheless, the Americans had succeeded in disrupting the Japanese resupply mission and the Japanese made no further attempts to reinforce or resupply the Aleutians with surface vessels. Afterwards, no more troops and only a trickle of supplies were delivered by Japanese submarines to Attu and Kiska before the American attack in May 1943. Rations on the island were restricted and by 16 May 1943 the Japanese were subsisting on one meal per day.[137]

Terrain and Weather

The Aleutian Island chain extends westward from Alaska 900 nautical miles. It ends at Attu, the westernmost island which is only 650 miles from what was then Japan's northernmost naval base at Paramushiro in the Kurile Islands. Devoid of trees but covered with grasses and snow, the island lies roughly 1,100 miles from the Alaskan mainland. The Aleutians were formed by geologic action, and the chain features forty-six volcanoes. The topography of Attu is characterised by numerous mountains, sharp cliffs, knife-edged ridges with 50-to-60-degree slopes, and elevations running between 2,000 and 3,000 feet above sea level. These descend to wind swept valleys with little vegetation other than the swampy muskeg, which quickly turns to thick, clinging mud when walked or driven over. Finally, comes the steep, rocky shoreline with its numerous obstacles and dangerous approaches.[138] The steep, rugged terrain is accentuated by glacier-like fields of ice in the passes, and permanent fields of snow on the slopes of the higher elevations. On Attu the snow line begins at approximately an elevation of 300 feet above sea level as does the fog line. The weather is typically snow, sleet and rain with gale force winds. Despite these high winds, the fog is persistent with only eight to ten clear days per year.[139] The ferocious winds that swept the island and the impenetrable fog that shrouded its formidable terrain severely limited the use and effectiveness of air power and artillery. The steep ridgelines and the boggy muskeg eliminated the use of vehicles. The burden of the fight thus fell squarely on the shoulders of individual American infantry soldiers, armed only with the weapons that they could carry, inexperienced in combat and short of food, water and ammunition to overcome a fanatical enemy defending well-prepared positions.

The American Attack Plan: 'Operation Land Crab'

By the end of January 1943, the US can be said to have gained the strategic initiative in the Pacific with its victories at the Coral Sea, Midway and Guadalcanal, but it wasn't until May 1943 that the US could muster the force necessary to achieve the military superiority at the operational echelon of war to counterattack in the Aleutians.

The 7th Infantry Division was activated for service in the Second World War on 1 July 1940 at Fort Ord, California, based on a core of prewar enlisted men and officers organised into two Regular Army infantry regiments and one National Guard infantry regiment. Most of the soldiers assigned had been recently inducted in the nation's first peacetime draft.[140] Just as most of the selective service soldiers were anticipating the end of their two-year tour of duty the attack on Pearl Harbor occurred. The soldiers were elated when the division's designation was changed to the 7th Motorized Division. They were going to be a modern, motorised force preparing to fight the Afrika Korps in Tunisia.[141] Manning, equipping and training activities to become a fully ready combat division were accelerated and they commenced six months of arduous training in the Mojave Desert in April 1942.[142] As a desert-trained, motorised force they expected that they were to fight the Afrika Korps in North Africa.[143] However, just over two months prior to conducting the invasion of Attu, they were surprised to be redesignated as a light infantry division. The vehicles and anti-tank guns were turned in and they began sixty days of intense amphibious assault training before sailing north from San Francisco in late March 1943. Little did they know that their mission had been changed to an invasion of the Aleutian Islands in May 1943.[144]

The Foundation of Tactical Culture – Training

The 7th Motorized Division had spent the spring and summer of 1942 training at Fort Ord, California in individual and small unit tasks under General Joseph Stilwell. They then moved to the Mojave Desert to train for three months under General George S. Patton on how to fight as a tank-infantry strike force. Mounted in armoured halftracks and jeeps with towed anti-tank guns they practiced how to move rapidly across the desert to seize and defend hills, ridgelines and defiles. They trained alongside tanks to conduct fast flanking attacks and deep envelopments of enemy forces in a desert environment.[145] Thus, there was no specific training regime for Attu. Rather than applying learned tasks and techniques to an anticipated situation, they would rely generally on the basic squad and platoon training that they had conducted at Ford Ord and on the specific individual and collective confidence and cohesion that they had earned in the inferno of the Mojave Desert to accomplish this new mission.

Their Japanese opponents on Attu were busy preparing the island's defences with deeply buried bomb shelters, machine gun positions, rifle trenches, hidden supply caches and barracks all meticulously camouflaged to blend into the natural terrain of rocks and tundra. Their additional training consisted of drills to quickly respond to the expected American attack from whatever direction it might come.[146]

The plan directed Regimental Landing Group 17 minus Battalion Combat Team 17-1 with Battalion Combat Team 32-2 attached to land on Beaches Yellow and Blue in Massacre Bay on 10 May 1943 to destroy the enemy in the Holtz Bay-Chichagof area. This Southern Landing Force would be the division's main effort. The Provisional Battalion composed of the 7th Scout Company and the 7th Reconnaissance Troop was to land on Beach Scarlet (Blind Cove) from the submarines USS *Narwhal* and USS *Nautilus*, and the destroyer USS *Kane*. Battalion Combat Team 17-1, together with the Provisional Battalion would form the Northern Landing Force and be the division's supporting effort. It was intended that from these positions they could attack the Japanese from the rear. The Southern Force was to 'advance rapidly' up Massacre Valley, seize the passes leading to Holtz and Sarana Bays, and then move into the Holtz Bay area where it was to join the Northern Force and destroy the enemy there. Upon completion of that task, they were to advance against Chichagof Harbor, while the Northern Force secured the valley running west from Holtz Bay. Fire support was to be provided by both naval gunfire and field artillery ashore. Naval aviation was to conduct long-range searches for Japanese naval forces bringing reinforcements. The 11th Army Air Force was to maintain a strike force of one-third of its heavy and medium bombers to attack any such forces discovered.[147]

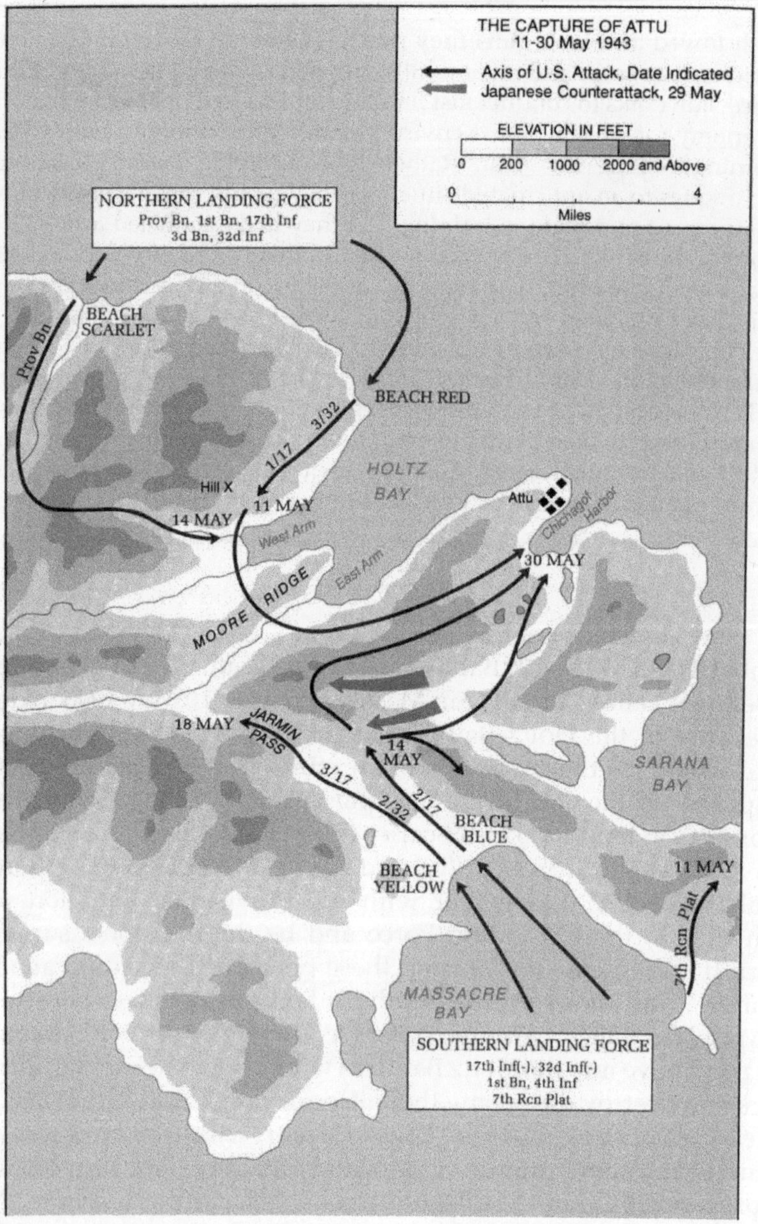

Figure 2-1: The Capture of Attu
Map. The Capture of Attu. (Map. Stetson Conn, Rose C. Engelman and Byron Fairchild, Guarding the United States and its Outposts. "Chapters IX/X/XI". The U.S. Army in World War II. Washington: Center for Military History, 2000, Public Domain, https://commons.wikimedia.org/w/index.php?curid=259311).

The Japanese Defensive Plan

The initial Japanese defensive positions were established at Chichagof Harbor, Holtz Bay, Massacre Bay and Sarana Bay. The Japanese commander, Colonel Yamasaki Yasuyo, was an experienced veteran of service in Siberia and China who understood how to best use the rugged high ground as natural fortification.[148] At Holtz Bay, beach defences were established to thwart any American assault on the harbour with each arm of the bay defended by a four-gun anti-aircraft battery. The concept of the operation in this sector was based upon four successive battle positions with a final position at the head of the valley.[149]

The Japanese intent was to conduct their main defensive effort in Massacre Valley in successive battle positions from the beach to the high ground, yielding in the centre in order to draw the American forces into a kill zone in Jarmin Pass.[150] There, key defensive positions were established on Cold Mountain and Black Mountain as well as at the Holtz-Massacre Pass (later renamed Jarmin Pass), which was further supported by a battery of mountain artillery.[151] In addition, Chichagof Harbor was defended by another four-gun anti-aircraft battery and beach positions. The defences of Sarana Valley followed this pattern with battle positions on Buffalo Ridge, Gilbert Ridge, Sarana Nose and Point A. The final battle position was established on Fish Hook Ridge.[152] All these defensive positions were well camouflaged, anchored on rugged terrain that gave excellent observation of the enemy below, and which offered no high-speed avenues of approach and little cover or concealment. Weapons, ammunition and supplies were cached in large quantities throughout the defensive sector to reduce reliance on resupply efforts across the rough terrain, which could be interdicted.[153]

This was a hybrid of their doctrine of defence *at* the shoreline with a defence *from* the shoreline, taking full advantage of the Aleutian terrain and weather.[154] Deception was a key element of their plan so numerous dummy positions were built elsewhere on the island to make a landing at Massacre Bay appear to be a more attractive course of action for the Americans. In fact, American photoreconnaissance efforts failed to detect any positions on the south side of the island and most of those on the high ground.[155] From hard-won experience, the Japanese knew that supplies, vehicles and heavy artillery would not be able to move off the beaches because of the swampy tundra and steep, mountainous terrain and this factored into their plan.[156]

The specific IJA units that defended Attu were identified as: the *HQ Second Sector Unit*, the *Yonegawa Independent Infantry Battalion*, the *303rd Independent Infantry Battalion*, the *33rd Independent Anti-Aircraft*

Battalion, the *6th Mountain Gun Battery*, the *302nd Engineer Company*, the *6th Shipping Engineer Company*, a Signal Unit, an Airfield Construction Detachment, a Naval Anchorage Detachment, a Field Hospital Section and a Machinegun Cannon Company.[157] This task organisation is typical of the Japanese 'Independent Mixed Brigade' numbering approximately 4,700 soldiers, deployed for garrison duty, although it included units like the shipping engineers, anti-aircraft, machine gun, airfield and naval detachments that were not standard to other independent mixed brigades.[158] The Japanese first occupied Attu in June 1942. They briefly shifted their forces to Kiska but then returned to Attu in October 1942.[159]

While it might appear that the Japanese force that defended Attu was a largely ad hoc force, it was organised in accordance with their doctrine. Imperial Japanese Army units were classified as 'standard', 'strengthened' or 'modified / special' and were specifically organised for varying roles and different types of terrain. The Japanese principle of organising units to fit operational conditions and requirements led to a common practice of creating 'independent mixed' units of various sizes which consisted of infantry units into which artillery, engineers, medical elements have been incorporated.[160] This seems to have been the case at Attu. The Japanese practice stands in contrast to American Army doctrine of organising and training regimental and battalion combat teams from a standardised base of organic units.

While there were no hard and fast rules for numbers of personnel assigned or types of equipment issued, the forces that were sent to Attu and Kiska came from Hokkaido. They were led by officers and sergeants who had combat experience in China and were equipped with the best cold weather gear available in the Japanese inventory.[161] Their two years of thorough training had inculcated an aggressive, self-reliant spirit, emphasising rapid encirclements and night attacks to conduct close combat.[162] Above all, Japanese training stressed the indoctrination of an almost fanatical spirit of self-sacrifice. This sentence from a letter found on a dead Japanese soldier exemplifies this spirit of the readiness to fight to the last round and the last man: 'When I received my mobilization [*sic*] orders, I had already sacrificed my life for my country you must not expect me to return alive.'[163]

Will to Fight – Morale

Whether the soldier has physical comforts or suffers physical hardships may be a factor but is seldom the determining factor in making or unmaking his morale. A cause known and believed

> in ... the individual's confidence and pride in himself, his comrades, his leaders; the unit's pride in its own will ... combine to weld a seasoned fighting force capable of defending the nation.'[164]

Throughout history, both military theorists and historians have recognised the importance of morale to combat effectiveness. Nevertheless, a definition of morale useful for analysis of tactical culture is hindered by the complexities and ambiguities of human psychology. Whether you define morale as the following, there are several factors found in combat that can contribute to our understanding of morale's impact on combat effectiveness and tactical culture:[165]

> the confidence, enthusiasm, and discipline', of an individual or group of people or as 'willing and dependable performance, steady self-control, and courageous, determined conduct despite danger and privations ... zeal, self-sacrifice, or indomitableness.

Massacre Valley and Holtz Bay

Poor weather had frustrated both the reconnaissance and aerial bombing campaigns from January through March and right up to the planned invasion date in May 1943. Storms and poor visibility continued to impede the invasion, forcing yet a delay of the attack until 11 May 1943. The bad weather gave an unexpected advantage to the Americans, however. Japanese submarines had observed the convoy depart from Cold Bay, Alaska and had reported the information to the forces on Attu and Kiska. The garrison on Attu went on alert on 3 May 1943 in expectation of an attack. However, after six days of waiting the alert was called off. The very next day, the American forces arrived offshore of Attu, unaware of how the weather delay had allowed them to surprise the Japanese.[166]

Ralph Eyde: The Letters

Clausewitz wrote that the art of war 'deals with living and with moral forces' and therefore the personal experiences of the combatants can offer insights into their motivations.[167] To assist in achieving analytical depth, I conducted a comparative content analysis of diaries, letters and interview statements made by the Japanese and American battle participants to discover patterns or biases which explore these questions and themes.[168] The language that people use in describing the experience and events of war is significant as it can not only express their emotions and opinions about war, but it can also help to shape and explain their actions.[169] The first of these comes from the letters of Ralph Eyde.

Ralph Eyde had quit his factory job in early 1941 to enlist in the US Army. Assigned to the 7th Infantry Division, he wrote to his brother John in April 1943 that he was preparing to deploy, as part of 'one of these outfits who make beach landings in the middle of the night on the roughest coastlines possible and seize airports, railroads, cities, and enemy coast defenses [*sic*].' He was wounded on the first day of fighting on Attu but refused to be evacuated, fighting until the battle's end. He was wounded again on Kwajalein, blown 20 feet out of his foxhole by a Japanese shell, with shrapnel wounds to the lung. Ralph was dizzy from his concussion and wounds but continued to throw hand grenades. Ralph's machine-gunner lost an eye, but both men survived. Discharged from the service after the war, Ralph worked for the CIA from the 1950s to the 1970s in clandestine operations all over the world, dying at the age of 85 in 2003.[170]

He warned his brother not to 'tell anyone out of family what our outfit has been doing cause all this training could be worthless if a pack of subs got ahold of us and all were sent to the bottom in Mid-Ocean.'[171] Ralph Eyde encapsulated the spirit of the 7th Infantry Division and its will to win when he wrote about Attu: 'It was plenty tough + rugged going with the weather against us + Jap snipers harassing us all the time, but we blew them from their foxholes + they all ended up 6 foot under.'[172]

Sustaining Morale – Mail

For the American combat soldier, mail to and from home represented a welcome distraction from the harsh realities of combat and a reminder of the lives and loved ones that they had left behind and yearned to return to. One soldier wrote to his sister that, 'Any little thing we do to divert our mind and keep us busy when the fighting comes to a temporary halt, relaxes the nerves and rests our bodies. That's why receiving mail from home is so important.'[173] The comforting psychological space that was created by sending and receiving words and mementos was essential to morale.[174]

Mail was equally important to the Japanese soldier. A letter written by First Class Private Tsukiji of the 303rd Independent Infantry Battalion on Attu illustrates his activities and his desire for mail from home:

> After leaving a harbor [*sic*] in Japan on November 3rd ... correspondence is delayed or else they are sinking to the bottom of the sea before reaching the mainland. The octopus are probably

> reading and laughing right this moment. Well, where am I located at the present time? Landed at Attu Island of the Aleutians on the 2nd of February (1943). I am to defend this island and construct an air port, [*sic*] and make it an advance base of Japan. There is constant bombing by enemy planes day after day. We are helpless to plane attacks, we run to our fox-holes, [*sic*] but don't know when we'll be bombed to bits. Please send me a watch, a pocket watch, if I'm not asking too much. There is no ink either. Please send me a safety razor. Living in isolation is an extreme hardship and there are a great deal of shortages. Also send some thread and needles. There is a shortage of cigarettes among my buddies, if you can spare some, please do so. Received your package, and it came just in time to help me out of my shortages. I shall end my letter now. Please take care of yourself. My regards to everybody.[175]
>
> From the content of this letter it appears that censorship to protect operational security was not applied by the Japanese.

Shrouded from their enemy by heavy fog, the 7th Infantry Division landed on Attu late on the afternoon of 11 May 1943. To retain the element of surprise no pre-invasion naval bombardment was conducted. At Massacre Bay in the south the Southern Force landed elements of four battalions and attacked up the valley, climbing the steeply rising terrain towards the ridges 1,500 to 2,000 feet high, slogging through the boggy turf against the highly camouflaged, well prepared Japanese defence. The Northern Force, with elements of two battalions, landed at Holtz Bay on narrow, rocky beaches that merged with tundra and mud so deep that not even tracked vehicles could move through the landing sites or the terrain beyond the beach.

Before dawn, the 7th Scout Company and the 7th Reconnaissance Troop paddled small rubber boats ashore commando-style from two submarines onto Beach Scarlet, 9 miles north-west of Chichagof Harbor. They met no opposition and moved inland. The unusual fact that the 7th Infantry Division had two reconnaissance units was a result of its rapid and incomplete transition from motorised to light infantry. The 7th Scout Company was the type of unit that a light division would have to infiltrate enemy lines to perform dismounted reconnaissance and surveillance missions. The 7th Reconnaissance Troop was a holdover from the motorised division structure; a cavalry unit designed to perform the traditional mounted missions of reconnaissance, screen, flank and guard. In addition to their initial mission of reconnaissance of the landing beach and the enemy's defences, the two units were to link-up to form a battalion-sized force and move to occupy positions at the head of one of the valleys running back from Holtz Bay. After landing their rubber boats on Beach Scarlet this Provisional Battalion began climbing a steep ravine up to the ridgeline above.

Meanwhile, the 1st Battalion, 17th Infantry Regiment landed at Beach Red as the nucleus of the Northern Force.[176] They faced a daunting task; they had to surmount two formidable obstacles. First was to thread their landing craft through the rock-studded approach to the narrow, rocky beach, there to unload only two or three boats at a time. Then, after slowly building up combat power, they had to scale a steep escarpment just 75 feet from the water's edge and rising to 250 feet above the beach. Because of the dense fog, H-Hour had been postponed twice in the hope of better visibility, and the men had been in their boats on the choppy water for seven hours. Luckily, the fog that was preventing their landing also concealed them from the Japanese. Finally, at 15.00 hours they were given the order to proceed. Once ashore they began to move down the west side of Holtz Bay. The landing had been unopposed, but the Japanese were waiting for them and just short of their initial objective Hill X, they were halted by heavy enemy fire.[177]

To the south, the 2nd and 3rd battalions of the 17th Infantry Regiment made the division's main attack in Massacre Bay. They landed unopposed on Beaches Blue and Yellow, approximately 6 miles south of Chichagof Harbor. Their landing had also been delayed because of high waves and dense fog, which caused the USS *MacDonough* (the fire control ship) to collide with USS *Sicard* (the landing control ship). *Sicard* towed the damaged *MacDonough* back to Adak.[178] The first and second waves managed to land between 15.30 and 17.00 hours but the 2nd Battalion, 32nd Infantry Regiment, was forced to wait aboard ship until the next day. This lessened the available attacking force by a third.[179]

As the Americans moved forward from Massacre Bay the boggy muskeg sagged under the weight of even a single man, slowing them to a snails' pace. They had to pause to rest every 300 to 400 yards. Trucks, jeeps, trailers and towed artillery quickly sank up to the under carriage within 100 yards of the beaches. The supporting 105-millimetre artillery never got off the beach.[180] In fact, the problem of cross-country movement was so severe that in the first six days of the operation the Americans only gained 4,000 yards of ground in their advance up Massacre Bay, and some of the landing force had to be diverted to moving supplies and ammunition by hand as all other means were defeated by the muck.[181]

Although the fog had initially concealed the attackers from the Japanese, by 10.00 hours on 11 May 1943, Colonel Yamasaki received the news that the American invasion force had finally arrived. Yamasaki responded by strengthening the defensive positions that guarded the passes leading out of Massacre Valley. Then, in the late afternoon he ordered his men to emerge from the protection of their caves to occupy the prepared outer defences surrounding Chichagof Harbor. Overall, their perimeter extended from Hill X on the west arm of Holtz Bay, southward to Jarmin Pass and then eastward to Sarana Bay.[182]

The Southern Landing Force, plodding through the slippery muskeg in Massacre Valley, came under enemy fire shortly after 18.00 hours. They discovered that the Japanese had withdrawn from the beaches to occupy defensive positions overlooking the valley from high ridgelines that were obscured in the mist. From these trenches they could see the attacking Americans without being seen and could pin them down in the waterlogged muskeg by fires from above.[183]

The Japanese defensive positions overlooked the valley from high ridgelines that were obscured in the mist. From these trenches they could see the attacking Americans without being seen and could pin them down in the waterlogged muskeg with mortars and mountain artillery joining the rifle and machine gun fire to stop the attackers.[184]

The Americans found themselves unable to manoeuvre in any direction, having advanced just 3,000 yards from the beach that they had landed upon five hours earlier.[185] To break the stalemate, they requested fire support from the 105 millimetre. howitzers back on the beachhead. The artillery fired at a target on the high ground at the head of the valley. The recoil from the gun jammed its trails eighteen inches into the tundra. As soon as the American artillery fire ended, the Japanese opened fire again and the American advance once more stalled. Neither battalion was to receive effective fire support from the field artillery, or from naval gunfire in the first few days because the thick fog made accurate, observed fires impossible.[186] One officer recorded that: 'Fired on call target …Visibility nil. Cannot contact spotter on radio. May have hit him instead of target.'[187]

While the main effort had been attacking up Massacre Valley, other small units had been sent out to reconnoiter and provide flank security under circumstances that would severely test their skill and tenacity. One platoon from Company F, 17th Infantry Regiment had been reinforced with a light machine gun section and a 60-millimetre mortar squad, with the mission of seizing a steep pass leading over Gilbert Ridge to Sarana Beach and the 'high ground along right flank' (i.e., Gilbert Ridge), to establish defensive positions in the Sarana end of the pass from which Sarana Beach and Lake Nicholas could be fired upon, and to 'clear the ridge of enemy.'[188] The force of fifty men had moved east along the shore of Massacre Bay and up into a steep pass leading over Gilbert Ridge to Sarana Beach. They were now out of contact with the main assault force and could not expect help.[189]

After climbing all night, the platoon found itself on the morning after D-Day on the Sarana Beach side of the mountains. They also found themselves with unexpected guests. Lieutenant Colonel William J. Verbeck, the intelligence officer of the Alaska Defense Command, was conducting a daring reconnaissance mission of his own with two Alaska Scouts. He spent the night with the platoon and provided them with insights into Japanese tactics and the Japanese language, which the platoon leader later used to his advantage to surprise the enemy during a later chance encounter in the fog.[190]

The next day, the Japanese discovered the platoon and for three days the Americans fought off strong enemy attacks while they struggled to move westward along Gilbert Ridge. They observed several hundred Japanese troops improving defensive positions on Sarana Nose but were unable to communicate with higher headquarters due to faulty radios. They continued to move along the ridge in the dense fog while fighting off superior enemy forces to physically link up with other American forces. For four long, cold, sleepless days and nights they persevered without food or water. They were finally able to link-up with the main force in Massacre Valley on 15 May 1943. They were all suffering from exposure, several were wounded and two had been killed in action, but they had accomplished their mission.[191]

By 21.30 hours on 11 May 1943, five hours after the main landings had begun, the 7th Infantry Division had a total of 3,500 men ashore. As the long day ended, the gathering darkness and the thick fog merged to obscure the terrain completely.[192] The Provisional Battalion had spent most of the day climbing up a steep valley leading away from Beach Scarlet. They reached what appeared to be the summit of the pass at an elevation of nearly 2,500 feet by midafternoon. From that point onward they found that their already sketchy maps were simply blank.[193]

Dr Paul Nobuo Tatsuguchi: The Diary

The records of lived experiences represent and explain the cultural, political and sociological perspectives of the participants. By interweaving the personal perspectives into the broader context, we see that people make choices, and those choices make history.[194] We see how ideas and emotions such as 'sacrifice', 'determination' and 'will' are internalised, expressed and shared. In this way these characteristics or qualities may be identified and subjectively measured and enhance our understanding of how strategic culture and the power of will were constructed and viewed by the soldiers.[195]

Dr Paul Nobuo Tatsuguchi was assigned to the *Northern 5216 Detachment, North Sea Defense Field Hospital* of the Imperial Japanese Army on Attu. Raised in the Christian Seventh-day Adventist faith, Tatsuguchi had immigrated from Hiroshima, Japan to Los Angeles, California in 1926 to attend college. He graduated from medical school there in 1937 and returned to Japan to work in the sanitarium founded by his father in 1939. He was conscripted into the Imperial Japanese Army in January 1942.[196] His personal diary, which was captured by the 7th Infantry Division at the end of the battle, recorded his observations and experiences throughout the battle. There he quietly recorded the tragedies of the war, his own suffering, his struggle to care for the wounded in his field hospital, and the last moments of Japanese troops on Attu.

His diary begins with the entry for 12 May 1943, which reads, 'Carrier based plane flew over, fired at it … Air raids carried out frequently … Infantry, American transports, about 41, began landing at Massacre Bay.'[197]

The diary is riddled with misspellings and grammatical errors induced in the process of its repeated translation and reproduction, until eventually the original version was lost altogether. Nevertheless, it offers a unique window into the Japanese perspective of the battle. As with any translation of a foreign language, care was taken to understand the problematic nature of the translation since cultural nuance and linguistic meaning may be lost or misunderstood. Language is more than just a tool for communication. It expresses how a culture views and expresses the realities of the world.[198]

Sarana Ridge to Jarmin Pass

The next day, 12 May 1943, the 7th Infantry Division continued its two-pronged attack toward Jarmin Pass. Although supported by naval gunfire and air support, the frontal assaults of the 17th Infantry Regiment failed to gain any ground. Because neither Gilbert Ridge nor Henderson Ridge had been cleared, both battalions came under fire from each flank as well as from the front. The 2nd Battalion, 17th Infantry Regiment, which had been ordered to hold its position to block the Sarana-Massacre pass, instead found it necessary to move forward over very rough terrain in the face of heavy fire. Valiant attempts by the 3rd Battalion, 17th Infantry Regiment on the south-west side of Massacre Valley to reach the pass, which was the regimental objective, failed with heavy losses. Among the casualties was Colonel Edward P. Earle, the regimental commander, who was killed by machine gun fire while moving with one of his forward elements. His death was a severe blow to the 17th Infantry Regiment and to the division as well, as General Brown was then forced to place Colonel Wayne C. Zimmerman in command of the regiment, thereby depriving himself of an extremely capable chief of staff just when he needed him the most to make sense of an increasingly complicated battle.[199] Both battalions sent patrols forward to probe the enemy positions in hopes of finding a way to outflank the Japanese defences. At that time, the 2nd Battalion, 32nd Infantry Regiment finally came ashore at Massacre Bay. This was a critical improvement in the tactical situation for the Americans, as they needed more combat power to overcome both the Japanese and the inertia induced by the terrain and weather.

Meanwhile, in the northern sector, the 1st Battalion, 17th Infantry Regiment had found that they had lost the initiative overnight. The high ground that the battalion had reached on the night of D-Day was 900 yards short of their initial objective, Hill X and that the enemy was now dug in on Hill X. The battalion conducted a double envelopment attack which succeeded in gaining a foothold on the crest of the hill, however, the Japanese held firm on the reverse slope. It took another two days before they were able to force the Japanese off the reverse slope of the hill. As they attempted to do so, one company that was moving south, down the western arm of Holtz Bay, began to climb up the nearby ridge. Upon entering a gully, they were attacked by enemy troops who had occupied the position only the night before. For twelve long hours, the company was pinned down by Japanese machine guns, mortars and artillery. Two other companies, supported by artillery and close air support, tried in vain to dislodge the Japanese. It was not until 17.00 hours, that the Americans slowly began to gain ground. Eventually, they took the ridge only to be confronted by a violent Japanese counterattack. As the Japanese charged, their own poorly aimed artillery fire fell indiscriminately on friend and foe alike. The fierce firefight lasted twenty minutes, but finally the Americans were able to stave off the Japanese counterattack and retain control of the ridge that they then named Bloody Point. At the end of the day, 1st Battalion, 17th Infantry Regiment, was only 300 yards closer to Holtz Bay. Meanwhile, the Provisional Battalion had moved down into the canyon leading to the rear of the Japanese positions in Holtz Bay, but had been halted in that location for nearly three days[200]

In Massacre Valley, the continuing efforts of the Southern Force to take Jarmin Pass failed, even though the 2nd Battalion, 32nd Infantry Regiment was now reinforcing the 3rd Battalion, 17th Infantry Regiment. American casualties mounted and the front-line positions remained almost in the same place as they were on D-Day. Naval gunfire and air support continued whenever weather conditions allowed, but the results were insubstantial. By 14 May 1943, the main effort assault in Massacre Valley appeared to be completely stalled.[201]

The terrible Aleutian weather had frustrated the American advance almost as much as the Japanese defenders. Although naval gunfire continued to attack reported enemy positions it did so without the benefit of observation to adjust the fires, and the American ships expended their ammunition without achieving measurable effects. The fog that obscured the targets was an even greater hindrance to close air support.

There were only eight days out of the nineteen in combat that even allowed for air support. Only two days of clear weather occurred.[202] When air and artillery support were available, gains were made as on 15–16 May 1943. However, most of the time the results were negligible and often had tragic costs. On 14 May 1943, two F4F Wildcat fighter-bombers crashed due to the high winds and one B24 Liberator bomber crashed into a ridgeline shrouded in the fog. A total of eleven US airmen were killed.[203]

The Americans attempted to hasten the capture of Jarmin Pass with a coordinated simultaneous attack by both the Southern and Northern Landing Forces. While the Southern Landing Force would continue to be the main effort in its continued attack up Massacre Valley, the Northern Landing Force would drive the enemy off the reverse slope of Hill X, seize Moore Ridge and attack the defenders of Jarmin Pass from the rear. With three battalions now ashore in each landing force it was felt that sufficient combat power could be brought to bear, even though several hundred men were still dedicated to the task of moving ammunition forward and the casualties rearward by hand.

Despite having more troops, the combined attacks quickly ground to halt. In fact, they never really got started. The Provisional Battalion in the north had moved for four hours in the pre-dawn darkness to a point where they could see the Japanese positions, but they could also be seen and they became stalled in a firefight and were unable to break out of the canyon that they were in as they sought to reach the similarly fixed 1st Battalion, 17th Infantry Division. When 3rd Battalion, 17th Infantry Division failed to even reach its attack positions on the line of departure on time, General Brown canceled the attack. In that evening's situation report to higher headquarters, Brown summarised the last four days of fighting thus:

> Reconnaissance and experience of four days fighting indicates Japanese tactics comprise fighting with machine guns and snipers concealed in rain washes or in holes or trenches dug in each side and at varying heights of hill along narrow passes leading through mountain masses. These positions are difficult to locate and almost impossible to shoot out with artillery. They produce casualties in excess of casualties, which can be returned. Number of machine gun positions out of proportion to estimated enemy strength. In addition, small infantry groups are dug in high up on sides of pass parallel to axis of approach through pass as well as all commanding terrain features in passes. Impossible to approach positions on sides of pass from above due to precipitous slopes more or less snow covered and extremely slippery footing. Progress through passes will, unless we are extremely lucky, be slow and costly, and will require troops in excess to those now available to my command.[204]

It was now day five of the planned three-day operation. The stress of the battle was felt all the way to the topmost leaders. The men were freezing, hungry and frustrated. In the 3rd Battalion, 17th Infantry Division all but one company commander had been killed or wounded and the battalion commander had been relieved.[205] Nevertheless, the situation was not as stalemated as it appeared. At 11.00 hours on 15 May 1943, the fog lifted in the northern sector to reveal that the Japanese had withdrawn to the centre of Holtz Valley. To accommodate their reduced strength, they shortened their defensive perimeter, leaving behind caches of food and ammunition that apparently could not be removed.[206] This withdrawal allowed the Provisional Battalion to break out of its positions. Low on food and suffering from the bitter cold, but no longer being under fire from above, they drove the Japanese from the high ground and linked up with the two other battalions of the Northern Landing Force near Hill X. The Northern Landing Force now entered Holtz Valley to chase the retreating Japanese only to find that the clear skies also benefitted the Japanese who could fire more accurately at them from their positions on Moore Ridge. Although slowed by this fire, the Americans continued to press their attack until the lead company was mistakenly hit by a friendly air strike that ended the pursuit.[207]

For the next two days, the Northern Force continued attacking the West Arm area of Holtz Bay and Moore Ridge. They captured

Moore Ridge itself during the night of 16 May 1943. This placed 1st Battalion, 17th Infantry and 2nd Battalion, 32nd Infantry directly in the rear of the Japanese defending the Massacre Valley Pass, and on the morning of 17 May 1943, the Japanese began to withdraw toward Chichagof Harbor.[208] With the east arm of Holtz Bay now free of the enemy, American resupply by the sea was possible. This greatly lessened the logistical strain on the Northern Force. In the southern sector, the other two battalions of the 17th Infantry also found that the Japanese positions in Jarmin Pass had been abandoned, and the Southern Landing Force moved to occupy the pass that had been their original D-Day objective.[209]

Dr Tatsuguchi provides a contrasting glimpse of the Japanese perspective of the battle at this point. On 13 May 1943, Tatsuguchi wrote,

> The enemy has advanced to the bottom of *Misuma Yama* … Have engaged them … upon the unexpected attack the AA Machine Cannon was destroyed and we have withdrawn. In the night attack we have captured 20 enemy rifles.[210]

Tatsuguchi continues his narrative:

> May 14, 1943. Battle. Our two subs from Kiska assisted us greatly … damaged two enemy ships. Lieutenant Sueyuki died by shot from rifle. Continuous flow of wounded in the hospital. In the evening the U.S. forces used gas, but no damage was done because of strong winds … Our desperate defense [*sic*] is holding up well.[211]

On 15 May 1943, Tatsuguchi wrote, 'Continuous flow of casualties into our field hospital caused by the fierce bombardment of enemy land and naval forces … In a raid, I was ordered to the West Arm, but it was called off.'[212] Tatsuguchi next recorded this:

> May 16, 1943. Battle. If *Shitagata Dai* is occupied by the enemy the fate of the East Arm is decided, so burn all documents and prepare to destroy patients. [*sic*] At that time, there was an order from headquarters of sect. unit. Proceeded to Chichagof Harbor by way of the *Umanose*. 0100 [hours] in the morning, patients from Ind. Inf. Was lost [*sic*] so accompanied with patient I started. [*sic*] There was an air raid so took refuge in the former field hospital cave. The guns of a Lockheed spitted fire [*sic*] and flew past our cave.[213]

Sustaining Morale – Food

'Nothing undermines morale more decisively than hunger', wrote Sir Basil H. Liddell Hart in his book, *Thoughts on War*. Lack of food, loss of sleep and being cold are stressors that can erode fighting spirit. Maslow's hierarchy lists physiological needs as the foundation for behavioural motivation.[214] The conditions of modern combat directly attack the attainment of these needs, threatening accomplishment of the mission unless the individual soldier and the unit can overcome these obstacles.

On Attu both sides had to surmount these challenges. Both adversaries faced shortages of food. The Americans suffered high casualties from exposure to the weather. They had failed to understand the adverse effects that the terrain and weather would have on their forces and thus were insufficiently supplied with food and appropriate clothing. The Japanese positions on the other hand were

> well supplied with ammunition and rations', however, it seemed that they 'never conceded that he would not regain lost terrain … (and thus) did not destroy his stores in retreat ... expected to recapture them … or, decimated had neither time nor manpower to destroy, hide, remove ammo, food, guns, *sake*, medicine.[215]

When discussing the 7th Infantry Division's will to fight, it is important to recognise what was their greatest challenge in this, their first fight. Four days into the operation, the combined effect of mistakes in logistical planning had reached a critical point, and the invasion almost foundered at this point solely on account of the logistical failures. By 14 May 1943, many soldiers were suffering from exposure, several had not eaten in days, and many of the key leaders were out of action.[216] Replacements or reinforcements were not available because the troops that might have fulfilled that role were fully employed performing logistical tasks like carrying ammunition, food and supplies to the front lines.[217] The American landing force had suffered the loss or damage of ninety of their ninety-three landing craft and boats due to the hidden shoals and rough weather. The planners had not understood that vehicles and artillery could not be moved over the muskeg. Nor did they anticipate that food, ammunition and casualties would then have to be carried by hand, by the infantry as they climbed the wind swept, icy ridges in slow movements of only a few yards per hour, often being forced to hold on to the man in front in order not to become separated in the wind and fog or fall down the steep slopes.[218] At this point in the fight, both the Japanese and the Americans were grimly hanging on.

Sustaining Morale – Logistical Planning

> It was difficult to furnish hot meals to the troops due to the demand for ammunition on this terrain. It takes hours to move a Battalion or at times even a company. 500 additional troops were used to hand-carry to the battalion in one day.[219]

The troops' bulky rucksacks and sleeping bags were landed after the initial force went ashore. The sleeping bags which were difficult to carry nevertheless could have helped prevent many exposure casualties, but these did not reach them until the fourth or fifth day of the operation. There is no indication that the Japanese suffered as much as the Americans because they had clothing better suited to the environment and they occupied caves and bunkers on the high ground and thus were not stuck in the icy water and slush in the valleys.[220]

Despite their change of operational area from the North African desert, the 7th Infantry Division did not receive a complete refit of equipment for the cold, wet and windy Aleutian environment. The most egregious lapse of judgment by the logistics planners was the failure to issue waterproof boots to all the troops which contributed to some 1,200 cold weather casualties that resulted from frostbitten feet.[221] The items that were subsequently issued did not sufficiently counter the special cold weather environment that the troops encountered.[222] Because of the lack of time to fully equip and train the force, the division went with what it had and did without the cold weather gear.

Sustaining Morale – Food

1SG Hamlin, of the 7th Scout Company recounted the challenges to maintaining the will to fight and win during this period:

> Fatigue, rations almost gone, cold, wet, the thick fog defeated the aerial resupply efforts. Fourth day without food, LT Stott found two old dirty pieces of candy in his pocket and shared them with SGT Petruska who affirmed, 'That was one of the best things that ever happened to me.'[223]

Several troops vomited green bile after several days without food while fighting the terrain, the weather and the Japanese.[224] The failure to supply proper cold weather gear and food both threatened combat effectiveness from cold weather injuries as well as from the adverse psychological effect of such sustained discomfort and deprivation. To have food was a comfort. To have hot food was a luxury in such circumstances.

Not only were the physical needs of the troops not properly addressed, the combined effects of the terrain and weather on the plan to logistically sustain the scheme of manoeuvre were not properly foreseen. In the first six days of the operation, a significant number of the American landing force had to be diverted to moving supplies and ammunition by hand to overcome the inertia of the muskeg. Fuel, food and water would need to be transported by hand over the muskeg, with two men devoted to that effort for every man engaged in combat operations.[225] A battalion sized force of 400 infantry soldiers was soon engaged in this non-combat mission, reducing the available frontline combat power by one third.[226] This was the only method capable of resupplying the division. This method was slow and cumbersome and, owing to its ad hoc nature, keeping it running required immense tenacity and hands on leadership.

The carrying parties were initially organised by randomly assigning individual soldiers to the task, without consideration of maintaining unit organisation. They were forced to pass ammunition, food and supplies up a steep mountain pass by hand. Later, they ingeniously rigged a pulley system to winch a jeep up over another steep escarpment.[227] They required strong leadership and lacked cohesion and morale suffered as the men quickly tired of the tedious and difficult task that required hours of effort to complete. Despite this prodigious effort, it took twenty-four to forty-eight hours for some forward infantry platoons to receive a resupply of food, water and ammunition.[228]

The evacuation of non-ambulatory casualties took about two days and up to eight litter bearers. Many patients had to be carried a mile or so from the front over very rough terrain. There was no other means of transportation.[229] Nevertheless, many prodigious feats of improvisation and ingenuity were accomplished in overcoming the challenges of sustaining the fight and overall, the 7th Infantry Division's will to fight and to win did not waver.

Sustaining Morale – American Medical Care

An important factor in maintaining will to fight is medical support:

> The object of an army, of course, is the defeat of the enemy, and to this everything else must give way ... The modern soldier is believed to fight better if he knows that in case of being wounded, he will receive prompt attention ...[230]

Knowing that competent and caring medical personnel would spare no effort and undertake enormous risk to treat and evacuate them gave soldiers courage and motivation to fight. American medics were heralded because they would go anywhere, at any time to rescue and treat the wounded. On average, one in twenty-nine wounded Americans died in the Second World War, a significant improvement from the First World War average of one in twelve.[231] On Attu, cold weather injuries accounted for 31 per cent of the Americans' total losses. There were 1,200 troops who suffered trench-foot, frostbite, or hypothermia versus 1,148 who suffered wounds from small arms and artillery. In twenty-two days of action there occurred a ratio of cold injuries to wounded in action of 1:1.[232]

Beyond the obvious practical purpose of restoring wounded fighting men to duty, medical care enhanced the soldiers mental and emotional well-being by showing them that they would not be abandoned and forgotten.

Clevesy Pass and Holtz Bay

The link-up of the northern and southern American forces at the pass between Massacre Bay and Holtz Bay on 18 May 1943 that followed the Japanese withdrawal to Chichagof Harbor marked the turning point of the battle. Seizing Clevesy Pass was an essential objective for the Southern Landing Force to gain access to Chichagof Harbor. The western side of the pass was dominated by Cold Mountain. Overlooking the eastern side of the pass was an escarpment named Point Able. With slow but steady resolution, the American infantry attacked and destroyed the Japanese machine gun nests and mortar pits on the frozen heights one by one, gradually tightening the noose around Chichagof Harbor.[233]

The initial attacks by the 17th Infantry Regiment and the 32nd Infantry Regiment ran into heavy machine gun fire that brought them to a halt. A second attack employed artillery firing smoke rounds, which allowed the Americans to defeat several Japanese positions on the lower edges of Cold Mountain and Point Able, but it was once again stopped by heavy Japanese fire.[234] However, thanks to the cover of the smoke and the fact that some of the Japanese fled their positions thinking that it was poison gas, one company of the 17th Infantry Regiment had managed to take a point of high ground within Clevesy Pass.[235] Colonel Zimmerman's inspiring leadership and aggressive spirit were instrumental to success. He directed his troops from front line positions while under enemy artillery, machine gun and small arms fire. He fully understood the challenges faced by his soldiers and he reported these forthrightly to higher headquarters, saying: 'I found most of a platoon – all dead – and identified Captain Jarmin's body.'[236]

Disregarding the danger, although assistants were wounded near him, his personal bravery and leadership restored confidence and aggressiveness to the soldiers, which had been badly shaken by battle casualties and exposure to the severe weather. He, himself, suffered from frostbite and swollen feet, but he concealed that fact from his men.[237]

Will to Fight – Leadership

Dr Paul Nobuo Tatsuguchi recorded an evocative account involving Japanese leadership in his diary on 21 May 1943:

> Nervousness of our Commander is severe, and he said his last words to his officers and men. He will die tomorrow. Gave all of his articles away. Hasty chap this fellow. Everyone who heard this became desperate and things became disorderly.[238]

When Tatsuguchi writes of the 'nervous C.O.', it is unclear whom this refers to, but it makes clear the importance of steady leadership. Leaders set the tone for morale and motivation in their units. Will to fight crumbles quickly when leaders lose confidence.[239] For the troops all that remains then is surrender or death.

Colonel Yamasaki recognised that his force was severely threatened now from both north and south by the converging American forces. He quietly withdrew his forces that were defending Jarmin Pass to new defensive positions on the ridgelines directly above Chichagof Harbor and the two American forces linked up at Jarmin Pass on 18 May 1943.[240] Tatsuguchi now describes what must have been a Herculean effort to move the Japanese field hospital:

> May 17, 1943. Battle. At night, under cover of darkness, left the cave. The stretcher went over muddy road, steep hills of no man's land. No matter how far or how much we went, we did not get to the pass. Was rather irritated in the fog by the thought of getting lost. Sat down every 20 or 30 steps. Would sleep, dream, wake up again. ... The patient on the stretcher, who does not move is frostbitten. After all the effort, met with sector commander Col. [Colonel] Yamasaki. The pass is a straight line without any width and a steep line towards Chichagof Harbor. Sitting on my butt and lifting the feet, I slide very smoothly and changed directions with the sword. Slid down in about 20 min[utes]. After that arrived at Chichagoff [*sic*] Harbor after straggling. Time expended was 9 hours for all this, without leaving any patients.[241]

Sustaining Morale – Japanese Medical Care

Examining the medical care provided to the Japanese soldier presents us with a paradox. During the Russo-Japanese War, the Imperial Japanese Army had perhaps the most efficient and sophisticated military medical system in the world. The IJA led the way in military medical planning, requiring medical support to be included in operations orders and their supply system provided the highest quality equipment and supplies to the front lines. This contributed the unprecedented result of there being fewer Japanese deaths from disease than those suffered from enemy fire.[242] An American doctor wrote admiringly after the war,

> The supreme test of an army's medical organization [*sic*] comes ... in time of battle ... the best record ever made in that direction ... was that of the Japanese in the war with Russia.[243]

However, preserving the force merely for desperate sacrifice in battle seems to negate these accomplishments. The fact that they were willing to absorb enormous casualties, losing 18,000 soldiers during the final assault of Port Arthur hints at future sacrifice.[244]

Tatsuguchi's diary entry for this date also records the report that the Imperial Japanese Navy had sunk an American battleship, three destroyers and six troop transports. However, no American ships were actually lost. The Tatsuguchi diary continues:

> May 18. Battle. The yonegawa [*sic*] Det. abandoned East and West Arms and withdrew to Umanose. About 60 wounded came to the hospital. I had to care for them all by myself all through the night. Heard that

> the enemy carried out a landing in Chicagof [*sic*] Harbor ... Had two grenades ready.[245]

From the position in Clevesy Pass that they had taken on 18 May 1943, two American platoons were able to seize another enemy position on Engineer Hill. On the afternoon of 19 May 1943, companies from both the 17th Infantry Regiment and the 32nd Infantry Regiment began to climb the snow-covered slopes of Cold Mountain. At this stage of the campaign, the infantry companies of the battalions were each reporting an average of fifty men available for duty.[246]

Advancing against heavy fire, they used hand grenades and bayonets to oust the Japanese from their defences. As the Americans tried to reach the north side of the mountain high explosive and smoke rounds were fired onto the enemy. Once again, the Japanese were frightened into thinking that they were under attack by chemical munitions which caused some to flee and others to don gas masks.[247] The Americans on Engineer Hill who were able to directly assault the northern slopes took the summit of Cold Mountain on the morning of 20 May 1943.[248] From the Tatsuguchi diary:

> May 19. Battle. At night there was a phone call from section unit headquarters. Was told to translate a field order presumed to have been dropped by an enemy officer in Massacre Bay. Was ordered to draw a detail map sketch of Massacre and Holtz Bay which was in possession of Capt. Robert Edwards, Adj. of Col.Smith. [*sic*] [249]

Tatsuguchi continues,

> May 20. Battle. The hard fighting of our 303 Bn. [Battalion] in Massacre Bay is fierce and to our advantage. Have captured enemy weapon and used that to fight. Mowed down 10 enemy closing in under fog. Five of our men and one medical N.C.O. [non-commissioned officer] died.[250]

The Americans now turned to the final obstacle, Point Able. On the night of 21 May 1943, the 32nd Infantry Regiment attacked through the thick snow and bitter cold. Despite the darkness, the soldiers could be seen from 200 yards away, silhouetted against the white backdrop.[251] Led by an officer who was yelling insults in English at the Americans, the Japanese lobbed hand grenades down on their attackers. In the chaos, the Americans sought cover in the rocks and returned fire.

In ones and twos, they began to manoeuvre to get a better shot at the machine guns that had them pinned down. When they pinpointed the location, a 60-millimetre mortar was brought up to fire and it dropped six shells right into the Japanese position. A lieutenant then led a squad of infantry in a bayonet and grenade attack that captured the strongpoint. While this was going on, the 1st Battalion, 4th Infantry Regiment and the 3rd Battalion, 17th Infantry Regiment cleared the remaining ridges surrounding the entrance to Chichagof Valley on the morning of 22 May 1943.[252]

Will to Fight – Leadership

Character and competence were found to be the hallmarks of effective combat leaders. In combat, American soldiers followed officers and sergeants as much because of confidence in their leadership as because of their rank.[253] Infantry soldiers held those leaders who were distant from the front line and out of touch with the reality of combat in contempt, but they absolutely respected leaders who, proven in times of crisis had given the unit confidence, cohesion and morale at a critical moment.[254] An imperturbable leader, cool and calm under fire, and undaunted by adversity, had the unqualified respect of the troops and was a substantial positive factor in a units' will to fight.[255]

Contemporary studies continue to find that strong leadership buoys the fighting spirit of men in combat. As recently as 2013, interviews with soldiers in Afghanistan found that when they were confident in the competence and caring of their leadership their individual morale and collective confidence in their unit effectiveness was equally high. Faith in competent leadership correlates across wars and is essential in soldiers having the will to fight.[256]

The Battle for Chichagof Valley

The way was now open for the drive against Sarana Valley and Chichagof Harbor. The Americans began to push against the two ridges that lead to the harbour, named Fish Hook and Buffalo Ridge. They were both heavily defended with numerous machine gun positions. The American advance was slow as the lengthening hand-carried supply lines were ever more challenged to keep up with the demand for ammunition, food and water. Casualties from enemy fire and the cold weather mounted. At this point, the intrepidity and tenacity of individual American soldiers sustained the attack. One such leader was Private First Class Fred M. Barnett of Company A, 4th Infantry Regiment. On 22 May 1943, his company was pinned down by heavy machine gun fire while attempting to cross a rocky, open mountainside on Fish Hook Ridge. Suddenly, Barnett jumped up and ran toward the nearest Japanese machine gun nest. Armed with a rifle and hand grenades he attacked nine different positions alone, shooting and tossing grenades as he went. The rest of the company began to follow him but by the time they caught up with him, Barnett had killed forty-seven enemy soldiers on his own.[257] When later asked why he had acted so boldly, all he had to say was, 'Hell, I dunno. Just got all fed up and disgusted and decided I'd get the damned thing over with, I guess.'[258]

At this point, Dr Paul Nobuo Tatsuguchi's description of the battle begins to reflect the mounting pressure on the Japanese defenders: 'May 21. Was straffed [*sic*] when amputating a patient's arm.'[259]

Will to Sacrifice – Belief in Immortality

The episode highlights a feature of the Japanese tactical culture and the willingness to sacrifice:

> 80 amputated arms found on ground outside of what was discovered to be hospital; *no indication of wounds to these extremities* [emphasis added] ... such high mystical patriotic fervor so great as to banish all thought of surrender ... ready to die, hoping for immortality their thoughts fixed on the Yasukuni Shrine. EPW [Enemy Prisoner of War] interrogation indicated that the Attu force believed that a submarine was tasked to take severed arms back to Japan for cremation.[260]

Japanese soldiers believed that their sacrifices would be immortalised. Then and now, most Japanese observe a mixture of Shinto and Buddhist funeral customs which involve a meticulously planned and executed ritual of cremation and inurnment.[261]

> May 22. 0600 [hours] air raid again. Strafing killed one medical man ... May 23. Friendly naval bomber destroyed an enemy cruiser off shore [*sic*] ... a hit was scored on tents for patients ... two died instantly ... Days ration 1 *go*, 5 *shaku*. Nothing else. Everybody looked around for food and stole everything they could find.

> May 24. It sleeted and was extremely cold ... a medical man died instantly by penetration of shrapnel through his heart ... May 25. The worst is yet to come ... Bn. [Battalion] Commander died at Umanose ... They cannot fully accommodate all the patients ... Am suffering from diarrhea and am dizzy.[262]

Will to Sacrifice – Enduring Privation

Ironically, for the Japanese this morale damaging hunger might have been avoided:

> For two months the Japs had been on half rations because of the American air and Naval blockade. Hunger and food were beginning to be major preoccupations of the garrison ... in particular, the enemy was suffering a shortage of rice ... nevertheless, dried foods were found in abundance, potato chips, squash chips, onions, kelp, and mushrooms. Dried flounder and dried salmon were also found, canned tuna, cod, and salmon, canned beef, canned peas, pickled carrots, mixed vegetables, some canned pineapple and large stores of tangerines.[263]

It is unclear why so much food went unused.

The advances along Buffalo Ridge and Fish Hook Ridge were time consuming and difficult. Artillery and mortars were firing in support of the American attack with some success, but it ultimately took individual infantrymen armed with carbines, Browning Automatic Rifles and hand grenades to assault each Japanese foxhole. The further the Americans advanced, the tougher the resistance became. The Japanese were dug in on high ground over watching every major avenue of approach from well-prepared defensive positions.

Once again, an individual soldier exemplified the heroism and fortitude of many. Private First Class Joe P. Martinez of Company K, 32nd Infantry Regiment helped break the stalemate twice when his battalion was pinned down on 26 May 1943. He advanced alone with his weapon, firing into Japanese foxholes, and calmly reloading as he went. At the crest of cliff, he stood in the open, firing into an enemy trench until he was fatally wounded. 'He stood there it seemed like an hour, exposed wide open and fired until the magazine was empty.' When the action was over his platoon consisted of twenty-four riflemen. They counted forty dead Japanese in the positions that they had won. Martinez was posthumously awarded the Medal of Honor for his bravery.[264]

It took six days for the Americans to advance just 4,000 yards in their attack up Massacre Bay. The steep, icy slopes were exceedingly dangerous. During one patrol on the 24 May 1943, five soldiers went out but only two returned. Three men had fallen to their deaths.[265]

Lacking the advantage of overwhelming firepower, it thus fell to the initiative of individual riflemen and aggressive manoeuvre by well-led fire teams and squads to take the attack to the enemy. The Unit Report of BCT 32-2 for 28 May 1943 reads simply: 'Cos [Companies] C and F assaulted Buffalo Ridge and seized their objective.'[266] This terse report belies the extraordinary valour of the men who accomplished this task. The unit had been attacking the ridge since 26 May 1943, and the Japanese had lashed them with machine gun fire from rocks and crags all along the slope.[267] Repulsed with heavy losses, the Americans attacked again on 27 May 1943. Once again, they took serious casualties and the attack stopped. As darkness fell, Company G found itself pinned down 200 yards from the rock ledge that companies F and C occupied. The battalion commander urged them to withdraw, but the lieutenant in command advised him that, although they were beaten up, they were alright. They were right in the Japanese laps and if they pulled back, they would have to retake the ground all over again in the morning. Thus, the seventy tired and frozen fighters scratched out holes between the rocks to rest before resuming the attack in the morning.[268] Before daylight, the senior officer in charge, Lieutenant Stice, conducted a leader's reconnaissance to find a new route of advance. Finding a Japanese soldier asleep in a foxhole, the lieutenant tried to take him prisoner. The Japanese soldier fought and was killed by the lieutenant's .45 caliber M1911A1 Colt pistol.[269] Instantly, the fight was on as the Americans found themselves in a close-range melee with the Japanese. Grenades, bayonets and rifle fire were exchanged in the furious charge as the rest of the battalion tried to support the hasty attack. Lieutenant Stice and Sergeant Ruiz led the way. When the fighting was over, they were both found dead just below a rocky ledge. Their quiet epitaph: 'Cos [companies] C and F assaulted Buffalo Ridge and seized their objective.'[270]

During the attack on what the soldiers called, 'Bloody Point' a sergeant led his squad right into the enemy command post and an artillery emplacement. In the ensuing bayonet fighting with the enemy, he was proud to see that his men did not hesitate and were doing their jobs well. He was particularly thankful that their hand-to-hand combat training had been so thorough and felt the 7th Infantry Division had the mark of confidence typical of a great unit.[271]

Tenno Heika Banzai! (Long Live the Emperor!)[272]

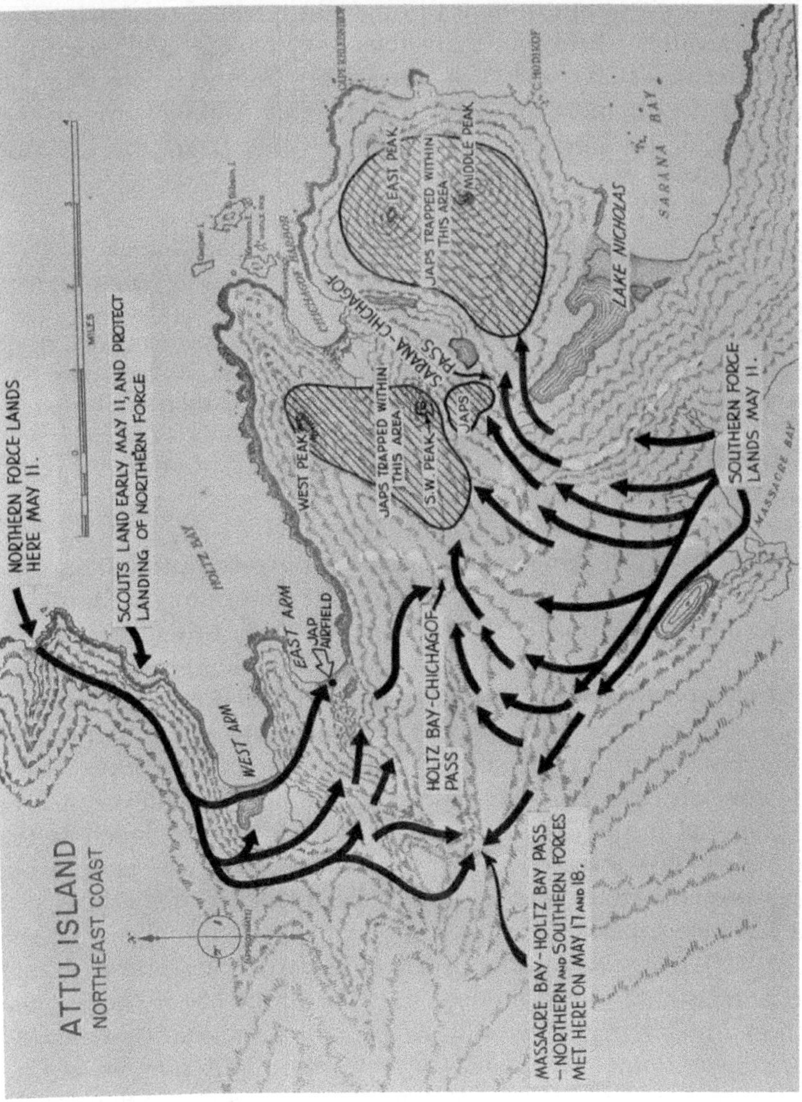

Figure 2–2: The Tactical Situation, 7th Infantry Division on Attu, 28 May 1943. (U.S. Army, Library of Congress. http://hdl.loc.gov/loc.pnp/fsa.8e01339. Public Domain.)

The Japanese were now pushed back into a couple of isolated areas near Chichagof Harbor. The Americans were positioned on the ridgelines to prevent any retreat through the various passes into one of the other valleys, however their lines in Chichagof Valley and the Sarana-Chichagof (Clevesy) Pass were thinly manned. The tragically apocalyptic denouement of the Japanese garrison was unforeseen. Dr Tatsuguchi described the final days events from the Japanese perspective thus:

> May 26 … it felt like the Misumi Barracks had blown up … Consciousness became vague … One tent burned down. Hirose, 1st Lt. [First Lieutenant] of Medical Corps is also wounded … The last line of Umanose was broken through. No hope for reinforcement. Will die for the cause of Imperial Edict … May 27. Diarrhea continues, pain is severe. Took everything from pills, opium, morphine, then slept pretty well. There is less than 1000 left from 2000 troops. Wounded from coast defense [*sic*] unit, field hospital headquarters, field post office, the rest are on front lines.[273]

On 28 May 1943, all American commanders were notified that the entire force was to attack no later than 05.00 hours on 29 May 1943. It was to be a maximum effort, with every soldier available. Those in the hospitals and aid stations who were capable of doing so were ordered to report back to their units for the final American push to victory.[274] On the Japanese side, Colonel Yamasaki's men had fought valiantly, but when all hope success or rescue was gone, he ordered a suicide attack for 29 May 1943. Knowing that he would never receive reinforcements and under threat of attack from his rear, he chose the destruction of his force over surrender. His order was simple but precise: 'We will attack and annihilate the United States Forces … I, in the advance for the attack, will be in the center [*sic*] rear of the front lines.'[275] Every remaining unit would participate, and each had a specific mission and terrain objective. From Chichagof Harbor, the 1,000 remaining Japanese would sweep down the lightly defended valley, retake Point Able and Clevesy Pass, and then seize the American artillery in Massacre Valley. It was hoped that they could then await reinforcements from Japan. Even the wounded and sick in the hospital would join in the attack if able. If they were not able, a doctor would execute them or give them a hand grenade with which to commit suicide.[276]

Sustaining Morale – Japanese Medical Care

Japan entered the war with a well-equipped and well-organised medical system, but it quickly broke down in combat. From New Britain to Holtz Bay, suffering abounded for the wounded Japanese soldier with numerous instances of the being abandoned or euthanised:

> We medics truly tried to save men's lives. Gangrene set in unless an amputation was performed quickly, so the doctor's operated on men using only partial anesthesia … We left an enormous number of them behind. There weren't any stretchers, so the more or less mobile ones were given a few days' rations and told to take off … get lost. The immobile ones, they were left behind. We had only a few hand grenades and a little medicine. Soon this was used not to cure but to kill our own men. We were five or six medics with one to two hundred patients to care for. What could we do with those without arms or legs? Carry them on our backs? Instead, we'd give them a shot of opium and then inject a 20cc [*sic*] solution of corrosive sublimate into a vein. It took only seconds to die. I could tell from their eyes that they knew what we were doing.[277]

The Japanese medical system was rife with contradictions: each soldier's blood was typed but it was not then recorded on dog tags; surgical instrument kits were exquisitely furnished and packed but haphazardly transported and distributed; sophisticated trauma surgery was done but convalescent care thereafter was lacking; finally, there was no comprehensive system for evacuating the wounded from the battlefield to the homeland. This seemingly paradoxical system that both treated and neglected the wounded may be attributed to the deeply embedded attitude expressed by a Japanese medical officer who told his interrogator that 'He could not return to his home or his parents, as all expect the soldiers to die at the front. When a soldier leaves home, he is not expected back anymore.'[278]

As the battle reached its terrible conclusion, Dr Tatsuguchi reported:

> May 28. The remaining rations is only for two days. Our artillery has been completely destroyed … The companys [*sic*] on the bottom of Attu Fuji (*Cold Mountain*) have been completely annihilated, except one … 303 Bn. [Battalion] has been defeated … Continuous cases of suicide. Half of sector unit headquarters was blown away. Heard that they gave 400 shots of morphine to severely wounded and killed them.[279]

While certainly reflecting the dire conditions that the Japanese faced at this point, Tatsuguchi's account cannot be taken as literal fact. His description and perception of the tactical situation and unit strength would lead one to the conclusion that the *banzai* attack could never have even been mounted due the complete lack of unit cohesion, to say nothing of having insufficient numerical strength. Notwithstanding the *in-extremis* nature of the attack, sufficient armed and healthy Japanese forces remained to commit to the operation. By physically massing his forces for the charge up the valley, Colonel Yamasaki was able to pit a phalanx of perhaps 800 soldiers against approximately 300 Americans spread across the valley and up onto Buffalo and Fish Hook ridges. The surprise, shock and speed of the charge gave the Japanese an even greater advantage.

Will to Sacrifice – *Sutegamari*

Yamasaki's attack plan had precedent in feudal Japanese history and culture. At the Battle of Sekigahara, 21 October 1600, Shimazu Yoshihiro decided to retreat, ironically in the only direction available by directly counterattacking the enemy headquarters, thus pushing through the opponent's lines to escape. They used a specific tactic called *Sutegamari*, a fighting retreat that required the commitment of a sacrificial force that would fight to the death to allow the escape of the leader. In execution, the *samurai* would delay pursuers by fighting from seated positions even at the risk of being overrun. This embodies a concept found in the *budo* and *bugei* of *sutemi*: to sacrifice or throw away oneself by physically yielding a defensible physical position to unbalance the opponent's attack; mentally it displays total commitment to the action without regard for the consequences.[280]

Dr Tatsuguchi's final diary entry reads:

> May 29. Battle. Today at 2000 we assembled in front of headquarters. The field hospital took part too. The last assault is to be carried out. All the patients in the hospital are to commit suicide. Only 33 years of living and I am to die here. I have no regrets. *Banzai* to the Emperor. I am grateful I have kept the peace in my soul which Ehkist [*sic*] bestowed on me. At 1800 [hours] took care of all the patients with grenades. Goodbye, Taeko, my beloved wife, who loved me to the last. Until we meet again, greet you God-speed. Misaka, who just became 4 years old, will grow up unhindered. I feel sorry for you Takiko, born Feb. [February] of this year and gone without seeing your father. Well be good. [*sic*] Matsuo, Ko-chan, Sake-chan, Massa-chan, Mitti-chan, Good-bye. The number participating in the attack is a little over 1000 to take enemy artillery positions. It seems that the enemy is expecting an all out [*sic*] attack tomorrow.[281]

On the night preceding the American attack scheduled for 29 May, Company B, 32nd Infantry Regiment had been ordered to move forward into Chichagof Valley through a gap between companies K and L of the 17th Infantry Regiment to establish a screen line across the valley. Having only fifty riflemen, this was to be a very thin line.[282] However, as the company pushed forward in the darkness, they suddenly found themselves in close combat with the Japanese. The company launched a hasty attack across the entire valley, but as they moved rapidly forward, the platoons began to get strung out. They felt that they were moving too fast; they first lost contact with the company command post, and then the individual soldiers began to lose contact with each other. Casualties were mounting, and as the company halted and consolidated its position to reorganise and evacuate the wounded, they received orders to withdraw.[283] The order seemed strange to the leaders and soldiers of the company and, because they didn't understand the reason for it, was passed on more as though it was a rumor than an actual order.[284]

Will to Fight – When Morale and Tactics Conflict

Both the 3rd Battalion, 17th Infantry Regiment and the attached B Company, 2nd Battalion, 32nd Infantry Regiment were assigned positions for the night on the floor of the valley near the southern end of Lake Cories. The reasons for the order to withdraw are obscure but there was no expectation of enemy action.

> It is said that the purpose was to permit the men to go back to the battalion kitchen ... so that they could get a hot breakfast ... At 0330 [hours] while the company was withdrawing, they were attacked and taken by surprise.[285]

This decision to rotate the company to the rear for a hot meal had an unintended impact. The battalion staff were not fully aware of the tactical situation faced by B Company and seemingly did not consider the fact that they were creating a vulnerability in the battalion battle position by ordering the withdrawal. This was an arguably poor decision and resultant tactical error undertaken in the sincere belief that it would improve the fighting spirit of the unit. Leaders must strike a balance between achieving the mission and looking after the welfare of their men. The willingness of men to trust and follow their leaders reflected the leaders' ability to strike this balance. Men felt they could trust a leader who was calm during crisis, who would not ask them to do anything that he would not do himself, and who genuinely cared for his men. One officer reflected, 'people are really looking for an opportunity to have confidence in others ... once [that] happens you have the troops in the palm of your hand.'[286] This incident on Attu illustrates both the nature of American leadership in its ingrained concern for the welfare of the troops as well as the resilience of these American soldiers who demonstrated the will to fight on without the hot food.

Nevertheless, while still in contact with the enemy, the company began a fighting withdrawal. Burdened with the wounded they moved back up the valley towards the aid station and the command post of the 3rd Battalion, 17th Infantry Regiment. The disorganised company was staggering back up the valley, shooting at small groups of the enemy, when red flares, grenade explosions and machine guns firing ahead of them heralded the *banzai* attack. Hundreds of Japanese troops charged through the company, breaking them into small, disconnected groups fighting from whatever cover they could find. The fight spread across the valley and up the ridgelines to the positions occupied by the 17th Infantry Division. Still, the main body of the Japanese attack hurtled onward towards the headquarters and support units in the American rear area.[287]

The charging mass of Japanese troops soon reached the command post of the 3rd Battalion, 17th Infantry Regiment where a desperate hand-to-hand fight ensued. The battalion commander, Lieutenant Colonel James Fish, was killed in the melee and the battalion headquarters was left in a shambles.[288] Captain Albert Pence was caught up in the swirling violence, first throwing hand grenades at the enemy and then physically grabbing one assailant, he plunged his knife into the man repeatedly until he finally realised that the blade had broken off inside the dead opponent's spine.[289] Lieutenant Dean Galles had been expecting replacements to arrive. Seeing the approaching forms of men in parkas in the misty darkness, he went to meet them only to be attacked by five Japanese soldiers. He was bayoneted four times but subdued one of his attackers with a headlock as his men up on the ridge killed the rest of the enemy.[290] Galles was left for dead by the enemy. Nevertheless, he dragged himself 2 miles to get medical care and alert other Americans of the danger.[291] The battalion aid station was stormed next; the medics and the wounded were trapped in their tent and many were killed. The rest feigned death for hours as the enemy attack continued around them.[292] The battalion surgeon, Captain Buehler, described it as 'a nightmare, a madness of noise and confusion and deadliness.'[293]

The Japanese main body continued through Clevesy Pass to attack the American artillery batteries on Engineer Hill at about 05.00 hours. There they were met by a hastily assembled defence force composed mostly of the 50th Engineer Battalion along with the gunners of the 49th Field Artillery Battalion and the medics of the 7th Medical Battalion. The Japanese made several direct attacks on the position only to be repulsed time after time by this force of American support troops that included cooks, drivers and headquarters staff.[294]

Somewhere in this maelstrom Dr Paul Nobuo Tatsuguchi was killed. There are conflicting stories of how he died. One claims that he was shot during the mopping up operation on 30 May by two American soldiers who were approaching a cave from which he emerged, yelling in English, 'Don't shoot! I am a Christian!'[295] The most plausible account was told by Dick Laird, who was a first sergeant in Dean Galles's unit. In 1984, he told his story to Tatsuguchi's surviving daughter. Laird was asleep in a tent on the morning when Yamasaki's troops attacked. He was awakened by the noise of the attack and had just emerged from his tent when the howling mob descended upon him.

Laird saw that a group of eight Japanese had captured an American mortar and were preparing to use it. Laird attacked them first with hand grenades and rifle fire and he eliminated the threat. Afterwards he examined the bodies for documents, and he found Tatsuguchi's diary and Bible. He was astonished to discover that Tatsuguchi was a physician and a father; a man that he felt should not have even been on Attu. Laird was awarded the Silver Star for his actions. However, the guilt of killing Tatsuguchi haunted Laird for the rest of his life.[296]

As their losses mounted, the Japanese lost momentum and became confused and disorganised. Daylight exposed them to effective counterattack by the now alerted American forces. Some began to run back down the valley toward Chichagof Harbor. Others stopped fighting altogether and began to commit suicide with hand grenades. By nightfall on 29 May, the majority had been annihilated. The few remaining pockets of Japanese forces were hunted down throughout the valley on the 30th.[297]

As the Americans moved forward to retake their overrun positions and mop up the remaining resistance, they were confronted with a ghastly sight at the base of Engineer Hill. The dead and wounded of both sides were heaped in piles and scattered everywhere like the fallen cherry blossoms so beloved in Japanese culture. This horrific sight caused a chaplain of the 7th Infantry Division to exclaim, 'I am glad they're dead, really glad. How can I go back to my church when I've got it in me to be glad men are dead?'[298]

The Foundations of Tactical Culture: The Fighting Spirit of the Seventh Infantry Division

Attu was the 7th Infantry Division's first experience of combat and showcased that the division was imbued with the will to fight and win under the most unexpected and adverse conditions. Intense unit training and dynamic leadership laid the foundation for the tactical culture that came to characterise the division throughout the rest of the war. The battle was extremely bloody; for every 100 Japanese killed on Attu, about 71 Americans were killed or wounded, making Attu second only to Iwo Jima in cost ratios.[299] The Americans suffered 3,829 casualties overall. In addition to the 549 who were killed in action and the 1,148 who were wounded, another 1,200 soldiers succumbed to frostbite and trench foot. Exposure to the cold and wet weather caused 614 more soldiers to be afflicted with pneumonia. Finally, accidents and injuries accounted for the loss of another 318 soldiers.[300] Cold weather injuries exceeded the number of casualties caused by wounds (1,148) and accounted for more than 31 per cent of all casualties from all causes.[301] The victors counted 2,351 Japanese dead and they had taken only 28 prisoners of war. The Americans estimated that another 300 to 500 Japanese had been buried in the mountain caves during the battle.[302] A soldier who fought at Attu summed up his experience of trying to retake that frozen terrain:

> It maybe wasn't such a big battle as battles go nowadays, but, brother, everything about it was done in a big way, including the way them Japs knocked themselves off. Believe me, that was the biggest, awfulest [*sic*] damned mess I ever saw in my life, so help me.[303]

The effects of the mountainous arctic terrain, bitter cold and dense foggy weather isolated and compartmentalised operations to small unit actions at the company level and below, while also denying the Americans the advantage of indirect fire support and close air support. While the Americans outnumbered the Japanese five to one overall, at the tactical level, the Americans could never bring the full division-sized force of the 7th Infantry Division eventually numbering some 11,000 (having initially embarked with only two infantry regiments) to bear on the Japanese all at the same time.

Furthermore, not all the soldiers of the division were combat infantry; the total strength of a US infantry regiment in 1943 was 3,118 soldiers.[304] In fact, about 50 per cent of the manpower in a US infantry division was in headquarters, artillery, engineers, military police, medical and quartermaster units. The infantry companies account for only about one half of a division's strength.[305] Therefore, for the first 6 days of the operation the Americans on Attu numbered approximately 3,500 against some 2,900 defending Japanese. At the actual point of attack the Americans enjoyed a correlation of forces of only 1.21:1.

In retrospect the American attack up Massacre Valley was precisely what the Japanese had planned and hoped for. The Japanese made maximum use of the terrain and weather to enhance their defences. Hidden in the heavy fog and mist, they always held the high ground, which dominated the barren valleys below. From these positions they were able to pour devastating fire onto the Americans as they struggled across the mushy tundra, steep slopes and heavy snow. There were no trees of bushes for concealment and the spongy muskeg offered little cover.

The Japanese were dug in on high ground over watching every major avenue of approach from well-prepared defensive positions. Most importantly, they were properly dressed and equipped mountain troops, trained in Hokkaido and north Manchukuo.[306] Having lived and trained in such an environment and being acclimatised to their conditions, these mountain troops would lay motionless for hours in camouflaged positions to ambush US soldiers as they passed by. The critical flaw in this otherwise tactically sound plan was in its technical execution. According to Japanese infantry tactical defensive doctrine, the machine gun was the primary weapon, each battle position being built around them.[307] At Attu, this technique of fire had less effectiveness because their positions were scattered and not physically connected, thus they were unable to concentrate and interlock their direct fires. The Japanese machine guns were however well emplaced to provide mutual support. They were usually supported by at least one other gun, 200 to 500 yards away. This required both positions to be attacked together which was a difficult task.[308] The Japanese also demonstrated a pattern throughout the battle for Attu of opening fire with their machine guns at a range of 1,000 yards, using the technique of plunging fire, which, although it slowed the pace of the American attack, proved to be ineffective in stopping them.[309] With their weapons positioned on the high ground, just inside the fog line, the Japanese were able to engage the Americans at the maximum effective range of their weapons from positions frequently invisible to the Americans exposed in the Valleys below.[310]

Japanese artillery was extensively used in the defence, with the individual field guns being tunneled into hillsides. The Japanese perspective on indirect fire support on Attu is somewhat illustrated by this excerpt from another captured diary:

> May 13th – Thursday. Clear. From about 0300 [hours] the enemy fired naval guns fiercely. Also heard rifle and machine gun firing very severely at West Arm. From about 0600 [hours] heavy fog lifted and about 10 enemy fighter planes attacked us. From about 0800 [hours] a formation of bombers dropped bombs on our positions vigorously, however, no damage. There were several severe battles today and many bombs were dropped around our protective position for artillery. We fired 117 rounds of ammunition ... May 16th – Sunday. Fine weather. Since we have been having heavy fog lately, everyone is full of pep and willing to fight hard. Fired at enemy skirmishers from our positions.[311]

This vignette illustrates that the Japanese volume of indirect fire was considerable, firing over a hundred rounds in approximately forty-eight hours. By noting that they fired at 'enemy skirmishers from our positions' it also appears that they also engaged the Americans with small arms. Despite 'heavy' fires by the Americans, decisive results were not often attained due to the weather and the terrain, which adversely affected their ability to deliver accurate, predicted fires. It also illustrates that these difficulties affected the Japanese as well, but these were further compounded by their practice of firing artillery as individual weapons rather than by massing indirect fires.[312] When coupled with poor communications between the Japanese positions and no concept of final protective indirect fires controlled by a fire direction centre, a coordinated combined arms defence was impossible.[313]

The actions of the 7th Infantry Division on Attu were cited for great skill in light infantry tactics in mountainous terrain, especially in conducting reconnaissance patrols and conducting squad/platoon/company attacks of a strongpoint. They used patrols to pinpoint enemy positions in the fog and small units to outflank and take enemy strong points. The leaders and soldiers quickly recognised the need to establish a base of fire to suppress enemy positions with direct fire and allow other forces to manoeuvre against the enemy's strong points. Whenever possible the Americans used artillery and mortar preparatory fires and smoke to support infantry manoeuvre. One particularly noteworthy method that they developed was the coordinated attack of riflemen supported by 37-millimetre anti-tank guns firing high explosive rounds to destroy enemy crew served weapons.[314]

Gradually, the Americans were able to manoeuvre to flanking positions where they would then isolate and suppress the Japanese battle positions and finish the defenders with a direct assault.[315] Numerous reports on Attu reflect the finding that suppressive fires kept Japanese forces pinned in their bunkers and 'spider holes/ octopus pots' (*takotsubo*) so effectively that American troops could fire right down into them in order to finish the assault.[316] Afterwards, 7th Infantry Division soldiers remarked on the bayonet and hand-to-hand fighting skills of their opponents in that they were not as dangerous as feared and that they were glad for the arduous training that they had received in preparation.[317]

Not only did the 7th Infantry Division emerge victorious from the Battle of Attu, but they did so without the aid of extensive logistical and close air support and in terrain and weather conditions that clearly favored a defensive stand by the Japanese. American soldiers successfully used the weapons at their disposal to close with and destroy the enemy. The American armed forces also proved their superior ability to operate effectively in a joint environment with air and naval forces.

Developing the Characteristics of Tactical Culture

Attu was the 7th Infantry Division's first experience of combat and showcased that the division was imbued with the will to fight and win under the most unexpected and adverse conditions. The chief of staff of the army, General George C. Marshall, personally selected the 7th Infantry Division as one of three units fighting in the Pacific theatre for inclusion in the study on 'Willingness for Combat'. The opinions of the troops in the study, quantitatively analysed, represented their attitudes and motivation in relation to their past and subsequent combat performance.[318]

In this study the 7th Infantry Division veterans gave high post-combat marks to their officers for leading by example, having personal interest in their men, and wanting to serve under them in combat again.[319] Cited by the study as having 'seen combat under the most arduous conditions' it was found that most of the soldiers of the 7th Infantry Division were proud of their unit and felt that the war was worth fighting. Their positive attitudes towards officer and non-commissioned-officer leadership were indicative of 'good combat motivation'.[320] It was further found that these soldiers who were very proud of their unit were also 'more confident in themselves the more times they went into combat.' Furthermore, 'combat became less frightening the more they saw of it.'[321]

Characteristics of Tactical Culture

Certain traits and characteristics appear common to successful combat units and leaders: They have an intuitive tactical and technical appreciation that allows them to judge terrain and visualise how to expertly employ their weapons and manoeuvre effectively; they are tenacious, displaying an imaginative intensity to win; they are imbued with a certitude about themselves and their mission that allows them to be audacious. The acme of tactical culture is expressed by a unit that promotes taking calculated risks and operates with controlled aggressiveness.[322] One interesting observation of the 7th Infantry Division on Attu illustrates their tactical culture. In contradiction to S.L.A. Marshall's contention that few American soldiers fired their weapons in combat it was reported that by the fifth day of the battle the troops had already fired 1,024,000 rounds of rifle and carbine ammunition and 2,442,000 rounds of machine gun ammunition.[323] Other studies have shown that units commanded by successful leaders take on the leaders' confidence and will to win. The leader is often the decisive factor in building a unit that displays audacity, aggressiveness, overcomes obstacles and refuses to accept defeat. Such units develop a unique cohesion largely brought about by good leadership.[324] Dynamic leadership laid the foundation for the 7th Infantry Division's high unit and task cohesion.

The fighting spirit of the American troops is exemplified by this excerpt from a letter written by Ralph Eyde of the 32nd Infantry Regiment. Eyde suffered a head wound early in the battle, but he shrugged it off and continued to fight:

> it was only a slight head wound + nothing more it's okay by me. It was plenty close [*sic*] but I was never out of the 18 straight days of action nor in any hospital or rest camp. Too many fellows worse off than myself at the time so I had it dressed the following day while eating my field ration (was hit the same day I landed – shell landing 15 feet away while pushing ahead). But all this a thousand times over never held up this outfit. Had plenty of calls as close + closer … If the people back home ever have any doubts about the fighting caliber of its soldiers, they want to see this outfit in action [*sic*] and I can assure you that all their doubts

would be erased. It was a rugged struggle and all the weather in the world couldn't hold us back.[325]

The tactical culture of the 7th Infantry Division was characterised by this type of stoic, grim, workman-like determination to accomplish the task; that embraced manoeuvre tactics as being more important than sheer firepower; that displayed individual stamina and tenacity, small unit cohesion, and competent and aggressive leadership.[326] These military strengths became unit traits and formed the foundations of the division's growing tactical culture.

Gyokusai

Attu established a paradigm for Japanese operations throughout the war; to endure horrific casualties and great privation, in steadfast perseverance and tenacious loyalty to the emperor. On 30 May 1943, the *Daihon'ei* (Imperial General Headquarters) addressed the defeat by announcing that the Attu force had accomplished a *gyokusai*, a phrase taken from classical Chinese literature. The earliest use of the word is found in a biography from the sixth century that expressed the desire to be 'a broken jewel rather than a whole tile', meaning that one should prefer to die gloriously rather than to live an inglorious life.[327]

Gyokusai is a poetic term, denoting a beautiful death in battle for a higher purpose. This was an electrifying concept for the Japanese, inspiring both the home front and other defending garrisons to see fighting to the death as entirely acceptable and it conveyed the feeling of 'the transcendent moral quality of such sacrifice.'[328] The men defending Attu became the first Japanese force to be destroyed during the war, but they would not be the last.

In Japan, their sacrifice was eulogised, and these 'shattered jewels' became the paragon of the will to sacrifice.[329] They were immortalised in a booklet titled *Yamasaki: God of Forces* (1944) that lists the name, rank, hometown and a photograph of every soldier killed on Attu.[330] In this depiction, the dead had not suffered a defeat. Rather, their spirits had been purified by their self-sacrifice. *Gyokusai* became synonymous in the Japanese lexicon for choosing death over dishonour and it thereby became a central feature of their tactical culture.[331]

Why did the Japanese soldiers choose death rather than accepting surrender? Why would the tragic and futile *gyokusai* be considered acceptable and even praiseworthy rather than being seen as an abject military failure? The answer lies in the Japanese national and cultural identity. The Japanese embarked on the war with a will to fight for glory in the service of the Emperor and the Nation. But this will to win was subverted by the tactical culture which emphasised the will to sacrifice as the paramount virtue of the soldier. In his final communique with headquarters, Yamasaki reported his situation and intended course of action:

> Under ferocious attack by enemy land, sea, and air, the two battalions to the fore were both almost smashed ... I arranged so the wounded and the ill in the field hospital were disposed of, the light ones by themselves, the serious ones by the medics ...We had them make a resolve [to die], lest we together suffer the shame of being taken prisoner while alive. It is not that there is no other way; I simply did not wish to sully the soldiers' last moments. We will carry out a charge with the heroic spirits [of those killed in battle].[332]

As Yamasaki indicates, surrender was viewed as shameful, the ultimate dishonour that could befall a soldier. Avoiding shame and displaying stoicism in the fulfilment of the debt owed to the nation and the emperor was deeply important.[333] Few Japanese were therefore taken as prisoners of war and the great majority of those who were told their captors that their greatest motivation for not surrendering was the shame and humiliation that they and their families would endure.[334] This belief derived from the *Senjinkun*, the Imperial Rescript to Japanese Soldiers and Sailors, first issued in 1882, that established a code of conduct on the battlefield. With the injunction, 'Die, rather than become a prisoner' the notion of honourable death in battle was embedded in the tactical culture of the Imperial Japanese Army and the Imperial Japanese Navy.

In conjunction with the powerful compulsion to discharge the burden of obligation was the Japanese attitude toward death. In the Japanese cultural world view, death was accepted as a tragic but inevitable consequence of life. Within Japanese society there is a strong sense of sorrow at the transient and impermanent nature of human life. This is expressed by the phrase '*mono no aware*' ('things of sadness'), and it embraces the sorrow that nothing will remain, that even the most glorious beauty will decay and disappear.[335] This Japanese resignation to ephemerality seems to have arisen from popular reaction to ancient feudal warfare. The epic *Heike Monogatari* (Tale of the Heike), believed to have compiled before 1330 CE, recounts the Genpei War (1180–1185 CE) fought between the Taira and Minamoto clans for control of Japan. The theme of impermanence is presented in the opening passage: 'The proud do not endure, they are like a dream on a spring night; the mighty fall at last, they are as dust before the wind.'[336]

This aesthetic of the sad beauty of life and death resonates throughout Japanese history in reaction to its many, long periods of near constant civil war and social upheaval and was deeply important in shaping Japanese culture. In the Second World War acceptance of the inevitability of death in combat was a commonly expressed theme. One Imperial Japanese Army lieutenant serving on Guadalcanal wrote in his diary, 'if we do not succeed in the occupation of these islands, no one should expect to return alive to Japan.'[337]

Contrast this view with the common American sentiment that the war was an unpleasant but necessary job to be accomplished before one could return home.[338] For the Japanese however, going to war was strangely celebrated for the certainty of death. One of the most important Japanese patriotic songs of the time was *'Umi Yukaba'* ('When Seagoing' or 'If I Go to Sea'), which expressed it thus:

> If I go away to the sea,
> I shall be a corpse washed up.
> If I go away to the mountain,
> I shall be a corpse in the grass
> But if I die for the Emperor,
> It will not be a regret.

This song, which became a semi-official national anthem during the war, invoked these ancient *samurai* attitudes and imagery about death.[339] In further affirmation of this sentiment was the immensely popular imagery of the *sakura*, the cherry blossom. The cherry blossom is a highly significant symbol in Japan, as it represents the evanescent nature of life, blooming for a short time and then dying at the height of its beauty.[340] The sad beauty represented by this transition from fullness to non-existence was viewed as the ideal philosophical approach to combat and death.[341] In this manner, the transcendence of life was confronted and accepted, as the soldier adopted a poetic cultural tradition to help him to confront the anxiety of death and the conflicting desire for immortality.[342]

Will to Sacrifice – Obedience

The keystone to *gyokusai* was strict obedience to orders. When ordered to commit mass suicide rather than surrender, Japanese soldiers obeyed unflinchingly. This stems from a common Japanese belief in the nobility of the act as demonstrated in the story of the *Chushingura*, an internationally known story in Japanese history. A group of forty-seven *samurai*, made indigent by the death of their master who committed ritual suicide as punishment for a transgression of the peace, waited for over a year to enact revenge on the man responsible.[343] It has become a legend and offers great insights into the national character highlighting the Japanese traits of loyalty, silent endurance, sacrifice and noble suffering.[344] The story idealises devotion to duty even unto death as the only correct choice for the *samurai*.

This fatalistic acceptance of death was nevertheless infused with a positive tone through the Japanese soldier's *seishin* (spirit, soul, intention, will), which always stressed the active attitude of the attack.[345] As soldiers killed in battle, they believed that they would be elevated to *kami* (a Shinto deity: 'a sacred spirit'), and thus be venerated at the Yasukuni Shrine.[346] This aesthetic influenced Japanese tactical culture, and *gyokusai* became the norm: 4,600 dying on Tarawa (17 surviving); 7,900 dying on Kwajalein (105 surviving); over 10,000 dying on Biak (520 surviving); and 29,000 to 32,000 dying on Saipan (921 surviving).[347] By declaring the martyrdom of the Attu garrison as an event to be revered, the Japanese leaders were able to ignore the reality of their failure and mobilise more men to sacrifice themselves. *Gyokusai* was the effect, but what was the cause of this trait of Imperial Japanese Army tactical culture? Part of the answer lies in *Bushidō*.

Chapter Three

THE BATTLE OF KWAJALEIN, THE *SAMURAI* LEGACY AND THE MYTH OF *BUSHIDŌ*

> 'As on Attu we lost some gallant young fellows whose heroic deeds against harassing snipers, pillboxes + blockhouses will never be forgotten. The Jap is a tough little fighter + no one in this outfit underestimates their fanatics [*sic*] fighting ability.'[348]

Introduction

Moving forward from victories in the Solomons and Gilbert Islands in 1943, Allied forces sought to penetrate the next ring of Japanese defences in the Central Pacific. Attacking into the Marshall Islands, the Allies occupied Majuro and then commenced operations against Kwajalein. The Battle of Kwajalein occurred from 31 January to 3 February 1944. Striking at both ends of the atoll, they succeeded in eliminating the Japanese opposition after brief but fierce battles. The triumph opened the way for the subsequent capture of Eniwetok and the campaign against the Marianas. This chapter will further explore how the respective American and Japanese tactical cultures evolved and what impact they had on combat.

The Operational Environment: The American's Central Pacific Advance

The over-all American objective to their attack of the Gilbert, Marshall and Caroline islands in the Western Pacific was to seize key positions that could be used to blockade Japan by air and sea and to provide launching points for an invasion of the Japanese home islands. When combined with the American advance through the Solomons and New Guinea, the Japanese were uncertain about which line of effort should be countered first.[349]

Terrain and Weather

Kwajalein is one of the world's largest coral atolls, being comprised of 97 islands enclosing a lagoon with an area of 839 square miles of water. It has a total land area of just over 6 square miles and an average height above sea level of 5 feet, 11 inches.[350] The main southern island is 4 miles in length overall, rising just 17 feet out of the sea and averages 800 yards wide.[351] Lying about 500 miles north of the equator, the atoll is 2,440 miles from Hawaii, 2,000 miles from Australia and 2,447 miles from Japan.[352] It has a tropical rainforest environment with average high temperatures of 85 degrees Fahrenheit during the month of January.[353]

The Air Campaign

Between 1932 and 1941 the Japanese had constructed several bases in the Marshall Islands, with Kwajalein as their principal base.[354] A prerequisite to seizure of these strategic points in the Gilbert and Marshall Islands was gaining air superiority. These island chains generally lay beyond the range of land-based aircraft. However, the Americans believed that their new Essex-class carriers could provide enough air power to isolate the islands from reinforcement or counterattack by the Japanese and once occupied would then extend the range of land-based bombers.[355]

An air campaign against the Japanese forces in the Marshalls was conducted between November 1943 and January 1944 to destroy the Japanese air forces and defences. Both aircraft carrier-based airstrikes and long-range bombing raids were conducted against the numerous facilities and airfields of the Kwajalein Atoll.[356] The campaign was highly effective, costing the Japanese approximately seventy-one aircraft and rendering them unable to launch air attacks against the coming amphibious invasion.[357] Additionally, extensive air reconnaissance was conducted to develop intelligence on the objectives.[358]

The American Attack Plan: 'Operation Flintlock'

On 4 September 1943, the 7th Infantry Division assembled on ships and prepared to leave the Aleutians. There was great speculation as to where they were going, but no specific target was revealed. The staff was only told to prepare plans for landings on coral atolls.[359] Their eventual target was the 'Eastern Mandates', the former German colonial possessions in the Pacific that had been mandated to Japan after First World War. They included the Marianas, the Palaus, the Carolines and the Marshalls. Under Article 22 of the Covenant of the League of Nations, Japan was prevented from establishing fortifications on the islands, however after withdrawing from the League in 1935 the Japanese conducted extensive clandestine military construction efforts in the islands to include naval support facilities and runways for aircraft.[360]

Once they moved from Attu to the island of Oahu in the Hawaiian Islands the staff of the 7th Infantry Division began to plan for attacks specifically on Wotje and Maloelap in the Marshalls. However, only six weeks before the landing the target was changed to the Kwajalein Atoll.[361] Dubbed Operation Flintlock, the American plan called for the US Navy's 5th Amphibious Force to deliver the V Amphibious Corps to the Kwajalein Atoll where the 4th Marine Division would assault the linked islands of Roi-Namur in the north while the 7th Infantry Division attacked Kwajalein Island in the south.

The Japanese had held the Marshall Islands for twenty-five years and it was assumed that elaborate defences were in place.[362] Kwajalein Island contained a new airfield, important supply dumps and repair shops and communications facilities. It had heavy beach fortifications running lengthwise down the island. The Americans expected a bitter fight just to gain the beach, followed by a fight to the death once on the island. American intelligence estimates were that between 8,000 to 9,600 Japanese troops were spread throughout Kwajalein Atoll in addition to a force of 1,200 to 1,600 Korean laborers.[363]

Intelligence Preparation

Preliminary intelligence assessments, supported by submarine reconnaissance and aerial photography had accurately located all beach defensive positions of significance. Before embarkation an amphitheatre at Schofield Barracks, Hawaii was used for intelligence briefings and large-scale model map studies. Once underway specific mission briefings were delivered to each battalion commander containing plans, orders and maps.[364] Detailed terrain models and photographs were used for planning and rehearsals while enroute. 'We could see each wave and wash, each frond of the palm trees, tire tracks on the road. We talked about the steep rise up the surf, the supporting fires and how that would change the landscape.'[365] Updated photos taken two days before the attack were delivered to the task force commanders on the day before the attack which were then used to confirm final details of the landing beaches and air and naval gunfire targets.[366]

As they studied the terrain and photographs of the enemy dispositions on Kwajalein Atoll the 7th Infantry Division's planners realised that most of the Japanese defenses faced either the ocean or the lagoon.[367] The lagoon shore is also protected by a wide reef. While there were gun positions constructed at each end of the island, the planners felt that a landing on the island's western extremity and a subsequent advance along the axis of the island would catch the main defenses from the flank and ease their task.[368] However, because the crescent of land is only 800 yards wide at the most, only two battalions or four rifle companies in total could be doctrinally employed together at any one time and therefore maintaining unit boundaries and alignment would be challenging.[369] The division's new commander, Major General C.H. Corlett explained his decision in the after-action report:

> The controlling reasons for the selection of the landing beaches ... was that the ones [eventually] selected were in the lee of the atoll from the prevailing wind, and the long axis of the island provided an ideal situation for a very strong attack with two regiments abreast in column of battalions, the narrowing dimension of the island to the northeast contributing to the strength of the attack.[370]

The Tyranny of Tropical Island Terrain

The topography of a Pacific atoll severely limits offensive manoeuvre options. There is no room for wide enveloping attacks and the small scale means that both friendly and enemy forces are all always within small arms range (0 to 500 metres) and mortar fire range (100 to 1,200 metres). Friendly units were often separated by a few yards, with only a building, trees, or vegetation to identify a unit boundary. Indiscriminate firing to the flanks will cause friendly casualties because of the close proximities of the adjacent forces. Attacking down the long axis as the terrain curves presents further challenges to maintaining proper weapons alignment towards the enemy. Neither force can retreat without risk of annihilation and repositioning is difficult.

The operation was to be conducted in four phases. Phase I was the capture of Carlson Island and the adjacent islets that guarded the best entrance channel into the lagoon. Phase II was the capture of Kwajalein itself as the main effort. Phase III was the capture of Burton Island and Phase IV was the mop-up phase.[371] Fire support was a matter of concern, based on the experience at Tarawa that naval gunfire preparation had been inadequate to destroy Japanese fortifications and

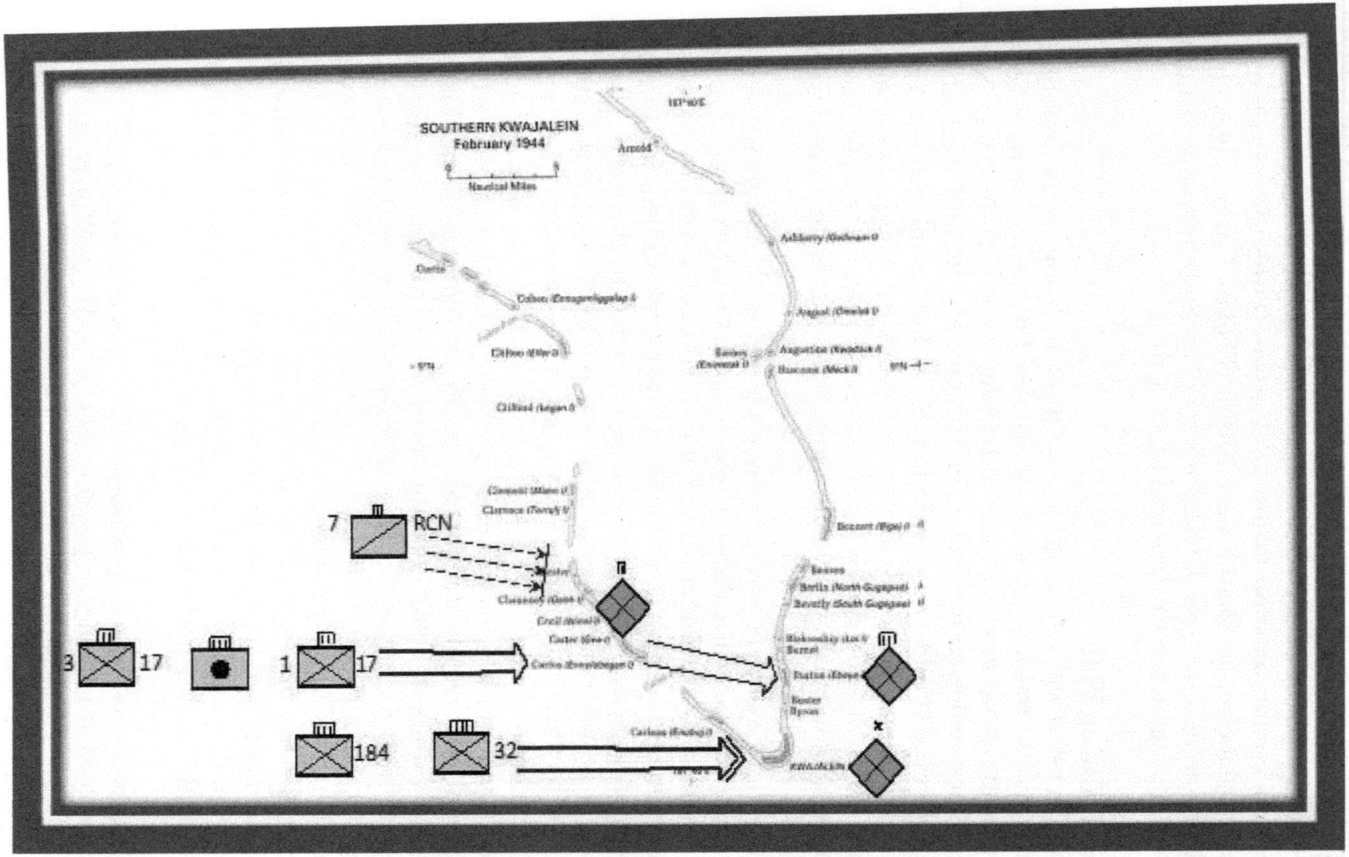

Figure 3-1: Operation Flintlock, Scheme of Manoeuvre, 31 January–4 February 1944. (The US Army Campaigns of World War II: Eastern Mandates, CMH Pub 72-23, downloaded and converted to PNG by US government. Public Domain, https://commons.wikimedia.org/w/index.php?curid=47139000.)

that, once the ground force was ashore, naval gunfire was no longer safe to employ.[372] The solution devised was to seize one or more of the adjacent, smaller islands to serve as firing positions for the division's artillery battalions. The two best nearby islands were the sites of a large Japanese communication facility on Carlson (Enubuj) and submarine and seaplane repair facilities on Burton (Ebeye). Carlson was chosen to be taken and used as the base for artillery support to the rest of the force landing on the western end of Kwajalein.[373]

The Training Plan

While the staff was planning the operation the troops were undergoing a four-month training program at Schofield Barracks. Leaders vowed to provide more mission focused training than was available before Attu. They reviewed the unit's performance at Attu and worked hard to perfect the latest techniques in jungle warfare, amphibious landings and fire and manoeuvre at the newly established Unit Jungle Training Center. The mission of this centre was to prepare troops for combat against the Japanese in difficult terrain, by day or night, under various weather conditions.[374]

They had many resources to draw upon. One of the characteristics of American tactical culture in the Second World War was seeking continuous improvement though the creation of a collective learning environment. All aspects of modern combat were studied, and relevant information and knowledge was disseminated to the force. The 7th Infantry Division's performance at the Battle of Attu was carefully studied by the War Department through numerous after-action reports, and the lessons that were learned were widely disseminated to the army's training bases and headquarters staffs and incorporated into doctrinal and technical publications. Improvements in amphibious cargo handling, training and equipping troops for harsh weather and mountainous terrain, and the use of forward air controllers in support of ground troops were carefully developed and applied successfully elsewhere.[375] The 7th Infantry Division emerged victorious from the Battle of Attu, but they did so without having been trained for that environment. Nevertheless, they were specifically commended for their initiative, agility and adaptability to successfully close with and destroy the enemy under adverse conditions:

> success depends more upon proper adaptation of available means to the terrain than upon their power. Maneuver [*sic*] of small units and the initiative and leadership of subordinate commanders are of the highest importance.[376]

This desire for continuous improvement was reflected in the 7th Infantry Division's subsequent training regimen. To prepare for Operation Flintlock the divisional training program first emphasised the physical conditioning of the troops through cross-country marches over the jungle terrain, low-level mountain climbing, and the completion of challenging obstacle courses. They advanced to specialised training in close-in fighting and 'hip-shooting', judo, map reading and land navigation through dense undergrowth, patrolling, ambushing, stream-crossing and jungle living. Training was also given in the assault of fortified positions and the use of demolitions.[377] Every non-commissioned officer received instruction in coordinated infantry-artillery operations in order that fire support missions could be planned and directed at the platoon and company level. Combined tank-infantry operations were also studied with an emphasis on improved communications to facilitate mutual support. New equipment in the form of the standard army six-wheel drive, 2.5-ton truck modified for amphibious operations and the tracked landing vehicle were integrated into the units and ingenious methods of using them for moving supplies and artillery were discovered and validated during the operation.[378]

Collective training built on these foundations. One officer recalled that

> The infantry battalions rotated through a round robin of specialized [*sic*] training. They had a week on the beach learning to swim, another week in a jungle training center [*sic*], next a week in an amphibious center [*sic*] where they went out to sea on landing craft and then returned, making full live ammunition landings. Next a week of intensive training in the use of explosives and the reduction of pillboxes and finally a week of practicing the exact tactics for this type of attack.[379]

Their training culminated with a week-long division level amphibious exercise on the island of Maui, from 11 to 18 January 1944, before returning to Oahu for final preparations for the assault.[380]

The Creation of Tactical Culture – Leadership and Training

How a unit trains contributes greatly to the development of its tactical culture. One of the quickest and most effective ways for a leader at any level to establish his organisational vision and performance standards is through his guidance of and direction for training. Leaders can use training to initiate or change tactical culture by emphasising how the organisation should operate, and how subordinate leaders are expected to plan, prepare and execute, and with this approach to thus build a cohesive team of teams. This gives the unit a definition of who they are, and that will in turn help them understand what to do and how to do it.[381] The 7th Infantry Division's Attu veteran officers and sergeants were promoted to positions of increased responsibility, and they undertook the task of training the unit for Operation Flintlock. The new commanding general was a passionate advocate of tough physical training and combined arms manoeuvre, telling his commanders:

> Our men are willing and enthusiastic if their orders are clear, definite, and based on common sense. In order to be worthy of the men we command, every leader must get in and push with all his might until victory is won.[382]

Leader focus on building both group cohesion and task cohesion developed the units' tactical culture.

The Japanese Plan

The Japanese had closed the Eastern Mandates off from the rest of the world in the 1930s. Authorised by the League of Nations mandate, they considered these newly acquired islands as vital Japanese territory. Their efforts to build visible facilities such as lighthouses were accompanied by clandestine projects to construct fuel oil and coal storage facilities to extend the effective range of the Japanese fleet into the Central Pacific.[383] Once the war with the US began their previous efforts to secretly build infrastructure were accelerated to create an integrated defensive zone that included airfields, docks, military barracks, generators, ammunition storage buildings, command posts, roads and water storage facilities.[384]

Imperial Japanese Army doctrine for island defense mandated defending at the shoreline. The intent was to annihilate the enemy before they could get fully ashore, and if an enemy were successful in landing on the beaches, the Japanese were to counterattack before the enemy could become firmly established.[385] Because of this orientation to defend at the shoreline and destroy the enemy on the beach, Japanese defenses behind the beaches were not usually planned in depth. This approach melded the offensive-minded character of Japanese doctrine with the limited topography of the coral atolls of the Pacific. Such thin, flat islands offered little terrain to provide physical depth to any defense.[386] At the time of the Kwajalein invasion, the Japanese had however begun to adjust their defensive strategy. On Kwajalein initially, the Japanese defenses indicated that they assumed that any attack would come from the ocean side. They apparently felt that the lagoon shore side of the island was inherently more defensible because its wide, shallow reef would preclude landings on the beach.[387] Their assumptions were revised after the American attacks on Makin and Tarawa in November 1943 made it clear that attacks could be made from the lagoon.[388] The Japanese seemed to recognise that they needed to create defences in depth and be able respond to attacks from unexpected directions and so they began to shift their defensive preparations to include the lagoon beaches, building trenches, gun positions and anti-tank obstacles, but these were not complete by the time of the American attack.[389] Most notably though, the passages into the lagoon were not mined, nor were supporting defensive positions emplaced on the adjacent islets.[390] The American threat was recognised but it was ambiguous because, as one Japanese naval commander put it:

> There was divided opinion as to whether you would land at Jaluit or Mille. Some thought you would land on Wotje but there were few who thought you would go right to the heart of the Marshalls and take Kwajalein.[391]

Kwajalein Atoll was defended mainly by the Imperial Japanese Navy's *6th Base Force* and the *Yokosuka 4th Special Naval Landing Force* numbering approximately 8,100 men and 110 aircraft under the command of Akiyama Monzo, Rear Admiral, IJN. The major Imperial Japanese Army combat unit was the *1st Amphibious Brigade,* reinforced by the *2nd Mobile Battalion,* totaling approximately 4,000 men. The other troops were electricians, mechanics, and communications specialists. This force also included many Korean laborers.[392] The defences on Kwajalein featured many bunkers and pillboxes, machine-gun positions and rifle pits, oriented mostly towards the ocean side beaches. The Japanese had installed 80-millimetre dual-purpose guns on both the ocean and lagoon sides of the island, 12.7-centimetre guns on each end of the island, a 20-millimetre anti-aircraft gun at the base of the seaplane ramp, and nearby two 13-millimetre single-mount machine guns, three 7.7-millimetre machine guns. Japanese pre-invasion training was focused on repelling an attack on the beach with cannon and machine gun fire followed by bayonet charges to destroy the survivors.[393]

The typical Japanese fighting position on the island was made of concrete and included an ammunition storage area and firing pit for a single machine gunner. A small window allowed an assistant gunner to pass ammunition to the firing position. The 7th Infantry Division soldiers faced approximately fifteen of these positions on Kwajalein.[394]

H-Hour Again for the 'Hourglass' Division

On 22 January 1944, the invasion force left Pearl Harbor enroute to Kwajalein, to seize the first Japanese-owned territory in the Pacific.[395] The 7th Reconnaissance Troop once again led the division onto Kwajalein with a pre-dawn assault against several of the smaller islands on 31 January 1944. They also boarded a beached Japanese vessel and there found a trove of seventy-five secret charts of lagoons and harbours across the Pacific, which provided extremely valuable intelligence for future operations.[396] At the end of the day, they had killed 106 Japanese and had taken 3 prisoners. Their losses were two killed, twenty-two wounded. Here, as at Attu, the 7th Reconnaissance Troop was highly effective in fixing the enemy, preventing surprise, and collecting intelligence.[397]

Intelligence Exploitation

Among the Japanese documents captured on Kwajalein was a complete set of secret maps and charts for Truk, the Imperial Japanese Navy's principal anchorage in the Central Pacific. These were exploited in the planning for an aircraft carrier strike against that base on 17–18 February 1944.[398] During that strike about 250 Japanese aircraft and 17,000 tons of fuel were destroyed and the dockyards, communications facilities and supply points revealed on the captured charts were attacked. Within the lagoon, two light cruisers, four destroyers, nine auxiliary ships and approximately two dozen cargo vessels were sunk. As a result, Truk was neutralised as a base of operations and rendered ineffective and isolated for the remainder of the war.[399] Quickly processing and exploiting such intelligence finds, helped the Americans to retain the strategic initiative over the Japanese.

Preliminary naval operations began early in the morning of 30–31 January 1944 when the battleships *Massachusetts*, *Indiana* and *Washington* bombarded the island followed by the *Pennsylvania*, *Mississippi*, *New Mexico*, *Idaho*, and three heavy cruisers. At 06.18 hours on 1 February 1944, covered by fire from the battleships, the destroyers *Ringgold* and *Sigsbee* entered the lagoon to protect the amphibious ships and landing craft.[400] The naval bombardment was thorough and intense. One observer, Commander Anthony Kimmins of the Royal Navy remarked:

> Nothing could have lived through that sea and air bombardment. [The bombardment] was the most damaging thing I have ever seen. [Ashore] I have never seen such a shambles in my life. As you got ashore the beach was a mass of highly colored [*sic*] fish that had been thrown up there by nearby explosions … [the bombardment was] the most brilliant success he ever witnessed.[401]

In addition to the main assault on Kwajalein Island, the 7th Infantry Regiment landed on several small nearby islands. The 2nd Battalion, 17th Infantry Regiment seized Carlson Island to establish artillery firing positions in support of the main assault. Despite taking fire from the Japanese batteries on Kwajalein, they cleared the way for the artillery to land and soon several batteries were in position to fire.[402]

The main assault force of 800 infantry landed on the western tip of Kwajalein at 09.30 hours on 1 February 1944. Within 15 minutes an additional 1,200 soldiers of the 7th Infantry Division landed to support the advance. The 184th Infantry Regiment led the assault along the lagoon side of the island with the airfield on their right flank, while the 32nd Infantry Regiment had the ocean to their right and the airfield on their left. In one outstanding action, Technical Sergeant Graydon Kickul of Company L, 184th Infantry Regiment destroyed a whole line of reinforced pillboxes by dropping grenades through the slits and then shooting the Japanese soldiers when they tried to escape.[403]

By the end of the first day the Americans had landed elements of six infantry battalions, four artillery battalions and one engineer battalion on the islands of the atoll, but the real fight was just beginning. Despite the impressive bombardment, the Japanese garrison had survived, and they fought from inside their bunkers, pillboxes and the many ruined buildings. As the Americans advanced, they found themselves pitted against a vast array of Japanese defensive structures situated both to their front and flanks.

Concrete bunkers and pillboxes built to employ several machine guns were emplaced along the shoreline and throughout the interior of the island. The entire area was so littered with destroyed foliage and shattered buildings that the Japanese defenders were often concealed until a surprise close range encounter yielded their location at the cost of another casualty. It became 'house-to-house' combat in the ruins on a tropical atoll. Throughout the

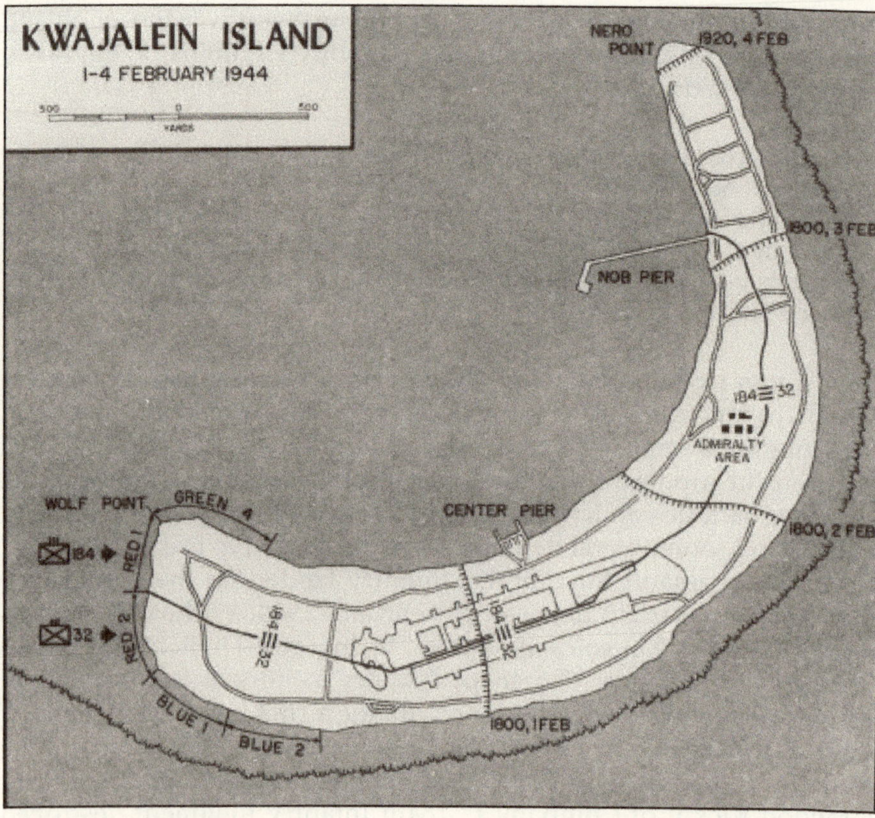

Figure 3-2: Assault Landings, Kwajalein, 1944. Map of the Battle of Kwajalein, February 1944. (James A. Walker, Lewis Bernstein, Sharon Lang, *"The Eastern Mandates Campaign: A Staff Ride Guide for Operation FLINTLOCK; The Seizure of Kwajalein Atoll", U.S. Army Space and Missile Defense Command Historical Office, 2004, 40.* Public Domain)

day the Japanese mounted stiff resistance from these positions and the American infantrymen were required to reduce each pillbox and strong point along the way.[404] After night fell, the Japanese fully emerged from their positions to counterattack with snipers, grenades, and mortars.[405]

Beginning the morning of 2 February 1944, both regiments continued their attack toward the north end of the island, coordinated with naval gunfire and air and artillery support. The 2nd Battalion, 184th Infantry Regiment advanced along the lagoon side of the island while the 2nd Battalion, 32nd Infantry Regiment continued to attack on the ocean side, overwhelming enemy strong points as they advanced. The Japanese responded with artillery and mortar fire, including white phosphorus shells which burned twenty men.[406]

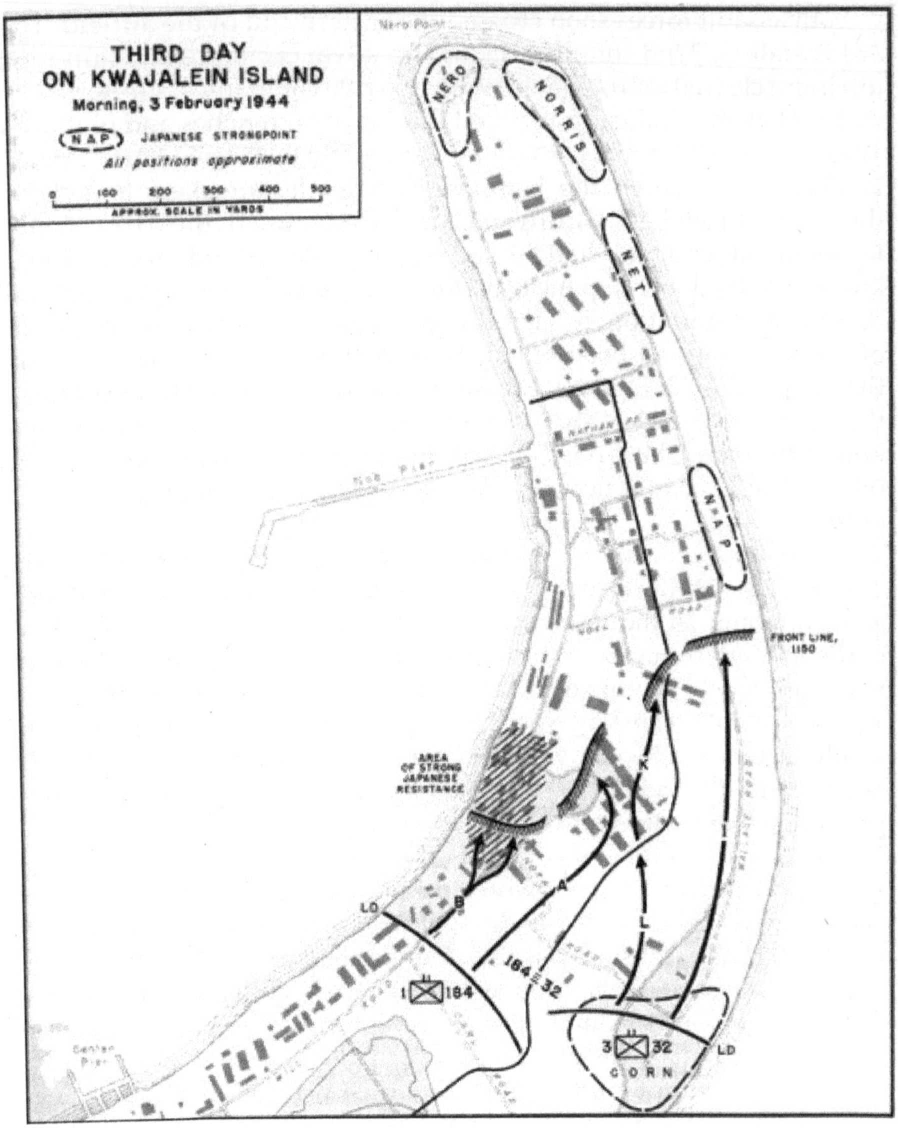

Figure 3-3: Third Day, Kwajalein, 1944. Map of the Battle of Kwajalein, February 1944 (James A. Walker, Lewis Bernstein, Sharon Lang, *"The Eastern Mandates Campaign: A Staff Ride Guide for Operation FLINTLOCK; The Seizure of Kwajalein Atoll", U.S. Army Space and Missile Defense Command Historical Office, 53, 2004, National Archives.* Public Domain, https://commons.wikimedia.org/w/index.php?curid=47139000.)

Both assault forces soon crossed the eastern end of the airfield. The 3rd Battalion, 32nd Infantry Regiment, advanced across an anti-tank ditch and cleared a strong point with two rifle companies, supported by tanks. They methodically attacked this maze of trenches and pillboxes, killing over 100 enemy soldiers without losing any Americans.[407] Having thus secured the Japanese airfield the attackers halted for the night. Elsewhere during the day, elements of the 7th Cavalry Reconnaissance Troop had landed on Chauncey Island and cleared it killing 125 Japanese. Japanese prisoners captured during the day said that their ammunition, food and water were gone and that over 1,200 of the garrison had been killed. With Attu still fresh in their minds, the men of the 7th Infantry Division were wary of a night attack from their desperate and trapped enemy. They warned one another, 'It's bound to come. The Jap [*sic*] makes his suicide counterattack at dawn on the day his cause becomes hopeless.' However, the night passed quietly.[408]

American expectations that final victory would be achieved on 3 February 1944, were not met. Instead, the Japanese resistance was stiffening as the defenders took full advantage of the cluttered battlefield environment. Specifically, their defence of the 'Admiralty Area' proved to be much more formidable than expected. This area was so called because it was the suspected location of the Japanese headquarters and its many administrative offices and warehouses had been reduced to rubble by American gunfire and bombing, ironically providing excellent cover for the Japanese defenders.[409]

The Admiralty area was by this time an almost hopeless maze of rubble, in which demolished wooden buildings, deeply revetted air-raid shelters and the mounds of still operative blockhouses and pillboxes were practically indistinguishable. Gunfire had torn and shredded the once thickly built-up area almost beyond recognition, and the litter of wreckage was a stumbling mass of splintered coral sand, blasted concrete, and the ever-present drying palm fronds. Added to the continuous cloud of gunfire and rising dust was the smoke from fires which broke out in the rubble. The Japanese continued to fight without pause: 'The mere fact that a position was being flanked or enveloped meant nothing to the Jap soldier. His psychology of fanatacism [*sic*] dictated that he kill as many Americans as possible before dying a "glorious death".'[410]

General Corlett called for a vigorous and speedy attack with the desire to 'finish the job at 1500 [hours].' The assault forces encountered both piles of wreckage and undamaged pillboxes and concrete blockhouses that required destruction in a zone of one mile in depth and 300 to

500 yards width.[411] Moving through this narrow, curved, tangled nest of hornets revealed challenges to command and control. So dense was the wreckage and smoke that units lost contact with each other and their headquarters. In one instance, even though only located 50 yards apart, two platoons were unaware that they were attacking simultaneously toward each other from different sides of a Japanese position.[412]

Numerous pockets of Japanese had been bypassed. Although outflanked these enemy forces would not surrender. The tactical cohesion of the Japanese defence was shattered, their communications and artillery destroyed, yet they stayed in the fight. Being outflanked or surrounded had no effect on the defenders. Even though the Americans had established a 'front line' of troops the follow-on echelon often found themselves fighting for ground already taken. Nominal 'mopping up' missions became full scale fire fights at one point even involving a battalion headquarters and the unit's support troops.[413] Hidden under the rubble piles and downed palm trees the Japanese survivors were fighting to the death at every point and thus the American advance was required to slowly destroy each position in turn as they moved forward. Some rifle companies were making progress, but others were bogged down and became isolated, receiving both friendly and enemy fire from all sides. Finally, the division ordered its units to halt and regroup to regain their momentum and finish the attack in the morning.[414] That night they faced small but fierce counterattacks as the Japanese emerged from their places of concealment. Heavy Japanese mortar and artillery fire from the far end of the island supported these infiltration attacks throughout the night.[415]

The sun rose on 4 February 1944, to find the Americans still encountering stiff resistance from the Japanese. Nevertheless, the Japanese defence was crumbling. As the 2nd Battalion, 32nd Infantry Regiment mounted an assault against the remaining Japanese 5-inch dual purpose gun, the 184th Infantry Regiment was collecting some ninety prisoners, among them Petty Officer Fujita Minoru, who had been on Rear Admiral Akiyama's staff. He reported to them that Akiyama had died two days earlier when he had ventured out of his bunker to watch the American bombardment, thus decapitating the Japanese command structure at the start of the battle. A high number of the surrenders were by Korean laborers who had been hiding in the rubble, merely hoping to survive.[416]

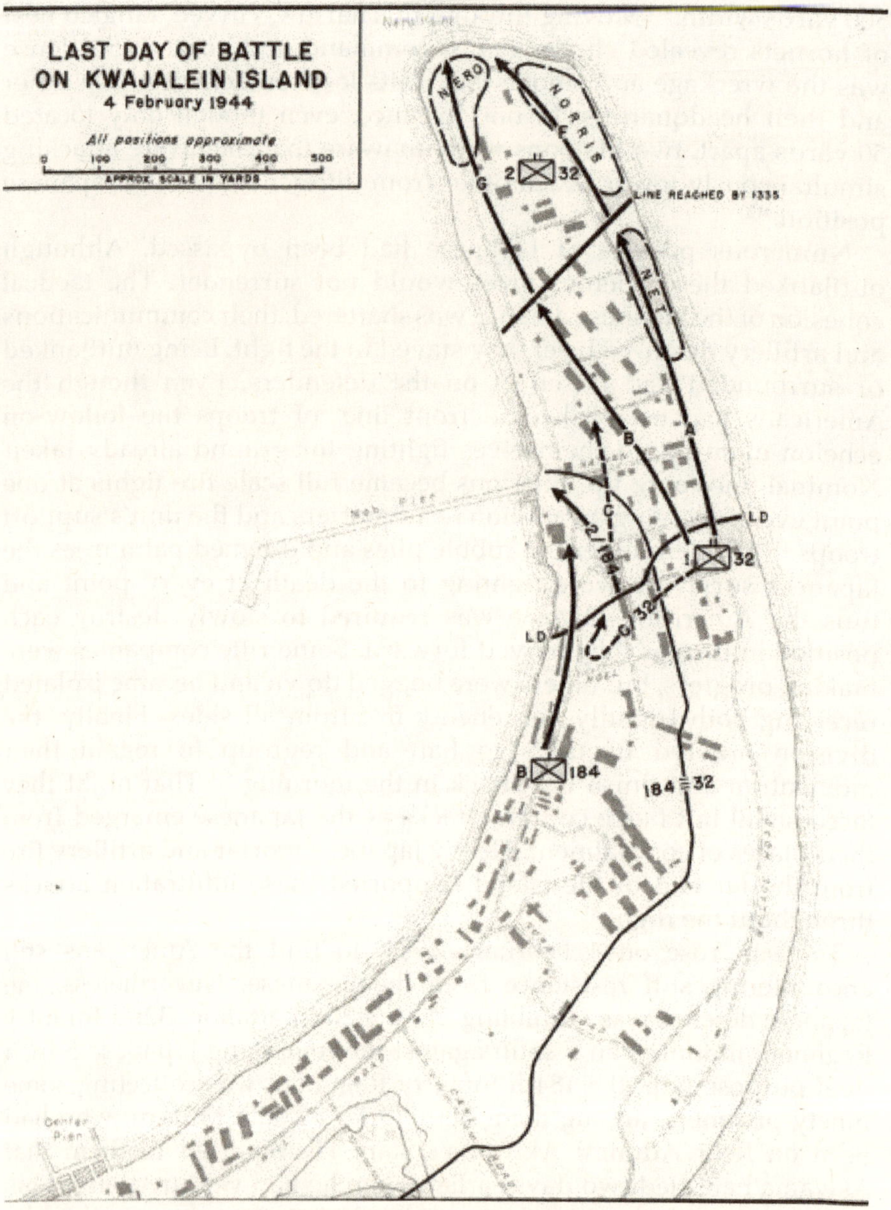

Figure 3-4: Last Day. Map of the Battle of Kwajalein, 4 February 1944. (James A. Walker, Lewis Bernstein, Sharon Lang, *"The Eastern Mandates Campaign: A Staff Ride Guide for Operation FLINTLOCK; The Seizure of Kwajalein Atoll", U.S. Army Space and Missile Defense Command Historical Office, 2004, 54. National Archives. Public Domain, https://commons.wikimedia.org/w/index.php?curid=47139000.)*

By the end of the last day, another 317 Americans would be killed or wounded from the stubborn but forlorn Japanese resistance. Attu veteran Captain Albert L. Pence would become one of the last American casualties when he was wounded at about 19.00 hours while leading the destruction of enemy bunkers in the final 150 yards of enemy fortifications.[417] Although smaller-scale operations occurred on the adjacent islands for the next three days, the main objective was secured by 21.00 hours. Various figures are given for the final costs of the operation, owing again to there being both few Japanese survivors and the destruction wrought by the Americans. The 7th Infantry Division had suffered 176 killed in battle and 767 wounded. Estimates of Japanese casualties vary greatly. According to the most authoritative sources, of the 5,112 Japanese defending Kwajalein Island 4,938 were killed, 79 were taken prisoner and with them 125 Koreans surrendered.[418] The grisly task of burying the dead revealed both the horror of modern war and a surprising facet of Japanese tactical culture. So many bodies were burned, mutilated and dismembered that there was little left to be interred: 'We'd pick up feet and arms and stuff, and it wasn't good and it all smelled horrible.'[419] The bodies and body parts were dumped into communal graves but there was no way to identify the individual soldiers; identification tags only revealed the name of the unit that the soldier had belonged to.[420] Their individual identities were of less value than their collective sacrifice as Japanese soldiers.

The Elements of Tactical Culture

When speaking of culture in a military context we can frame it as the values, beliefs and behaviours expected of the members of the military. This culture is composed of shared basic assumptions, which inform the beliefs and values of the group. These then shape the expected behavioural norms that the group follows and enforces. Dr Edgar Schein argues in *Organizational Culture and Leadership*:

> Culture: A pattern of shared basic assumptions learned by a group as it solved its problems of external adaptation and internal integration, which has worked well enough to be considered valid and, therefore, to be taught to new members as the correct way to perceive, think, and feel in relation to those problems.
>
> Basic Underlying Assumptions: Unconscious, taken-for-granted beliefs and values that determine perception, thought, feeling, and behavior [*sic*].
>
> Values: Articulated publicly announced principles and values that the group claims to be trying to achieve.
>
> Norms: Implicit standards and values that evolve in working groups.[421]

For an army and its subordinate units to have a unique identity it must have a culture that exists as the core of its sense of purpose, providing the why and how it serves. Tactical culture includes characteristics like pride, cohesion, loyalty and initiative. It also includes capabilities like leadership, planning, and individual and collective skills. Tactical culture expresses an organisation's beliefs about its duties, roles and relationships, its preferred operational style and the guidelines for how it will fight.

Imperial Japan: The Samurai Legacy and the Myth of *Bushidō*

> *Bushidō* can be seen as expressing the most remarkable feature of our national morality. To embrace life and death as one, to fulfill the Way of Loyalty [to the emperor], that is our *bushidō*.[422]

The ideology of the 'way of the *samurai*' or *bushidō* has been the subject of much debate in terms of its connections to and influence on Japanese thought and identity.[423] Many have claimed that it represents the very 'soul' of the Japanese people, and that its motivating tenets of courage, selflessness and loyalty represent the best characteristics of the *samurai* class long after they had ceased to exist.[424] Although both popular culture and some scholarly works have portrayed *bushidō* as a traditional system of ethics bequeathed from the *samurai*, its historical pedigree shows it to be a modern invention originating in the confluence of cultural, social and political trends beginning in the late 1880s.[425] The *bushidō* that had such profound effects on Japanese attitudes and actions during the Pacific War sprung from Meiji era efforts to create a national ethos that would blend personal sacrifice and martial virtues with State Shinto.[426] Their exploration of a quasi-feudal code of ethics arose in response to the need to define the national identity and character during Japan's rapid period of societal change and modernisation. Influenced by contemporary English discourse on European chivalry *bushidō* was intended to provide Japanese society with new moral guidelines to mobilise the populace in service of the state as Japan leapt into the modern world.[427] The most influential work on the subject remains Nitobe Inazo's *Bushidō: The Soul of Japan* (1899). Historians have not found evidence of medieval *samurai* ethical thought that connect to modern *bushidō* or of historical conduct that reflects this.[428] The ideology seems to have first originated in the 1880s in 'a confluence of intellectual and social trends of journalist and politician Ozaki Yukio', who developed the concept as a 'potential counterpart to English chivalry and the English "gentlemanship" that he idealized [*sic*].'[429]

Rather than a classical system of ethics, imperial *bushidō* should be understood as a modern ideology, deliberately invented to indoctrinate the theory of Japanese nationalism as 'a traditional *samurai* ethic and/or defining trait of the Japanese 'national character.'[430] Tokugawa era *bushidō* had been a transactional feudal system in which the *samurai* received benefits from his lord in return for his services. Imperial *bushidō* demanded that soldiers were to give their all, in service to the emperor because it was a duty of birth. This theory of Japanese nationalism was consistent with the overall Meiji approach of cosmopolitan chauvinism and radical nostalgia that shaped much of the restoration through a synthesis of adopting or emulating a foreign trait, policy or philosophy and yet adapting it to become Japanese in nature.[431]

This was also a response to the unique circumstances of the formation of the modern Japanese state from the 'compound state' that existed in which the *daimyo* were semi-independent states under Tokugawa authority. Tokugawa Japan was not a fully unified nation state in the modern sense, and Meiji Japan needed *bushidō* to create both a national identity and modern statehood.[432] In the process of creating the modern Japanese state and its military often one tradition was shattered while another was restored. The *samurai* class was abolished, and the wearing of swords outlawed but the sword remained an essential talisman for the Japanese soldier. Commoners were conscripted to form the new Imperial Japanese Army, but they were inculcated with the purported traditions of the hereditary warrior elite.[433] The strategy of the Meiji state for integration into the modern world was to emulate what they saw as best practices in the West but create Japanese analogues and rituals to claim legitimacy as a Japanese version of the thing.[434] *Bushidō* became a part of the process of asserting an essential cultural identity for the Japanese nation state with the ruler and the ruled bound together by a common language, culture and heritage. Portrayals of the ideology were easily blended with contemporary theories on what constituted Japanese spirit and identity and many in academia and the government worked diligently to give *bushidō* widespread acceptance through the education system, military training and government policy. From 1901 to 1945, the discourse laid out the foundational principles of

> government-sanctioned and emperor-focused 'imperial bushidō' as a uniquely Japanese ethic with no equivalents in other cultures or nations, [that] most importantly, called for absolute loyalty to the sovereign and nation and sought to instill a willingness to die for these causes.[435]

Imperial *Bushidō* and National Identity

Bushidō has been called an 'invented religion'; a *Meiji* interpretation that did not reflect the ideals or the conduct of *samurai* in the historical record. It was a simplification of the values of the *samurai* intentionally manipulated to strengthen the 'fighting spirit' of the Japanese soldier particularly in its emphasis on loyalty and self-sacrifice centred on the emperor.[436] The soldiers of the Imperial Japanese Army in the Second World War nevertheless revelled in the myth that they were now members of the modern *samurai* class; elevated to a status that their ancestors could never have achieved.[437] As a racist and militaristic code of conduct it thus facilitated some of the atrocities perpetrated by the Imperial Japanese Army during the Pacific War.[438]

The invention and adoption of *bushidō* thus mirrored the processes found in other societies that also grappled with the processes of modernisation, nationalism and imperialism in the late nineteenth and early twentieth century. Modern invented traditions seek to synthesize modernisation, tradition and national identity to establish social cohesion, legitimise institutions and authorities, and inculcate beliefs and conventions of behaviour.[439] Imperial *Bushidō* (the form conceived during the Meiji era and refined during the Showa era) served all three functions in the modernisation of Japan, being presented as the unifying expression of the unique Japanese national character, and used as an ideological tool of the Japanese government to inculcate national identity and unity. Furthermore, its philosophically strident nationalism and militarism came to be a form of spiritual guidance for the Japanese people.[440]

Of note was its emphasis on loyalty as it sought to change the traditional culture of allegiance to feudal clan to devotion to the emperor. It built on the legend of the founding of the empire by the sun-goddess and the mythical intervention of divine winds that saved the nation from the Mongol invasions to craft a narrative of a polity whose core goal was to repay the debt owed by the people to the nation for being so blessed.[441] Imperial *bushidō* gave loyalty a special meaning of being an absolute duty and it established a direct relationship between the people and the imperial state. This created a value system intended to motivate the Japanese people to selfless devotion to duty and to endure extraordinary sacrifice for the emperor by elevating, intensifying, and in some cases, distorting or reinterpreting these traditional values and symbols.[442] A remarkable feature of the adoption and dissemination of *bushidō* was that well over 90 per cent of the population were descendants of classes that had generally resented the *samurai*. Yet this residual class consciousness was broken down gradually through public education and military training which encouraged identification with the martial ethic associated with the former *samurai* elite.[443]

The Forty-Seven *Rōnin*

The widely held Japanese cultural belief that the fullest expression of loyalty is in self-sacrifice was foregrounded in the famous *Akō* Incident of the Forty-Seven Masterless *Samurai* (*Rōnin*). The story tells of a group of *samurai* who were left indigent after their feudal lord was compelled to perform ritual suicide (*seppuku*) for assaulting a court official. After a year of planning, the *Rōnin* avenged their master by killing that official. They were then obliged to commit *seppuku* for the crime of murder. They were subsequently immortalised in Japanese culture as paragons of the warrior virtues of loyalty and sacrifice.[444] Throughout the Meiji and Showa periods their personal fealty and self-sacrifice was venerated as being central to Japanese national identity and political morality.

The degree of acceptance of *bushidō* by the general populace was expressed by claims that 'to insult *bushidō* is to insult all Japanese', and that '*bushidō* did not die with the *samurai* … it entered all Japanese and is especially pronounced in the soldier spirit.'[445]

Japanese Tactical Culture: A Cult of Loyalty, Obedience, Self-Sacrifice and Self-Destruction

> *Bushidō* is a single straight way to death, practicing over and over again every day and night how to die a *samurai*'s death on every possible occasion and every possible cause. Readiness to die at the call of one's duty should be kept ever fresh and alive by repeating the vow every day and every moment.[446]

Extolled as the great classic of imperial *bushidō, Hagakure* ('hidden leaves' or 'hidden by the leaves') was however written in the early eighteenth century. A previously obscure collection of maxims, *Hagakure* glorifies the warrior virtues in a distinctively Japanese way that reflects both Japan's long history of feudal warfare and its 300 years of peace and deliberate isolation from Western influences.[447] Its central theme is that only the warrior who is prepared and willing to die at any moment for his lord is worthy of the title. Beginning with the sentence that, '*Bushidō* is a way of dying', it asserts that one should live as though one is already dead, free from attachment to worldly things and thus being fully capable of the ultimate sacrifice that feudal loyalty demanded.[448]

Hagakure came to be viewed by the Imperial Japanese Army as canonical *samurai* behaviour and *bushidō* was the basis for the ideology of the emperor-centric militarism held as the national spirit.[449] The *bushidō* that was invented in the Meiji era and evolved during the Showa period was a hybrid ideology that successfully merged the concept of the national warrior identity with the central theme that the values and spirit of the *samurai* were the ethnic birthright of all Japanese.[450]

The ultranationalist ideologue and theorist Yasuoka Masahiro identified *bushidō* as the ultimate expression of the 'Japanese spirit' ('*Nihon seishin*') and promoted it as the Japanese nationalist ideology. He wrote and lectured extensively on this theme by citing from *Hagakure*, exhorting Japanese men to embrace a self-sacrificial '*samurai* spirit' and to act as exemplary 'men of character' (*jinkakusha*), loyal to the emperor-centred state. Yasuoka believed that *Hagakure* expressed the spirit of the ideal Japanese warrior and claimed that by following this example modern Japanese soldiers could demonstrate the selfless spirit of fidelity and sacrifice needed for Japan to be victorious.[451] Yasuoka further asserted that Japanese soldiers should feel no regret in dying. He referenced the famous eighth-century poem '*Umiyukaba*' ('If I Go to Sea'), to argue that the true goal of a Japanese soldier was to serve loyally and to die well:

> It is most regrettable for a person to live idly and end their days having achieved nothing of value. Truly, what is a life without deep passion? The desire to die a hero is the passionate spirit of the people: If at sea, a watery corpse, if in the mountains, a verdant corpse, to die at the side of our lord – this is the oath of the Japanese subject.[452]

As the ideology of *bushidō* developed there were heated debates amongst Japanese thinkers concerning combat effectiveness and how to win against more militarily advanced European nations. An army composed of conscripts needs a motivation to fight. *Bushidō* was used for the ideological indoctrination of these conscripts, and this helped to shape the national character that began to emerge in this period. The predominant view developed that while other nations fought with technology, Japan fought with a unique spirit, inspired not only by their sense of duty but also with the honour of their ancestors in mind.

> The battle cry of the Japanese pierced the heart of the Russians and filled them with terror ... Several sudden assaults, throwing one human

> bullet after another against the enemy's defenses [*sic*], ended with the blood of heroes spattered, their bones shattered ... I must admit that the first attack ended in failure, but those human bullets who had been used to this end became integral initial stepping stones for smashing the enemy's battlements.[453]

This officer, Sakurai Tadayoshi, stressed that such defeats were not needless tragedies. They were the first necessary steps towards victory.[454] He expressed what would become the common belief that by serving as loyal subjects of their divine emperor and placing their faith in the power of 'spirit over matter' the Japanese would eventually triumph.[455] Victory over the Russians seemed to vindicate the theory that despite their materiel and technological deficiencies, Japan would always triumph because of its superior *bushidō* 'spirit and the self-sacrifice of the 'human bullets'.[456]

> Despite the great number of projectiles and the large quantity of human bullets that were spent, the storming of the forts ... ended in utter failure. ... however, this apparently useless sacrifice of a large number of lives was not without its effect. Strategically we needed to reduce the great fortress as quickly as possible, however great the damage to our army might be; so, therefore, the commanding general resolved with tears to offer the necessary sacrifice, and his subordinates willingly offered their lives and stormed the enemy with bullets of their own flesh. And these first fruitless assaults proved the necessary first step and a valuable preparation for our final success.[457]

Human Bullets

Considered by some to be the defining work of Russo-Japanese era war literature, Sakurai Tadatoshi's *Human Bullets* described the emotions of the Japanese soldiers in vivid and lyrical language that stressed the nobility of suffering and the superior élan of the Japanese soldiers. The work was immensely popular in Japan and was translated into English for a wider audience:

> This battle is our great chance of serving our country. To-night we must strike at the vitals of Port Arthur. Our brave assaulting column must be not simply a forlorn-hope ('resolved-to-die'), but a 'sure-death' detachment ... Do your best, all of you.
>
> Yes, we were all ready for death when leaving Japan. Men going to battle of course cannot expect to come back alive. But in this battle to be ready for death was not enough; what was required

of us was a determination not to fail to die. Indeed, we were 'sure-death' men, and this new appellation gave us a great stimulus.[458]

This spirit of self-sacrifice was pervasive and carried the highest endorsement. In his introduction to Sakurai's book, former prime minister Okuma Shigenobu wrote: '[Our] soldiers vie with each other in offering themselves on the altar of their country, the spirit of sacrifice prevails to a marked degree. This is the true characteristic of the race of Yamato.'[459]

The war with Russia caused the Japanese to consider the technological advances in warfare that they experienced.[460] Despite revising their large unit doctrine to reflect modern weapons and tactics they maintained their belief in the power of individual devotion to duty and self-sacrifice to achieve victory.[461] Paramount to Japanese military thought was their steadfast belief in the power of offensive action to quickly overwhelm an enemy. The success of their attacks against the Russians was attributed to their intangible and unique *samurai* ethos and a tactical bias for attack. This led to a doctrine built on the idea of close quarters combat characterised by overwhelming speed and violence conducted by elite infantry shock troops supported by mobile artillery.[462]

While acknowledging the advances that had taken place in arms and materiel because of the First World War, the Imperial Japanese Army nevertheless maintained the view that victory was solely dependent on the intangible factors of patriotism, devotion and self-sacrifice. Still, the Japanese did strive to develop a doctrine that would encompass the advances in technology, mobility and firepower while maintaining the philosophy of the innate power of spiritual training. As a result, subsequent doctrine advocated offensive mobile warfare exemplified by envelopments but maintaining the dogma that the bayonet in the hands of a soldier imbued with the intangible and indomitable powers of the fighting spirit would overcome any shortcomings or disadvantages in materiel and firepower.[463]

The Creation of Tactical Culture – Imperial Japanese Army Training and Indoctrination

The Japanese relied on the gruelling training that produced quality infantrymen to compensate for the inferior material and technological support. It was this combination of obedience and ferocity that made the Japanese Army so formidable.[464]

Japanese Army doctrine and training revolved around the infantry with all other elements in support. Training and exercises emphasised flanking movements, night attacks and bayonet charges by small units.[465] Japanese training for both soldiers and officers focused on the Red Army rather that the Americans or British who were seen as far lesser threats. The core curriculum from basic training to the Imperial Army War College centred on tactics and battle drill, which produced instinctive tactical actions but stifled operational level innovation and creativity.[466] The basic traits that permeated Japanese 'tactical' culture were strict obedience, and their faith in victory based on the belief in their 'fighting spirit'. They considered the Japanese soldier ideal because he had mastered Western technology and melded it with the unique martial spirit of the Japanese people.[467] All military training was linked to *bushidō*, yet it was not mentioned in the Army Regulations because it existed on a higher plane – as a creed, a faith and an existential guide to life and death.[468]

This approach fully manifested itself with the publication in 1928 of the *Infantry Manual*. Here the German infiltration tactics of First World War were revised to incorporate the Japanese infantry-centric style of warfare that emphasised destroying the enemy with 'cold steel' utilising speed and surprise, under the cover of night. Combined arms fire and manoeuvre was not practiced. Instead, the concentration of attacking manpower and firepower on a narrow front was favored to achieve a breakthrough. All of this was based on an ideology and tradition that allowed for no retreat and no surrender.[469] Any reference to surrender, retreat or defence had been removed from the regulation as unauthorised manoeuvres.[470] They instead emphasised mobile combat tactics by dismounted infantry against Soviet forces; encircling attacks, night attacks and close combat. Lessons learned from the difficult battles against the Soviets at Changkufeng in 1938 and Nomonhan in 1939, were also eventually incorporated into their combat training.[471] However, it wasn't until much later in 1943 that the Army General Staff directed that there be training to counter American and British tactics, which led several instructors to lament the fact that they didn't even know what those tactics were![472]

Influence on Tactical Culture – Japanese Anti-Intelligence Bias

Throughout the war Allied intelligence collection and analysis consistently outperformed the Japanese system. The greatest reason for this seems to have been enculturated biases. There was a marked propensity by the Japanese to underestimate their opponents and overrate themselves. An example from a captured Japanese document entitled 'Land Warfare Tactics to Use against U.S. and British Forces' states that

> because the character of the American is simple and lacking in tenacity, in their tactics and battle leadership they also lack tenacity; and if they meet with one setback, they have a tendency to abandon one plan for another. For this reason, we must not fail to hammer at this weakness.

The prevailing theme was that 'lack of equipment gave us Japanese a chance to demonstrate our superior spirit and valor [*sic*].' When paired with a bias in their tactical culture that subordinated intelligence and its practitioners as an inferior warfighting function, Japanese intelligence suffered from the effects of flawed assessments that spiritual superiority would triumph (confirmation bias) and from poor intelligence security and sharing.[473]

The Imperial Japanese Army came to rely on surprise, speed and aggressive infantry tactics to attack and seize terrain in the Pacific, but in the defence its neglect of fully developing a modern combined arms doctrine and organisation made them very ineffective. Japanese tactical doctrine always emphasised offensive action characterised by speed, surprise and mobility. Japanese doctrine for defensive operations was less well developed.[474] The machine gun, supported by grenade launchers, was the primary weapon for the defence. Snipers augmented defensive positions and counterattacks were quickly launched to regain lost positions or to repulse the attackers. Artillery was generally less used in the defence, with the individual field guns being tunneled into hillsides or emplaced in fortified positions. When deployed in this manner and under the tactical control of infantry commanders, they were unable to mass the effects of their indirect fires.[475] When on the defensive the Japanese strove to surprise the attacker by remaining silent and concealed. This was achieved by their highly skilled camouflaging of their battle positions and their effective deception measures like using decoy positions. They also made extensive use of snipers to disrupt the American advance.[476] Their reverence of rank and the hierarchy of command, also suppressed initiative, and stifled low-level decision making that might have allowed for more successful defensive operations.

The Japanese displayed no innovations in tactics on Kwajalein. In general, their defence amounted to a slow retreat through a maze of previously prepared positions: pillboxes, trenches, air-raid shelters, blockhouses, log emplacements and ruined buildings. It was, in effect, a static defence with short periods of active operations as evidenced in nightly limited counterattacks by small units and attempts at infiltration.[477] For the Japanese, the battle should have demonstrated that beachline defences were too vulnerable to attack and that defence in depth was necessary if they hoped to stop Allied assaults.

The Japanese drive to modernise their weapons, doctrine and training was contrasted with the antithetical belief that success in future battle was primarily reliant on non-materiel means. They believed that victory would be assured if *bushidō* was fully inculcated into the Japanese soldier.[478] Japanese tactical culture thus focused on the legacy of *samurai* identity and the values of discipline, obligation or duty, martial spirit, loyalty and a willingness to sacrifice one's own life. *Bushidō* had an essential effect on influencing Japanese will to fight and will to sacrifice because it portrayed the quintessential trait of the Japanese soldier as his self-effacing and even self-destructive loyalty to the nation.[479] Their tactical culture embraced the belief that death in man-to-man combat was glorious because of the importance placed on honour and reputation codified by *bushidō*.[480] In his widely published interpretation of *Hagakure*, Watsuji Tetsuro contended that the Japanese have historically valued purity of intent more highly than effective outcomes. He argued that exhibiting *seimyōshin* (a 'pure spirited heart/mind') in the execution of the task is more important that whether one is successful. Thus, the failed *gyokusai* at Attu was heavily romanticised as an inspirational example of the fighting spirit of the nation.[481] The public was manipulated into believing that suicidal acts like this were the ultimate proof of loyalty and devotion to duty.[482]

IJA Tactical Culture and *Bushidō*

The warrior ethos of loyalty and self-sacrifice was thoroughly enculturated in Japanese society and the people fully believed that obedience, service and sacrifice was their debt to society:[483]

> Victory and defeat are matters of the temporary force of circumstances. The way of avoiding shame is different. It is simply in death. Even if it seems certain that you will lose, retaliate … A real man does not think of victory or defeat. He plunges recklessly towards an irrational death. By doing this, you will awaken from your dreams.[484]

> Because the most vital and expected quality of the Japanese soldier was his willingness to die, this removed all limits on what his leaders could demand. As the war worsened the acceptance of death became essential.[485] For the Imperial Japanese Army it seemed that there were no unacceptable losses.

Imperial *bushidō* forbade surrender or retreat as incompatible with the Japanese martial spirit. Obeying this spirit included the obligation to 'giving one's most valuable life for the imperial nation (as) a duty' even in the case of committing suicide rather than being captured.[486] This attitude was strongly tempered by the Japanese aesthetic of *wabi-sabi* (the appreciation of beauty and life as imperfect and impermanent) and *mono no aware* (the embrace of sorrow as the essential character of life) with their fatalistic and melancholic view of the beauty of impermanence and loss, as well as the Zen influenced beliefs on transcendence and nothingness.[487] In 1943, Lieutenant General Ryotaro Nagai described this philosophy of stoicism and fatalism:

> It is a fact that victory or defeat in warfare is ascribable to something transcending logic, fate or the grace of heaven. I presume there is hardly a commander who, being responsible for many lives does not fall into the idea of doing his best, then praying for the grace of heaven.[488]

This spiritual indoctrination was not the only factor that kept Japanese soldiers from surrendering when the situation was clearly hopeless. Peer pressure and group think were also highly influential factors with many Japanese soldiers fearing that their comrades would kill them if they attempted to surrender.[489] Because of Imperial Japanese Army indoctrination 84 per cent of one group of Japanese prisoners interviewed thought that they would be executed or tortured by their captors; 66 per cent thought that they would be executed or punished by Japanese authorities.[490] It appears that while many Japanese soldiers refused to surrender because they believed in *bushidō* others feared being killed by the Americans or their own side for surrendering. For the Japanese soldier group cohesion was a coercive force for collective sacrifice.

Imperial *bushidō* evolved into an ideology that inspired loyalty, obedience and self-sacrifice for the nation. The manipulative indoctrination of *bushidō* reinforced values already accepted throughout Japanese society.[491] It endured as an accepted ideology for the Japanese people despite its demand for their suicidal sacrifice because it was interwoven with traditional cultural values and popular nationalism, each promoting the other in terms of goals and ideals.[492] The result was the creation of a tactical culture that believed and operated as though victory could be attained through sufficient sacrifice.

American Tactical Culture: Inculcated With a Will to Win

As we examine the variables affecting combat motivation, especially in comparing the American and Japanese forces in the Pacific War we must consider the political context. In this case we find a democracy opposing a totalitarian empire. Research indicates that when faced with an existential threat strong democracies demonstrate a powerful will to fight. (For example, France in the First World War.)[493] When combined with a strong national identity and will to fight nations can endure high casualties. (For example, France in the First World War; the Soviet Union in the Second World War.)[494] Having a strong will to fight increases the chances of victory and fully totalitarian and democratic governments show the strongest will to fight. (For example, the United Kingdom and the Soviet Union in the Second World War.)[495]

After the trauma of the First World War, the failure of the League of Nations, and the debilitating effects of the Great Depression America chose neutrality and nonintervention. Despite strong public opinion against involvement in foreign conflicts this isolationist approach to foreign policy was gradually eroded as rising tensions and open conflict in both Europe and Asia caused the United States to become an undeclared participant through the Lend Lease Act and the Atlantic Charter.[496] The Japanese attack on Pearl Harbor and the subsequent declaration of war by Nazi Germany eradicated any remaining isolationist sentiment. Nevertheless, many soldiers still felt great disillusion and frustration with war as evidenced by this reflection on the twenty-fourth anniversary of Armistice Day: 'Well, it is hard to sit here + [*sic*] think that World War I was to end all wars. What am I doing here?'[497]

Recognising the potential impact on combat effectiveness of the previous anti-war mood of the country American sociologists conducted detailed studies of the attitudes, motivations and combat performance of American soldiers during the Second World War. Based primarily on these contemporary research surveys the prevalent theory has since been that ideology plays little role in modern combat motivation and that it is generally accepted that the cohesive primary social group that is the combat unit provides the key motivation and support for the combat soldier.[498] Numerous historians have also affirmed the pivotal role played by primary group dynamics on combat performance. The fulfillment of basic physiological needs followed by unit cohesion and teamwork were generally seen as more important to the soldiers of the Second World War than ideology and patriotism.[499]

Will to Fight – Fundamental Influences

The existence of a strong national identity is a foundational element of will to fight. Because it permeates almost every other aspect of will to fight governments will frequently try to strengthen or, if necessary, create a national identity through indoctrination and propaganda.[500] In status-based Japanese society, belonging to the group, maintaining loyalty to the group and conforming to group expectations is essential. Group orientation governs individual behaviour and group cohesiveness is a core value.[501] This identity structure extends vertically to embrace the Japanese national polity. Showa era *bushidō* was intended to provide the needed Japanese national identity.[502] Many consider the American Creed, first formulated by Thomas Jefferson, as the core of American national identity. Its principles of liberty, equality, justice, representative government and humanity represent the uniquely American interpretation of the Enlightenment and the Reformation.[503] Its tenets were summarised in 1917 by William Tyler Page:

> I believe in the United States of America, as a government of the people, by the people, for the people; whose just powers are derived from the consent of the governed; a democracy in a republic; a sovereign Nation of many sovereign States; a perfect union, one and inseparable; established upon those principles of freedom, equality, justice, and humanity for which American patriots sacrificed their lives and fortunes. I therefore believe it is my duty to my country to love it, to support its Constitution, to obey its laws, to respect its flag, and to defend it against all enemies.[504]

Despite these observations an alternative hypothesis exists that proposes there is a deeper foundational element involved. Charles Moskos proposed that the strength and effectiveness of the primary group is reliant on a latent ideology, the shared values of the group. There is an underlying commitment to the societal values that the soldier brings to the unit and thus to the fight. In these surveys, American soldiers expressed a common belief in American war aims and in American ideology and 'the cause'. Generally, speaking, America's war goals and national philosophy were perhaps best expressed by President Franklin D. Roosevelt's speech to the nation of the Four Freedoms. The ideas of freedom of speech, freedom of worship, freedom from want and freedom from fear symbolised both America's foundational principles and its national identity as defenders of universal human rights.[505]

While the link between beliefs and combat motivation is uncertain it seems to be affirmed in studies that found that when asked questions about their ideological motivations, 'majorities in the neighborhood of ninety per cent said that they felt that the United States was fighting for things they personally felt were worth fighting for.'[506] The cohesion concept explains soldier motivation very well, but we should not overlook the explanatory power of latent ideology and commitment to national goals in our understanding of what gives soldiers the will to win.[507] Tactical culture seems to be built on a fabric of relationships interwoven with belief in the cause. The bonds of belonging to the group give the safety and strength of shared identity, values and goals which become both what one is and what one does.[508] The strongest warriors are armed with belief.

A holistic interpretation of will to fight seems to indicate that ideology and belief in the cause will get soldiers to the battlefield, and thereafter their commitment to each other sustains them through combat. This was best expressed for me in a lecture given by Lieutenant General Hal Moore:

> American soldiers fight for each other. We discovered in that depressing, hellish place, where death was our constant companion, that we loved each other. We killed for each other, we died for each other, and we wept for each other. And in time we came to love each other as brothers.[509]

To further illuminate the questions of will fight and will to win, I will examine one of Ralph Eyde's letters to his brother written after the battle. By drawing on this personal account I hope to reveal his underlying attitudes, emotions and beliefs. I will highlight the variables of will to fight that I think are revealed within the original text. Having recovered from his wounding on Attu, Eyde fought again on Kwajalein. On the last night of the operation, he was hit by a Japanese mortar round suffering shrapnel wounds to his lung:

> You already know we've been in action again + we really gave 'em hell on Kwajalein island in the Marshalls + though it was taken in only a few days there were still plenty of those yellow b---- giving us a bad time even after all the bombarding our navy + air corps gave them. Things were going along in good shape in the early stages of the campaign and then we pushed the Japs in one corner of the island. This was the scene of close in fighting on the last night of hell. Believe me, it was a regular nightmare!! My job in this operation was a heavy machine gun squad leader, as it was on Attu. I was in a foxhole with a buddy + the machine gun was well concealed. Wham! Shell just missed us. Wham! Another right behind us. The machine gun lets go with a roar mowing down some Japs several yards away. My machine gun keeps mowing 'em down all night. It's getting near dawn now. We let go with hand grenades to wipe

out a bunch of Japs in a trench just in front of us. What's this? The Japs are throwing everything they've got at us and they're on both sides of us and closing in! Shells landing all around my gun. Looks like they've found my position. Some of the fellows are getting their knives ready. The machine gun is still barking. [Here his narrative reveals the variable of desperation in the moments of fearing death during this night of combat.] Then wham!! A shell lands right in my foxhole, blowing us both up in the air. Don't know how high I went and I guess it doesn't make much difference as I got up and made my way to a nearby shellhole as best I could cussing. There a medic fixed the shrapnel wound in my left side as best he could. Just then the Japs were rushing screaming wildly and our gunners were just pouring it into them. [Eyde stays in the fight despite his wounds, providing leadership to his team.] I guess I'll never know the many of those slant-eyed heathens my gun mowed down all that night.

But when dawn came and the tropical sun was shining brightly, the Japs were piled in lines near our position [*sic*] and it would have taken an adding machine to total them up. My gunner was shaken up + lost one eye, but he's in good shape now + in high spirits. I'm laid up in a hospital somewhere in the Hawaiian Islands now & getting along fine + eating the best of chow. [Both Eyde and his gunner show good morale despite their wounds, the natural result of having survived.] So don't worry about me Johnny, cause everything will be okay with me. Don't know how long I'll be here + the rest is a bit of okay. This is sure different than my foxhole with its rain + mud, lizards, land crabs, + insects, with no sleep + little food in 4 days. [The level of a soldiers' morale is relative to his changing circumstances and conditions. He appreciates the rest and food because he has endured the privations of combat.] Glad it's over + it's a great bunch of fighters – these American lads and we bested the smart, tricky, + cunning Japs at his own game-night close in fighting. [Here he demonstrates his sense of pride in his identity as an American soldier in the 7th Infantry Division and in their fighting skills.]

Boy, it was a beautiful operation, Johnny, and we had the best support an outfit could get – the navy, air corps, + artillery [*sic*]. [Again, he expresses his feelings of pride, identity, and cohesion with the larger American force and its accomplishments.] And believe me they did a great job of bombarding. As on Attu we lost some gallant young fellows whose heroic deeds against harassing snipers, pillboxes + blockhouses will never be forgotten. [This is an example of the quality of cohesion that Lieutenant General Moore spoke of when he cited the power of love for one's fellow soldiers.] The Jap is a tough little fighter + no one in this outfit underestimates their fanatics [*sic*] fighting ability. Every man in my company is receiving a citation for breaking up the enemy's last big counterattack on that last night which meant saving our already hard-earned gains. [Here he reveals both social and task cohesion and pride in unit identity.]

> The General was here yesterday + pinned an Oak Leaf Cluster on me which is an addition to my previously earned Purple Heart. But I'll never forget that last night in the Marshalls. Those medics on the battlefield are a great bunch + deserve all the praise in the world. Scared? There's too much going on to be scared. There were no atheists in the foxholes on Kwajalein + somehow a fellow can feel God is close in combat + in tight spots it's good to know He's there. [Eyde's religious beliefs helped sustain his will to fight.] One Jap yelled 'Cease Firing' in good English. He popped up again + was about to yell something when a hail of lead brought him down. We kept firing.
>
> Ralph Eyde, M/3-32 IN[510]

Schein's 'Model of Organizational Culture' establishes that 'any group's culture can be studied at three levels' from a shallow outer level (*artifacts*, for example, uniforms, emblems, salutes), a middle level (*espoused beliefs and values*), and a deeply embedded core level (*basic underlying assumptions*).[511] The core layer is formed when consistent beliefs and values are ingrained in the collective unconscious and held by the group to be absolute truths. This 'group identity [is a] key component of culture' and the shared assumptions guide behaviour, and 'tell group members how to perceive, think about, and feel about things.' These assumptions become so strongly felt that group members find any other behaviour inconceivable.[512] To have a tactical culture, the members must be trained to think and behave in a common way, using homogenous doctrine, requiring the same values and skill sets for all.[513]

The tactical culture provides stability and order for the group members; 'Disorder [and] senselessness' lead to anxiety, so people cope with that anxiety by cultivating cultures that support 'consistent and predictable views of how things should be' and providing the individual with the protective structure of stability, consistency and meaning. Group culture ties together group assumptions, ethic, identity, values, beliefs, norms and behaviours into a coherent whole.[514]

For the men of the 7th Infantry Division their tactical culture and will to win seemed to reflect a synthesis of identity, ideology and cohesion. Shared values and the desire for revenge propelled them *to* the battlefields of the Pacific. The foundation of their combat effectiveness and group and task cohesion was established in training. Their love for each other kept them together *on* the battlefield. Their will to win, tempered to a razor's edge, allowed them to emerge victorious *from* the battlefield. Their actions expressed the shared conviction that 'we all know that the quickest way home is to put a bullet between the eyes of every (enemy) we can find.'[515]

Chapter Four

THE BATTLE OF LEYTE AND THE INFLUENCE OF THE *SENJINKUN* ON JAPANESE STRATEGIC CULTURE

> 'My father, appearing in a dream, urged me, "Come home in death."'[516]

Introduction

The Battle for Leyte Island, fought from October 1944 to January 1945 was one of the largest and most difficult ground campaigns of the Second World War. The Americans assembled a force of over 700 warships to carry some 150,000 soldiers of the US Sixth Army to Leyte. Although Leyte had been an 'advanced depot' area for the Japanese, defended by only 23,000 troops of the Imperial Japanese Army *16th Division*, they quickly committed a force that would grow to over 250,000 soldiers.[517] The Imperial General Headquarters had correctly anticipated that the Americans would take offensive action in the Philippines and decided to make Leyte the 'decisive battle' for the Pacific with land and naval counteroffensives supported by all available air power.[518]

The Operational Environment

After their victory at Kwajalein the 7th Infantry Division returned to Hawaii. There they integrated replacements, repaired and replaced equipment, and made personnel changes. Leadership skill and success in combat were recognised with promotions and transfers to positions of increased responsibility.

Combat Leadership

Will to fight is the result of the combination of morale, cohesion, ethics and leadership. Of these, leadership is the 'lightning in a bottle'. The commanders of the 7th Infantry Division recognised the skills and superior performance of its key leaders and consistently elevated the best for their character and competence. Attu and Kwajalein veterans like Lieutenant Colonel John Finn had risen from battalion to regimental command, Lieutenant Colonel Francis Pachler had risen from company to regimental command and Lieutenant Colonel Delbert Bjork had risen from company command to battalion command, to name just a few. Recognising and developing competent combat leaders is essential.

From February to September 1944, the division again conducted intensified training at the Unit Jungle Training Center while higher headquarters planned for their next mission.[519] Between June and August 1944, several options were considered and finally on 11 September 1944 the division embarked for an invasion of Yap Island. While underway, however, the target was changed to Leyte. The division was now to spearhead General Douglas MacArthur's return to the Philippines.[520] For the Americans, the Philippines were the ultimate objective of both the Central and Southwest Pacific offensives. Taking Leyte offered the Americans a central launching point to invade both Luzon and Mindanao and a base for American air power.[521] For the Japanese, controlling Leyte was essential to protect vital supply lines from Southeast Asia and to maintain the lines of communication with their isolated forces further south. In response, the Imperial Japanese Army rushed their best available units from Manchuria, Korea and Japan itself to conduct a counteroffensive so ambitious that they envisioned capturing General MacArthur and achieving a decisive victory that would salvage their hope for a negotiated peace.[522]

Sustaining Morale – The Impact of Training on Unit Cohesion

Studies conducted during the war suggested that the two biggest factors in lowering morale were the American individual replacement system and the lack of rotation from frontline duty. Replacements joining a group of strangers and lacking their sense of unit pride and cohesion had a tougher time becoming fully integrated than soldiers who entered combat with men they had known through prior service and training. The replacements felt isolated and often needed orientation and additional training before entering combat. Those that didn't get this opportunity generally suffered higher casualty rates when they entered combat.[523] However, many soldiers who successfully endured combat felt that the bonds of loyalty, feelings of security and sense of unit pride that had been instilled in them by previous service and training in a cohesive unit had sustained them in combat. When given additional training and mentoring by veteran unit members, replacements performed better.[524]

Prolonged combat operations also undermined morale. When soldiers experienced long periods of danger, mental/physical stress, emotional anxiety, food and sleep deprivation combat effectiveness was degraded. In divisions that were able to rotate units or even just individual soldiers off the line morale was boosted.[525]

Because the 7th Infantry Division was able to rest, integrate replacements and conduct individual and collective training in Hawaii before both the Kwajalein and Leyte operations they enjoyed better morale and combat effectiveness. The division sought to maintain these practices on Leyte and Okinawa although there was less time and fewer opportunities for integration training or rest and relief during those combat operations.

Terrain and Weather

The island of Leyte is the third largest in the Philippine Archipelago. Its land mass is 115 miles long and 45 miles at its widest point. A tropical island with profuse swamps and rainforest, Leyte is dominated by a mountain range that rises to 4,500 feet above sea level along its west coast. The valleys to the east are rich agricultural areas crossed by streams descending from the mountains. Heavy rains are common, especially from October to December. Its capitol, Tacloban is 100 miles to the south-west of Luzon and 350 miles from Manila.

Leyte is dominated by the mountain range that rises to 4,500 feet along its west coast. Two large, fertile valleys spread out on the eastern half of the island; the flat and swampy Leyte Valley in the south and the Ormoc Valley to the north. The only important towns were the capital city of Tacloban (then with a population of approximately 20,000), Dulag on the east coast, the port of Ormoc on the west coast, and Dagami nestled at the foot of the mountains. Leyte had been a territory of the United States for 43 years, with a population of 916,000 according to the 1940 Census, yet little was known about it because of the general lack of effort to develop the area. The only real contributions by the American authorities were a modern water reservoir and an improved road system that consisted of only one paved highway linking Tacloban and Dulag, a 'good' cross-island trail over the mountains to Baybay, and a road running from Tacloban to Dulag and Burauen. As a result of this logistical and administrative apathy the invasion forces had no accurate maps of the island.[526]

The American Attack Plan: 'Operation King II'

The American plan for the invasion of Leyte was straightforward; the US Sixth Army, consisting of four divisions would land on the eastern beaches of the island, seizing the capitol city of Tacloban and the key terrain of four Japanese airfields.[527] In roughly the same manner as they had on Kwajalein, the 7th Infantry Division would land four battalions abreast, capture the airfield at Dulag and push inland to the town of Dagami.[528]

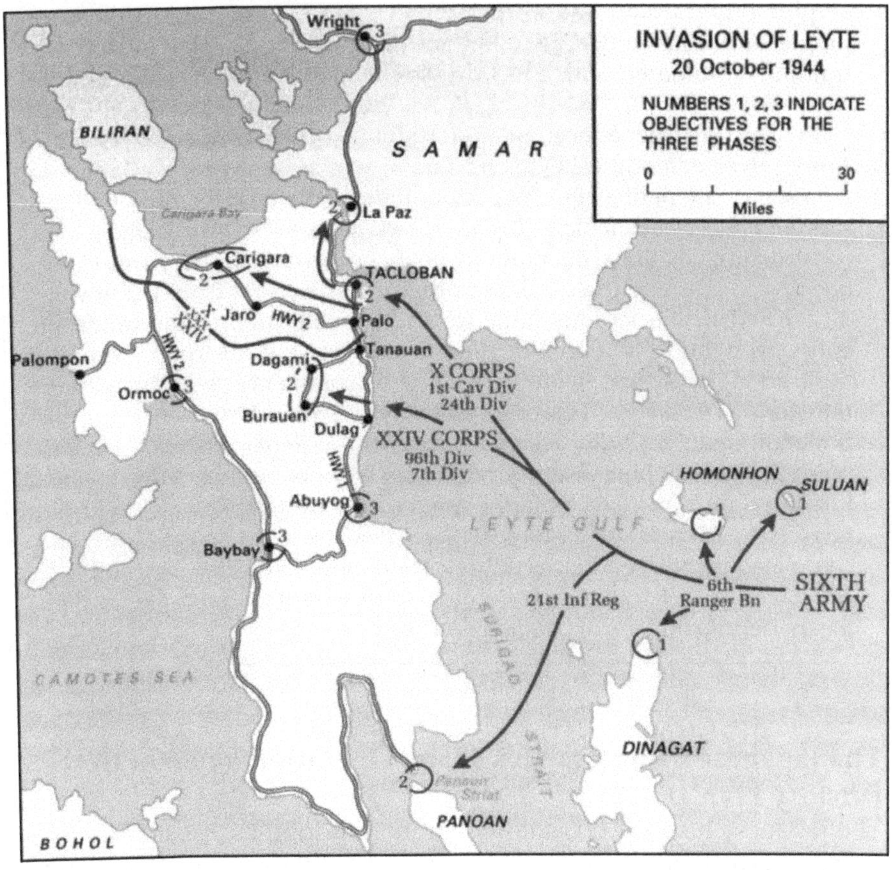

Figure 4-1: Invasion of Leyte, 20 October 1944 ('US Army Campaigns of World War II', via ibiblio.org. Downloaded from http://www.ibiblio.org/hyperwar/USA/USA-C-Leyte/maps/USA-C-Leyte-3.jpg, accessed 19 November 2021. Public Domain.).

Reinforcing Success – Training for Combat Effectiveness

Building on their experiences at Attu and Kwajalein, the 7th Infantry Division conducted training that focused on further development of tank-infantry team tactics, and the control and massing of indirect fire by forward observers. Showing excellent forethought, they also trained on tactics in tropical mountain terrain, cane fields and swamps, and in the conduct of aerial resupply to isolated infantry units. Replacements who had missed Attu and Kwajalein were given special amphibious training and all personnel attended training at the Unit Jungle Training Centre. Just as they did prior to Kwajalein division training culminated with a full-dress rehearsal amphibious landing in August 1944.[529]

In contrast, the education and training of the Imperial Japanese Army forces defending Leyte and Luzon was assessed by the Japanese themselves as 'poor'. Unit inspectors judged that the 'combat method was not taught satisfactorily' because 'each unit was so busily engaged in constructing positions, maintaining peace and order that they were in no position to improve their training program'.[530] Experts from Japan were dispatched to the various units to teach 'fortification, communication, anti-tank fighting' but lack of time meant that not all troops received the training and thus 'were compelled to commence fighting without the proper training.' This deficiency was particularly acute for the Imperial Japanese Army reserve forces sent as replacements.[531] At this point in the war Japanese reserve forces were being hurriedly pushed into the fight. They were often a mix of ages ranging from 21-year-old recruits to 35-year-old family men recalled to active duty. They had completed just three months of basic training before being sent to Leyte but it was expected that their fighting spirit would compensate for their inexperience and lack of competence.[532]

The Japanese Counterattack Plan: 'Operation *Sho Ichi Go* (Victory Plan 1)'

The Japanese had 432,000 soldiers in the Philippines, most of them on Luzon. Because of the successful American offensives in New Guinea and the Marshall Islands as well as increasing air strikes on Leyte the need for additional air bases was recognised and construction on these began in March 1944. From May to July 1944, the *14th Army Group* established its headquarters in Manila and began to prepare defences oriented on protection of the airfields with enough ammunition to supply ten divisions.[533] When the Americans invaded Leyte General

Yamashita decided to shift the main effort there and he directed the Imperial Japanese Army *35th Army* to coordinate its efforts with the Imperial Japanese Navy in what was intended to be the decisive battle against the Americans.[534] Japanese preparations for defensive operations in the Philippines were practically nil and the strength of the garrisons were relatively low, consisting of only two divisions until June 1944.[535] Between 23 October and 11 December 1944, the Japanese reinforced Leyte with five divisions, three independent mixed brigades and one regimental sized infantry unit.[536] Three lines of defensive positions were constructed along the seashore by the Japanese *16th Infantry Division,* but these were incomplete. Few other defensive positions were completed before the invasion because the priority of effort was given to airfield construction.[537] The Japanese *Southern Leyte Defense Force,* based on the *16th Infantry Division,* was composed of the *20th Infantry Regiment,* less one battalion, the *2nd Battalion of the 33rd Infantry Regiment, the 7th Independent Tank Company* and two platoons of the *16th Engineer Regiment.* They had established a loose system of strongpoints composed of log pillboxes, machine guns and 70-millimetre mountain howitzers with radiating trenches and spider holes like those used at Kwajalein.[538] They had also destroyed many of the bridges on Route 1, the main highway between Tacloban in the north and Abuyog in the south.[539]

The American Landings and the Battle of the Stone Bridge

The 7th Infantry Division made its third amphibious assault of the Second World War at 10.00 hours on 20 October 1944. The 32nd Infantry Regiment and the 184th Infantry Regiment landed abreast between the Calbasag and Daguitan rivers. Upon landing the 3rd Battalion, 32nd Infantry Regiment ran into heavy fire from Japanese machine gunners entrenched in bunkers hidden in hedgerows and banana groves. In just the first fifteen minutes, two officers and fifteen men were killed, and one officer and eighteen men were wounded. In a combined series of tank-infantry attacks, this strongpoint was destroyed without further casualties.[540] To the south the 184th Infantry Regiment landed directly in front of Dulag encountering surprisingly little resistance, allowing them to quickly capture the town and its airfield. The 2nd and 3rd battalions of the 17th Infantry Regiment landed after midday, successfully securing the bridge over the Daguitan River at Dao.

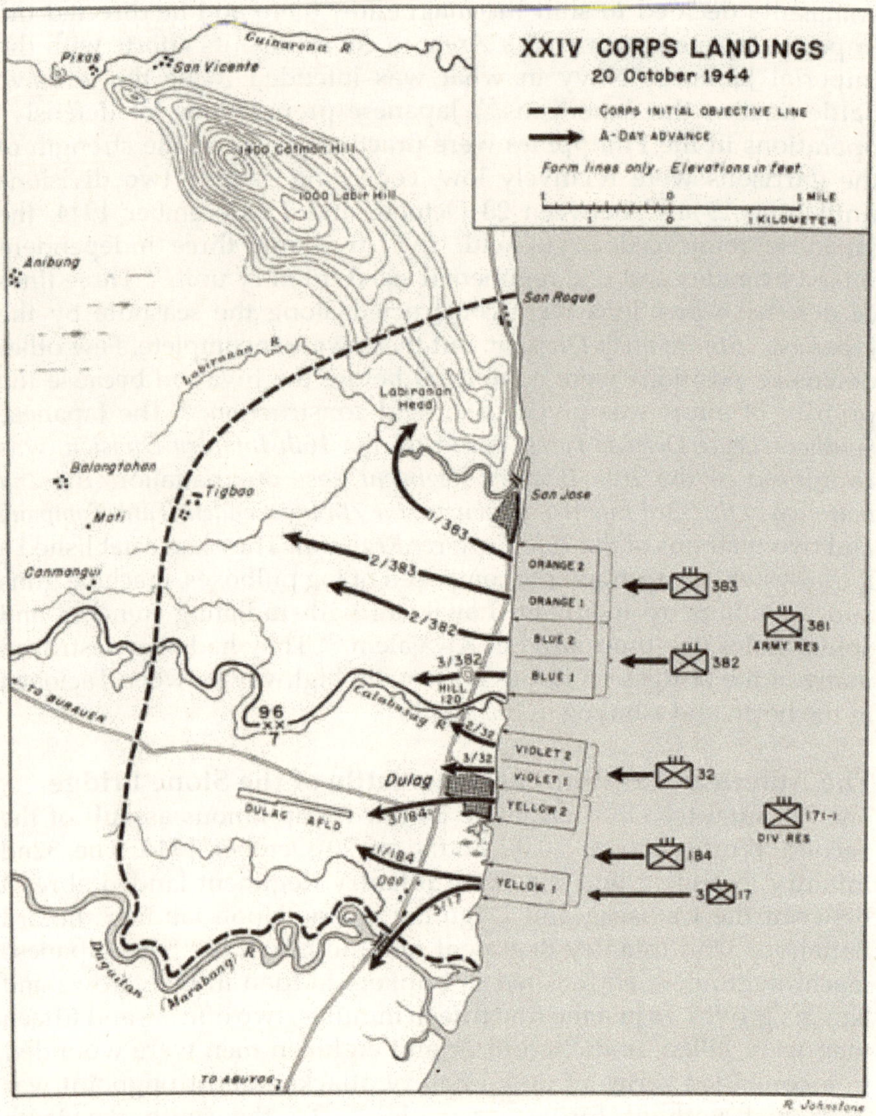

Figure 4-2: XXIV Corps Landings, 20 October 1944 (M. Hamlin Cannon, *Leyte: The Return to the Philippines*, US Army in World War II, The War in the Pacific, 73. *https://www.gutenberg.org/files/48991/48991-h/48991-h.htm#m08. Accessed 19 November 2021. Public Domain.)*

By nightfall the leading battalions had fought through moderate resistance to secure a beachhead deep enough to receive vehicles and supplies. It had been an auspicious day for the 7th Infantry Division; overall, it held a beachhead a mile and a half deep, with artillery, engineers, medics and anti-aircraft guns in place supporting the infantry. The division was thus poised to seize the next four airfields at San Pablo, Bayug and Buri.[541] The division planned to continue their attack west along the Dulag-Burauen road in a zone bounded by the Calbasag and Daguitan rivers. The 184th Infantry Regiment would be south of the road, the 32nd Infantry Regiment would be north of the road, and the 17th Infantry Regiment with tanks attached would attack along the road. At Burauen the road turned north towards Dagami which was the 17th Infantry Regiment's next objective.[542] The greatest obstacles to their progress had come from the tall, thick cogon grass, the numerous streams and the large swamps in the area that had stymied an entire battalion for a time.[543] Well hidden in the tall grasses and situated to take advantage of the swamps' restriction on mobility, several sharp fights ensued as the Americans moved forward to eliminate these battle positions.

As night fell on 20 October 1944, the Japanese counterattacked. They launched their only tank unit, the *7th Independent Tank Company* equipped with obsolete Type 89B tanks in three piecemeal attacks that the Americans quickly defeated. Of the eleven tanks available, eight were destroyed and three broke down without causing any damage to their opponents.[544] For the next two days the American 32nd Infantry Regiment and the 184th Infantry Regiment ground their way forward through the swamps around Dulag destroying enemy positions, and an armoured strike force of tanks and infantry under the command of Lieutenant Colonel Frances T. Pachler of the 17th Infantry Regiment attacked west along the Dulag-Burauen-Dagami road. The 'flying wedge' of tanks advanced rapidly, often outrunning the infantry which had to contend with the swamps and dense undergrowth closely lining the road, seizing San Pablo Airfield Number 1 by nightfall.[545] Together, all three regiments continued their attack, with the tanks reaching Burauen and the adjacent airfield the next day. The Japanese were hard pressed to stop them, and the commander of the *20th Infantry Regiment* was killed during the day.[546]

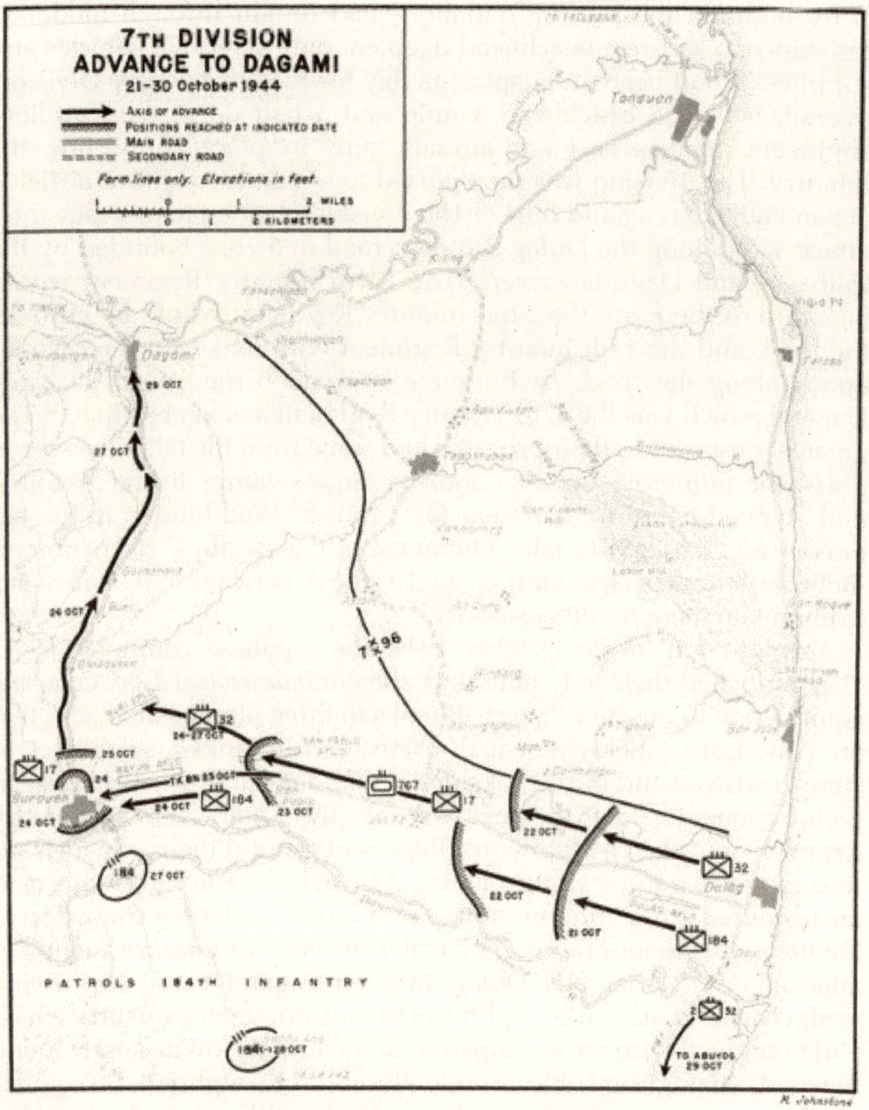

Figure 4-3: The 7th Infantry Division's Advance to Dagami (M. Hamlin Cannon, *Leyte: The Return to the Philippines, US Army in World War II, The War in the Pacific,* 125. *https://www.gutenberg.org/files/48991/48991-h/48991-h.htm#m08. Accessed 19 November 2021. Public Domain.)*

Devotion to Death

On 21 October 1944, an unidentified Japanese soldier on Leyte wrote in his diary:

> Finally the enemy's gunfire and bombardment has reached our field and road area (except the runway). Gunfire seems to fade to Dulag area during the night. It seems that enemy tanks are approaching San Pablo vicinity. We are preparing for them. Barracks and fuel dumps are to be burned. I am awaiting the opportune moment. I feel alive during the night and dead during the day. Though life and death are separated by a thin sheet of paper I will not die until I see a face of a Yankee.[547]

After capturing Burauen and San Pablo Airfield Number 2 and the 17th Infantry Regiment turned north. As night approached on 23 October 1944 the task force confronted a heavily wooded ridge, 50 feet high and 700 yards long that parallelled the road 250 yards away. A platoon sent to investigate was hit by fire from several machine guns, wounding eleven men. As they sought to remove the wounded the Japanese counterattacked getting close enough to bayonet the wounded. They were driven off and the Americans withdrew to their perimeter.[548] Defensive positions were carefully prepared for the night with concertina, trip wires, and flares positioned and artillery fires planned. As enemy mortar and machine gun fire began hitting the American positions, patrols of twenty to thirty Japanese began to probe the perimeter. The well trained and experienced veterans of Attu and Kwajalein held their fire, using only grenades and close in artillery to deter and disorganise these probes. After midnight, the Japanese made a head-long company sized charge which was met with an awe-inspiring spectacle of defensive fire that shattered the attack. The enthusiastic volume of fire was so great that it took fifteen minutes for the American leaders to bring it to an end. Fifty Japanese were killed and no further attacks were attempted.[549]

While the 17th Infantry Regiment was driving toward Dagami, the 32nd Infantry Regiment was attacking cross country. Moving through the swamps on 24 October 1944 they deployed to attack Buri airfield. At the edge of the airfield, they surprised a Japanese company digging defensive positions. As the Americans organised a hasty attack the Japanese commander ordered his own immediate attack. There ensued a hand-to-hand melee with some units moving forward, others moving back, and officers trying to find and direct their forces. Heavy casualties were suffered by both sides including the American battalion commander. Both opponents withdrew to reorganise during the night.[550] Continuing the attack on 25 October 1944, the Americans faced twenty strongly constructed pillboxes, well manned by 1,000 infantry and engineers, and found the airfield mined with 100-pound bombs buried in the runway and fused for remote detonation.[551] The fight went on from 08.00 to 17.00 hours with 2nd Battalion 32nd Infantry Regiment having gained 800 yards but they were unable to take all the enemy bunkers that defended the airstrip.[552] The 3rd Battalion manoeuvred to the flank to capture the airfield but was stopped by heavy machine gun fire. As they established a night defensive position they were attacked by a company of Japanese charging through the gap between the battalions. In five minutes of combat the Japanese lost seventy-five men in a futile effort that inflicted no casualties on the Americans.[553] At 08.10 hours on 26 October 1944, the 32nd Infantry Regiment continued its attack now with two battalions against the trenches and pill boxes. An attempt to send tank support via a detour around the swamps had begun at 06.30 hours but they did not arrive until 14.00 hours at which time the enemy positions were swiftly destroyed. The defence of Buri airfield had cost an estimated 400 Japanese lives.[554]

The Japanese Scheme of Manoeuvre

Although characterised by some contemporary observers as an 'Organized [*sic*] withdrawal covered by suicide units', it appears more likely that the Japanese were conducting a delay on successive positions.[555] In this type of defence, the unit fights from a battle position and then moves rearward to the next prepared position, following withdrawal criteria to hold until a specified time or until ordered to withdraw. A delay trades space for time, making best use of the terrain and obstacles, inflicting maximum damage on the enemy, and avoiding decisive engagement. The withdrawal breaks contact to free the unit for

Japanese troops on Attu, well equipped for the Aleutians, winter of 1943. Photograph was captured by US forces. *(U.S. Army.).*

Ralph Eyde of the 32nd Infantry Regiment, 7th Infantry Division. *("Brothers in Arms", The Washington Post, Dan Lamothe, Dec. 6, 2017, accessed January 2018.).*

Massacre Bay, Attu, 11 May 1943. The first wave penetrates the fog on its way to the beach. The destroyer USS Pruitt used her radar and searchlight to guide the boats nine miles through the fog. The searchlight beam is faintly visible pointing aft from atop her pilothouse. *(U.S. Navy.).*

Dr Paul Nobuo Tatsuguchi after his induction into the Imperial Japanese Army, 1941. *(Laura Tatsuguchi-Davis - Hays, Otis, Jr., Alaska's Hidden Wars, University of Alaska Press, 2004, p. 35., Public Domain, https://commons.wikimedia.org/w/index.php?curid=3996281. Accessed March 16, 2016. https://en.wikipedia.org/wiki/Paul_Nobuo_Tatsuguchi).*

American infantry fighting in the Jarmin Pass area, Attu, 26-27 May 1943. *(U.S. Army Signal Corps.).*

7th Division troops after taking a Japanese trench in the snow and ice on Attu. May 1943. *(U.S. Army Signal Corps.).*

American troops hauling supplies forward to units fighting the Japanese in the Jarmin Pass- Chichagof area, May 1943. *(U.S. Army Signal Corps.).*

Evacuating an American casualty, May 1943, Massacre Valley, Attu, *(U.S. Army Signal Corps.).*

Colonel Zimmerman and Captain Mapes, Attu, May 1943. *(U.S. Army Signal Corps.).*

American 60mm mortar firing in support of riflemen, May 1943, Chichagof Ridge, Attu. *(U.S. Army Signal Corps.).*

Attu, May 1943: Aerial photograph of American troops moving into the attack single file across the steep slope of Fish Hook Ridge. Here the number of men in the fight was less important than the amount of fight in the men. *(U.S. Navy.).*

Attu, 29 May 1943 – The Japanese dead. *(U.S. Army Signal Corps.).*

Colonel Yamasaki Yasuyo, Commander of the Japanese garrison on Attu. *(Accessed March 19, 2016, Public domain. https://en.wikipedia.org/wiki/Yasuyo_Yamasaki.).*

7th Infantry Division training at the Jungle Training Center, Schofield Barracks, Hawaii, 1943. *(United States Army in World War II, Pictorial Record: The War Against Japan, The U.S. Army Center of Military History, 224.).*

The effects of the bombardment of Japanese defenses on Kwajalein atoll. *(United States Army in World War II, Pictorial Record: The War Against Japan, The U.S. Army Center of Military History.).*

Kwajalein, 1944. *("The Eastern Mandates Campaign: A Staff Ride Guide for Operation FLINTLOCK; The Seizure of Kwajalein Atoll", U.S. Army Space and Missile Defense Command Historical Office, 2004, National Archives.).*

Japanese bunker. *("The Eastern Mandates Campaign: A Staff Ride Guide for Operation FLINTLOCK; The Seizure of Kwajalein Atoll", U.S. Army Space and Missile Defense Command Historical Office, 2004, National Archives.).*

7th Infantry Division fighting on Kwajalein Island, January 1944. *(United States Army in World War II, Pictorial Record: The War Against Japan, The U.S. Army Center of Military History.).*

7th Infantry Division soldiers use flamethrowers to drive Japanese soldiers from a blockhouse on Kwajalein atoll. *(United States Army in World War II, Pictorial Record: The War Against Japan, The U.S. Army Center of Military History.).*

7th Infantry Division soldier eating lunch behind a destroyed Japanese pillbox, Kwajalein. Note: dead Japanese soldiers to his right. *("The Eastern Mandates Campaign: A Staff Ride Guide for Operation FLINTLOCK; The Seizure of Kwajalein Atoll", U.S. Army Space and Missile Defense Command Historical Office, 2004, National Archives.).*

The victors on Kwajalein Island. *(United States Army in World War II, Pictorial Record: The War Against Japan, The U.S. Army Center of Military History.).*

Invasion of Leyte, 20 October 1944, *(U.S. Army Campaigns of World War II: Leyte. National Archives.).*

American infantrymen in cautious advance against enemy machine gun nest, Leyte, 21 Oct 1944. *(U.S. Army Campaigns of World War II: Leyte. National Archives.).*

Mortarmen fire 60mm mortar in attack, Leyte, 1944. *(U.S. Army.).*

The Pinnacle, 5-6 April 1945. *(Roy Appleman, James M. Burns, Russel A. Gugeler, John Stevens, Okinawa: The Last Battle, The U.S. Army in World War II, Washington DC: Center of Military History, 1948/2000.).*

A 7th Infantry Division rifleman examines a firing position on the Pinnacle. *(United States Army in World War II, Pictorial Record, The War Against Japan, U.S. Army Center of Military History, 402.).*

A typical Japanese defensive position on Okinawa. On this ridgeline there are thirty-two separate firing positions. *(United States Army in World War II, Pictorial Record, The War Against Japan, U.S. Army Center of Military History, 403.).*

Attacking the Rocky Crags. *(U.S. Army. United States Army in World War II, Pictorial Record: The War Against Japan, The U.S. Army Center of Military History, 322.).*

A tank-infantry team breach a minefield as the approach enemy defenses, Okinawa, April 1945, *(United States Army in World War II, Pictorial Record: The War Against Japan, The U.S. Army Center of Military History, 403.).*

Japanese rocket fire in support of the 4-5 May 45 counteroffensive. *(U.S. Army. Roy Appleman, James M. Burns, Russel A. Gugeler, John Stevens, Okinawa: The Last Battle, The U.S. Army in World War II, Washington DC: Center of Military History, 1948, 2000, 293.).*

Night attack on Yaeju Dake by the 1st Battalion, 17th Infantry on 12 June 45. Company A went up the path in the center and occupied the coral ridges in center. Company B moved up the slope to the left and swung back to the right to take the top of the escarpment. Note the lack of cover and concealment and the deceptively benign appearance of the heavily defended hill. *(Roy Appleman, James M. Burns, Russel A. Gugeler, John Stevens, Okinawa: The Last Battle, The U.S. Army in World War II, Washington DC: Center of Military History, 1948, 2000, 448.).*

Japanese soldiers emerge from a cave to surrender to the 7th Infantry Division. *(U.S. Army. United States Army in World War II, Pictorial Record, The War Against Japan, U.S. Army Center of Military History, 405.).*

another mission.[556] The Japanese *2nd Battalion 33rd Infantry* had been successfully withdrawn from Dulag to a position 1,000 yards south of Dagami where they had established well prepared defence in depth with elements of the *16th Engineers* and the *9th* and *20th Infantry* also committed giving a total strength of 2,500 to fight a delaying action from Burauen to Dagami.[557] On 27 October 1944, Lieutenant Colonel Kakuda, the commander of the Japanese Central Area Unit ordered the *20th Infantry Regiment* to take a position south-west of Dagami and annihilate the Americans.[558] Another group of approximately 600 soldiers composed of the *98th Airfield Battalion* and the *54th Airfield Company*, and air-ground service units were given the mission to defend key positions of the high ground west and south of Burauen, and the Buri airfield. The engineers were to demolish road bridges between Dagami and Burauen and between Dagami and Tanauan.[559] The Japanese were successful in their mission because they gained time for reinforcements from two new brigades to arrive by 25 October 1944 which made up for their losses at the beachheads.[560] However, the Japanese tactical culture of being willing to sacrifice themselves in combat influenced their chosen method of defending each strongpoint without planning for a withdrawal. Instead, they chose to counterattack directly at the enemy without supporting indirect fires which generally caused the final destruction of the Japanese force.

The Capture of Dagami

The 17th Infantry Regiment continued its drive along the road toward Dagami. The narrow corridor formed by the swamps and rice paddies restricted both freedom of manoeuvre and the size of the force that could be brought to bear.[561] On the morning of 28 October 1944, the Americans approached a swamp 100 yards across. The road crossed the swamp on a causeway with a stone bridge in the centre. On the far shore of the swamp lay a cocoanut grove. The Americans first tried to wade through the swamp but could not push through. They were forced to risk an advance along the narrow bottleneck formed by the causeway.[562] The company commander recalled:

> The Japs [*sic*] had destroyed all he bridges between Burauen and Dagami. Engineers worked under fire to rebuild the bridges … The Japs figured they had us where they wanted us. They had 42 pillboxes in the area on both sides of the road. Between the road and their positions on either side were 400-yard stretches of waist deep swamp.[563]

Upon reaching the far side of the causeway the Americans were met by a hail of fire. They attacked the bunkers, pillboxes and spider holes in small teams, taking casualties as they went but moving continuously forward. At 10.45 hours a second infantry company crossed the causeway and entered the fight and were immediately hit by heavy rifle and machine gun fire from previously unknown positions. The Japanese pillboxes, trenches and spider holes were so well-camouflaged that they could not be seen from more than 20 yards away.[564] At 11.30 hours three light tanks joined the fight and from 13.15 to 17.00 hours fought through the swamp and grove meticulously searching and destroying fourteen strongpoints. Private First Class Leonard C. Brostrom was a rifleman with Company F, 17th Infantry Regiment. As the enemy machine-gun and rifle fire caused severe casualties in his platoon, Brostrom realised that a key pillbox in the centre of the strongpoint would have to be knocked out if they were to advance. Without orders and completely ignoring his own safety, he attacked the pillbox with hand grenades. Six enemy soldiers made a bayonet charge against Brostrom, but he killed one and drove the others off with rifle fire. Throwing grenades from his completely exposed position he was wounded several times. Although suffering intense pain he slowly rose to his feet and completed his attack. As he collapsed, the enemy began fleeing from the fortification and were killed by riflemen of his platoon. Private First Class Brostrom died while being carried from the battlefield.[565]

Company G, 17th Infantry Regiment was sent on a flanking movement around the swamp. Private First Class John F. Thorson, acting on his own initiative, advanced far in front of his platoon. He came upon an enemy trench defended by several Japanese soldiers. Disregarding the intense fire directed at him, Thorson attacked alone and fell seriously wounded just short of the trench. Just as the remaining members of his platoon reached him, the enemy threw a hand grenade into their midst. Private First Class Thorson shouted a warning and rolled onto the grenade, smothering the explosion with his body. He was instantly killed, but his company was successful in causing the enemy to abandon their positions to face this threat.[566] By 17.30 hours, all Japanese resistance ended. It was estimated that two full companies of Japanese had died defending the stone bridge and a prisoner informed the Americans that the Japanese forces were being reinforced by troops landing at Ormoc.[567]

At 08.00 hours, 29 October 1944 the 1st and 3rd battalions, 17th Infantry Regiment, passed through the 2nd Battalion to seize

Dagami. With artillery support, they destroyed the Japanese force on their left flank, killing more than 120 and entered the southern section of Dagami.[568] By 10.40 hours, the town was in American hands, but sweeps continued for the rest of the day. The 3rd Battalion encountered no opposition until it had passed halfway through a cemetery. There, amongst the derelict graves and 7- to 10-foot-tall weeds awaited a Japanese infantry company. As the American unit was establishing night positions within and beyond the cemetery they were surprised by the enemy, who were literally rising from the graves.[569] A headstone tilted back, and four Japanese soldiers opened fire. Others quickly joined in from graves that had been converted to fighting positions. The battalion commander later said, 'They opened the graves and made each one a pillbox. We didn't know where the Japs [*sic*] were until one jumped out of his grave, swinging a sword.'[570] The Americans broke into small teams to hunt down and eliminate the enemy. Because they were protected from gunfire by the stone crypts, the Americans brought forward flame throwers to drive the Japanese out.[571] One Japanese officer charged three Americans, firing his pistol and wounding two before his weapon jammed. Drawing his sword, he wounded the third American before he was himself killed.[572] At the apex of the fight the American regimental headquarters, hearing the noise, called to ask for a situation report. Unable to reach the beleaguered battalion commander, they called a company commander to ask whether the Japanese had broken through the American lines. The company radio operator's laconic reply was, 'Hell no. We're just fighting for a bivouac area.'[573]

The Battle of Shoestring Ridge

In mid-November 1944, the 7th Infantry Division moved to the west coast of Leyte to confront the fresh Japanese forces that had been sent into the battle.[574] The elite Japanese *1st Infantry* and *26th Infantry* divisions had landed at the port of Ormoc to counterattack the Americans. The 7th Infantry Division responded by moving to stop them in the mountains and valleys of west Leyte. The poor, single-lane roads and torrential rains of October 1944 had created such constraints on the logistical system that the battle became known as 'Shoestring Ridge' to reflect the limited supplies and forces available.[575]

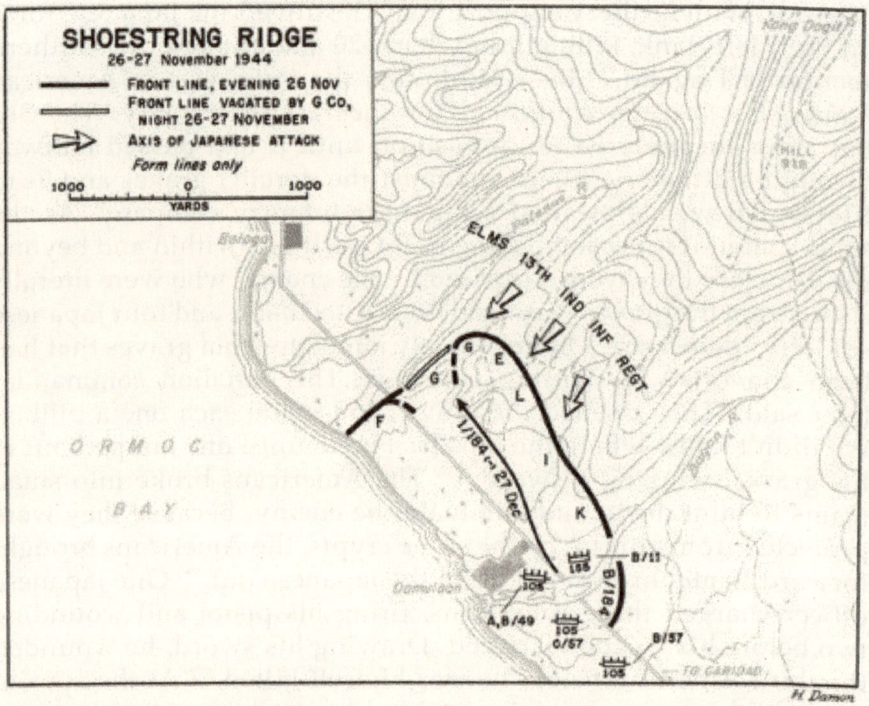

Figure 4-4: Battle of Shoestring Ridge. (M. Hamlin Cannon, Leyte: The Return to the Philippines, US Army in World War II, The War in the Pacific, Chapter XV, Battle of the Ridges, 255; https://www.ibiblio.org/hyperwar/USA/USA-P-Return/maps/USA-P-Return-13.jpg. Public Domain.)

By 23 November 1944, the 32nd Infantry Regiment having already seen thirty-five days of hard combat without replacements had only two understrength battalions available. They were defending the most prominent terrain feature, a ridgeline on the south side of the Palanas River valley, astride the road between Ormoc and Baybay, from which the whole coastal area and the town of Damulaan could be observed.[576] From there they could see enemy ships and barges in Ormoc Bay. On the night of 23–24 November 1944, the Japanese *26th Infantry Division* attacked across the river with four infantry battalions supported by three artillery battalions to seize the airfields near Burauen.[577] On this bright, moonlit night the Japanese infantry, supported by artillery seized the high ground of Hill 918 but had not pierced the American lines. The Americans counterattacked on 24 November 1944, regaining most of Hill 918.[578] A rhythm was established for the next four days and nights of battle: By day, they would toil to dig fighting positions and bring up ammunition, food and water. By night, they would defend against strong Japanese infantry attacks supported by heavy artillery fire. Ground was gained and lost by both sides as the Japanese first sought to overwhelm and then to outflank the Americans. For the Americans, ammunition resupply became a critical since there were no fresh troops available. They were indeed 'operating on a shoestring'. The 32nd Infantry Regiment commander later observed, 'The old slogan, 'too little and too late' became 'Just enough and just in time' for us.'[579]

The battle reached a crescendo on the night of 26–27 November 1944 when companies E, G and H of 2nd Battalion, having only thirty men altogether, faced an assault by two fresh Japanese battalions.[580] Preceded by artillery fire the Japanese advanced against heavy fire to engage in hand-to-hand fighting. Just when it appeared they would overwhelm the Americans, the Japanese withdrew. The Americans quickly filled the gaps in their lines and with all officers wounded Technical Sergeant Melvin H. Raabe took command. Skillfully directing his men's fires and moving forces to thwart any penetration he managed to hold the line. He led a bayonet attack down the hill to sweep the remaining enemy from their positions. Meanwhile, when the critical left flank machine gun became jammed with mud, Staff Sergeant Lewis V. Pulver and Private First Class Dee Taylor took it apart, cleaned it, and resumed firing while Private First Class Rufus F. Pate stood over them throwing grenades, thereby saving the whole left side of the position.[581]

Combat Effectiveness – Conducting Maintenance Under Fire

Weapons require constant cleaning and lubrication in a tropical environment. Doing so successfully during a firefight, in the pitch darkness is an emergency event, but it speaks well of the training, competence and self-confidence of the American soldiers.

They thwarted Japanese attempts to infiltrate the rest of the night. For his leadership Raabe was awarded the Distinguished Service Cross and promoted to Second Lieutenant.[582] Both sides were exhausted, but the Americans held the key terrain and the Japanese had lost an estimated 75 per cent of the six battalions that attacked.[583] The next morning the defenders counted 400 Japanese dead in front of their positions. Despite the heavy fighting, the 32nd Infantry reported only four officers and fifteen enlisted men wounded and one enlisted man killed.[584] On the night of 27 November 1944 the Japanese launched their last attempt to force their way across the Palanas River. Their only success came at the point where Company G, 32nd Infantry Regiment defences joined those of Company A, 184th Infantry Regiment. Here the enemy climbed to within 20 yards of the American foxholes. The Americans two light machine guns fired continuously until they became too hot to function. While the gunners sought to fix them, they were overrun and five of the defenders were killed in hand-to-hand combat. By morning the Japanese had managed to gain a foothold on the ridgeline, but they had no more men to throw into the attack. Colonel Finn's understrength and weary 32nd Infantry Regiment had held the line against six Japanese battalions for five days, preventing the *26th Infantry Division* from attacking southward in their best opportunity to win the Battle of Leyte.

General Arnold then ordered the 7th Infantry Division to push northward through the enemy with the 184th Infantry and 17th Infantry regiments abreast. The 32nd Infantry Regiment was withdrawn to rest and resupply.[585]Although several days of hard going still lay ahead the backbone of the Japanese resistance had been broken. The 7th Infantry Division had achieved something that the Japanese had considered impossible. It had pushed through Leyte over the tortuous single lane mountain road between Abuyog and Baybay, it had stopped the enemy divisional attack at Shoestring Ridge, and it had then counter-attacked north across the ridges and hills, destroying the right flank of the *26th Division*, which was crucial for the defence of Ormoc, thus tightening the noose on the remaining Japanese on Leyte.[586]

In a period of four months the 7th Infantry Division had fought the enemy through 37 miles of swamps, jungles and mountains, dominating over 105 square miles of Leyte, Panoan Island and the Camotes Islands. A total of 16,559 Japanese were killed by the 7th Infantry Division and 233 were taken prisoner at the loss of 582 killed in action and 2,102 wounded or 18.85 per cent of the division's total strength.[587] Overall, the Battle of Leyte was a tragic blow for the Japanese, losing four divisions and several separate combat units.[588] With them the Japanese also lost any real hope of retaining the Philippines as General Yamashita realised that 'the decisive battle was impossible'.[589]

Combat Effectiveness – Mastering Force Employment

Returning to the premise that explaining success in battle cannot be reduced to technological asymmetry and/or industrial overmatch, and that non-material factors must also be considered we examine the Japanese doctrine and tactics used on Leyte.[590] American observations were that the

Japanese made skilful use of terrain in the defensive with positions dug in deeply and expertly camouflaged. The Japanese employed reverse slope defence tactics with great skill and made good use of caves and other natural formations. The Japanese frequently sacrificed clear observation and fields of fire for better cover and concealment, a fact which made it very difficult for the Americans to locate hostile positions.[591]

The Japanese pillboxes weren't as solid as those on Kwajalein because they were made of concrete rather than logs:

> They are all connected by deep trenches so the Japs [*sic*] can run back and forth, concentrating firepower where they need it the most. But once a pillbox falls, the whole damned system seems to break down.[592]

Their use of wire obstacles to deter, delay, or disrupt attackers was almost non-existent. Mines were poorly used, usually being surface laid and were thus easy to detect and remove. Japanese artillery was used in high volume in several attacks but not to best effect. The gunnery techniques were 'remarkably undeveloped' and inefficient. Their guns fired singly or in pairs, rarely as batteries, and their fires were not massed.[593] Japanese troops were highly motivated and well led by officers extremely devoted to duty. Consequently, 'as long as any officers remain alive, the remnants of a force are capable of determined action.' Sometimes they fought fiercely, other times they gave up as soon as the first pillbox fell, or the last officer died. 'I've seen Japs [*sic*] throw down their rifles and run, but I've only seen one actually surrender on Leyte.'[594] To win, any force that is fighting when outnumbered must exhibit full mastery of the interrelated battlefield operating systems of command and control, manoeuvre, fires, protection, mobility and counter mobility, depth and reserves in a synchronised and synergistic manner.[595] An effective defence is characterised by best use of terrain to protect the force and maximise observation and fields of fire. Obstacles, mines and barriers must be employed to slow the attacker and break up his formations. They deny his mobility, preventing him from moving on the defender's positions, and they fix him in place to destroy him with massed fires and counterattacks. A reserve force must always be available to repel any penetrations and reinforce threatened areas as needed. The Japanese defences on Leyte lacked these essential features and thus they were less combat effective than the Americans because of their ineffective force employment, and not just from an unfavourable correlation of forces ratio. The Japanese view of American methods was summarised:

> The strong points of the American strategy in the Leyte Operation were numerous but the two outstanding points were (1) the overwhelming striking power of the American Army, and (2) the American operations were planned in minute detail and on the whole were carried out scrupulously.[596]

Imperial Japanese Army Ideological Indoctrination

> We vow to be first to die.
> We vow to be first to achieve glorious deeds.
> We vow to be first to follow orders.[597]

In just seventy-seven years, the Imperial Japanese Army grew from a handful of royalist *samurai* to an army of 5.9 million soldiers. During this time, both it and Japanese society underwent radical change and explosive growth, and it fought three successful conflicts but finally ended in ashes.[598] I will examine the crucial connections between Japanese ideological indoctrination and their strategic/tactical culture. The Japanese army adopted the modern methods, uniforms, and weapons used by Western armies, but they adapted centuries old traditional Japanese values of obedience, loyalty, discipline to create an army that would fight to the death … uselessly.

Yamagata Aritomo, father of the Imperial Japanese Army, was tasked to quickly create a national army from a force of undereducated conscripts. The primary goal was a force that would be loyal to the emperor and embody the romanticised warrior values of the former *samurai* class. To accomplish this great emphasis was placed on establishing an ethos that espoused loyalty, bravery and obedience.[599] The method chosen was intense indoctrination via the *Gunjin Chokuyu* (The Imperial Rescript to Soldiers and Sailors). Issued on 4 January 1882 by Emperor Meiji, the *Gunjin Chokuyu* declared the emperor as the Japanese military's supreme commander and commanded complete loyalty to him.[600] The Imperial Rescript to Soldiers and Sailors was the foundational doctrine on loyalty to the emperor, obedience to superiors, *esprit de corps*, filial piety, and veneration of Shinto *kami* (deities; spirits) and the *kokutai* (polity).[601] A long and complex document, written in obscure language, it was studied daily by recruits who were required to recite it aloud. As reinforcement, the entire document was read to the troops on several special occasions during the year. All soldiers memorised the short version of the Imperial Rescript which contained these five principles:[602]

1. The soldier and sailor should consider loyalty their essential duty. Bear in mind that duty is weightier than a mountain, while death is lighter than a feather.
2. Inferiors should regard the orders of their superiors as issuing directly from Us.
3. The soldier and the sailor should esteem valour.
4. The soldier and the sailor should highly value faithfulness and righteousness. Faithfulness implies the keeping of one's word and righteousness the fulfillment of one's duty.
5. The soldier and the sailor should make simplicity their aim.

The indoctrination of the troops was further enhanced by a parallel effort that began in the school system. The Imperial Rescript on Education of 1890 (*Kyōiku ni Kansuru Chokugo*) designated the emperor as the 'father' of all Japanese children, explained the mythical origins of the Japanese polity, and stressed the importance of obedience to parents and loyalty to emperor. To prepare these children for a life of service to the nation it was stressed that it was a duty to give one's life for country and emperor, and that even as children they should not fear sacrificing themselves.[603] Japanese society was carefully shaped to adopt these values by government propaganda, and they were institutionalised in the mandatory national educational curriculum for school children called National Morality from 1910 onward.[604] Through the school system, government propaganda and adherence to cultural norms the Imperial Japanese Army was thus imbued with standards and values falsely claimed to be derived from the ancient warrior traditions of the *samurai* that were then held as a faith and a creed.[605] This was further reinforced by the mandate for preparatory military training in the secondary schools beginning in 1925. This promoted the importance of the military and its high place in Japanese society. Absolute obedience to military superiors as direct representatives of the emperor, and the importance of the polity over the individual were key elements of this indoctrination.[606]

This indoctrination was solidified once the Japanese boy entered the military. The strict hierarchy of military life became accepted as a natural extension of that of family and society. Soldiers were required to serve those soldiers senior to them by preparing their food, caring for their bedding, rifle and boots, and even washing their non-commissioned officers' underwear. At the same time, they were frequently beaten for any mistake or error as a means of instilling blind discipline and loyalty.[607]

By characterising the army unit as another family, situated within the larger hierarchy of family relationships in Japanese society, with the emperor as the ultimate head of family, the Imperial Rescripts codified the chain of special relationships and loyalty to higher authority extending from the individual to the emperor.[608] By using the ancient cultural norms of the agrarian feudal Japan, Meiji leaders developed support for a new nationalistic system of behaviour.[609] Loyalty, obligation and obedience were ideas central to all Japanese people and by interpreting all these smaller loyalties as leading to one enormous loyalty to the emperor it allowed them to demand and expect enormous acts of self-sacrifice, loyalty and obedience from the Japanese people.[610]

> they drove loyalty and patriotism, that sort of ideology home … the country of Japan is, well, the country of God. It is the absolute best country in the world – that idea was thoroughly planted into us … it means to despise other races … Another reason is, like I said before, to give your life to the leader, His Majesty the Emperor, of what is absolutely the greatest country in the world, Japan, is a sacred duty and the highest honor [*sic*]. And this ideology, when you go into the military, is strengthened more and more, and your personality is taken away … When it's time to go to battle – at those times, when you were ordered by a superior, you couldn't resist. So, the humanitarian ideology I learned about in college just couldn't win out over the ideology of 'loyalty and patriotism' that had been drilled into me from the time I was small.[611]

The *Senjinkun*, 'Instructions for the Battlefield' first issued on 8 January 1941 was regarded as a supplement to the Imperial Rescript to Soldiers and Sailors.[612] The *Senjinkun* was both a code of conduct and a field manual with sections devoted to 'Reverence for the Spirits; Salutes and Manners; Duty; Outlook on Life and Death; The Maintenance of One's Honour; and Gallant Behavior [*sic*]'. The *Senjinkun* gave official approval to the belief in 'death before dishonour' by proclaiming that it was impermissible for Japanese soldiers to become prisoners of war. 'Never live to experience shame as a prisoner. By dying you will avoid leaving behind the crime of a stain on your honor [*sic*].'[613] The *Senjinkun* is known mostly for this one sentence. It has been interpreted to describe capture as both a shameful act and a crime, but is ambiguous on how one should die to atone for this.[614] Nevertheless, for the Japanese soldier the *Senjinkun* made it clear that there was no middle ground between victory and death; therefore, they believed that it was 'critical for us to die manfully on the battlefield.'[615] The indoctrination of the Imperial Rescripts made respect for the chain of command and the orders of superiors, even orders to commit suicide, fully accepted. When faced with such a preposterous dilemma the response was found in a Japanese cultural predisposition to resign themselves to fate. This fatalistic attitude, shared by most Japanese was that *shikata ga nai* ('it can't be helped'), encouraged stoicism and acceptance.[616] This attitude may be shocking, but many cultural studies have noted that suicide was widely seen in Japanese arts and literature as an acceptable response to the irreconcilable conflict between personal desires and societal demands to the extent that it was codified in ritual form as *seppuku*.[617] But, these were just documents. How could a piece of paper, no matter who signed it, have had such compellent force? Group culture is one of the most powerful forces in human history. When people are working toward a shared goal their actions can become not just something that they are doing together but something that they are. The bonds of belonging, and the shared burdens and risks, create both group values and purpose as well as individual identity.[618] Group membership and group action in Japanese society governs individual behaviour. Since cohesiveness is a core value consensus is essential and the individual's needs and desires are minimised.[619]

The Japanese Cultural Matrix: Social Debts and Obligatory Behaviour

The *Kokutai* ('national essence'), is an ideology that defined the State as the extended family to which Japanese people are indebted. 'This is our eternal and immutable national entity ... all the people, united as one great family nation in heart and obeying the Imperial Will.'[620]

The *Senjinkun* carried more than the insuperable weight of the divine majesty's command. It was supplemented by the inexorable power of the unique Japanese social traits of *giri* and *on*. Japanese society is built on a foundation of social debts. *Giri* means 'duty', 'responsibility' or 'obligation', and carries with it a sense of honour in the performance. A debt of loyalty becomes a duty to be repaid and that duty includes self-sacrifice on behalf of others.[621] *Giri* is one of the most fundamental values in Japanese society and the sense of responsibility and effort that are required to fulfil this obligation are immense.[622] *On* is the corresponding burden of the obligation, a debt of gratitude and the further honourable duty to repay that debt. It exists in the complex, Confucian maze of hierarchical societal relationships which are given coherence through the deep responsibility each person has, to maintain order and harmony (*wa*). Recognising both one's place and one's obligations in this network is essential.[623]

This complex construct subsumes all human relationships in Japan. Serving one's superiors with self-effacing devotion was ingrained in Japanese culture from its feudal era.[624] *On* and *giri* attach to a relationship, whether between individuals or to society as a whole and are authoritarian in nature. There is an ethical requirement to be aware of the *on/giri* one has incurred and to repay the debt which is carried in one's heart and is not fully discharged short of death.[625] There were three principal *on* in Shōwa Japanese culture: to the emperor, to one's parents and to one's teacher. These *on* were viewed as immeasurable and limitless; 'higher than a mountain, and deeper than the sea.'[626] The relationship between people and these values is also seen as being enduring and cyclical. If one has received an *on*, *giri* demands that it be repaid. And in the example of the ultimate *on/giri* relationships, those with teachers, parents, or the emperor the magnitude is that of a lifelong and endless debt.[627] These social values are integral to Japanese society and are thought by some sociologists to be rooted in the static agrarian culture of feudal Japan. (A hunter-gatherer culture may tolerate a higher degree of individualism than one wherein the cultivation of rice requires the mutual dedication and shared commitment of the entire community to succeed).[628]

To fulfil such an all-encompassing debt requires enormous devotion and self-sacrifice.[629] Their personal beliefs, and society's affirmation of their duty to sacrifice themselves held enormous motivational and coercive power over the Japanese soldier:

> Those who consider the great principles of sincerity, self-sacrifice, and martyrdom to country as mere slogans ... who disgrace the absolute trust of the Emperor, are the pinnacle of unfaithfulness ... if this fact be known by the parents, brothers and relatives ... their condemnation and long hatred will be extremely regrettable.[630]

The effect was to urge the Japanese masses to sacrifice. *Giri* and *on* prescribe individual behaviours and have an enormous impact on group dynamics and decision making, even today.[631]

It has been argued that Japanese wartime aggression was caused by the exaggeration of many 'national characteristics' especially the importance of societal cohesion.[632] Despite having developed a modern economy and polity since the Meiji Restoration primary personal relationships in Japanese society have remained quite traditional. To be Japanese is to be involved in close, complex and enduring personal relationships in an expanding matrix beginning with the family and extending to other primary groups. Traditionally, each member subordinates his personal desires to the requirements of the group. Group identity and cohesion is an essential element of Japanese society. Group values supersede personal values and group loyalty and rigid vertical hierarchy predominate. Correct behaviour is viewed in context of fulfilling one's obligations to the group.[633] The strictly hierarchal Imperial Japanese Army relied on top down decision making and centralised command and control. The culture of traditional group orientation supported consensus based decision making. This enhanced vertical cohesion, but innovation and initiative were subordinated to group thinking and the desire to avoid the shame and embarrassment of reporting bad news ultimately undermined combat effectiveness.[634] Modernisation did not alter the fact that the Imperial Japanese Army was ritually bound in hierarchical relationships in which the appropriate responses were grateful dependency and loyalty.[635]

The Dilemma: Die With Honour or Live in Shame?

> I wanted to die in the action of the battle. I cannot apologize to my fellow soldiers who have died in action, when I am captured and nursed here. I do not feel like living now.[636]

The *Senjinkun* exerted a powerful effect on Japanese soldiers' actions throughout the war. Fighting to the death remained a common outcome. The Imperial Japanese Army routinely fought and died, believing this to be the honourable choice. But what of those initial few, growing over time, who chose a life of shame? What caused them to go against their training?

Japanese survivors and the diaries of those who died, revealed that their motivations to sacrifice their lives were not as simple as believed. On one level, their unquestioning obedience and loyalty to the emperor reflected *tatemae* (a façade; the behaviour and feelings one presents in public) in accordance with the group orthodoxy. Public disapproval and shame are scrupulously avoided and hiding one's true feelings in the presence of the group is common.[637] On another level their *honne* (the true, hidden feelings of the individual) were focused on the avoidance of shame, dishonour and punishment for their families. Due to their ideological indoctrination meant that Japanese soldiers believed that they would be executed or banished if they returned from war after committing the crime of being captured.[638] Their strong identification with the group and fear of letting others down or appearing cowardly ultimately propelled them toward sacrifice more than dedication to a distant imperial deity.[639] A summary of the personal accounts of some Japanese prisoners provides some insights on unit cohesion, leadership and cultural attitudes: Matsubara Shunji, Kojima Kiyofumi, Ooka Shohei and Kobayashi Shigehiko.

Matsubara Shunji

A non-commissioned officer in a maintenance unit fighting as infantry, surrendered on Leyte. When other nearby units conducted *gyokusai*, he and his colleagues sought a way to avoid throwing their lives away. Finally, they surrendered, and he was amazed at the kind treatment that he received and the feeling that he could become friends with the Americans. Still, when asked which country would win the war he replied, 'As a Japanese noncommissioned officer, I must believe that in the end Japan will win.' Despite this, he felt utterly powerless and fell into a deep depression.[640]

Kojima Kiyofumi

A naval officer, transferred to Clark Field after the Japanese defeat at the Battle of Leyte Gulf. He was ordered to lead a platoon of sailors fighting as infantry after the unit had already been decimated by combat and malaria.[641] He received an order to withdraw, with the directive to kill the wounded who could not be moved. Kojima escaped this moral dilemma because the wounded sailor committed suicide, leaving Kojima a cigarette case upon which was written 'Long Live the Emperor' and 'I pray for the platoon leader's eternal military good fortune.'[642] Kojima was struck by the sailors' generosity and his devotion to the *Senjinkun*, but he concluded that the war was lost and that he had to survive in order to inform the Japanese people that their leaders were to blame. After weeks of evading the enemy without food he surrendered himself and his few remaining men.[643]

Ooka Shohei

A reservist and university graduate. Ooka was one of the few prisoners of war who confessed to having questioned the *Senjinkun*. 'To arrogantly choose a needless death' seemed delusional and he concluded that 'sacrificing one's life in pursuit of absurd tactics was simply insignificant, nothing more.'[644] Nevertheless, he followed orders, moving with his unit as they tried to avoid the Americans until he was too sick from malaria to proceed. He tried and failed to commit suicide due to faulty weapons and was discovered unconscious by the Americans.[645] Even though he questioned the *Senjinkun* he had been sufficiently indoctrinated that he proudly said that he had not surrendered, rather he had been taken prisoner when he could not resist: 'My personal pride did not permit me to submit in such a way to the enemy.' Still, he felt shame at being alive when his brothers in arms had died.[646]

Kobayashi Shigehiko
Surrendered on Saipan after coming to the inescapable conclusion that Japan would lose the war and rather than commit suicide, he could do more for his country by remaining alive. Nevertheless, in doing so he 'lost his life, his homeland, his race, his honour and knew shame. I had lost everything.'[647]

Strategic Culture and Path Dependence

The strategic culture of the Imperial Japanese Army was succinctly expressed by the *Gunjin Chokuyu*: 'Duty is heavier than a mountain (and so to be much regarded), while death is lighter than a feather (and therefore to be despised).'[648] Orders will be followed; sacrifice is expected. Their societal adoption of this explicit philosophy suggests that later outcomes were influenced by it. Historical outcomes are rarely determined by pre-existing conditions; however, some social structures exert substantial resistance to contingency and once a long-term institutional pattern is set into effect inertia takes hold and causal processes result.[649] The indoctrination of the Imperial Rescripts and the *Senjinkun* had the intended effect of inculcating unquestioning obedience and unassailable loyalty to the Emperor and the Japanese nation. However, they also had the unanticipated consequence of encouraging the self-destruction of the Imperial Japanese Army. When faced with defeat, rather than surviving to fight and win on another day, they chose to 'Die, and leave no ignominious crime behind you.'[650] Whether sacrificing their lives in units committing *gyokusai* or as individuals committing suicide, the Imperial Japanese Army followed this injunction to its eventual doom. Even when units withdrew, they lost cohesion, killing the wounded and abandoning equipment thus becoming combat ineffective. Soon there remained only individuals seeking to evade and escape, tormented by the shame of having survived. The Imperial Japanese soldier did not merely accept his obligations within the hierarchical social structure but obsessively demonstrated the need to define and validate oneself in accordance with that structure, identifying so strongly with its mandates of its tactical culture to respond reflexively with a willingness to fight to the death. Japanese strategic culture was heavily based on their reliance on the 'spiritual superiority' of the Japanese soldier and sailor, particularly their spirit of selflessness. The glorification of death in service to the emperor was an integral element of their strategic culture.[651] The believed that in a prolonged war they would ultimately defeat the Americans who lacked their 'spiritual quality' to sacrifice all for the cause. Their strategic force assessments assumed that the Americans had a 'simplistic belief in weaponry and materiel superiority'. In response the Japanese would rely on the Japanese soldier's readiness to endure any hardship and fight to the death to ultimately wear down the Americans.[652]

Chapter Five

THE BATTLE OF OKINAWA, STRATEGIC CULTURE AND *'YAMATO DAMASHII'*

'The only course left is for Japan's one hundred million people to sacrifice their lives by charging the enemy to make them lose the will to fight.'[653]

Introduction

In early January 1945, the 7th Infantry Division was alerted of its new mission, the invasion of Okinawa. By 12 February 1945, all elements were relieved of tactical missions on Leyte and began to plan, train and organise for the new operation.[654] Just as before Attu, the lack of time given, and the competing deployment tasks prevented the execution of a tailored training plan. Nevertheless, in just one month the division received and trained replacements, repaired, or replaced equipment, gathered supplies, and conducted rehearsals. Using their past training regime at the Unit Training Center in Hawaii as a guide as well as recent combat experience they focused on individual and small unit tasks. Lacking port facilities, they loaded out across the same Leyte beaches that they had assaulted in October of 1944, in a reverse movement of troops and vehicles to the beaches and on to the landing craft and then the landing craft returning to the transports. Embarkation began on 12 March 1945 and the division then conducted two practice beach landings with the navy before getting underway for Okinawa on 27 March 1945.[655]

The Operational Environment

In late October 1944, the Americans were faced with several choices of where to strike the Japanese next. Should they attack Luzon or invade Formosa? General MacArthur favored Luzon. Admiral King argued for Formosa. Admiral Nimitz endorsed Luzon. The decision was made to conduct a three-pronged campaign, attacking Luzon on 9 January 1945, Iwo Jima on 19 February 1945 and Okinawa on 1 April 1945. All told, the Americans would send a land, sea, and air armada of some 500,000 troops against the Japanese at Okinawa.[656]

The Japanese, meanwhile, were uncertain of the Americans' next move and wavered between preparing for attacks on Formosa and Okinawa. The capture of either island would put American bombers within 350 miles of Kyushu. Thus, both islands were strategic key terrain. While Formosa gave the Americans a stepping-stone to China, the Japanese recognised that with its multiple airfields and excellent anchorages for an invasion fleet Okinawa was ideal for an invasion of the home islands. In the end, the Imperial General Staff directed that both be defended equally, diverting their best infantry division, the *9th Infantry Division,* previously in Manchukuo and thus fresh and fully equipped, from Okinawa to Formosa which they considered to be the more likely American target.[657]

Terrain and Weather

Okinawa is a rugged and mountainous island, 60 miles long and ranging from 2 to 16 miles wide. The island is heavily vegetated and narrows at the middle to a central plateau. From there the land rises in the south towards a series of hills, ridges, ravines and steep escarpments. The ridges are ideal for defence and generally run east to west, with no north to south avenues of approach, thus providing successive natural lines of defence. Numerous caves of natural rock and coral provide the defender with ready-made fortifications. The climate is subtropical and humid with frequent, heavy rains in the spring and summer.[658]

The American Attack Plan: 'Operation Iceberg'

The American plan for the invasion of Okinawa built on the successful practices, training and experiences of Kwajalein and Leyte. The US Tenth Army, initially consisting of four divisions would land on the eastern beaches at Hagushi, seizing the key terrain of the four Japanese airfields. Reminiscent of the plan they had executed on Leyte, the 7th Infantry Division would land four battalions abreast, capture the airfield at Kadena and then attack south towards the towns of Yonabaru and Shuri.

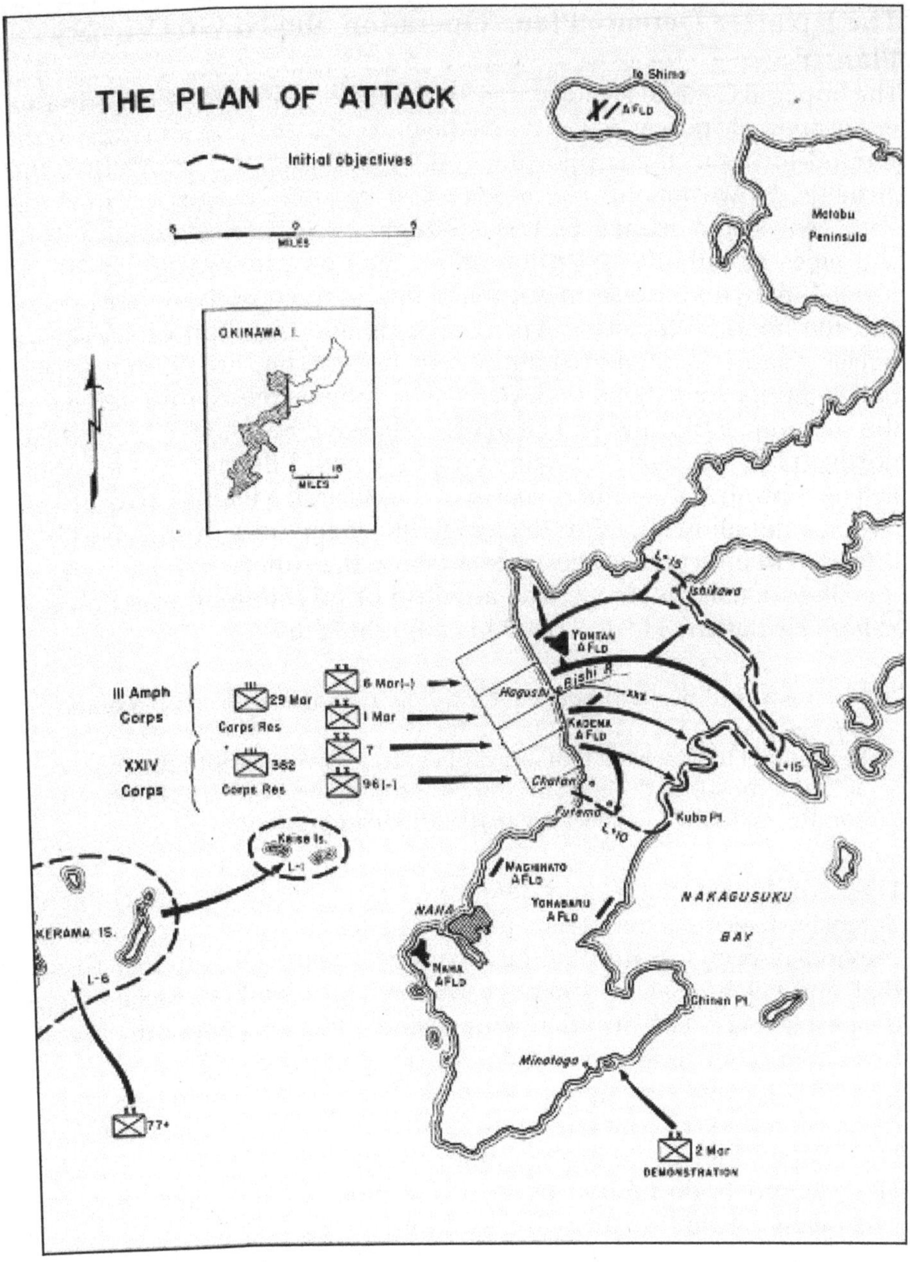

Figure 5-1: Tenth Army Invasion Plan, Okinawa, April 1945. (Roy Appleman, James M. Burns, Russel A. Gugeler and John Stevens, *Okinawa: The Last Battle*, The US Army in World War II, Washington DC: Center of Military History, 1948, 2000, 30. Public Domain.)

The Japanese Defence Plan: 'Operation Sho Ni Go (Victory Plan 2)'

The Imperial General Headquarters strategy for the defence of Okinawa envisioned air power as the mechanism to defeat the Americans with ground forces in the supporting role of building and protecting the airfields. However, the *Thirty-Second Army* staff recognised that the ends, ways and means of this strategy were incompatible; severe shortages of aircraft and pilots made this air strategy infeasible.[659] Instead, they undertook an approach that ignored both higher orders and the Imperial Japanese Army doctrine and tradition of seeking a 'decisive battle' in favor of a battle of attrition.[660] The *Thirty-Second Army* had carefully considered their defensive options: they could defend at the shoreline as normal and be overwhelmed; they could retreat to the north and be passively contained; or they could defend strongpoints in the central and southern parts of the island, yielding two of the airfields but allowing them to engage the enemy in a protracted fight intended to inflict the highest casualties on the Americans. They chose the latter defensive plan.[661] The architect of this strategy was Colonel Yahara Hiromichi. He described his thoughts thus,

> Japan was frantically preparing for a final decisive battle on the home islands, leaving Okinawa to face a totally hopeless situation. From the beginning I had insisted that our proper strategy was to hold the enemy as long as possible, drain off his troops and supplies, and thus contribute our utmost to the final decisive battle for Japan proper.[662]

They would conduct a fluid defence in depth using the pre-eminent defensive feature of the terrain, the cave system. Cave fortifications had previously been a feature of the Japanese defences at Attu and Kiska, Biak and Peleliu, Saipan and Leyte but on Okinawa they reached their deepest level of sophistication with 60 miles of connecting tunnels and their integration into the undulating ridge lines to create a series of reverse slope and strongpoint defences. The planned intent was to dig deep, contest every foot of ground, and only counterattack selectively. They hoped thereby to impose unacceptable costs on the Americans. They would trade human treasure for time and the hope that the Americans would lose the will to continue the fight.[663]

Combat Effectiveness – The Integration and Training of Replacements

The 7th Infantry Division had only a month to plan, equip and load aboard ships for the movement from Leyte to Okinawa. This resulted in a scramble to provide limited post-battle rest and rehabilitation to the veterans of the unit as well as to receive, stage and integrate replacements arriving fresh from the United States. The short training period focused on eliminating faults and deficiencies identified during the Leyte campaign by educating the non-commissioned officers on the needed corrections and training the replacements and veterans alike on demolitions, night perimeter defence and new weapons like the infra-red sniper scope.[664]

In contrast, the *Thirty-Second Army* had been activated on Okinawa on 1 April 1944 and over the next twelve months it had received a steady stream of reinforcements eventually numbering over 77,000 troops. In addition, there were an estimated 20,000 Okinawan Home Guards present. They were primarily devoted to the construction of elaborate fortifications including concrete pillboxes, tank traps, tunnels and other positions.[665] The training that they conducted when not otherwise engaged in building defensive positions included practicing unit counterattacks against amphibious landings and artillery live fire exercises on the expected beachheads.[666]

Lacking time and resources for a full-scale training program, the veteran American units heading to Okinawa had to rely on the knowledge and expertise of the old soldiers in the ranks to teach and guide the new men while enroute to battle. In these exigent circumstances tactical culture comes to the fore. Tactical culture is built on pride, cohesion and loyalty, and reflects the goals and objectives, beliefs, values and expected behaviours of the unit. Capable leaders at all levels can bridge the gaps in training by communicating the standards and explaining how the unit intends to meet current and future challenges. On Okinawa the 7th Infantry Division skillfully displayed the tactical culture that first emerged on Attu.

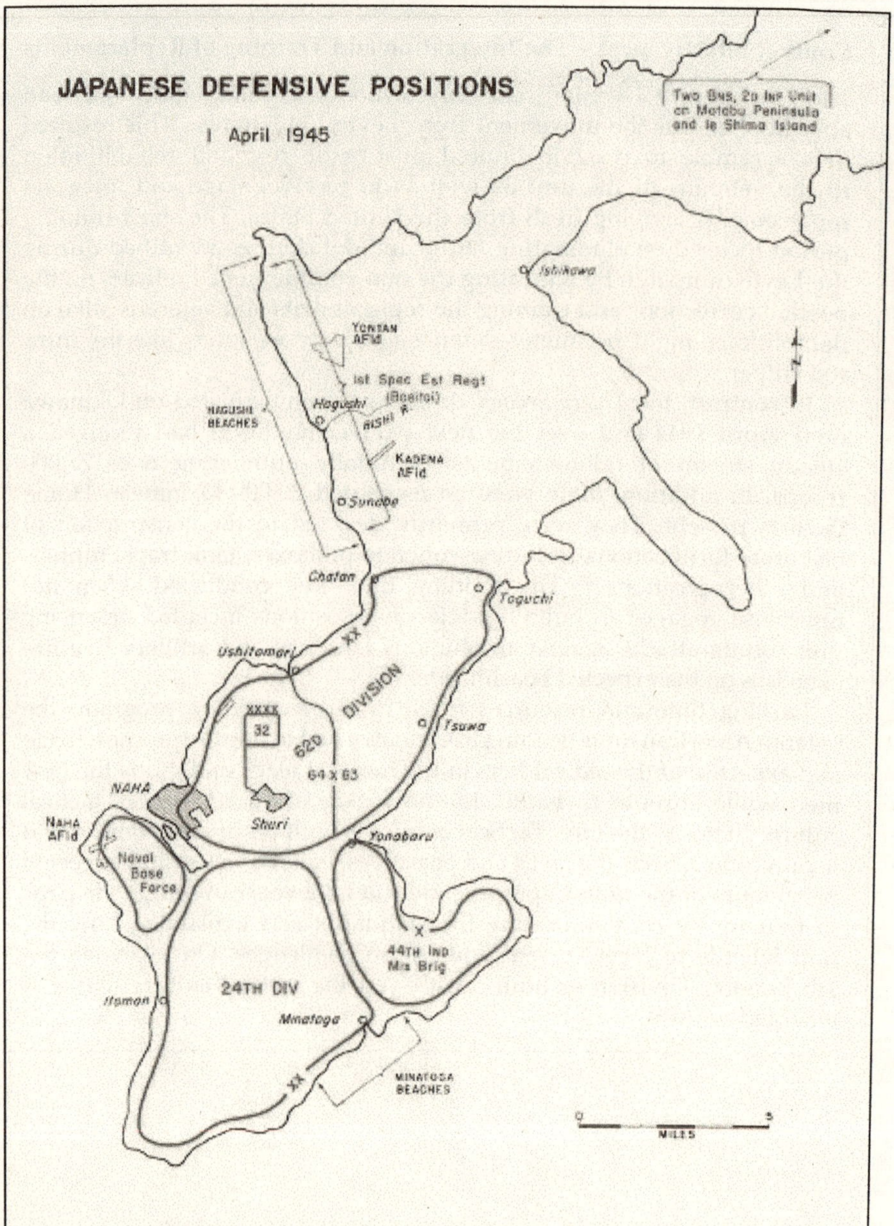

Figure 5-2: The Japanese Thirty-Second Army Defensive Plan. (Thomas Huber,' Japan's Battle of Okinawa, April–June 1945', Leavenworth Papers Number 18, Combat Studies Institute, US Army Command and General Staff College, Fort Leavenworth, Kansas, 1990, 36. Public Domain.)

From April 1944 to March 1945, the *Thirty-Second Army* devoted immense effort to the construction of elaborate defensive positions using the extensive natural cave system as a starting point. They built concrete pillboxes, gun emplacements, headquarters, and dormitories underground with ventilation shafts, connecting tunnels and electrical power. Tank traps and minefields were constructed along avenues of approach.[667] The defence was centred on the town of Shuri, a cultural centre and site of the ancient royal palace. Although the Thirty-Second Army protested doing so, they complied with Imperial General Headquarters orders to also complete the airfields, even though there were no aircraft to use them.

The Japanese force consisted of the *24th Division*, a heavy division with artillery and three infantry regiments; the *62nd Division*, a light division with two brigades, each with five infantry battalions, each with five rifle companies per battalion, but with no artillery; the *44th Independent Mixed Brigade*; and the *27th Tank Regiment*. Additional forces such as naval personnel, engineers, communications troops and other miscellaneous units brought the estimated strength of the Thirty-Second Army to over 77,000 Imperial troops. In addition, there were about 20,000 Okinawa Home Guards (*Boeitai*), and even 750 male Okinawan middle-school students who were organised into 'Blood and Iron for the Emperor' ('*Tekketsu*') volunteer units and trained for combat. Many thousands of other Okinawan civilians were conscripted for construction and logistical duties. Because of inaccurate data and destruction of the records the exact Imperial Japanese Army strength is not known, but it probably exceeded 100,000 men.[668]

The American Landings and the Outposts of the Shuri Defences

The 7th Infantry Division made its final amphibious assault of the Second World War at 08.00 hours on 1 April 1945. For the first time in the war, they landed without significant opposition. The 7th Infantry Division quickly moved inland, seizing the Kadena airfield many hours ahead of schedule and continued to the east coast 14 miles away on the second day. The ease of this phase of the operation surprised the Americans. One soldier from the 7th Infantry Division expressed what many might have felt, saying: 'I've already lived longer than I thought I would.'[669] At this point, rather than chronicle the entire eighty-two-day operation I will synopsise the battle narrative, highlighting a few significant actions.

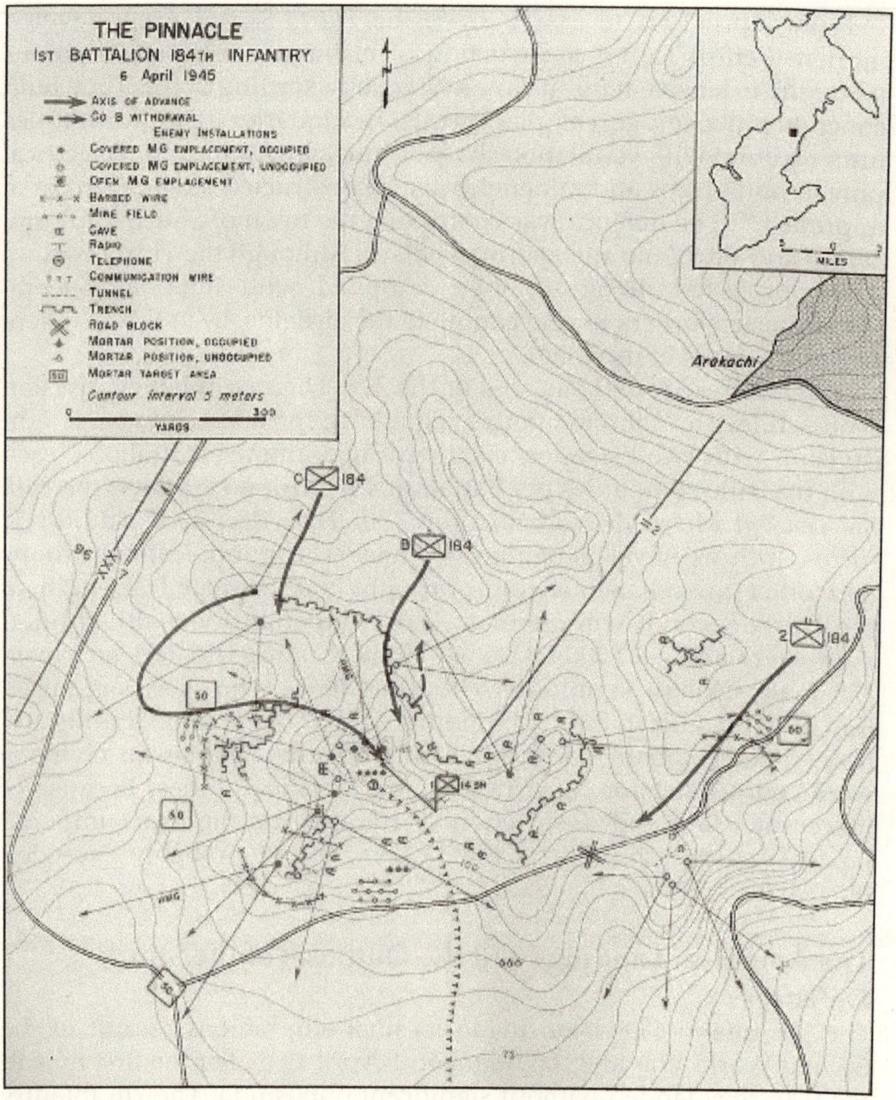

Figure 5-3: At the Pinnacle: Fighting through the outposts to the Shuri Line, 4–6 April 1945. (Roy Appleman, James M. Burns, Russel A. Gugeler and John Stevens, Okinawa: The Last Battle, The U.S. Army in World War II, Washington DC: Center of Military History, 1948/2000, 107–109. United States Army Center of Military History. Public Domain.)

Assaulting the Shuri Line

Located just 2 miles from the town of Naha and the western coast of Okinawa is the site of the ancient castle of Shuri. It is surrounded by the most rugged terrain in the southern half of the island, offering excellent observation both north and south down to the coasts. It is ideal for defensive operations due to the steep slopes, abrupt ravines and sharp escarpments. The *Thirty-Second Army* would make this area the keystone of their defensive effort by constructing a network of pillboxes, tunnels, caves and fortified tombs. The Americans called it the 'Shuri Line'.[670]

The initial attempts to pierce the outposts of the Shuri Line served as preview to the bitter struggle to come. On 5–6 April 1945, the 1st Battalion, 184th Infantry attacked 'The Pinnacle', a 30-foot-tall spire atop a 100-yard-long coral ridge that was defended by Lieutenant Tanaka Seiji's *1st Company, 14th Independent Infantry Battalion* of 110 men, 8 light and 2 heavy machine guns, and 7 50-millimetre mortars.[671]

Fighting from trenches and gun pits and protective caves, interconnected by tunnels, and strengthened by barbed wire and mines, the defenders were able to repulse three attacks until the Americans used a difficult route to surprise the Japanese in a flanking manoeuvre. Of the 110 defenders only 20 escaped. The Americans lost one killed and ten wounded including a company commander.[672] 'The Pinnacle' had been a difficult position to take but it was only one of several outposts in front of the main defence. Similar fights ensued at Red Hill, Triangulation Hill, Hill 178, and Tomb Hill from 6 to 10 April 1945, involving intense Japanese artillery and machine gun fire and mines which disabled several American tanks and frustrated both frontal attacks and flanking manoeuvres.

On 7 April 1945, for Captain Dean Galles, who had served with the 7th Infantry Division from Attu to Okinawa, the war came to an end. Ignoring personal hazards, he moved across open, fire-swept terrain directing the successful attack of his company. As he advanced, Galles was wounded by machine-gun fire that nearly killed him. The first bullet hit his left shoulder joint. The next four bullets went into his left shoulder, chest and stomach. Another bullet pierced his helmet and grazed his skull and neck. Galles spent a year recuperating in hospitals. Sixty years later, when reflecting on why he persevered he said, 'I just served my country and did the best job I could. What about all the others, particularly those who gave their lives?'[673]

Overall, the *62nd Infantry Division* outposts had successfully delayed the Americans for 8 days at the cost of 4,489 killed and 13 captured.[674] In the first 10 days of the battle the 7th Infantry Division had taken 20,000 yards of terrain and suffered 120 killed, 696 injured and 13 missing, most in the last 3 days of the period.[675] Between 10 April and 19 April 1945, there began a cold and steady rain which turned the primitive roads and trails to slick mud and made any movement very difficult. Constant Japanese shelling helped create a quagmire that made resupply and medical evacuation herculean tasks. The 7th Infantry Division was now directly up against the Japanese main line of resistance.[676]

From 19 to 24 April 1945, the division fought to take the Rocky Crags and Skyline Ridge. Attacking with two battalions, the Americans faced a Japanese force of 1,000 men, fortified in caves, tombs and tunnels.[677] Attacks with artillery, mortars, flame throwers and hand grenades were met with fierce counterattacks. The Japanese did not give up a single foot of ground, fighting until they were killed. On just 19 April 1945, the 3rd Battalion, 32nd Infantry had lost about 100 men on Skyline Ridge. Two companies of the Japanese *11th Independent Infantry Battalion* had been annihilated and a Japanese company commander had committed suicide.[678]

Combat Effectiveness – Intelligence Successes and Failures; Processing, Exploitation, Dissemination

The Americans had very few detailed maps of the rugged terrain on Okinawa. Most were based on photography from aerial reconnaissance which often failed to reveal terrain features hidden under the clouds and foliage. The extent of the cave defensive system was therefore completely unknown until they encountered the Shuri outposts. On the evening of 17–18 April 1945, the XXIV Corps Military Intelligence Service team received a detailed topographical map found on the body of a dead Japanese artillery forward observer that showed all Japanese artillery and heavy mortar positions in their sector. Knowing that an American attack was planned for the next morning, the Nisei interpreters worked straight through the night to translate the chart, finishing just two hours before the attack. The translated document was delivered to the corps assistant intelligence officer but the attack went on as scheduled. The attack failed; at no point did the Americans break through. The corps lost 720 dead, wounded and missing in a single day. While this map was not exploited in time to affect the attack on the Shuri Line it was still valuable. It was quickly sent to Hawaii where 12,000 copies were printed for issue to every unit on Okinawa and the information it provided may have contributed to the successful American counter-battery fires during the Japanese counterattack of 4–5 May 1945.[679]

On 21 April 1945, Sergeant Theodore Roosevelt MacDonnell, infuriated by the losses attacked alone three times up a 20-foot embankment alone armed only with grenades. He then borrowed an automatic rifle to attack an enemy machine gun, but the weapon jammed. Returning to attack a fifth time armed with a carbine, he fired point-blank into a machine-gun position, killing the gunner and two enemy riflemen. He then hurled the machine gun and a captured mortar down the hillside. His actions inspired others to advance, and he was awarded the Distinguished Service Cross.[680] After four days of heroic effort, the first ring of the Shuri defence was broken. On the night of 23–24 April 1945, the Japanese fired 4,500 rounds of artillery as the remnants of the 11th Battalion withdrew under the cover of fog. Within the maze of tunnels under Skyline Ridge the Americans found 500 dead Japanese and 250 rifles, four heavy machine guns, nineteen light machine guns, twenty mortars, a 20-millimetre anti-aircraft gun and a 75-millimetre field gun.[681]

Assaulting the Second Shuri Line

After penetrating the first ring of the Shuri defences the 7th Infantry Division encountered the 500-yard-long Kochi Ridge. There they fought the fresh Imperial Japanese Army 22nd Regiment in what they regarded as the most resolute defence they faced on Okinawa. The masterfully emplaced reverse-slope defence was well integrated with nearby supporting positions and the excellent unit leaders kept the Japanese spirit high.[682] From 25 April to 10 May 1945, elements of all three of the division's regiments attacked Kochi Ridge without the usual artillery, tank and air support. Rain had reduced tank mobility by turning the poor, narrow roads into slippery bogs and the opposing forces were too close to one another to avoid fratricide from indirect fire. The terrain limited the fighting to close range rifle and grenade battles with more hand-to-hand combat than the men of the 7th Infantry Division had seen in their three previous campaigns.[683]

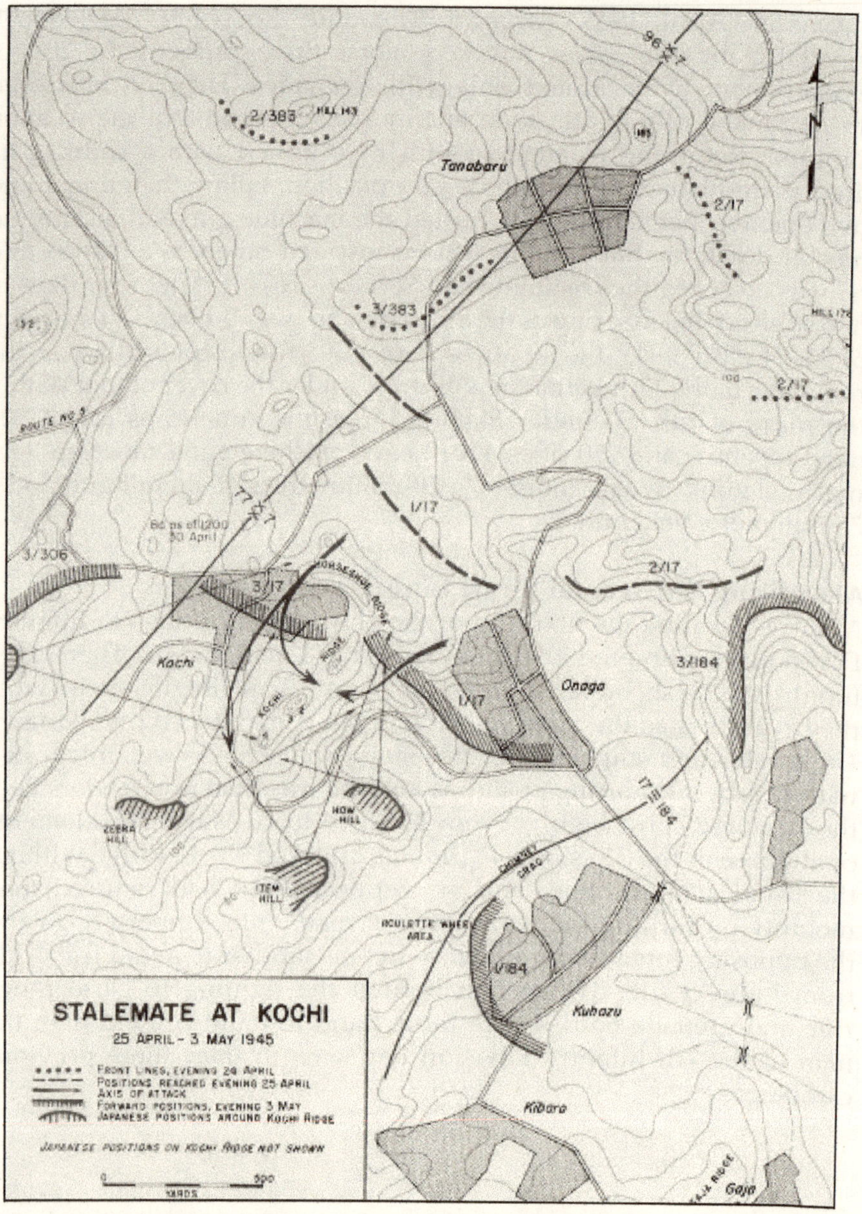

Figure 5-4: Stalemate at Kochi Ridge, 25 April–3 May 1945. (Roy Appleman, James M. Burns, Russel A. Gugeler and John Stevens, Okinawa: The Last Battle, The US Army in World War II, Washington DC: Center of Military History, 1948/2000,Map XXIX. Public Domain.)

Combat Effectiveness – Caves Versus Tanks

Okinawa represents an interesting study in the role, influence and adaptation of doctrine. Japanese island defence doctrine in previous campaigns mandated the annihilation of the attacker before he got ashore, and counterattacks to eliminate his toeholds. Japanese units had used natural caves as supplemental defences at Attu, Biak, Peleliu, Saipan and Leyte but on Okinawa their cave warfare doctrine came into full maturity.[684] The Japanese built strong points to take full advantage of the rugged terrain creating a series of mutually supporting, concentric positions that fortified both the forward and reverse slopes of hills. Pillboxes and gun emplacements were built into the hills, escarpments and caves, connected with elaborate tunnels, and skilfully camouflaged. The ancient Okinawan castles and tombs were also incorporated into the defences. Overall, the Thirty-Second Army built 60 miles of underground formations.[685]

When they landed the Americans did not know that the cave pillbox defence system existed, nor did they have doctrine for how to attack them.[686] The American answer to these defences was the tank-infantry team, using flame thrower tanks, supported by artillery. Learning on the ground how to infiltrate small teams of men into the 'dead spaces' between caves took a couple of weeks at a high cost in casualties. Mortars and artillery would suppress or obscure the Japanese fighting positions so that assault groups of tanks, riflemen and demolition squads could creep up to point-blank range to attack the position with flame and explosives while fighting off the Japanese 'close-quarters attack troops' who sought to destroy the tanks with their own demolitions, and drive off the American infantry with their machine guns and mortars.[687] The fighting became a duel between American infantry with a mobile, but vulnerable fortress (the tank) versus Japanese infantry within an immobile but nearly impregnable fortress (the cave).[688] This kind of toe-to-toe fighting requires indomitable courage to achieve victory. The side that yields first, even for a moment, usually loses.

On 30 April 1945, while one platoon was preparing to advance, a Japanese counterattack killed two machine gunners, destroyed the gun and wounded the platoon leader and most of the riflemen. Although himself wounded, Sergeant Alois Mand took command and killed eight enemy infiltrators with carbine fire. Out of ammunition, Sergeant Mand recovered a BAR from a wounded comrade and fought until the weapon jammed. He then reorganised the remainder of the section and with the few remaining riflemen held off the foe while the wounded were evacuated, and another platoon helped secure the hill.[689] Attempts to use supporting fires led to two friendly fire mishaps with artillery fire striking one company and a Marine Corsair fighter plane attacking another unit. As a result, the 17th Infantry Regiment suffered sixty casualties from friendly fire.[690]

The Japanese Counterattack

Meeting on the night of 2 May 1945, General Ushijima's staff debated their defensive strategy. General Cho, the chief of staff, who was never in support of the chosen defensive course of action argued for the traditional Imperial Japanese Army solution: an immediate counterattack, saying that it was time for a decisive blow against the Americans. The chief architect of the defensive strategy, Colonel Yahara, had faith in the defensive tactics and opposed the counter-offensive as premature. Most of the subordinate Japanese commanders were impatient with defensive fighting, seeing it as a battle of attrition that they were doomed to lose. Colonel Yahara was overruled, and General Ushijima ordered a full offensive on 4 May 1945.[691] The *24th Division* was to make the main attack with 15,000 soldiers. This would be supported by all available artillery and coordinated with amphibious attacks on the beaches of both coasts behind American lines by several hundred men who were detached from their shipping engineer regiments and ordered not to return. Finally, the Japanese assault was to coincide with an attack by *kamikaze* aircraft and suicide boats against the American fleet.[692]

This was not to be a simple but desperate *banzai* charge as on Attu. The attacking units were given precise instructions with clear objectives. The efforts of the supporting artillery were planned to be well integrated with the infantry. Better knowledge of the terrain and accurate locations of the American units should allow the attackers to exploit weak points, especially that of the seam between the American 7th Infantry Division and the 77th Infantry Division.[693]

The details of the manoeuvre and fires planning reflect that some Imperial Japanese Army officers, like Colonel Yahara, were willing to recognise past mistakes and employ better methods and more sophisticated approaches but the overall strategic/tactical cultural bias to attack undermined both the overarching defensive strategy and the operational approach meant to ensure that tactical actions are not random in nature but united in the pursuit of the strategic objective.[694] The result was an ambivalent response to the attack order: 'The time of the attack has finally come. I have my doubts as to whether this all-out offensive will succeed, but I will fight fiercely with the thought in mind that this war for the Empire will last 100 years.'[695] The Japanese will to sacrifice soldiers in another risky attack represented a 'romantic aspiration against reality and rosy doctrine against harsh fact.'[696]

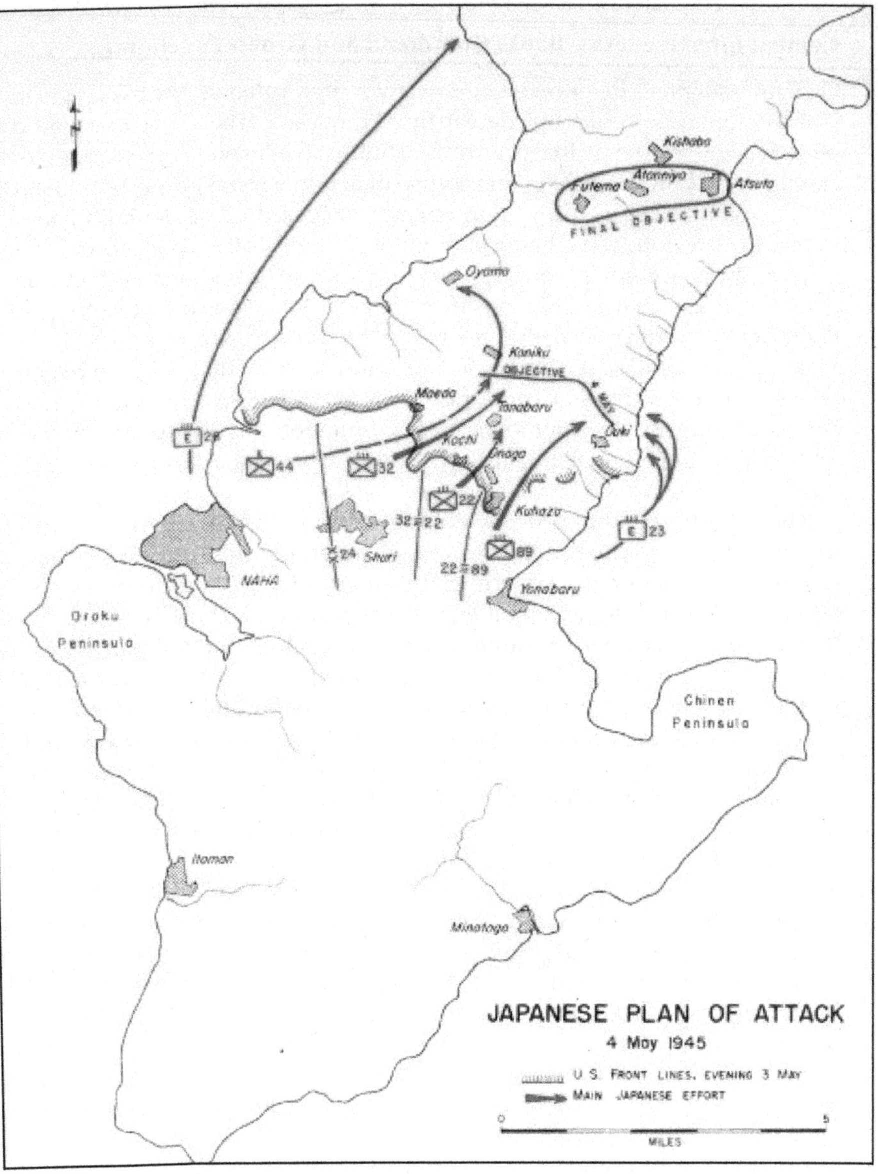

Figure 5-5: The Japanese Counteroffensive. (*U.S. Army. Roy Appleman, James M. Burns, Russel A. Gugeler, John Stevens, Okinawa: The Last Battle, The U.S. Army in World War II, Washington DC: Center of Military History, 1948/2000, 293, 'Map XXIXI', last modified 2012, Accessed 27 May 2022 at http://www.ibiblio.org/hyperwar/USA/USA-P-Okinawa/maps/USA-P-Okinawa-37.jpg. Public Domain.*)

Combat Effectiveness – Battle Command and Group Psychology

General Ushijima's defence of Okinawa was predicated on the assumption that the Japanese could not defeat the Americans. The most that could be done was to delay the enemy and inflict the maximum number of casualties on him. Ironically, this course of action was taken in the context of the larger strategic culture that remained focused on achieving victory in one decisive offensive battle that would establish the conditions for a favourable peace settlement.[697] These conflicting goals resulted in the operational and tactical decisions that directed the Japanese troops to give the ultimate sacrifice of their lives to outlast the American's will to fight. Making such pivotal decisions based on counterfactual thinking and biases seems like an example of cognitive dissonance. In 1959, Leon Festinger described this unique pathology as a situation involving conflicting attitudes, or beliefs which often gives rise to irrational and sometimes maladaptive behaviour.[698]

The decision-making process whereby the Thirty-Second Army chose to conduct their counteroffensive is a tableau of cognitive dissonance and group think. Seemingly forgetting that their strategy was to delay the Americans for as long as possible at the highest cost, the Thirty-Second Army staff advocated for a counteroffensive. 'Each soldier will kill at least one American devil ... Advance even to the last man.'[699] Even though their defence was succeeding as envisioned, General Cho argued that the Americans had the upper hand and that the Thirty-Second Army would eventually be destroyed. He felt they should wage an offensive while they still could. But their eventual defeat had been tacitly acknowledged all along. Nevertheless, Cho's forceful personality overwhelmed the younger officers who enthusiastically agreed, especially since a superior was goading them to this response. It was rationalised that this was supported by the doctrine that 'one Japanese division with a robust spirit of attack could defeat three Soviet divisions with superior equipment.'[700] There was an ingrained belief that aggressive attack would catch the enemy off guard, offset his advantage in fire power, and win the battle. This exaggerated belief in the effectiveness of the attack was in stark contrast to all experience, but most Japanese officers lacked the intellectual framework to think about alternatives and implications; they were instead biased toward action not analysis.[701]

Colonel Yahara argued for continuing the war of attrition and avoiding an offensive. Yahara pointed out that in modern warfare a force ratio of three to one was usually needed for successful attack. 'To take the offensive with inferior forces is reckless and would lead to certain defeat.' In that case, Thirty-Second Army's reduced forces would be unable to hold Okinawa for a long period and thus delay the US invasion of Japan. Ultimately, Cho declared that the consensus was in favour of the attacks and Ushijima gave his tacit approval. Yahara was coerced into ending his dissent. This example of Japanese battle command represented the

Japanese societal characteristic of consensus-based decision making and submission to group think because maintaining group solidarity was considered a prime virtue.[702]

The Japanese fired more than 5,000 artillery rounds against the 7th Infantry Division on the night of 3–4 May 1945.[703] Nowhere else in the Pacific had the 7th Division experienced such artillery and mortar fire. In the darkness the Japanese infantry crept forward to attack from close range, but the initial surprise that they achieved was short-lived. The veterans of the 7th Infantry Division had been anticipating a *banzai* charge for several days, in some cases quite eagerly. They knew that in such past events loss ratios heavily favored the Americans. In this case they would be fighting from protected positions while the enemy exposed themselves to advance.[704]

Combat Effectiveness – The Integration of Fires

A crucial element of the Thirty-Second Army's defence was the integration of both artillery and mortars emplaced in the caves and tunnels.[705] The Japanese had 3 artillery regiments, a separate artillery battalion, 1 mortar regiment and 2 light mortar battalions, comprising a force of 287 guns and 30 mortars of 75- to 150-millimetre calibre together with hundreds of 60-millimetre mortars. This allowed the Thirty-Second Army to bring to bear a volume of defensive fires never seen before in the Pacific War. On 23 April 1945, the 7th Infantry Division alone received more than 4,500 rounds of high explosive shells in just 6 hours.[706]

Yet, despite this formidable force, well protected in their fortifications, the Japanese artillery could not bring decisive indirect fire to the fight. This was chiefly because their communications system did not enable responsive and agile fire support. Fire requests were sent by telephone and runners. Telephone wire was vulnerable to damage and runners could take up to six hours to deliver a fire request. The Imperial Japanese Army did not employ a centralised fire direction centre or use forward observers attached to infantry units and therefore could not start, stop and shift fires in minutes like the Americans did.[707] The best that they could provide was pre-programmed bombardments in support of either attack or defence that were unobserved or unobservable and could not be adjusted. And although many rounds were fired over time, they were not truly massed fires because of the fear of American counterbattery fire. Typically, a gun would fire a few rounds and then withdraw into a cave for safety before firing again. When they did remain exposed, the Japanese artillery suffered. During the 4–5 May 1945, counteroffensive seventy-eight artillery pieces were destroyed by American counterbattery fire.[708]

Thus, night after night the Japanese fired harassing fire against the Americans. Day after day they sought to support the defending infantry, but they could not stop the American advance. Although they produced a high volume of fire on occasions like on the 23 April 1945, the Japanese generally achieved only light casualties and little damage, thus often inadvertently boosting American morale with their ineffective fire.[709]

Advancing stealthily under the cover of darkness and the supporting artillery barrage some units attacked the American positions directly and were driven off. Others moved around the American positions, avoiding, or missing them, but were then spotted in the open. A group of 2,000 was observed by one American company commander who tried to call artillery on the enemy. When he reported the target to the 184th Infantry regimental command post, the response was one of elation, but he pointed out that there were 200 Japanese just 100 yards from the colonel's observation point aiming two 75-millimetre howitzers at him at that very moment. Within a few moments artillery, tank and machine-gun fire rained down and the Japanese scattered.[710] On the east coast, the 7th Reconnaissance Troop spotted enemy boats offshore and fired on them. Only the broken remains of eight boats were found on the reef at dawn.

Other units were not attacked at all. The battalions on Kochi and Horseshoe Ridges and Hill 178 saw no action until daylight. Overall, the Japanese were driven back but remained in the open, flat ground exposed to mortar and machine gun fire.[711] At one point, carnival atmosphere developed as artillery and infantry attacked the broken and disorganised Japanese who reluctantly abandoned the attack. In the same way that the heavy but ineffective Japanese artillery barrages had boosted American morale, so too did the experience of having decimated this night attack with little loss further strengthen American confidence and sustain their will to fight. By nightfall, the 7th Infantry Division's casualties were 26 killed against 1,051 Japanese killed.[712]

The only bright spot for the Japanese was found by the *1st Battalion, 32nd Regiment* that had infiltrated through the gap on the 7th Infantry Division's flank. They were unseen at first, but as they progressed the Americans reported their movement but could not fire on them without endangering friendly forces. The Japanese attacked the American 1st Battalion 17th Infantry Regiment's supply dump and motor pool at the base of the Tanabaru escarpment, mined the road and took up positions in the caves on the escarpment.[713]

This success owed largely to the decision of the battalion commander, Captain Ito Koichi to abandon the frontal attack he had been ordered to make in favor of infiltration into the American rear area. Ito had carefully reconnoitered the American positions at night and adjusted his orders in response.[714] Thus they had successfully penetrated 1,500 metres but now they were isolated and unsupported. At dawn on 5 May 1945, the American 2nd Battalion 17th Infantry Regiment counterattacked, first with just one company and then with a second company waging a furious 2-day fight against Ito's 600 men.[715] On the night of 6–7 May 1945, the 200 Japanese survivors were ordered to slip away, taking refuge for the remainder of the battle in the caves of an isolated valley.[716] The 17th Infantry Regiment resumed the attack on Kochi Ridge from 7 to 10 May 1945, at which time the 7th Infantry Division was sent into corps reserve after 40 days of continuous combat in which it had suffered more casualties than in the entire 110-day campaign on Leyte.[717]

Combat Effectiveness and Battle Fatigue: 'flung into hell's own cesspool'[718]

> 'Stress was the essential factor we had to cope with in combat, under small-arms fire, and in warding off infiltrators and raiders during sleepless, rainy nights for prolonged periods; but being shelled so frequently … seemed to increase the strain beyond that which many otherwise stable and hardened Marines could endure without mental or physical collapse. From my experience, of all the hardships and hazards the troops had to suffer, prolonged shell fire was more apt to break a man psychologically than anything else.'[719]

The battle for Okinawa produced the heaviest American casualties of the Pacific war. By the end of May 1945, the two Marine divisions had suffered 1,718 killed, 8,852 wounded and 101 missing in action. The four Army divisions fighting for two months on the Shuri front suffered 2,871 killed, 12,319 wounded and 183 missing. Altogether, the XXIV Corps and the III Amphibious Corps had lost a total of 26,044 killed, wounded or missing. This amounted to approximately one American killed for every ten Japanese killed.[720] Non-battle or neuropsychiatric casualties were occurring at a higher rate on Okinawa than in any previous operation in the Pacific. Again, the 2 Marine divisions had suffered 6,315 nonbattle casualties by the end of May 1945; the 4 army divisions had suffered 7,762 nonbattle casualties.[721] Overall, non-battle casualties occurred at a higher level in the Pacific than in Europe because of the higher stresses of living in isolated, tropical environments for long periods.[722] The increase in 'combat fatigue' cases on Okinawa was attributed to the rain and mud from which there was no protection or relief and the high volume of Japanese artillery and mortar fire. The fighting on Okinawa represented the first time that the Americans in the Pacific had experienced the quantity of artillery fire that was characteristic of the fighting in Europe. The stress of fighting a close-in battle with a fanatical foe all day in the rain and mud and then being shelled all night while maintaining constant vigilance against infiltrators and counterattacks placed the soldiers and Marines under enormous stress.

> 'The bodies lay pathetically just as they had been killed, half submerged in muck and water, rusting weapons still in hand. Everywhere lay Japanese corpses, killed in the fighting. Swarms of big flies hovered above them ... For several feet around every corpse, maggots crawled about in the muck ... To be under a barrage of prolonged shelling simply magnified all the terrible physical and emotional effects of one shell. To me, artillery was an invention of hell ... To be killed by a bullet seemed so clean and surgical. But shells would not only tear and rip the body, they tortured one's mind almost beyond the brink of sanity ... I found it more difficult to go back each time we squared away our gear to move forward into the zone of terror ... And it wasn't just dread of death or pain, because most men felt somehow, they wouldn't be killed ... Each time we went up, I felt the sickening dread of fear itself and the revulsion at the ghastly scenes of pain and suffering among comrades that a survivor must witness. The increasing dread of going back into action obsessed me. It became the subject of the most tortuous and persistent of all the ghastly war nightmares that have haunted me for many, many years. The dream is always the same, going back up to the lines during the bloody month of May on Okinawa.'[723]

Three factors that bear on the causation of battle fatigue have been attributed to retaining the will to win in these situations. These are faith and trust in the command, self confidence in the soldiers' training and readiness for combat, and unit and task cohesion.[724] Well trained units with high military knowledge, skills and abilities, deep trust in the competence and capabilities of their leaders, and sincere affection and respect for their comrades combined with pride in the units' accomplishments and their own individual contributions to the success of the mission show far greater resilience against battle fatigue.[725] Such units fight *for* each other as much as *against* the enemy. The 7th Infantry Division displayed such comradeship, and they had a conviction in victory born of each soldiers' belief in his own competence, trust in his peers, and collective pride in the unit's effectiveness. This is expressed in the comments of several veterans during interviews about Okinawa: 'The willingness to keep fighting (was from) training, experience, and anxious to get the job done and go home.' Another who had previously fought on Guadalcanal and Bougainville, rising from private to lieutenant believed his personal training and experience had helped him to survive and to lead and that the soldiers of the 7th Infantry Division who he joined as a replacement officer 'were a sound, well trained and experienced group ... (they) had the ability to fight all day and take heavy artillery fire at night.'[726]

Conquest of the Shuri Line

Beginning 12 May 1945, replacements joined the division and thereafter they conducted weapons firing, combat lessons training, and patrolling to orient and integrate the new men.[727] On 21–22 May 1945, the 7th Infantry Division conducted a night attack towards Yonabaru by the 184th Infantry Regiment. They completely surprised the Japanese who had not expected a night attack and in two rainy days they gained over 2,000 yards.[728] The 32nd Infantry Regiment joined in the action on 23 May 1945 to conduct an envelopment of the Japanese right flank, but the constant rain slowed progress and the supporting tanks were immobilised in the mud. The Japanese counterattacked at night to retake Yonabaru but failed and were forced to withdraw.[729]

The last ten days of May 1945 saw a torrential downpour. Over 1 inch of rain fell each day with 3.5 inches on the 26 May 1945 alone. The narrow dirt roads and trails turned into impassable quagmires and the American tanks continued to be neutralised by the weather. The 32nd Infantry Regiment tried to break the enemy resistance without them, but in a fierce encounter it was thrown back with heavy casualties. The fighting became so intense and confused that at one point five Japanese soldiers broke through the American lines and attacked the only remaining medic in one company as he was treating wounded men in an exposed forward area. Sergeant William Goodman killed all five Japanese with a pistol and then protected the wounded until they were evacuated.[730] Finally, from 28–31 May 1945, the American attack gained 2 more miles and Shuri was almost enveloped. At this point the *Thirty-Second Army* decided to retreat south.[731]

Night Infiltration Attack of Yaeju Dake

The Japanese assessment of the Americans was, 'The enemy generally fires (its guns) during the night, but very seldom takes offensive action.'[732] This was accurate, but it was about to change. The Americans were adapting and evolving their tactics. In mid-April 1945, the 27th Infantry Division surprised the Japanese with a successful night attack. These were followed by others by the 77th Infantry Division, the 96th Infantry Division and the 7th Infantry Division in May 1945 with mixed successes.[733] As the rainy weather had slowed advances to a mere 300 yards per day, the 7th Infantry Division decided to take the Yaeju Dake escarpment in a daring night infiltration attack. The Yaeju Dake was a cliff and ridgeline that anchored the Kiyan defensive line from which any American movement below was easily observed and quickly fired upon.[734]

The 17th Infantry regimental commander, Colonel Pachler, sought to negate the Japanese observation and fields of fire from the 170-foot-tall coral escarpment by infiltrating at night to take the high ground while the enemy was sheltering in his protective caves. Extensive reconnaissance of the trails, minefields and known cave positions was followed by meticulous planning and coordination of the scheme of manoeuvre. The attack emphasised stealth and surprise, with no artillery preparation. Company A took a path directly up the face of the cliff. Company B had to travel south to a break in the escarpment face and then, once on the high ground, turn right. The 3rd Battalion was to support by attacking the south-east end of the escarpment.[735]

Ever mindful of the possibility of confusion and disarray in the dark, Colonel Pachler ensured that all the troops were briefed on the details. There was some apprehension the night before the attack when the 7th Infantry Division intelligence officer reported interception of an enemy radio message which said, 'Prepare to support the attack at 2300 [hours].' And another which said, 'If there are any volunteers for the suicide penetration, report them before the contact which is to be made one hour from now.' That night the Japanese fired an extremely heavy artillery concentration in support of an attack which was stopped by the 32nd Infantry Regiment.[736]

The 17th Infantry Regiment moved out silently at 04.00 hours, 12 June 1945 and, as if it had been planned, a heavy fog settled over southern Okinawa, providing extra concealment without obscuring their route. Unobserved, the 1st Battalion was in place by 05.30 hours without a shot being fired. The 3rd Battalion also reached its objective without a fight and taking further advantage of the fog, took another nearby small hill. As the sun rose, the Japanese started to move back into positions now occupied by the Americans. Between 06.00 and 08.00 hours both battalions easily fought off the Japanese in the culmination of a masterfully executed night attack. The Japanese defenders were taken completely by surprise and a significant terrain feature had been captured with minimal loss to the attacking force.[737] Private First Class Roland Lea, a new replacement described his experience thus:

> In the later hours of darkness my company and others crossed the valley ... The escarpment was scaled with such stealth that not a shot was fired. The Japs awakened with dawn's light [*sic*] and we had a day in killing a surprised enemy. A real turkey shoot. This firefight will always remain vividly in my mind.[738]

Sustaining the Will to Fight – American Technological Improvements

The tank-infantry team that was the American answer to the Japanese cave and tunnel defence system found success in the use of a new weapon, the armoured flame thrower; an M4 Sherman tank capable of shooting napalm up to 125 yards. Using flames and demolitions to assault and seal the caves in a 'blowtorch and corkscrew' method boosted US morale because of its effectiveness and its psychological effect on the enemy. A captured Japanese commander of an anti-tank battalion stated that he did not see how any defence line could not be penetrated with this combination of weapon and tactics.[739]

Another weapon introduced on Okinawa in limited numbers was the infrared-sight equipped T3 carbine. Developed for the sole-purpose of thwarting Japanese night infiltration a soldier could see in the dark to a range of about 70 yards. Although heavy and bulky, when used in a defensive position, the Americans could see and engage Japanese soldiers creeping forward in the dark. These carbines were a welcome tool to counter the danger of the legendary Japanese night attack, and some credited that up to 30 per cent of the total Japanese casualties inflicted in the first weeks of action on Okinawa were due to the infrared scopes.[740]

The Death of the Imperial Japanese Thirty-Second Army

From 12 to 21 June 1945 the American forces steadily compressed the remaining Japanese defenders, collapsing the flanks of the overall defence. The depleted Japanese fought on bravely with fewer weapons and ammunition now being wielded by combat support and service troops.[741] On 21 June 1945, the 7th Infantry Division found and attacked the guard posts of the *Thirty-Second Army* headquarters hidden inside Hill 89. With no forces left to command the surviving brigade and division staff officers were ordered to conduct 'honourable death' attacks. General Cho, however, ordered that his *Thirty-Second Army* staff was to refrain from suicidal actions. Instead, they should escape and wage guerilla warfare. Some did so but others remained in the headquarters out of loyalty to the generals. Thus, it was that the ritual suicides of General Ushijima and General Cho were witnessed by these survivors and later reported to the Americans.[742] Colonel Yahara summarised the situation thus:

> Our 32nd Army was now faced with this situation. Must one hundred thousand soldiers die because of tradition? From this point on it was but a battle to kill the remaining Japanese soldiers for nothing. We could cause the enemy little damage; they could walk freely on the field of battle. The war of attrition was over, and we would simply be asking the enemy to use this formidable power to kill us all.[743]

The reason that we have so much detail on the Japanese side of the Okinawa battle is because Colonel Yahara obeyed his final orders from General Cho to escape and convey to Imperial General Headquarters the lessons learned to prepare for what they presumed would be a fight to the death on the home islands. After the war, an embittered Yahara, having borne the brunt of postwar contempt from other Japanese veterans for not having committed *seppuku*, wrote that the Japanese thus lacked a consistent war plan, 'tormented by the strategic thinkers who dreamed of air war priorities – not to mention absurd suicide tactics ... a futile illusion as the war drew to a close.'[744]

The 7th Infantry Division searched for Japanese and Okinawans in hiding and made direct appeals for their surrender using leaflets, loudspeakers and other surrendered soldiers. Many committed suicides but increasingly, surrender became the chosen course. During the first seventy days of the battle Tenth Army captured only four Japanese per day on average. On 19 June 1945, 343 surrendered and on 20 June 1945, 977 Japanese surrendered. Eventually, the number reached 7,400.[745]

Captain Ito, who had led the only successful action of the May 1945 counteroffensive, held out in caves until 22 August 1945 when he responded to an approach by a Japanese linguist officer from the 7th Infantry Division who told him the war was over. He then listened to Emperor Hirohito's radio message and spoke directly with Colonel Yahara who confirmed to him that the war was over. Ito then surrendered 400 soldiers and 105 civilians on 29 August 1945 and convinced another 300 troops to surrender as well.[746]

Strategic Culture and '*Yamato damashii*'

> I wondered whether the army's leaders really understood the importance of modern weapons. They thought Japan could win a war solely by reliance on spiritual strength.[747]

The term *Yamato damashii* (sometimes also expressed as *Yamato gokoro* or 'Japanese heart/mind') is a compound of the ancient word for the Japanese people and the word for 'spirit' and/or 'heart' ergo, the Japanese spirit. Its genesis was a Heian era (794–1185 CE) philosophical effort to describe and assert a superior 'Japanese Way' as distinct from Chinese culture and the influences of Confucianism and Buddhism.[748] *Yamato damashii* extols certain qualities and virtues held to be unique to the Japanese people. These national spiritual qualities included being brave, loyal, industrious and obedient. As nationalism and militarism rose in Japan in the 1920s and 1930s *Yamato damashii* expressed a specific nationalistic ideology that propagandists used to build and strengthen national identity in the assertion of imperialism.[749]

The Japanese obsession to dominate Asia began in the early years of the Meiji Restoration. The dogma that Japanese military and technological superiority was a natural consequence of their innate spiritual and racial superiority contributed to the belief that they stood at the apex of the hierarchy of Asian nations and peoples and were thus entitled to rule them all. This became a core element of their strategic culture.[750] A secret Japanese government report created in 1943 outlines the theories, themes and rationale for Imperial Japan's policy of racial superiority. Titled, 'An Investigation of Global Policy With the *Yamato* Race as Nucleus' ('*Yamato Minzoku wo Chūkaku to suru Sekai Seisaku no Kentō*'), the document mirrored contemporary Nazi theories on race but took a Confucian approach to its themes on colonisation and imperialism by stressing that the other peoples of Asia should naturally conform to a hierarchy that placed the Japanese at the top with all others in their 'proper place'.[751] In this patriarchal family metaphor, other Asians were the 'children' of the Japanese, who as the racially superior people were destined to rule. Nationalists syncretised the *Yamato damashii* philosophy with the myth of the founding of the nation and the prestige of the emperor to create the national identity of Japan as a sacred land, and a special people with a special spirit. This was the ideological and psychological motivation for the Japanese in the Pacific War; a racially motivated war to ensure 'living space' for the Japanese and to secure their political, economic and cultural dominance.[752]

Yamato damashii expressed a strong consciousness of how special it was to be Japanese, having 'superior Japanese spirituality unequaled in any other country', that thus required 'a pure mind to render good service to the Japanese nation'.[753] Philosophically, *Yamato damashii* encouraged belief in Japanese racial superiority to mobilise support for Japan's ultra-nationalist ideology and to justify its purported destiny to rule Asia.[754] Knowing that Japan's success as an empire required the absolute commitment of the people, the Imperial Army sponsored a series of pamphlets promoting the concepts of *kokutai* (the national polity), *kogun* (the emperor's army) and *Yamato damashii*. They persuaded soldiers and civilians alike to place unquestioning faith in their leaders and to trust in the invincibility of the army and navy, inspiring greater levels of devotion and sacrifice as the Pacific War expanded.[755] Thus, *yamato damashii* weaponised racism and a sacrificial spirit for the sake of the nation as the essential spiritual weapon wielded by the Imperial Japanese Army.[756]

The Power and Limitations of Fighting Spirit

The Imperial Japanese Army wrestled with a dilemma throughout the Pacific War: how to overcome their deficient military capability? Their answer was that their spiritual superiority was a power that would overcome the modern firepower and mechanisation that they lacked. Despite the mounting evidence to the contrary this dogma was perpetuated until the end of the war. One Japanese reservist was astonished by the sentiment,

> that lack of equipment gave us Japanese a chance to demonstrate our superior spirit and valor [*sic*] ... Leaders totally ignorant of the scientific and mechanical excellence of the enemy and their weapons praised the waste of priceless human lives for the sake of the cause.[757]

Nevertheless, both the Japanese and the Americans believed in the potential power of elusive concepts like the 'will to fight' and the 'will to win'. The Americans never assumed that victory would come from mere numerical superiority, knowing that valour and fighting spirit were also essential. The Japanese denied that there was an American fighting spirit and believed they lacked the will to fight. Americans were believed to be 'selfish and egoistic', and they regarded America as 'a decadent nation in which pacifism and isolationism practically ruled.'[758] The Japanese fervently believed that the unique national qualities expressed in *Yamato damashii* would defeat the technologically strong but spiritually soft Americans.[759]

The soldiers of the 7th Infantry Division consistently repudiated this ethnocentric contempt. They approached Okinawa with mixed feelings. For the new soldiers there was eagerness to get into the fight. For the veterans of Attu, Kwajalein and Leyte there was sober acceptance of what they knew would be a tough fight but an essential step on the way to the final victory. They knew that they could handle the job and were determined to win.[760] This prompts the question: Is there an American fighting spirit? If there is, how would one describe it? I believe that the following is a good expression of the American fighting spirit:

> Americans love to fight. All real Americans love the sting and clash of battle … Americans play to win all the time … The very thought of losing is hateful to Americans. Battle is the most significant competition in which a man can indulge. It brings out all that is best and it removes all that is base … An army is a team. It lives, eats, sleeps, and fights as a team. This individual hero stuff is bullshit. The bilious bastards who write that stuff for the Saturday Evening Post don't know any more about real battle than they do about fucking. And we have the best team … the best spirit and the best men in the world … Sure, we all want to go home. We want to get this war over with … The quickest way to get it over with is to get the bastards who started it … The quicker they are whipped, the quicker we go home. The shortest way home is through Berlin and Tokyo.[761]

Patton described an American fighting spirit characterised by aggressiveness, team action and selfless service. He affirmed the collective American faith in the righteousness of their cause, the soldier's conviction that his job was worthwhile, and their confidence in eventual victory.[762] Philosophically, he acknowledged that the romantic notion of '*Dulce et decorum est, Pro patria mori*' no longer motivated American soldiers. Instead, they recognised the bitter truth of what Wilfrid Owen, called 'The old Lie' when he said:

> My friend, you would not tell with such high zest
> To children ardent for some desperate glory,
> The old Lie: *Dulce et decorum est.*[763]

For the Japanese, fighting a hemispheric war of attrition but thinking that a single decisive battle would result in victory because their innate 'spiritual superiority' would compensate for their materiel inferiority, represents a profound conflict in beliefs and behaviours juxtaposed with flawed interpretation of the evidence to justify seemingly irrational decisions. The Americans had a will to fight and a will to win, but they rejected needless human sacrifice as a substitute for competent doctrine, logical strategy, effective leadership, and modern firepower. The Americans did not start the war with all these advantages but their will to win motivated the creation of a force that fully embodied these attributes.

Chapter Six

CONCLUSION

'In the changing of the times, they were like autumn lightning, a thing out of season, an empty promise of rain that would fall unheeded on fields already bare.'[764]

Introduction

For as long as historians have explored the question of how nations field and operate effective fighting forces there has been a bias towards technology and mechanisation as the chief explanatory factors in modern warfare.[765] This military power analysis approach is perhaps best epitomised by John Keegan's *The Face of Battle* where he analysed the fighting at Agincourt (1415), Waterloo (1815) and the Somme (1916) to study the battles through the effects of the weaponry. Keegan showed us the soldiers' reactions to various weapons, the lance and the long bow, the sword and musket, and poison gas and machine guns. Keegan said that it was, 'my purpose to demonstrate what warfare of hand, single-missile, and multiple-missile weapons was (and is) like and to suggest how and why men face these weapons.'[766]

Some historians have focused specifically on the weapons, organisation and technology of war to argue that operational history reflects the clear influence of technological determinants, particularly in the twentieth century.[767] For instances of this interpretation there are, S.T. Possony and J.E. Pournelle's *The Strategy of Technology: Winning the Decisive War* (1970) and Martin van Creveld's *Technology and War: From 2000 BC to the Present* (1989), wherein he declares, 'every part of technology affects war.'[768] This approach becomes more pronounced when discussing the technological advances in air and naval warfare and the countermeasures developed against them during the Second World War, such as in Lee Kennett's *A History of Strategic Bombing*

(1982), V. E. Tarrant's *The U-Boat Offensive,1914–1945* (1989) and Ian Hogg's *The Weapons That Changed the World* (1986). These authors have strongly influenced military professional thinking that weapons alone can decide the course of battle or create war-winning breakthroughs. 'From ancient times when the Bronze Age superseded the copper only to fall to the iron, technological superiority has most often provided the margin for victory.'[769]

This focus on the operational history of military technology ignores the fact that war is a human activity, saturated with social, political and psychological influences that intertwine with technology.[770] The narrow, weapon and battle- centred approach that dominates misses an opportunity for more complex interpretations and thus a more profound understanding of warfare.[771] Beliefs and behaviours concerning violence and war are culturally constructed, and the meanings of victory, defeat and suffering vary considerably. Norms concerning the appropriate use of force, acceptable levels of risk and the willingness to accept casualties differ between cultures. Comparing the strategic and tactical cultures of competing states and their militaries, especially their goals, social contexts, ethos and practices reveals a more nuanced view of combat effectiveness than a straightforward correlation of forces and means formula alone.[772]

It is relatively easier, and thus has been far more common, to assess historical combat effectiveness by taking a functional / technological approach that measures the relative capabilities of warring nations and militaries by comparing the quantity and quality of their weapons, and their proficiency in their use. The simple belief is that the side that can launch the greatest number of projectiles has the best chance of winning. However, this assumes that there is a universal scale of technological capacity or proficiency that can be quantified, and that combat effectiveness is not affected by any other factors.[773]

There is no consensus on how to define combat effectiveness nor of how to evaluate historical examples of combat effectiveness. Some have claimed that unit combat effectiveness can be mathematically represented by the attritional effects of its offensive firepower, some by the ability of a unit to accomplish its mission to advance or to deny the enemy's advance and to cause casualties greater than its own losses, while others judge by their willingness to engage the enemy.[774] It has been conceded that overall studies so far 'have been based on a measurement of casualty effectiveness, but casualty effectiveness is an outcome … we have no means of directly measuring combat effectiveness.'[775]

Peter Mansoor has offered a forthright definition of combat effectiveness as the 'ability of a military organisation to achieve its assigned missions with the least expenditure of resources in the shortest amount of time.'[776] He explains:

> since war involves the vagaries of human behavior [*sic*] under extreme stress, accurate quantification of combat effectiveness is not possible, but it is possible to examine successful military organizations [*sic*] to determine what makes them work, for in the end, success in war is the only standard by which to judge military organizations [*sic*].[777]

Warfare is more 'art' than 'science' and that the historical analysis of mission accomplishment is arguably the most straightforward and objective evaluation of combat effectiveness.

Strategic Culture

The use of culture as a lens through which to view war has a long lineage. Thucydides recorded that both the Athenians and the Spartans linked the capabilities of their militaries to the character of their state.[778] In choosing the concept of culture as an analytical approach I recognise that many definitions contend and that inferring or even implying connections or causation with historical events is challenging. I approach it from the belief that war is a form of cultural activity and that as such, culture can shape how militaries develop a command structure, adopt technologies or implement their strategy and tactics. Even if you cannot make a case for a causal relationship between concepts and phenomena, being aware of cultural values provides greater historical context.[779]

For this work I accept the definition that

> strategic culture exists as an integrated system of shared symbols, values, behaviours, and traditions that works through commonly understood decision-making processes that are shaped or influenced by societal perceptions and preferences, which thus informs and influences how decision-makers envision and respond to the strategic environment.[780]

These respective beliefs and behaviours illustrate how it shaped their respective objectives, means, organisation and actions.[781]

Strategic culture was as important to the outcomes of the Pacific War as the imbalance of power. The battle performance of 7th Infantry Division illustrates the decisive importance of willpower. Will to win is the bedrock upon which military success is founded. Effective weapons and equipment are vital to success, but they are only one element of combat effectiveness. American forces, fighting as cohesive teams, were driven by a fierce will to win that gave them immense combat effectiveness.

The Strategic Culture of Imperial Japan

Overall, Japanese strategic and tactical culture was affected by pervasive cultural conditioning that inculcated the belief that Japan was a unique and special nation with a divine mission to rule the world.[782] While the Japanese understood that the US had tremendous material resources that could produce massive firepower the they felt that the Americans lacked fighting spirit, tactical finesse and operational skill.[783]. Their belief in Japan's unique martial culture, its proud tradition of military virtue and preference for death over humiliation or defeat led them to believe they could win the war despite the mismatch in capabilities.[784]

Japan's physical separation from the rest of Asia and its deliberate isolation from Western influences for almost 300 years, helped to create an unusually homogenous society and culture. Many different elements have interacted to define Japanese culture. The themes and events that were most formative in their strategic culture are:

The Myth of Divine Providence

The myth that the Japanese people are descended from the sun goddess, Amaterasu, and as a divine race they were specially favoured by the gods. When the very survival of the Japanese people was threatened by the Mongols the spiritual power of their living god, the emperor had saved them. This led to their belief in having a divine right to rule others.[785]

The Veneration of Imperial Authority

The Japanese developed a reverence for imperial authority and a belief in the Confucian tenets that emphasised law, ritual and hierarchy as essential to maintaining social order. This melded well with native Japanese concepts of loyalty to family and clan.[786]

The Legacy of the Japanese Feudal Era

The turmoil, intrigue and military rule of the 700-year Japanese feudal era gave rise to the unique *samurai* warrior class that promoted the qualities of loyalty, bravery and selfless sacrifice as the supreme virtues in society. Every vassal was expected to give his life freely in service to his lord, even if the sacrifice was futile.[787]

The Influence of the Tokugawa Shogunate

The Tokugawa Shogunate provided the longest period of peace and stability in Japanese history, but it did so by the imposition of a rigid police state that isolated Japan from the rest of the world. As a result, the nation failed to modernise in step with the rest of the world. The *samurai* became a legally defined hereditary class and Japanese society became accustomed to obedience to central authority and strict adherence to norms of social behaviour. Within this closed society the Japanese sense of nationhood was awakened, and veneration of the emperor began to supersede loyalty to clan or *shogun*.[788]

The Transformation of the Meiji Restoration

The Meiji Restoration caused massive social upheaval as the nation rushed to transform itself from a feudal society with seventeenth-century technology into a modern industrial nation. Japan underwent rapid modernisation in its industry, technology and institutions to match the Western liberal democracies, but it tried to preserve the traditional values and behaviours of their hierarchical society. The pace and scale of Japan's modernisation was astounding, but it rested on shaky foundations. In particular, the *samurai* had reached a crisis point as an effete caste of feudal warrior bureaucrats struggling to remain relevant, while the masses beneath them chafed at having to support an unproductive hereditary aristocracy that had outlived its function.[789]

Victory over Russia in 1905 led the Japanese to embrace several fallacious ideas that shaped their doctrine and organisation for the next forty years.[790] The most significant legacy of this experience was the absolute belief in the value of the offensive as the way to quick and decisive victory. The Imperial Japanese Army was conceived, trained and equipped as a light force that used bold manoeuvre to close with and attack its enemies in hand-to-hand combat with the bayonet.[791] This faith in the ineluctable power of offensive operations was only exceeded by the deeply rooted belief that the Japanese people were uniquely gifted with a singular warrior ethos that gave their attacks an awe-inspiring and devastating power that could cause opponents willpower to falter. The Japanese military's emphasis on the power of spiritual superiority was both simplistic and complacent, callously ignoring the realities of modern firepower.[792]

The Strategic Culture of the United States

Having its foundations in the Enlightenment and the Reformation, American philosophy and culture expressed a world view that was skeptical of orthodoxies, rebelled against authority, celebrated individual autonomy, and was confident in the power of human intellect and technology. American culture envisioned a new form of society, based on self-evident truths of individual liberty and of a government that replaced monarchical power, rejecting collectivism with the duty to secure the rights of the people and to bring an end to oppression.[793]

American strategic culture exhibits an almost which optimism, strategic impatience, a deep faith in technology as a solution and a tendency to view every conflict as an existential crusade in defence of democracy, motivated by the need to overthrow foreign tyranny.[794] It is *sui generis*, however, in its reflection of certain beliefs and habits found in American culture such as showing respect for human life and individual political rights, equal opportunity and equal burden sharing, the defence of free market capitalism, isolationism and unilateralism.[795] A particularly American strategic view is that war represents the failure of policy rather that its continuation as held by von Clausewitz.[796] This translated to the American strategic military philosophy that,

> Politics and strategy are radically and fundamentally things apart. Strategy begins where politics end. All that soldiers ask is that once the policy is settled, strategy and command shall be regarded as being in a sphere apart from politics.[797]

These unique cultural determinants have influenced American strategy and military operations.

Russell Weigley interpreted American strategic thought as following two basic types of strategy: attrition and annihilation. He characterised early American strategy as relying on attrition over time to exhaust stronger opponents, as in the 1781 campaign of General Nathaniel Greene.[798] Weigley portrayed the strategy of the American Civil War as one of overwhelming force to 'grind down opponents with firepower and mass.'[799] Brian Linn has challenged his definitions of attrition and annihilation as being confusing and simplistic (for example, at what point does continual attrition result in inevitable annihilation?)[800] Linn has described other schools of American strategic thought as: attrition, Napoleonic, annihilation, partisan war, sea-power and air power.[801] John Lynn has also suggested that there are 'three related tendencies' as historical characteristics of American strategic culture:

'1) abhorrence of U.S. casualties, 2) confidence in military technology to minimize [*sic*] U.S. losses, and 3) concern with exit strategies.'[802]

While a nation's strategic culture may exhibit certain fixed preferences, in the larger historical context there does appear the ability to evolve in response to geo-political, technological and societal change.[803] American strategic culture has certainly changed as new weapons and tactics were introduced. We can see that there is an existential danger when this does not happen or when such evolution is too slow to respond effectively to external threats. The ability to change from obsolete concepts of operation to overcome unforeseen battlefield challenges and asymmetric adaptability, or the lack thereof, in strategic culture explains much of the disparity between the Japanese and American forces in the war.[804]

Tactical Culture

Just as there is an ontological hierarchy that extends from strategy to operations to tactics, I believe that there is a relationship between a nation's 'way of war' and its 'way of warfare'. The former reflects a nation's values regarding the proper use of force. The latter represents how a nation's military wants to fight wars.[805] Strategic culture (the way of war) is implemented through a tactical culture (the way of warfare) that expresses prevailing military attitudes and beliefs through actions taken on the battlefield. Many studies of cultural, behavioural and identity science have shown how culture can influence individual and organisational performance.[806]

As strategic culture flows from a nations' geography, history and competitive advantages so then does tactical culture derive from the choice of tactics and technologies used, how they have been employed in the past, how they will be employed in the present, to achieve what effects and with what expectations.[807]

Tactical culture is rooted in the history, traditions and customs of the service and the unit, and it reflects the goals and objectives, values and behaviours of that unit. These distinctive traits and accompanying patterns of thought, actions, or set of practices become the units' tactical culture, which in turn provide the foundation for planning, training and operations.[808] Every military unit: every squad, platoon, company and battalion has a unique personality and a distinctive character that are the result of that cohort's training and experiences. There is an intersectionality between tactical culture and military organisational culture and the way that it defines and shapes how an organisation functions as expressed through the 'habitual practices ... hidden assumptions, and unreflected cognitive frames' that support its actions.[809] Tactical culture is also a synthesis of a unit's past experiences, lessons learned and shared beliefs that becomes the foundation of their methods of warfighting and establishes their confidence of success on the battlefield. It is an expression of how the unit views itself and the battlefield and how they intend to meet current and future challenges.[810]

The military techniques, procedures and operational style used by a unit are the artifacts of its tactical culture. These values, missions and preferred technologies are carefully taught to new members of the organisation.[811] Doctrine influences tactical culture in concert with the unit's organisational scheme by providing the framework for action. Some characteristics of tactical culture include intangible elements like esprit de corps, pride, cohesion, loyalty, morale and will power. It also includes capabilities like leadership, and proficiency in individual and collective tasks. Tactical culture reflects the philosophy and ethos of the unit and is more likely to influence how a unit acts on the battlefield than any policies or directives from higher headquarters.[812]

Japanese Tactical Culture

Japan adopted Western weapons, military organisation and strategy but not Western concepts of discipline and motivation.[813] The Imperial Japanese Army was deeply imbued with the glorification of ritualised death, and Japanese culture was manipulated to create what was essentially a state-sponsored death cult.[814] 'Duty is heavier than a mountain; death is lighter than a feather.'[815]

The result was a paradoxical hybrid tactical culture that sought to compensate for disadvantages in modern firepower by applying an ancient approach of substituting humans for weapons, in the belief that the power of the superior Japanese spirit would prevail by simply persevering.[816]

The Imperial Japanese Army was an infantry-centric force that emphasised offensive action as the keystone of its doctrine. Japanese tactics called for flanking or enveloping attacks that relied on massed, mobile light infantry attacking under the cover of darkness. Decisive effects were to be achieved through close quarters battle with the bayonet. Surrender was prohibited and counterattacks were launched whether there were sufficient forces available or not. IJA tactical culture idealised the *samurai* warrior virtues of courage, loyalty and self-sacrifice and embraced hand-to-hand combat in an age of mechanised warfare.

One of the most notable characteristics of Imperial Japanese Army tactical culture was its tenacious adherence to doctrine, especially its bias for the attack. The Japanese soldier was believed to be uniquely effective in 'always attacking, courageous, selfless, and victorious.'[817] Despite constant defeats Japanese officers refused to change doctrine. Even though they suffered defensive defeat from late 1942 onward, it was not until August 1944 that Imperial General Headquarters issued a tactical manual that rescinded the counter-amphibious doctrine that invaders would be stopped at the waterline, and then counterattacked and destroyed.[818] Generally, however, defensive doctrine was never enthusiastically embraced; officers at all echelons looked for opportunities to attack even when insufficient forces were available, thus reinforcing defeat, and ultimately squandering lives in hopeless efforts.[819]

The most striking element of Japanese tactical culture was how it extolled the preference for death in battle over the humiliation of surrender or defeat.[820] The avoidance of the shame of surrender overruled the need for preserving the force for future battles.[821] The Field Service Code or *Senjinkun* issued in 1941 put it explicitly: 'Do not live in shame as a prisoner. Die, and leave no ignominious crime behind you.'[822] The *Senjinkun* was intended to indoctrinate the IJA soldier with the unique spiritual attributes of Japanese tactical culture whereby: 'death in battle became the standard by which to measure fighting spirit.'[823]

> The Japanese tended to regard 'spirit' as their main strength, with almost mystical potency – an amulet, whose loss would be fatal. Beyond doubt it carried them to some startling early victories; but at the same time, it carried within Japan's undoing.[824]

Seishin (spirit/mind/soul/heart) was viewed as being unyielding and resilient; the belief in the ability to succeed or survive through sheer will alone. The Japanese sincerely believed that this unique cultural value was the answer to their qualitative and quantitative inferiority in the face of more modern forces.[825] Stoicism was encouraged to motivate both unit and individual resistance past the point where it might have been of any tactical benefit or in the best interest of the individual, the unit or the nation.

The basic characteristics that permeated Japanese tactical culture; strict obedience, endurance of hardship, faith in their 'fighting spirit', their innate racial superiority and the morality of honourable death to repay the debt owed for being Japanese underscored everything with the paramount importance and nobility of sacrifice, even in failure.[826] Japanese tactical culture demonstrated the will to sacrifice; to kill the enemy and if that was not possible then to die instead. A commonly expressed sentiment illustrates this: 'Come home in death' (*Shinde kaere*) meaning, 'Fight with resolve to die on the battlefield and come home only as a soul.'[827]

American Tactical Culture

> It was plenty tough + rugged going with the weather against us + Jap snipers harassing us all the time, but we blew them from their foxholes + they all ended up 6 foot [*sic*] under.[828]

In the course of its history the American army has had a long and often acrimonious debate over its self-identity and vision of warfare. Through this process three traditions of thought have developed.[829] One of these philosophies holds that war is both an art and a science and that with mastery of the science one could practice it as an art. In this view, war is a project in which skilled technicians, applying the scientific principles of warfare, are guaranteed success.[830]

The second philosophical tradition emphasises the human element in war and espouses the critical importance of intangible factors like courage, discipline, morale and experience gained in training. This tradition encourages adaptability and innovation to cope with the chaos and violence of an ever-changing battlefield. This concept of war holds that 'Wars are fought with men, not weapons. It is the spirit of the men who fights, and of the men who leads which gains the victory [*sic*].'[831]

The third tradition sees modern warfare as the result international rivalry over political and economic issues that require full national mobilisation of a mass army to conduct large-unit operations. It is a von Clausewitzian view of industrial scale war that requires skilled managers to organise the force, create the weapons, and direct the operations of this juggernaut. To achieve success requires rational coordination of both human and materiel resources on a large scale.[832]

These three martial philosophies combine to provide an intellectual and practical framework for American tactical culture, weaving together a belief in precise planning, superior administration and the application of all available resources, while embracing the romanticism of heroic human virtues as the keys to victory.[833] American tactical culture favored aggressive action, combining firepower and manoeuvre to overwhelm and destroy the enemy to achieve a quick and decisive victory with the least casualties.[834] This approach was a practical combination of operational art, supported by technology and logistics to project power over long distances, and sustained by its belief in a righteous cause.[835]

American tactical culture in the Second World War focused on definite and tangible goals and held that 'the battle is the ultimate payoff.'[836] The attitude that all actions should be directed toward a clear task and purpose permeated the army, and soldier and unit morale suffered when it was perceived that they did not. Loyalty to comrades / group solidarity, prestige / pride in unit and working to end the task and get home were broad characteristics of American tactical culture. Both primary group cohesion and task cohesion were essential elements of American tactical culture that contributed to individual survival and unit success in combat.[837] The shared experiences of training and combat created peer (horizontal), leader (vertical) and cross-organisational bonds that focused on the capability and capacity for teamwork in the accomplishment of the common task.[838] This task cohesion was as much a driving force for the American soldier as social cohesion, allowing them to maintain their combat effectiveness and the will to win. When asked, 'What was most important to you in making you want to keep going?' Thirty-nine per cent of soldiers said, 'ending the task' while fourteen per cent said, 'solidarity with the group.'[839]

Another facet of American tactical culture is the ferocity that America brings to war. 'The American tends to be an extremist on the subject of war: he either embraces war wholeheartedly or rejects it completely. For the American a war is not a war unless it is a crusade.'[840] Once engaged, Americans prefer a fight to the finish. Thus, feelings of hatred, vindictiveness and revenge towards the Japanese were notable elements of the tactical culture of units in the Pacific area.[841]

Unit Will to Fight – Assessing the 7th Infantry Division

Returning to *The American Soldier: Combat and its Aftermath*, we see many of these will to fight variables quantified by the soldiers of the 7th Infantry Division themselves in a contemporary survey of their attitudes. Sixty per cent were 'very proud' of their company. Fifty-four per cent thought their unit teamwork was 'very good'; forty per cent thought it was 'fairly good'. Eighty-one per cent expressed confidence in their leaders. On the question of supplies, 68 per cent felt that they 'usually got' what they needed. On the question of mail delivery, 44 per cent felt that the army tried 'hard enough' to get mail to the battle front; 29 per cent did not. Sixty-four per cent of the soldiers of the 7th Infantry Division thought that the army tried 'hard enough' to get them good food; twenty-four per cent did not. When asked, 'When the going was tough, how much did it help you to think that you had to finish the job in order to get home again?', their answers were 'Helped a lot = forty-five per cent; Helped some = twenty-one per cent; Helped a little = nine per cent; Didn't think of it = twenty-one per cent.' When the soldiers of the 7th Infantry Division were asked, 'When the going was tough, how much did it help you to think that you couldn't let the other men down?', their answers were 'A lot = sixty-four per cent; Some = nineteen per cent; A little = five per cent; Didn't think of it = ten per cent.' Less importance was given to thinking of 'what we're fighting for: A lot = thirty-five per cent; Some = twenty per cent; a little = eight per cent; Didn't think of it = twenty-eight per cent'; and to 'hatred for the enemy: A lot = thirty-nine per cent; Some = twenty-three per cent; a little = eleven per cent; Didn't think of it = nineteen per cent'.[842] Overall, task and group cohesion, leadership and morale were the highest rated variables in the will to fight model for the 7th Infantry Division in the Second World War.

Will to fight and winning always matter in combat. Soldiers and the units they are members of develop a tactical culture that includes the disposition to fight or not fight, when faced with imminent death. Combat almost always ends when one opponent loses the will to fight. With these evaluative criteria as a guide, not a model nor a formula, to compare the belligerents in the Pacific War, it is apparent that both sides had a tremendous will to fight. However, there seems to be an ironic disparity in how that will fight was translated into action. In the case of the Japanese during the Pacific War, their fighting until total annihilation suggests an extraordinary will, but what motivated this requires cultural analysis.[843]

Strategic Culture: The Will to Win Versus the Will to Sacrifice

The Will to Sacrifice

We recognise that individual nations have distinct cultures with respect to religion, the arts and literature. These are expressions of their shared traditions and their common ways of life.[844] Strategic behaviour should also be approached in the context of the culture that has shaped it.[845] To fully understand a nation's 'way of warfare' requires looking beyond battle narratives or debates on the merits of firepower, mass or mobility to examine how a nation perceives and interprets its military traditions; how it views strengths and weaknesses, and threats and opportunities.

The Japanese failed in the Second World War because of their strategic culture. Why? There were hidden, fatal flaws in Japanese strategic culture that emanated from specific cultural values and social behaviours. The Japanese chose an anachronistic approach to the war that was rooted in their cultural values of unquestioning obedience, group loyalty and self-sacrifice. In the face of unanticipated and changing operational conditions the Japanese were unable to make effective changes in doctrine, technology and tactics because of their dependence on a strategic path that assumed American willingness to accept defeat and to seek a negotiated outcome. Perceiving the Americans to be a racially and spiritually inferior people, the Japanese underestimated their will to fight and overestimated their own military prowess and capabilities with tragic consequences.[846] Adapting their strategy and tactics to address their faulty assumptions was obstructed by the very core beliefs in Japanese cultural superiority upon which they stood. I further believe that Japanese strategic and tactical culture reflected a deeply ingrained will to sacrifice which unintentionally undermined their will to fight, in contrast to the American strategic and tactical culture of the will to win, and that this difference strongly determined the outcomes of the war.[847]

Ultimately, Japanese strategic culture caused them to be mesmerized by short-term operational opportunities but blind to the long-term strategic consequences. They acknowledged American materiel superiority but failed to recognise that they were not the only people with willpower and courage. Their 'theory of victory' (or more appropriately hope of victory) was based on their faith that spiritual superiority would neutralise materiel superiority. They were confident that the unique Japanese qualities of national will, discipline and sacrifice would defeat the Americans. Japan's failure in this regard was because their strategy implicitly accepted annihilation of their tactical forces as a substitute for victory. The Japanese government motivated the people to endure extraordinary sacrifice by elevating, distorting or reinterpreting core Japanese values of loyalty, obedience, stoicism and fatalism, to create an idiosyncratic Japanese strategic culture with the unintended outcome of consistently and blindingly adhering to failed courses of action to the point of defeat.[848] This may be the ultimate failure of Japanese strategic thinking which doomed their soldiers and led to the crushing defeat of the nation.

Legendary historical acts of sacrifice in battle like Thermopylae, the Alamo, Balaclava, Port Arthur and Camaróne still resonate across cultures precisely because they are so uncommon. The Japanese converted suicidal battlefield sacrifice into a religious and ideological keystone of both their strategic and tactical culture.[849] The leaders of the Meiji and Showa eras invoked the precept that 'duty is heavier than a mountain; death is lighter than a feather' and promoted the myth of imperial divinity and the sacred origins of their land and people.[850] In support of this the philosophy of *bushidō* was carefully shaped and manipulated to represent the 'national essence' of the Japanese to help build a unified, modern national army from the conscripts of a fundamentally feudal society.[851] Japanese soldiers were taught that 'the essence of *bushidō* was that the young warrior *should aim at dying*.'[852] Inculcated with this mythological belief in their racial superiority, and a social Darwinist influenced philosophy of manifest destiny, the Japanese believed that the ultimate expression of devotion to the emperor was to seek honourable death in battle.[853] Imperial soldiers, sailors and airmen understood the preciousness of life and the gravity of their choice to die but they were nevertheless motivated by their sense of duty and the traditional aesthetic of '*mono no aware*' ('the poignant beauty of things'), which expressed the melancholic beauty of life's evanescence.[854] The few Japanese survivors shared a profound, lifelong sense of loss and pity.[855]

> It cannot end in our favor [*sic*], we have been defeated. I find myself thinking these thoughts often. Death ... How easy is it ... how disappointing. It is not especially dreadful or tragic ... death compared to life is peaceful and simple.[856]

As the war continued to turn against Japan, more contrived and desperate rationales for giving the ultimate sacrifice began to arise:

> we are turning the disaster into a fortunate event. We are now searching for something like a phoenix which rises out of ashes. Even if Japan gets defeated once or twice, as long as the Japanese survive, Japan will not be destroyed.[857]

Paradoxically, there was an ancient tradition that venerated the struggle of such 'failed heroes' who died nobly in crushing defeat yet achieved a transcendent form of death. Japanese had traditionally viewed such acts of individual voluntary death as honourable acts of supreme agency and the assertion of control over one's destiny. In consequence, encouraged by the belief that their deaths were transcendent because of the deep nobility of their martyrdom, Japanese officers often seemed more obsessed with demonstrating the proper way of dying in combat than they did for winning the battle.[858] The Imperial General

Headquarters eventually acknowledged the constant succession of sacrificial defeats by merely announcing that 'all achieved a heroic death in battle.'[859]

The awful consequences of this 'death cult' are reflected in the death rates of Japanese soldiers in the Pacific War. An analysis of the eleven primary island battles of the Pacific Ocean reveals that the average loss ratio of the Japanese forces was 97 per cent.[860] These death ratios were consistent across differing terrain whether sandy atolls or mountainous jungle covered island or sub-artic muskeg. Even had retreat been permitted (which it was not) on most islands there was nowhere to go; stand and die was the order. For comparison, in North Africa the British defeated a force of approximately 100,000 Germans and Italians of whom about 5,000 were killed. At the Battles of Imphal and Kohima the British faced a 100,000-man Japanese army of whom about 70,000 died. As General Slim observed, 'Everyone talks about fighting to the last man and last round, but only the Japanese actually do it.'[861]

Despite the supporting cultural foundation, and government indoctrination, by 1945 support for the war was eroding. The Japanese soldier found himself in a double bind; vitally dependent on his culture and society as the source of his identity and social support but receiving false and contradictory information from them with respect to the wartime situation and his existence. His inner psychological and spiritual sense of what was correct was incompatible with the scientific metacommunication he received from the physical world. Thus, he was placed into an impossible situation by the Japanese government wherein they could not win the war, nor could they end it. Trapped in a mutually enforced prison of alienation, unable to escape their dilemma, self-sacrifice seemed the only answer.[862]

The Will to Win

The Americans succeeded in the Second World War because of their strategic culture. Why? The America of the Great Depression and the Second World War had evolved from an eighteenth-century agrarian society with a small republican government into a modern industrial giant with a large and efficient central government capable of organising and directing the economy in full mobilisation. The United States had historically chosen to avoid the political and economic costs of maintaining a large standing army instead relying upon its large population and industrial capacity to respond to the crisis in the moment. The struggle against the fascist tyranny of the 1940s was seen as an existential threat to the American ideals of freedom, equality, democracy and reason.[863]

Just as the American economy and government evolved and matured over time so did its strategic culture. The insistence on unconditional surrender of the Axis powers as a strategic goal led to the historically dominant American operational approach of massing forces and means for a direct assault on enemy centres of gravity. The American frontier constabulary experience of managing logistics and providing engineering support across continental distances put a premium on the use of machines and abundant natural resources to surmount obstacles. This in turn inspired the American approach to the support and sustainment of expeditionary warfare, particularly in the Pacific theatre where moving mountains of supplies to the far-flung battlefields was a massive undertaking.[864] Perhaps the best contemporary expression of this strategic culture is this:

> America, as a nation, has the greatest ability for mass production of machines. It therefore behooves us to devise methods of war which exploit our inherent superiority. We must fight the war by machines on the ground, and in the air, to the maximum of our ability, particularly in view of the fact that the two races left which we may have to fight are both poor mechanics but have ample manpower. While we have ample manpower, it is too valuable to be thrown away.[865]

Much has been made of the overwhelming industrial superiority that the Americans enjoyed over the Japanese and rightly so. Many historians have assumed that American industrial power made their victory inevitable.[866] However, the deterministic supposition that mere numerical preponderance assures victory is false. To bring superior numbers to bear a force must survive long enough to make their numbers tell. A force that is poorly managed, manoeuvred or employed will not be able to take full advantage of its greater numbers and / or superior weapons.[867] Matériel factors are only part of the story of victory and defeat.

This is not to deny the dominance of American military industry, and its resultant staggering air and sea power but the many transport ships produced only delivered troops *to* the fight, they did not *win* the fight for them. Tanks, bombers and warships are the tools of war, but to be effective they must be properly wielded by trained and dedicated soldiers.[868] Alone, they have no power. The will to win the fight displayed by the soldiers, sailors, airmen and Marines enabled them to turn raw American industrial power into successful combat performance.

Furthermore, despite assumptions on the qualitative superiority of their technology, American weaponry, particularly that of the ground forces was not markedly superior in all respects to that of the Japanese. Japanese machine guns and grenade launchers were deadly. The Zero fighter plane and the Type 99 torpedo were highly effective and greatly feared. The ubiquitous M4 Sherman tank with its low velocity, short-ranged gun and light armour was rugged, reliable and manoeuvreable but still suffered numerous losses against simple Japanese defences like mines and demolition charges. The Americans responded differently to their equipment deficiencies than did the Japanese. The Americans overcame their capability shortcomings not by relying on 'spiritual power' or by massing forces but by creating massed effects; 'we compensate for our inferior equipment by the most efficient use of artillery, air support, and manoeuvre.'[869]

A Subjective Evaluation of Combat Effectiveness

'More than most professions, the military is forced to depend upon intelligent interpretation of the past for signposts charting the future.'[870]

At the beginning of the war the Allies were stunned by the speed and effectiveness of Japanese forces and the advanced technology of many Japanese weapons. Yet, the prevailing belief among many historians is that the Japanese were always doomed to failure because they could never match the industrial might of the United States.[871]

Was Japan's Defeat Inevitable?

Most historians of the Pacific War have expressed a teleological approach to the war's outcome. For example, John Toland's *The Rising Sun: The Decline and Fall of the Japanese Empire, 1936–1945,* Dan van der Vat's *The Pacific Campaign: World War II, the U.S.-Japanese Naval War, 1941–1945* and Ronald H. Spector's *Eagle against the Sun: The American War with Japan.* However, as Richard Overy points out:

> Why did the Allies win World War II? This is such a straightforward question that we assume it has an obvious answer ... Allied victory is taken for granted ... Explanations of Allied success contain a strong element of determinism ... To ask why the Allies won is to presuppose that they might have lost or, for understandable reasons, that they would have accepted an outcome short of total victory. These were in fact strong possibilities. There was nothing preordained about Allied success.[872]

> The common belief holds that the outcome of the war was predetermined simply because Japan lacked the resources to win, discounting their strategic plan to attack, occupy and defend a resource rich enclave that consisted of Thailand, Sumatra, Borneo, Malaya and Java.[873] Their stunning success in this plan gave them a small window of opportunity in 1941 to accomplish their strategic goals. However, overconfidence encouraged them to expand beyond this planned perimeter in 1942–1943, motivated chiefly by the Imperial Japanese Navy's desire to fight and win a decisive battle with the US Navy.[874] This deviation from the basic plan was demanded by Admiral Yamamoto and he specifically altered the plan to include the strike on Pearl Harbor and the invasion of the Philippines.[875] To have been successful the Japanese needed better integrated planning, communication and cooperation between the Imperial Japanese Army and Imperial Japanese Navy, earlier and greater repositioning of ground and air assets from China to the Pacific Ocean areas, and a submarine warfare campaign to attack America's long and vulnerable sea lines of supply while protecting their own sea lanes against American submarines.[876] This did not happen and the Imperial Japanese Navy's ambitions to expand the perimeter into the Southwest and Central Pacific exceeded the Imperial Japanese Army's resources requiring the diversion of resources from China.[877] Finally, the surprise attacks on the American forces ignited an unquenchable thirst for revenge that drove their will to win the war. The great irony of the Pacific War is that the virtually flawless execution of Japan's initial strategic plans resulted within less than a year not in victory but in a series of significant defeats that left the strategic initiative in the hands of the enemy. The fact that this dramatic reversal took place even before the balance of power had tipped in favour of the Allies might appear to be evidence that Japan's entry into the war had indeed been a terrible mistake. Not only could the outcome have been different, but it was also within the power of the Japanese to have made it different.[878]

Do the biggest battalions always win? The prevailing argument that the largest and best-equipped force will dominate clashes with the theory that the way a force is used, in conjunction with the weapons it employs is what produces positive outcomes in combat. I contend that the Japanese lost the war not merely because of their materiel disadvantages but in part because they never fully mastered the 'modern way of warfare', which Stephen Biddle defines as the method of force employment that maximises friendly firepower while shielding one's own forces from the enemy's lethal capabilities.[879] At the tactical level, independent small unit manoeuvre and combined arms operations that maximise cover, concealment and dispersion allow mission success in the face of modern lethality. Close and deep fires shape the battle by providing both suppressive and destructive effects and depth and reserves provide flexibility at the operational level of war.[880] Superior numbers and technological advantages are nullified if the force cannot be brought to bear or if they are ineptly led. Thus, in modern battle, both materiel and nonmaterial factors interact to influence battle outcomes, but neither is predominant. In this view doctrine and tactics are just as important as industrial production and technological innovation because they shape how those factors are used.[881] The Imperial Japanese Army did not fully understand and apply 'the modern system' of tactics, the essence of which (in the offense) is 'cover, concealment, dispersion, small-unit independent manoeuvre, suppression and combined arms integration' and (in the defence) a similarly complex use of 'ground, deep positions, reserves and counterattack'.[882] In fact, the modern system represents a distinctive element of tactical culture that was more clearly demonstrated by the US Army.

Combat effectiveness is the subjective measure of the ability of a military force to accomplish its mission based on assessments of its behavioural, operational and leadership qualities. To be effective a military unit must have proper equipment and personnel who are trained to follow orders, make full use of their weapons and equipment, and be able to execute the battlefield tactics as a coordinated team. Simply having a large or well-equipped force does not guarantee success on the battlefield.[883]

In making a subjective evaluation of combat effectiveness I acknowledge that by focusing on a single US infantry division is narrow in scope and thus may not be fully representative of the rest of the US Army. Nevertheless, I believe that the 7th Infantry Division was highly representative of the US Army as a whole and that their actions demonstrate the importance of the human factors of tactical culture: personality, character and emotions.[884] I have organised this qualitative comparison of the American and Japanese forces by using a few of the major battlefield operating functions as a framework to evaluate and assess their relative combat effectiveness.

Battle Command and Leadership

Leadership is crucial to combat effectiveness. The leaders of the 7th Infantry Division established the vision, values and standards that built the division's shared identity and cohesion. In battle their personal example provided the inspiration to overcome the inevitable fear, uncertainty and confusion that comes with combat.[885]

Battle command and staff planning were not strong points for the Japanese. Based on their belief in the spiritual and racial superiority of the Japanese soldier, Japanese operational thinking was essentially unscientific, narrow, simplistic and arrogantly complacent. Throughout the war they pursued unimaginative, counterproductive, and ultimately suicidal policies.[886] Both Japanese historians and generals later admitted that there was a qualitative failure in Imperial Japanese Army leadership with its repetitive use of failed tactics and slavish devotion to faulty plans and that ultimately it was their deficient strategy rather than inferior arms that explained Japanese defeat.[887]

For Japanese officers an assignment to a headquarters staff lacked the prestige of other assignments and most avoided staff duty, therefore very few were experienced or more importantly talented as staff officers.[888] Japanese headquarters and planning staffs were smaller than their American counterparts and their contributions were severely denigrated by commanders and line officers, and they were not seen as adding value to the effort.[889] Lacking skilled planners, Japanese headquarters staffs were frequently unable to synchronise logistics, communications and fire support as force multipliers and thus were unable to positively influence combat outcomes.[890]

The senior American commanders and staff, the generals and colonels, had served as junior officers in the First World War, but they lacked experience in the command and control of large units because of the small size and limited resources of the army during the interwar era. In this regard, the Japanese had an advantage having gained command experience in combat against both the Chinese and the Soviet Union since 1937. The Americans relied on the intensive staff planning problems and lessons learned studies they had undergone in the army's professional education program to bridge the gap. For the most part, American commanders at the division level and below displayed great ability, and the citizen soldiers who filled the ranks as sergeants, captains and majors demonstrated an unparalleled ability to quickly learn, adapt, improve and innovate to accomplish any mission that they faced. They combined units and used weapons in inventive ways, devising ingenious tactics and techniques to defeat the enemy on various battlefields and under extremely diverse and challenging conditions.[891] The expertise in planning, coordination and leadership displayed by the 7th Infantry Division's battalion and company commanders was exemplary. Despite having no previous combat experience, when leaders were lost in battle, sergeants took over platoons, lieutenants stepped forward to command rifle companies, and captains assumed command of battalions. The 7th Infantry

Division served as a forge for army leaders, with five of the generals who served with the division going on to higher commands, three colonels becoming generals, and nine lieutenant colonels and fourteen majors moving to command other units to spread their experience.[892]

In contrast, when faced with unexpected circumstances or the loss of leadership, the Japanese soldier displayed admirable tenacity and a willingness to die but rarely the capacity to take independent action to change the situation or to alter their plans or methods to achieve success.[893] For example, numerous US after-action reports reflect the finding that suppressive fires kept Japanese forces pinned in their bunkers and 'spider holes/octopus pots' (*takotsubo*) so effectively that American troops could manoeuvre on top of them and fire right down into them to finish the assault. 'If you get their heads down ... suppress by fire ... they stay down; if there are no officers present/alive, they don't know what to do (they) take no action.'[894] Their tactical culture inhibited initiative and innovation. Junior officers were trained to follow orders and execute the chosen plan without deviation. For Japanese company and battalion commanders 'the appreciation of a new and sudden situation seems to be beyond the ability of junior commanders.'[895]

The American superiority in battle command was even more clear at the higher operational and strategic echelons. The US was much more successful than Japan in operational command and control, campaign planning and joint operations. Frequently, the Imperial Japanese Army did not know what the Imperial Japanese Navy was planning or doing so any attempts at synchronisation or synergy were fruitless. This was in part because the autonomy of each service was firmly established in their relative perspectives of the operational environment. Japanese strategy envisioned three enemies: China, Russia and America. The former two were the responsibility of the Imperial Japanese Army, the latter the responsibility of the Imperial Japanese Navy. Although each service had its own air arm the navy had insufficient ground forces to control all the land in the Pacific Ocean area that they had invaded to create the Greater East Asia Co-Prosperity Sphere, thus the navy had to borrow forces from the army. There were no fully integrated joint campaign plans. Each service prepared separate plans, coordinating with each other only when needed. Although the Imperial General Headquarters was established in response to the 1937 Marco Polo Bridge incident to control strategy and operations, there were no joint intelligence or logistical relationships and the Japanese never established geographic joint commands or a unified command structure to prioritise and de-conflict competing demands.[896] As their defeats continued the army and the navy expressed disappointment in each other's performance:

> There is no doubt that a major portion of the responsibility for Japan's' failure at Guadalcanal, Bougainville, the Gilbert Islands, and later at all-important Saipan may be traced to the failure of the Army and Navy to set aside their differences when the future of the nation was at stake.[897]

They sought refuge in their enculturated values of loyalty to the group, obedience to the emperor and collective self-sacrifice to stay the course.[898]

The Americans were consistently able to achieve complementary effects through coordinated campaign planning. As an example, while the 7th Infantry Division was attacking Kwajalein during January and February 1944, the 4th Marine Division was simultaneously assaulting Roi-Namur to the north.[899] Most significantly, the Japanese never resolved the differing strategic views of the Imperial Japanese Army which favored the initial plan for a smaller, shorter fortified perimeter to parry American counterattacks and the Imperial Japanese Navy desire to push out farther, seeking a decisive fleet engagement. After the war Admiral Fukudome explained this divergence:

> From the very beginning there were two divergent views: (1) holding a long line; (2) the other, compact … the Navy favoring the former and the Army the latter ... with the Navy's [*sic*] view prevailing … with the hope of getting a chance to strike a heavy blow against your fleet from one of the outlying bases … and through that line we intended to gain time. Time, we felt, was very important. If the war could be continued long enough, we expected there might be slips on your side of which we could take advantage.[900]

Despite inevitable interservice friction, disagreements and misunderstandings, the Americans avoided the consequences that result from uncoordinated operations of the magnitude that the Japanese did.[901] The US Army, US Navy, US Army Air Force and US Marine Corps were able to transform the individual services into a joint force that could bring all the elements of combat power to bear in a synchronised and synergistic effort. This 'revolution in joint operations' provided logical and flexible planning.[902] Complex compromises were adopted to address command and control, supported and supporting relationships and doctrinal differences over the employment of mechanised and light amphibious forces during joint operations evolved continually from Guadalcanal to Okinawa.[903] The Battle of Okinawa marked the full maturation of joint force doctrine and the apex of cooperation, confidence and trust, particularly between the US Marines and the US Army. This transformation of the American joint force, perhaps more than the mobilisation of America's industrial capacity, provided the overmatching power that resulted in victory.[904] The result was a 'team of teams' that had an advantage in lethality and operational effectiveness because it had mastered modern warfare.[905]

Leadership is crucial to combat effectiveness. The leaders of the 7th Infantry Division established the vision, values and standards that built the division's shared identity and cohesion. In battle their personal example provided the inspiration to overcome the inevitable fear, uncertainty and confusion that comes with combat.[906]

Manoeuvre and Fire Support

In battle after battle and campaign after campaign American combined fires and manoeuvre were successful, but the Imperial Japanese Army response was to rely on fighting spirit and close-quarter battle. Their tactical culture was based on the spirit of offensive action and the belief in their superiority in man-to-man combat in the age of mechanised warfare.[907] Japanese combined arms actions were rare, with tanks generally providing fire support to the infantry but not operating with them as a well-coordinated team. Their belief was that aggressive infantry manoeuvre would infiltrate, envelop and outflank the enemy where close combat with rifles, machine guns and hand grenades would prevail.[908]

The Japanese took steps to strengthen their infantry capabilities but improvements in supporting arms firepower remained unaddressed. This is not because Japanese military technology was incapable of producing new, better weapons. Throughout the war Japanese fighter aircraft continued to evolve and improve, but little was done to improve tanks and artillery. Ironically, Japanese army officers are recorded as having said that 'lack of equipment gave us Japanese a chance to demonstrate our superior spirit and valor [*sic*].'[909] Thus they paid less attention to the development and employment of modern supporting weapons in a combined arms team than did the Americans.[910]

Japanese employment of artillery was generally poor due to an inadequate supply of ammunition and the failure to coordinate and deliver massed destructive fire.[911] In contrast, the US Army enjoyed an enormous advantage in indirect fire support to infantry operations. American advances in fire support coordination, through centralised fire direction centres and forward observation teams, made field artillery support rapid, flexible and responsive. Well-trained American tank-infantry teams supported by accurate and fast artillery fire, integrated manoeuvre tactics with protection and firepower to win.[912]

Japanese tactical doctrine and culture considered night attacks a more important force multiplier than artillery. 'The night is worth a million reinforcements', but they squandered the effectiveness of this tactic by their disjointed commitment of forces, adhering to a practice of: 'commit ten soldiers when one was killed; and another 100 when those ten were wiped out.'[913] They thus reinforced failure rather than created success. When this operational approach was combined with their no surrender policy and their abhorrence of defensive operations, they were doomed to be less effective than the Americans irrespective of their materiel disadvantages.[914] By habitually conducting operations without concern for casualties, fighting to the death could actually play into the hands of American troops if they were well trained and skillfully led to be confident in their abilities to outthink and outfight their opponents.[915]

Intelligence

At the very heart of Japanese operations and planning was a flawed intelligence system that was unable to provide a comprehensive picture of American capabilities and intentions. This resulted in the continuous underestimation of their enemy's will to fight and the belief that their own spiritual power was a greater asset than any technological advantage possessed by the Americans.[916]

Strategic analysis and threat estimates on both sides were influenced by racist stereotypes, flawed assumptions and faulty research which contributed to poor planning.[917] Estimates of enemy capabilities and skills and willpower were often inaccurate. Racial biases adversely influenced planning and unreasonable expectations led to overconfidence and hubris.[918] The Americans underestimated the Imperial Japanese Army and Navy as second-rate forces. This view quickly changed: 'with more than a year of war behind us and with experience gained in fighting we can begin to see how much we have misunderstood the [Japanese.]'.[919] A similar contemporary Japanese assessment of American tactics reveals both insight and prejudice:

> because U.S. tactical ideas are simple, deceptive displays of force are one of the most valuable of all anti-U.S. strategic weapons … because the character of the American is simple and lacking in tenacity, in their tactics and battle leadership they also lack tenacity; and if they meet with one setback, they abandon one plan for another. We must search

> for ways of attack and defense [*sic*] against the Americans with their superior firepower ... we must avoid a stationary defense [*sic*] as much as possible. The Americans make much of firepower, especially the power of artillery, and lay small stress on bayonet charges.[920]

The Japanese generally suffered from selective perceptions of reality, only seeing, and accepting information about the enemy and the operational environment that met their expectations and desired outcomes. Intelligence was undervalued and usually inaccurate, which hindered planning and operations.[921] Intelligence was considered a secondary function and Japanese operations officers distrusted intelligence officers as untrained, second-rate men, relegated to the background, except when their estimates agreed with the chosen course of action.[922] One Japanese general summarised the situation by saying, 'Operations had no confidence in intelligence and until that was changed there would be little use in assigning good men.'[923]

Although Japanese intelligence collection was good, dissemination was poor, and their analysis was often superficial, with the underestimation of the effects of terrain and weather and potential enemy capabilities and intentions being common.[924] Japanese decisionmakers belittled contradictory information and rejected evidence and opinions that did not conform to their expectations or intended plans:

> the Japanese military mentality tended to nullify the work of intelligence. Corrupted by their own propaganda, military planners ... bestowed (with) Japanese invincibility, overemphasized [*sic*] the importance of the attack ... suppressing information ... bending it to serve political ends ... and they became blind to objective intelligence.[925]

The Imperial Japanese Army and Navy did not merely ignore the intelligence that was provided, they chose to twist the information to fit their preconceptions and refused to allow negative views to alter decision making.[926] Their intelligence apparatus was as disjointed as their command structure as Ken Kotani notes:

> In addition, there was no communication between the Army and Navy Intelligence Departments ... although the codebreaking section of the IJA succeeded in breaking the Strip Ciphers, they did not share the method of deciphering with the IJN ... the Army General Staff were angry when the Army codebreaking section provided the method of breaking the US mechanical codes to the NID [Naval Intelligence Department] it was difficult for the Intelligence Departments to cooperate with each other.[927]

Overall, they showed a lack of ability to conduct comprehensive strategic thinking.[928] IJA officers persisted in forlorn operations attacks long after it was clear that the effort would fail, instead desperately seeking an opportunity to 'deliver the enemy a decisive blow by attacking.'[929] Wishful thinking and deliberate misperceptions of reality led to easy acceptance of beliefs that met desires.

Much like their Japanese opponents, The US Army and US Navy had separate intelligence services and differing geographic foci, the army concentrating on Europe and the navy on the Pacific. The critical difference with the Japanese system was the deliberate effort to synthesise and share intelligence. The Americans full-spectrum intelligence effort provided tactical intelligence in support of battlefield missions as well as strategic indications and warnings to inform planning.[930] In addition to their superiority in signals intelligence, having broken several Japanese radio codes, human intelligence gained from the interrogation of prisoners often yielded good intelligence.[931] On Leyte an artillery observer from the Imperial Japanese Army 26th Division provided immediately exploitable information on Japanese artillery methods of reconnaissance, observation and fire control.[932] Captured documents were equally useful because the Japanese depended heavily on written plans that described every aspect of their operations in detail. 'The Japanese disposition of troops, distribution of artillery units, casualties following engagements, hospital records, and numerous other points were found in large numbers.'[933]

Cultural Intelligence and the Military Intelligence Service

During the Second World War, the US Army recognised the need for soldiers with foreign-language proficiency and quickly took steps to address its deficiencies through the creation of the Military Intelligence Service, an intelligence-gathering unit composed of a German-speaking section and a Japanese-speaking section primarily made up of second-generation Japanese Americans (Nisei).[934] The Nisei soldiers translated intercepted Japanese communications and captured documents, and interrogated prisoners of war but their greatest contribution to intelligence analysis was their ability to place the information in its cultural context. By September 1945, they had translated 18,000 captured enemy documents, printed 16,000 propaganda leaflets, and interrogated more than 10,000 Japanese prisoners of war.[935] Military Intelligence Service personnel served with the 7th Infantry Division with distinction, earning the respect and admiration of their fellow American soldiers. On Attu, Staff Sergeant George T. Hayashida crawled alone into a cave to induce ten Japanese soldiers to surrender.[936] A 7th Infantry Division soldier on Kwajalein wrote to the *San Francisco Chronicle* in praise of a Nisei soldier who entered an enemy position armed only with a trench knife,

> The enemy immediately started popping out of the other entrance with no desire to fight. From these prisoners our interpreter learned of more. Just take it from this G.I. that our interpreters have plenty of nerve and their services are invaluable.[937]

Training and Education

After the Japanese-Soviet clash at Nomonhan in 1939 the Japanese high command saw that they were not prepared for enemies that had both superior technology and modern tactics, but their strategic culture obstructed changes in training to meet these threats.[938] Instead, they overestimated their own effectiveness and underestimated the effectiveness of potential enemy forces, continuing to rely on outdated tactics and outmatched forces hoping for successful outcomes.[939]

As the war progressed, the education and training of the Japanese forces was not entirely ignored but various efforts to improve tactical effectiveness were thwarted by circumstance and culture. Instructors sent from Japan to teach 'fortification, communication, anti-tank fighting' assessed that the 'combat method was not taught satisfactorily' because 'each unit was so busily engaged in constructing positions, maintaining peace and order ... that they were in no position to improve their training program.' The lack of time meant that not all troops received the training and thus 'were compelled to commence fighting without the proper training.'[940] This deficiency was particularly acute for the IJA reserve forces sent as late war replacements.[941]

Tragically, Japanese attempts to gather, analyse and disseminate lessons from battle were defeated by fact that so few survived the battles to provide information; most senior Japanese officers committed suicide to atone for defeat. Thus, nobody returned from Tarawa and Kwajalein to warn those at Leyte and Luzon against defending on the beaches. However, some information was received at higher headquarters allowing some Japanese officers to seek lessons from their past defeats and to attempt to develop new doctrine and tactics as demonstrated at Okinawa by the decision not to defend at the shoreline. The Japanese did learn from combat and eventually adjusted their tactics, techniques and procedures to confront the Americans, but they did so at a pace too slow to regain the initiative.[942]

Early American after-action studies quickly concluded that to achieve success against the Japanese would require the US ground forces to rely less on fire power and more on the efficient manoeuvre of infantry units in coordination with their supporting arms.[943] The American system of 'Unit Interviews After Combat' drew on the shared experiences of soldiers to rapidly reinforce learning in combat, bolster unit cohesion and share best practices. This method found its way into widely distributed training pamphlets such as the series, *Combat Lessons 'Rank and File in Combat: What They're Doing; How They Do It'* and the *U.S. Army Infantry Combat Pamphlet-Tactical and Technical Trends.*[944]

The 7th Infantry Division conducted training that built on their previous battle experiences, new developments in enemy systems and new trends in enemy operations, further development of tank-infantry team tactics and special amphibious training.[945] Between campaigns units conducted orientation programs to sustain morale and the will to fight with,

> training about U.S. and Japan (history) military strategy; duty, honor [*sic*], and country; patriotism; current events; the role of the different services in the Pacific; battle tactics of the enemy; and postwar goals ... when faced with the rigors [*sic*] of battle they could reach into their innermost being and find the wellsprings of dedication and conviction that would enable them to carry on.[946]

Logistics and Sustainment

The Japanese could not afford the modernised land, sea and air forces needed to achieve their strategy of hemispheric supremacy. The debate over modernisation and reform centred on whether Japan should plan for a short decisive war or mobilise for a long total war raged throughout the 1920s and was never fully resolved.[947] 'In war there are two factors – human beings and weapons. Ultimately, though, human beings are the decisive factor.'[948]

They chose to prioritise production of aircraft and warships and to bridge the quantitative and technological gap in ground forces with the only resource that remained: manpower and spiritual strength.[949] The Japanese army's preoccupation with the Asian mainland blinded them to the fact that the strategy they contemplated in the Pacific was on a larger scale than the Japanese economy could support, and it required resources that Japan simply did not have.[950]

Japanese operational planning was impatient with the cautious, deliberate and detailed work involved in logistics. Their philosophy was that 'Logistics follows operations.'[951] However, Japanese industry was incapable of producing the quantity of ammunition, armour and artillery that could sustain a modernised army fighting throughout Asia and the Pacific.[952] As a result logistical planning and preparations were seriously deficient most of the time. Even if Japanese logistics had been a higher priority and better planned by the Japanese, they could not move the quantities of weapons, equipment, food and supplies needed to sustain their forces. This was a perpetual problem for the IJA and a strategic weakness that was continually exploited by the Americans.[953] One American officer described the emaciated few Japanese survivors of one battle thus:

> disorganized, demoralized [*sic*] and starved. Malnutrition had weakened the average Jap to the point of death. Many had died in their shelters. Bodies without visible wounds were found by the hundreds. When approached by our men, many of the surviving Japs could be counted on to make a feeble grab at a weapon. Some offered no resistance at all – they simply remained sitting or lying, looking glassy-eyed.[954]

The Americans placed heavy emphasis on logistics. Influenced by geography as a continental nation protected by two oceans and by the experiences of past warfare such as the First World War and the Civil War, that required the supply and movement of forces on a scale equal to the distance from Paris to Moscow, the projection and sustainment of men and materiel across oceans was a part of American strategic culture.[955]

Conclusion

The Second World War was perceived by those who fought it as the ultimate moral and ideological crusade. The Allies regarded it as the defence of freedom and democracy against fascism and militarism. The Axis partners saw it as a righteous struggle for the national destiny that their racial and cultural superiority entitled them to.[956]

The success of the American military in the Second World War came from its systematic preparation via doctrine and education, its demanding field training and competent leadership that inspired their men to fight and win as a team. Both sides underestimated their opponents at the beginning of the conflict, but the Japanese continued to manifest this fatal mistake. The Americans responded to their initial surprise at Japanese success by overestimating their opponents' capabilities and subsequently elevated their own efforts to achieve victory. They soon recognised that superior arms and equipment would have to be matched with ferocity, tenacity and human will to triumph in this fight to the finish.[957] The Japanese, however continued to underestimate the Americans will power and denigrated American fighting spirit as being inferior to their own.[958] The Americans maintained the force of will to skillfully use their capabilities wisely to destroy the enemy's capacity and will to fight.

The 7th Infantry Division was comparatively more combat-efficient than its Japanese opponents because of an American 'tactical culture' characterised by superior leadership and tough, realistic training, that resulted in highly effective tactical performance. Both the Japanese and the Americans displayed the will to fight. Both sides wanted to win. Both sides believed in the ineffable power of their unique fighting spirit as an asymmetrical advantage. The Americans' will to win was centred in the belief that they were fighting for a profoundly moral cause and was exemplified by a grim determination to accomplish the job and return home while the Japanese will to win was subverted by a strategic/tactical culture that promoted a will to sacrifice which became popularly misconstrued by Japanese soldiers and leaders alike that their death in battle was the method of winning.[959]

The 7th Infantry Division displayed a strong sense of shared identity and a determined purpose that gives a force the will to fight and succeed. They had excellent organisational cohesion with strong horizontal bonds within squads, platoons and companies that was consistently demonstrated as individual soldiers integrated as teams, and the teams operated as effective fighting forces. This team of teams fought with the goal of winning not by dying for America but rather by making their enemy die for his country. The American individuality thought by the Japanese to be a weakness was harnessed to serve the goals of the team yet still allowing the innovation and initiative that finds new ways to succeed.[960]

The 7th Infantry Division's distinctive unit identity arose from their common experiences and became a foundational element of their tactical culture. Their shared battle history strengthened their comradeship and pride. Before Okinawa, 40 per cent of the division's original Attu 1943 component was still present. After Okinawa, only 20 per cent remained. Nevertheless, Attu was the yardstick by which all other campaigns were measured.[961] That legendary performance had passed into the division's tactical culture and supported each soldier's belief in his own competence, his trust in his peers and the collective pride and conviction in the unit's effectiveness. They had high confidence in their combat skills and were driven to accomplish the mission and 'end the task' before them.[962]

This extended beyond the unit. Throughout the Pacific Theatre the 7th Infantry Division was widely known as a 'Fighting Division'. It was respected for its high morale and combat performance including by the Marines. During a US Army versus US Marine Corps debate at the end of the war a Marine was asked, 'Well, what about the Seventh Division?' The response: 'Well, I guess the Seventh is kind of different. They're almost like Marines.'[963]

Japanese strategic culture caused them to believe that they were not the only people with real willpower and courage. Their hope of victory was based on their faith that spiritual superiority would neutralise materiel superiority. They were confident that the unique Japanese qualities of national will, discipline and sacrifice would defeat the Americans. Japan's failure in this regard was because their strategy implicitly accepted annihilation of their tactical forces as an acceptable substitute for victory.

Will to win is the bedrock upon which military success is founded. Effective weapons and equipment are vital to success, but they are only one element of combat effectiveness. American forces, fighting as cohesive teams, were driven by a fierce will to win that gave them immense combat effectiveness.

General of the army George C. Marshall summarised the superior effectiveness of the American will to win thus:

> It is not enough to fight. It is the spirit which we bring to the fight that decides the issue ... The soldier's heart, the soldier's spirit, the soldier's soul, are everything. ... not in reliance on things of steel and the super-excellence of guns and planes and bombsights ... We are building it *on belief,* for it is what men *believe* that makes them invincible. We have sought for something more than enthusiasm, something finer and higher than optimism or self-confidence, something not merely of the intellect or the emotions but rather something in the spirit of the man, something encompassed only by the soul. This army of ours already possesses a morale based on what we allude to as the noblest aspirations of mankind – on the spiritual forces which rule the world and will continue to do so ... With your endorsement and support this omnipotent morale will be sustained as long as the things of the spirit are stronger than the things of earth.

NOTES

Chapter One: Strategic Culture and the Will to Fight in the Pacific War

1 Russell F. Weigley, *Eisenhower's Lieutenants: The Campaigns of France and Germany, 1944–45* (Bloomington: Indiana University Press, 1981), 727–30; Michael D. Doubler, *Closing With The Enemy: How GIs Fought the War in Europe, 1944–1945* (Lawrence: University Press of Kansas, 1994), 6; Peter R. Mansoor, *The GI Offensive in Europe: The Triumph of American Infantry Divisions, 1941–1945* (Lawrence: The University Press of Kansas, 1994), 7–8; Brian M. Linn, 'The American Way of War Revisited', *The Journal of Military History*, Volume 66, Number 2, April 2002: 502; John C. McManus, *Fire and Fortitude, The U.S. Army in the Pacific War, 1941–1943* (New York: Dutton Caliber, 2019), 50.

2 Cole Kingseed, 'The Pacific War: The U.S. Army's Forgotten Theater of World War II', *Army* 63, Number 4 (April 2013): 50–56; Louis Morton, *Strategy and Command: The First Two Years. The United States Army in World War II.* (Washington: Government Printing Office, 1962), 88.

3 Ardant du Picq. *Battle Studies: Ancient and Modern Battle,1921 (1870)* (Kingston: Legacy Press Books, 2008), 40–41, 324. Ardant du Picq felt that placing emphasis on 'mathematical and material dynamics' and ignoring the intangible factors in war like will to fight led to illusions about the real nature of war.

4 Peter R. Mansoor, *The GI Offensive in Europe: The Triumph of American Infantry Divisions, 1941–1945* (Lawrence: The University Press of Kansas, 1994), 8.

5 Robert W. Coakley, Chapter 23: 'World War II: The War Against Japan', Army Historical Series, American Military History (Washington DC: Office of the Chief of Military History, 1989), 503; John T. Kuehn, 'The War in the Pacific, 1941–1945'. Chapter 15, *The Cambridge History of the Second World War*, John Ferris (editor), University of Calgary, Evan Mawdsley, University of Glasgow (Cambridge: Cambridge University Press, 2025) 420–454, DOI:10.1017/CHO9781139855969.019.

6 Ronald Spector, *Eagle Against the Sun: The American War With Japan* (New York: Vintage Books, 1985), 560; Phillips Payson O'Brien, *How the War was Won: Air-Sea Power and Allied Victory in World War II* (Cambridge: Cambridge University Press, 2015), 3, 5, 11, 13.

7 McManus, *Fire and Fortitude*, 50.

8 Major General Oscar Griswold, letter to Lieutenant General Lesley McNair, 30 November 1943, Record Group 337, Entry 58A, Box 9, The National Archives.

9 Richard Frank, *Guadalcanal: The Definitive Account of the Landmark Battle* (New York: Random House, 1990), 595–596.

10 Kingseed, 50.

11 Division level *esprit de corps* is an essential element of combat effectiveness. General Eisenhower wrote, 'the Army *esprit de corps* centers [*sic*] around a division much more than it does any other echelon.' (Alfred D. Chandler Jr and Louis Galambos (editors). The Papers of Dwight David Eisenhower, Occupation, 1945, Volume 6, Baltimore, MD: Johns Hopkins University Press, 1978, entry 107).

12 Clausewitz, *On War*, 101.

13 Richard A. Burklund, 'Hell in the Mists', 'The U.S. Seventh Infantry Division and the Forgotten Battle of Attu'; unpublished master's thesis, Southern New Hampshire University, Manchester, New Hampshire, 2015, 10–11.

14 Ben Connable, Michael J. McNerney, William Marcellino, Aaron Frank, Henry Hargrove, Marek N. Posard, S. Rebecca Zimmerman, Natasha Lander, Jasen J. Castillo, Dan Madden, Ilana Blum, Aaron Frank, Benjamin J. Fernandes, In Hyo Seol, Christopher Paul and Andrew Parasiliti, *National Will to Fight: Why Some States Keep Fighting and Others Don't* (Santa Monica, Calif.: RAND Corporation, RR-2477-A, 2018), xii.

15 Ben Connable, Michael J. McNerney, William Marcellino, Aaron Frank, Henry Hargrove, Marek N. Posard, S. Rebecca Zimmerman, Natasha Lander, Jasen J. Castillo and James Sladden, *Will to Fight: Analyzing, Modeling, and Simulating the Will to Fight of Military Units* (Santa Monica, Calif.: RAND Corporation, RR-2341-A, 2018), xi, xxi.

16 Michael Howard, 'The Use and Abuse of Military History'; Royal United Services Institution, Journal, Volume 107, Issue 625, 1962, based on a lecture by Professor Sir Michael Howard to the Royal United Service Institute on 18 October 1961 and published in their journal, Number 107 in February 1962, pp.4–8, reprinted in *Parameters,* Journal of the US Army War College, Volume XI, No. 1, pp.9–14.

17 Laurie M. Johnson Bagby, 'The Use and Abuse of Thucydides in International Relations', International Organization, Volume 48, Number 1, Winter 1994: 133. Rashed Uz Zaman, 'Strategic Culture: A Cultural Understanding of War', Comparative Strategy, 10 February 2009: 70–72.

18 H. Shultz, Jr's, Adapting America's Security Paradigm and Security Agenda (Washington DC: National Strategy Information Center, 2010), p.35.

19 Jack Snyder, *The Soviet Strategic Culture: Implications for Nuclear Options* (RAND R-2154-AF, 1977).

20 Harry R. Yarger, 'Strategic Theory For the 21st Century: The Little Book on Big Strategy', Strategic Studies Institute, U.S. Army War College, Carlisle, Pennsylvania, February 2006, v.

21 Carl von Clausewitz, *On War*, Michael Howard and Peter Paret (editors and translators) (Princeton: Princeton University Press, 1989), 128.

22 Carl von Clausewitz, *On War*, Michael Howard and Peter Paret (editors) (Princeton: Princeton University Press, 1976), 142–143.

23 Michael Howard, *Clausewitz* (New York: Oxford University Press, 1986),16; Carl von Clausewitz, *On War*, 127–132.

24 Carl von Clausewitz, *On War*, 111. 'In the highest realms of strategy ... there is little or no difference between strategy, policy and statesmanship.' Ibid.,178. Winston Churchill reaffirms this point: 'The distinction between politics and strategy, diminishes as the point of view is raised. At the Summit true politics and strategy are one.' Winston S. Churchill, *The World Crisis 1915* (New York: Charles Scribner's Sons, 1929), 6.

25 Carl von Clausewitz, *On War*, Michael Howard and Peter Paret (editors and translators) (Princeton: Princeton University Press, 1976), 87, 141.

26 Williamson Murray and Mark Grimsley, 'Introduction: On Strategy', *The Making of Strategy: Rulers, States, and War* (Cambridge: Cambridge University Press, 1994; 1997), 22.

27 Yarger, 3,5.

28 Arthur F. Lykke, Jr, 'Toward an Understanding of Military Strategy', chapter in *Military Strategy: Theory and Application* (Carlisle Barracks, Pennsylvania: Department of National Security and Strategy, US Army War College, 1989), 3–8.

29 Murray and Grimsley, *The Making of Strategy*, 1, 13; Carl von Clausewitz, *On War*, 86, 89.

30 Michael D. Krause, 'Moltke and the Origins of the Operational Art', in *Military Review*, Volume ixx, Number 9, September 1990, 28–44; and Douglas A. MacGregor, 'Future Battle: The Merging Levels of War', in *Parameters*, Volume xxii, Number 4, winter 1992–93, 33–47.

31 Gregory D. Foster, 'A Conceptual Foundation for a Theory of Strategy', *The Washington Quarterly*, winter 1990, 43, 56–56; Lykke, 38.

32 Aaron P. Jackson, 'The Roots of Military Doctrine: Change and Continuity in Understanding the Practice of Warfare', Combat Studies Institute Press, US Army Combined Arms Center, Fort Leavenworth, KS, 2013, 3.

33 Ibid., 6, 11.

34 Alfred Vagts, *A History of Militarism* (New York: Scribners & Sons, 1937; revised edition 1959).

35 There have subsequently been many treatments on national ways of war. See Antulio Etchevarria II, *Toward an American Way of War* (Carlisle: Strategic Studies Institute, 2003); Robert M. Citino, *The German Way of War: From the Thirty Years' War to the Third Reich* (Lawrence: University Press of Kansas, 2005); Victor Davis Hanson, *The Western Way of War: Infantry in Battle in Classical Greece*, second edition (Berkeley: University of California Press, 2000); Richard M. Harrison, *The Russian Way of War: Operational Art, 1904–1940* (Lawrence: University Press of Kansas, 2001).

36 Thomas Mahnken, 'United States Strategic Culture', Defense Threat Reduction Agency Advanced Systems and Concepts Office, 13 November 2006, 1; see also Julian S. Corbett, *Some Principles of Maritime Strategy* (London: Longmans Green and Co., 1911), 38.

37 Sir Basil H. Liddell Hart, *The British Way in Warfare* (London: Faber & Faber Limited, 1932), pp.25–38; and Lawrence Sondhaus, *Strategic Culture and Ways of War* (New York and London: Routledge, 2006), p.1.

38 Valerie M. Hudson, 'Culture and Foreign Policy: Developing a Research Agenda', in editor Valerie M. Hudson, *Culture and Foreign Policy* (Boulder, Co., and London: Lynne Rienner Publishers, 1997), p.2.

39 Colin S. Gray, *Out of the Wilderness: Prime-Time for Strategic Culture*, National Institute for Public Policy, United States Nuclear Strategy Forum, National Institute Press, October 2006, iii.

40 Alastair Iain Johnston, 'Thinking About Strategic Culture', *International Security*, Volume 19.4, spring 1995: 50.

41 Forrest E. Morgan, *Compellence and the Strategic Culture of Imperial Japan: Implications for Coercive Diplomacy in the Twenty-First Century* (Westport and London: Praeger, 2003), pp.19–20.

42 Clifford Geertz, *The Interpretation of Cultures* (New York: Basic Books, 1973), 33.

43 Jeffrey S. Lantis, 'Strategic Culture: From Clausewitz to Constructivism', *Strategic Insights*, Volume IV, Number 10, 2 October 2005, 5.

44 Ruth Benedict, *The Chrysanthemum and the Sword: Patterns of Japanese Culture* (Boston: Houghton Mifflin, 2005), 1, 2, 18–19, 49.

45 Jeffrey S. Lantis, 'Strategic Culture: From Clausewitz to Constructivism', Comparative Strategic Cultures Curriculum, Defense Threat Reduction Agency, 31 October 2006, 3.

46 Colin S. Gray, 'Comparative Strategic Culture', *Parameters*, Volume 14, Number 4, winter 1984: 27.

47 Ken Booth, *Strategy and Ethnocentrism* (New York: Holmes & Meier Publishers Inc., 1979), 5.

48 Ken Booth, *Strategy and Ethnocentrism* (New York: Holmes & Meier Publishers Inc., 1979), 5.

49 Jack Snyder, *The Soviet Strategic Culture: Implications for Limited Nuclear Options* (Santa Monica, CA: RAND, 1977), pp.6–9.

50 Colin Gray, 'National Style in Strategy, International Security (Fall 1981); 'Out of the Wilderness: Prime Time for Strategic Culture', paper prepared for the Defense Threat Reduction Agency, Advanced Systems and Concepts Office's Comparative Strategic Cultures Curriculum (2006), 8–14.

51 C. Gray, *Modern Strategy* (Oxford: Oxford University Press, 1999), 138.

52 Elizabeth Kier, *Imagining War: French and British Military Doctrine Between the Wars* (Princeton: Princeton University Press, 1997), 7.

53 Alastair Iain Johnston, *Cultural Realism: Strategic Culture and Grand Strategy in Chinese History* (Princeton, New Jersey: Princeton University Press, 1995): 1,7–8, 36.

54 Ibid., 46–48.

55 Ibid., 4–22.

56 Jacques E.C. Hymans, *The Psychology of Nuclear Proliferation* (Cambridge: Cambridge University Press, 2006), p.17; see also Stephen Saideman, 'Thinking Theoretically About Identity and Foreign Policy', in Shibley Telhami and Michael Barnett (editors), *Identity and Foreign Policy in the Middle East* (Ithaca, NY: Cornell University Press, 2002), 169–170.

57 Ted Hopf, 'The Promise of Constructivism in International Relations', *International Security* 23, Number 1 (Summer 1998), p.914; Valerie M. Hudson (editor), *Culture and Foreign Policy* (Boulder: Lynne Rienner, 1997): 28–29.

58 C. Gray, *Modern Strategy* Oxford: Oxford University Press, 1999), 138 and A. Johnson, 'Thinking About Strategic Culture' in *International Security, 19 (4)*, 1995, 28.

59 Richard H. Shultz, *Strategic Culture and Strategic Studies: An Alternative Framework for Assessing al-Qaeda and the Global Jihad Movement*, JSOU Report 12-4, 3, The JSOU Press, MacDill Air Force Base, Florida, 2012.

60 Linn, *The Echo of Battle*, 4.

61 John R. Galvin, 'Uncomfortable Wars: Toward a New Paradigm', Parameters, Volume 16 (winter 1986): 2.

62 Bernard Brodie, *War and Politics* (New York: Pearson, 1973), 332, 'good strategy presumes good anthropology and sociology. Some of the greatest military blunders of all time have resulted from juvenile evaluations in this department.'

63 Jeffrey S. Lantis, 'Strategic Culture and National Security Policy', *International Studies Review* (Number 3, 2003), 11.

64 Antulio J. Etchevarria II, *Reconsidering the American Way of War: U.S. Military Practice from the Revolution to Afghanistan* (Washington DC: Georgetown University Press, 2014), 27.

65 A. Johnson, 'Thinking About Strategic Culture' in *International Security, 19 (4)*, 1995, 46–48; Etchevarria, 27.

66 Alastair Iain Johnston, *Cultural Realism: Strategic Culture and Grand Strategy in Chinese History* (Princeton, New Jersey: Princeton University Press, 1995): 1.

67 Miriam D. Becker, 'Strategic Culture and Missile Ballistic Defense', *Air and Space Power Journal* (Special Edition, 1994). A postulate to my study is that previous country-specific historical studies have established that a unique and specific strategic culture does exist for both Japan and the US.

68 Forrest E. Morgan, *Compellence and the Strategic Culture of Imperial Japan: Implications for Coercive Diplomacy in the Twenty-First Century* (Westport and London: Praeger Publishers, 2003), 28.

69 A corollary: 'When the Germans shoot, the British duck. When the British shoot, the Germans duck. When the Americans shoot, everybody ducks.'

70 Michael A. Bonura, *Under the Shadow of Napoleon: French Influence on the American Way of Warfare from Independence to the Eve of World War II* (New York: NYU Press, 2012), 3–4.

71 Isabel V. Hull, *Absolute Destruction: Military Culture and the Practices of War in Imperial Germany* (Ithaca: Cornell University Press, 2006), 2.

72 Edgar H. Schein, *Organizational Culture and Leadership* (San Francisco: Jossey-Bass, 2010), 3–11.

73 Edgar H. Schein, *Organizational Culture and Leadership*, fourth edition (Jossey-Bass Business and Management, 2010), 18, 24.

74 Schein, *Organizational Culture and Leadership*,16, 28, 29.

75 Schein, 16, 17, 18, 24, 29.

76 Thomas Mahnken, *Technology, and the American Way of War Since 1945* (New York: Columbia University Press, 2008), 3, 4-6, 223–225.

77 Hull, *Absolute Destruction*, 92.

78 Robert M. Citino, *The German Way of War* (Lawrence: University Press of Kansas, 2005), xiv.

79 Ben Connable, Michael J. McNerney, William Marcellino, Aaron Frank, Henry Hargrove, Marek N. Posard, S. Rebecca Zimmerman, Natasha Lander, Jasen J. Castillo and James Sladden, *Will to Fight: Analyzing, Modeling, and Simulating the Will to Fight of Military Units* (Santa Monica, California: RAND Corporation, RR-2341-A, 2018), xi.

80 Forrest E. Morgan, *Compellence and the Strategic Culture of Imperial Japan: Implications for Coercive Diplomacy in the Twenty-First Century* (Westport and London: Praeger Publishers, 2003), 8.

81 Marion J. Levy, Jr, *The Structure of Society* (Princeton, NJ: Princeton University Press, 1952), 147–148.

82 Morgan, 8–9.

83 Ann Swidler, 'Culture in Action: Symbols and Strategies', *American Sociological Review* 51, Number 2 (1986): 273–86.

84 Morgan, 10.

85 Adrian Lewis, *The American Culture of War: The History of U.S. Military Force from World War II to Operation Iraqi Freedom* (New York: Routledge, 2018), xvii, 34–35; Echevarria, 16, 23.

86 Weigley, *American Way of War*, 6–7, 467–477.

87 F.G Hoffman, *Decisive Force: The New American Way of War* (Westport: Praeger, 1996), xii.

88 Brian M. Linn, 'The American Way of War Revisited', *The Journal of Military History*, Volume 66, Number 2, April 2002: 502.

89 Linn, 'American Way of War Revisited', 502–503, 530.

90 Max Boot, *The Savage Wars of Peace: Small Wars and the Rise of American Power* (New York: Basic Books, 2002), 287, 352.

91 Forrest Morgan, *Compellence and the Strategic Culture of Japan*, 10, 37.

92 Benedict, 117, 133, 136–137; Morgan, 63–64, 75.

93 Morgan, 1.

94 Edward J. Drea, *Japan's Imperial Army: Its Rise and Fall, 1853–1945* (Lawrence: University Press of Kansas, 2009), 320, 593; Allison B. Gilmore, *You Can't Fight Tanks with Bayonets: Psychological Warfare against the Japanese Army in the South West Pacific* (Lincoln: University of Nebraska Press, 1998), 87.

95 David Hunter-Chester, 'Imperial Japanese Army Culture, 1918–1945: Duty Heavier than a Mountain, Death Lighter than a Feather', Chapter 9, in *The Culture of Military Organizations*, Peter R. Mansoor and Williamson Murray (editors), 208–25. (Cambridge: Cambridge University Press, 2019), 208–225.

96 Ibid., 11, 227, 228; Thomas Cleary, *The Japanese Art of War: Understanding the Culture of Strategy* (Boston and London: Shambhala, 1991), 1–2.

97 Sir Basil H. Liddell Hart, *Strategy* (New York: New American Library, 1974), 323.

98 James M. McPherson, *For Cause and Comrades: Why Men Fought in the Civil War* (New York: Oxford University Press, 1997), 46.

99 Ibid., 27.

100 William Darryl Henderson, *Cohesion: The Human Element in Combat* (Washington DC: National Defense University Press, 1985), 9.

101 Wayne M. Hall, *The Power of Will in International Conflict: How to Think Critically in Complex Environments* (Santa Barbara: Praeger, 2018), xxi.

102 Carl von Clausewitz, *On War* (Princeton: Princeton University Press, 1976), 75; Ben Connable, *et al, Will to Fight: Analyzing, Modeling, and Simulating the Will to Fight of Military Units.*

103 Connable, *et al, Will to Fight*, 34.

104 Ibid.

105 Ben Connable, Michael J. McNerney, William Marcellino, Aaron Frank, Henry Hargrove, Marek N. Posard, S. Rebecca Zimmerman, Natasha Lander, Jasen J. Castillo, and James Sladden, *Will to Fight: Analyzing, Modeling, and Simulating the Will to Fight of Military Units* (Santa Monica, California: RAND Corporation, RR-2341-A, 2018), xi.

106 Connable, *et al, Will to Fight*, 3. Note: RAND is a name, not an acronym.

107 Connable, *et al, Will to Fight*, xi.

108 U.S. Army, Army Doctrine Publication (ADP) 3-0, *Operations*, 2017.

109 Connable, *et al, National Will To Fight*, xiii–xvi.

110 Ibid., xii.

111 Ibid., 34.

112 Ibid., 13, 38; note: RAND is not an acronym.

113 Ibid., xiv; note: Connable *et al*, points out that cohesion is an important factor that influences will to fight but there is no accepted empirical proof that it is the most important factor in every case.

114 Ibid., 19.

115 Oxford English Dictionary Online, January 2021, Oxford University Press. http://www.oed.com/view/Entry/122088?redirectedFrom=morale.

116 Connable, *et al*, 13, 'Combat almost always ends when one side quits. Even total annihilation suggests extraordinary will on the part of the defeated foe. Will to fight always matters in combat. Winning at the tactical level hinges on will to fight.' They represent this with an equation: Capabilities + Casualty infliction + Will to Fight = Victory/Stalemate.

117 Ibid., xvii.

118 Ibid.

119 Ralph Eyde, 'Brothers in Arms: Letters from War', *The Washington Post*, Dan Lamothe, 6 December 2017, accessed January 2018; letters and family photos courtesy of Joe Alosi, https://www.washingtonpost.com/podcasts/letters-from-war/.

120 Mark Obmascik, *The Storm on Our Shores: One Island, Two Soldiers, and the Forgotten Battle of World War II* (New York: Simon & Schuster, 2019), 5, 10, 36.

121 Dean E. Galles Collection (AFC/2001/001/88536), interviewed by Christine Seifert, Veterans' History Project, American Folklife Center, Library of Congress.

122 Albert V. Hartl, 'Hartl Still Remembered as United States War Hero', Tom Hintgen, 25 July 2011, https://www.fergusfallsjournal.com/opinion/columnists/hartl-still-remembered-as-united-states-war-hero/article_3d80da72-5037-534c-b920-620297c48591.html/?utm_medium=internal&utm_source=readerShare&utm_campaign=bButton.

123 General Orders Number 31: Headquarters, US Army Troops, APO 726 (Attu Landing Force), 1943. Citation to accompany the Award of the Distinguished Service Cross to Lieutenant Colonel Wayne C. Zimmerman.

124 The Hourglass Newsletter, December 1990, Special Announcement: Major General Francis Pachler, https://www.7ida.us/documents/Hourglass%20NL%27s/HG_1990.pdf.

125 Mark Obmascik, *The Storm on Our Shores: One Island, Two Soldiers, and the Forgotten Battle of World War II* (New York: Simon & Schuster, 2019), 137–138.

126 Yahara, Hiromichi, *The Battle for Okinawa*, Roger Pineau and Uehara Masatoshi (translators), with an introduction and commentary by Frank B. Gibney (New York: John Wiley & Sons, 1995), 49.

Chapter Two: The Battle of Attu: Tactical Culture and *Gyokusai*

127 John Dower, *War Without Mercy: Race & Power in the Pacific War* (New York: Pantheon Books, 1986), 231: Translation of a poem found on the body of one of the Japanese casualties on Attu, May 1943.

128 Richard A. Burklund, 'Hell in the Mists', 'The U.S. Seventh Infantry Division and the Forgotten Battle of Attu'; unpublished master's thesis, Southern New Hampshire University, Manchester, New Hampshire, 2015, 1–4, 15–18.

129 Edgar H. Schein, *Organizational Culture and Leadership* (San Francisco: Jossey-Bass, 2010), 1, 7–8.

130 Alvin D. Coox, *Nomonhan: Japan Against Russia, 1939* (Stanford: Stanford university Press, 1985), 2–3.

131 Brigadier General Billy Mitchell, official testimony to the U.S. Congress; *Air Defense Bases*, Hearings before the Committee on Military Affairs, House of Representatives, Seventy-Fourth Congress, First Session on H.R. 6621 and H.R. 4130, 11, 12, 13 February 1935, Washington DC: US Government Printing Office, 51–52.

132 John Haile Cloe, *Attu: The Forgotten Battle,* National Park Service (Washington DC: Department of the Interior, 2017), 19.

133 Paul S. Dull, *A Battle History of the Imperial Japanese Navy (1941–1945)* (Annapolis: Naval Institute Press 1978), 157.

134 Japanese Monograph 46, Aleutians Operations Record, June 1942–July 1943, 8-5.1 AC46, CMH, 111-118; Japanese Monograph 88, Aleutian Naval Operations, March 1942–February 1943, not dated, HQ Army Forces Far East, Mil Hist Section, Japanese Research Division; Sewell Tyng, 'The Capture of Attu: As Told By The Men Who Fought There', United States War Department (Washington DC: The Infantry Journal, October 1944), 2.

135 James, D. Clayton. 'American and Japanese Strategies in the Pacific War'. in *Makers of Modern Strategy from Machiavelli to the Nuclear Age,* Peter Paret (editor) (Princeton, New Jersey: Princeton University Press, 1986), 703–732.

136 Paul S. Dull, *A Battle History of the Imperial Japanese Navy (1941–1945)* (Annapolis: Naval Institute Press 1978), 261.

137 Ibid.; William J. Verbeck, 'Action on Attu: A Summary of Information of the Enemy Obtained During the Operations of the Force on Attu' (G-2 Alaska Defense Command, 30 July 1943), 35.

138 Stan Cohen, *The Forgotten War: A Pictorial History of World War II in Alaska and Northeastern Canada* (Missoula: Pictorial Histories, 1981), 110.

139 *Western Regional Climate Center.* https://earthobservatory.nasa.gov/images/6715/attu-island-alaska; https://www.britannica.com/place/Aleutian-Islands.

140 John B. Wilson, *Armies, Corps, Divisions, And Separate Brigades* (Washington DC: United States Army Center for Military History, 1999), 217.

141 Ibid., 10, Wilson, *Armies, Corps, Divisions, and Separate Brigades,* 217.

142 Bruce Gardener, Barbara Stahura, *Seventh Infantry Division: 1917–1992, World War I, World War II, Korea, and Panamanian Invasion* (Nashville: Turner Publishing Company, 1997), 10.

143 Ibid., 10. Wilson, *Armies, Corps, Divisions, And Separate Brigades,* 217.

144 Ibid., 10, 112.

145 Ibid.

146 Stetson Conn, Rose C. Engelman and Byron Fairchild, *The United States Army in World War II: The Western Hemisphere, Guarding the United States and its Outposts, U.S. Army in World War II* (Washington DC: United States Army, Center of Military History, 2000), 16–17, 223–270.

147 Stetson Conn, Rose C. Engelman and Byron Fairchild, *The United States Army in World War II: The Western Hemisphere, Guarding the United States and its Outposts, U.S. Army in World War II* (Washington DC: United States Army, Center of Military History, 2000), 16–17, 223–270.

148 Ibid., 277–280.

149 Ibid.

150 Ibid.

151 Ibid.

152 Ibid.

153 William J. Verbeck, 'Action on Attu: A Summary of Information of the Enemy Obtained During the Operations of the Force on Attu' (G-2 Alaska Defense Command, 30 July 1943), 99.

154 Ibid.

155 Ibid., 21–23; 7th Infantry Division, G2 Estimate of Enemy Situation, April 26, 1943, Robert Fergusson Collection, Box 1.

156 Japanese Monograph 46, Aleutians Operations Record, June 1942–July 1943,8-5.1 AC46, CMH, 111–118; Conn, *et al*, *Guarding the United States and Its Outposts*, 268-275; Mitchell, *et al*, *Capture of Attu*, 2–6; Garfield, *The Thousand Mile War*, 217–219.

157 William J. Verbeck, 'Action on Attu: A Summary of Information of the Enemy Obtained During the Operations of the Force on Attu' (G-2 Alaska Defense Command, 30 July 1943), 99. These unit identifications and their estimated strengths were developed after the battle from the analysis of the few surviving documents and interviews with the eleven enemy prisoners of war that were captured. This primary source places the total estimated strength at 2,359 and the total number of enemies killed as 2,350. Secondary sources conclude that Yamasaki had 2,650 men.

158 Leland Ness, *Rikugun: Guide to Japanese Ground Forces, 1937–1945* (Solihull: Helion and Company, 2014), 174–180; 327–328. The machine cannon units were equipped with both dual purpose 20-millimetre cannons and 13.2-millimetre guns capable of engaging air and ground targets with great effect.

159 Japanese Monograph 46, Aleutians Operations Record, June 1942–July 1943, 8-5.1 AC46, CMH, 111–118; Conn, *et al*, *Guarding the United States and Its Outposts*, 268–275.

160 Ibid., 44.

161 TM-E-30-480, 'Technical Manual: Handbook on Japanese Military Forces', War Department: Washington DC, 15 September 1944, 19; Cloe, 41.

162 Japanese Monograph Number 45, 22–23.

163 *Tactical and Technical Trends, Number 33, 9 Sep[tember] 1943*, Military Intelligence Service, War Department, Washington DC 25–27.

164 James A. Ulio, 'Military Morale', *American Journal of Sociology*, Volume 47, Number 3 (1941): 321.

165 Oxford English Dictionary Online, accessed June 2021, Oxford University Press, http://www.oed.com/view/Entry/122088?redirectedFrom=morale; Paul Fussell, *Wartime: Understanding and Behavior in the Second World War* (New York: Oxford University Press, 1989), 144.

166 Craven and Cate (editors), *The Pacific – Guadalcanal to Saipan*, 380–383.

167 Clausewitz, *On War*, 86.

168 Leedy, 142–143.

169 John Shy and Thomas W. Collier, 'Revolutionary War', *In Makers of Modern Strategy from Machiavelli to the Nuclear Age*, Peter Paret (editor), Craig Gordon A. and Gilbert Felix, 817 (Princeton: Princeton University Press, 1986). 31.

170 Ralph Eyde, 'Brothers in Arms: Letters from War', *The Washington Post*, Dan Lamothe, 6 December 2017, accessed January 2018, https://www.washingtonpost.com/podcasts/letters-from-war/.

171 Ralph Eyde, personal letter dated 15 April 1943; 'Brothers in Arms: Letters from War', *The Washington Post*, Dan Lamothe, 6 December 2017, accessed January 2018, https://www.washingtonpost.com/podcasts/letters-from-war/.

172 Ibid.

173 PFC Ernest Uno letter to his sister Mae, Andrew Carroll, *War Letters: Extraordinary Correspondence from American Wars* (New York: Scribner, 2001), 225.

174 Frank Walker, 'The Postal Service at War', United States at War, 7 December 1942–7 December 1943 (Washington: *Army & Navy Journal*, 1943), as reproduced by Kurt Greenbaum in 'Wartime Postmaster Details the Work of Mail Delivery in WWII'; Monica Cronin, 'U.S. Combat Morale in the World Wars: The European Theater of Operations' (2017), Undergraduate Honours Thesis Paper, College of William and Mary. https://scholarworks.wm.edu/honorstheses/1104, 49–50.

175 Excerpts from the diary/letter of an unknown Japanese private found on Attu. The translation was done by 7th Infantry Division G-2, http://aleutians.hlswilliwaw.com/Attu/html/attu-tsukiji-diary-translation.htm, (Tokai University Peace and War On Line, Torikai Lab Network website, accessed 20 March 2016), http://torikai.starfree.jp/1943/attu.html.

176 From messages recorded in the G-3 Journal File, HQ TF 51.4, and G-3 Journal vouchers, 11 May 1943, Manoeuvre Center of Excellence Libraries, HQ Donovan Research Library, Fort Benning, Georgia, author's collection; Smith, *Preliminary Report on Attu Landing*, 6–7; ONI Combat Narrative, *Aleutians Campaign*, 79–81; and *Attu Operations* (General Brown's report), 20.

177 HQ TF 51.4, G-3 Journal File, 11 May 1943; Smith, *Preliminary Report on Attu Landing*, 6–7; ONI Combat Narrative, *Aleutians Campaign*, 79–81.

178 *The Aleutians Campaign*, Combat Narratives, Publications Branch, Office of Naval Intelligence – United States Navy, Washington DC, 1 March 1945, 77–78.

179 Smith, *Preliminary Report on Attu Landing*, 6–7.

180 Brian Garfield, *The Thousand-Mile War: World War II in Alaska and the Aleutians* (Juneau: University of Alaska Press, 1995), 222; Boyes, 9. Eventually, two batteries (twelve guns) of 75-millimetre howitzers were laboriously moved 1,000 yards inland by hand.

181 Brian Garfield, *The Thousand-Mile War: World War II in Alaska and the Aleutians*. (Juneau: University of Alaska Press, 1995), 224. At times, almost half of the attacking force was instead occupied with moving supplies by hand onto the island and up to the forward line of troops.

182 Japanese Monograph 46, 111–18; Morison, *Aleutians, Gilberts Marshalls*, 43.

183 US Army Medical Department, Office of Medical History, Chapter V, 'The Aleutians', http://history.amedd.army.mil/booksdocs/wwii/ColdInjury/Chapter05.htm.

184 US Army Medical Department, Office of Medical History, Chapter V, 'The Aleutians', http://history.amedd.army.mil/booksdocs/wwii/ColdInjury/Chapter05.htm.

185 BCT 17-2, After Action Report and Unit Journal (11 May 1943); RLG 17, After Action Report (11 May 1943).

186 BCT 17-3, After Action Report and Unit Journal (11 May 1943).

187 Garfield, 230. From Colonel William Alexander's operations log, 13 May 1943. The observer was not hit.

188 Ibid.

189 BCT 17-2, Action Report and Unit Journal (11 May 1943); RLG 17, Action Report (11 May 1943).

190 Tyng, 'The Capture of Attu: As Told By The Men Who Fought There', 31-32; US Army Infantry Combat Lessons Learned: Attu, 11–12; Verbeck, 'on his own initiative … personally led a reconnaissance party over the island … greatly assisted by the advance information he obtained … used his knowledge and familiarity with the language and customs of the Japanese to trick and outwit the enemy.' William Jordan Verbeck Obituary, *The Taro Leaf*, Volume 19(4), 1965–1966, The 24th Infantry Division Association; 'General Verbeck War Hero Dies, Post Standard of Syracuse, N.Y. undated'.

191 RLG 17 Action Report, Overlay, 11–14 May; Personal Narratives by Lieutenant Charles K. Paulson, Corporal Mike M. Brusuelas and Corporal Paul H. Doty, in 'The Capture of Attu: As Told By The

Men Who Fought There', 27–31. The quotations are from Field Order Number 1, Plan E (corrected copy), 2 May 1943, in Landing Force (Task Force 51.4) G-3 Journal Vouchers (2 May).

192 BCT 17-1, Unit journal for 11 May 1943; Smith, *Preliminary Report on Attu Landing*, 6–7; ONI Combat Narrative, *Aleutians Campaign*, 81. The Smith report places the first encounter with the Japanese at 1900, which does not quite correspond with the unit journal.

193 Maj Gen Eugene M. Landrum, CG Landing Force, 'Report of Operations-Attu, 22 Jun[e] 43', 3–4; ONI Combat Narrative, *Aleutians Campaign*, 78–79; Drummond, *Attu Operation*, 1, 99–102; Personal Narrative by First Sergeant Fenton Hamlin, in the War Department's 'The Capture of Attu: As Told By The Men Who Fought There' (Washington DC: Infantry Journal Press, 1944), 64–68.

194 James MacPherson, *For Cause and Comrades: Why Men Fought in the Civil War* (New York: Oxford University Press, 1997), 12; William Darryl Henderson, *Cohesion: The Human Element in Combat* (Washington DC: National Defense University, 1985), 6, 9–11; David Hackett Fischer first advanced the construct of the 'braided narrative' in *Albion's Seed* (New York: Oxford University Press, 1989).

195 See John Keegan, *History of Warfare* (New York: Knopf, 1994), 22–23; 'We all find it difficult to stand far enough outside our own culture to perceive how it makes us, as individuals, what we are.'

196 Mark Obmascik, *The Storm on Our Shores: One Island, Two Soldiers, and the Forgotten Battle of World War II* (New York: Simon & Schuster, 2019), 5, 10, 36.

197 Paul Nobuo Tatsuguchi, 'Diary', captured 29 May 1943. Historians have discovered as many as ten differing translations of the diary. I have used the one found in Verbeck, 'Action on Attu: A Summary of Information of the Enemy Obtained During the Operations of the Force on Attu', G-2 Alaska Defense Command, 30 July 1943. I think it is the most accurate translation because it was done soon after it was obtained. A Japanese language version from the Tokai University, Peace and War On Line, Torikai Lab Network web site was also consulted; http://torikai.starfree.jp/1943/attu.html.

198 Paul S. Dull, *A Battle History of the Imperial Japanese Navy (1941–1945)* (Annapolis: Naval Institute Press 1978), xiv.

199 Brian Garfield, *The Thousand-Mile War: World War II in Alaska and the Aleutians*. (Juneau: University of Alaska Press, 1995), 228.

200 BCT 17-1 Unit Journal and Overlays; Smith, *Preliminary Report on Attu Landing*.

201 RLG 17, Action Report and Overlays (11–14 May); BCT 17-2, Unit Journal; and BCT 17-3, Unit Journal.

202 Cloe, 118,

203 Ibid., 83–84.

204 Memo, General Brown for CTF 51 (Admiral Rockwell), 14 May 1943, HQ TF 51.4, G-3 Journal Vouchers (Item 35, 14 May 43).

205 Edmund G. Love, *The Hourglass, A History of the 7th Infantry Division in World War II* (Washington DC: Infantry Journal Press, 1950), 50–54.

206 *Combat Lessons Number 2, 'Rank and File in Combat: What They're Doing; How They Do It'* (Washington DC: Operations Division of the War Department General Staff, 1943), 4.

207 BCT 17-3, After Action Report and Unit Journal (15–16 May 1943); RLG 17, After Action Report (17 May 1943).

208 BCT 17-3, After Action Report and Unit Journal (17–18 May 1943); RLG 17, After Action Report (18 May 1943).

209 RLG 17, After Action Report (19–21 May 43).

210 Paul Nobuo Tatsuguchi, 1; The Americans referred to Misuma Yama as 'Hill X'.

211 Paul Nobuo Tatsuguchi, 1; The claim of the American use of gas was carefully investigated at the direction of LTG Simon B. Buckner. It is probable that smoke rounds that were fired by the Americans to visually mark targets or to obscure friendly movements in the valley below were misidentified by the Japanese as chemical munitions.

212 Paul Nobuo Tatsuguchi, 'Diary', 1; captured.

213 Paul Nobuo Tatsuguchi, 'Diary', 1; captured; the '*Umanose*' or the Horse's Back referred to is Jarmin Pass; *Shitagata Dai* or *Shiba Dai* ('Grassy Knoll' in Japanese) was known as Hill X to the Americans.

214 Abraham H. Maslow, *A Theory of Human Motivation, Psychological Review* (1943), 50, 370–396.

215 Tyng, *et al*, *Action on Attu*, 3, 15.

216 Lynn D. Smith, *Preliminary Report On Attu Landings* (Presidio of San Francisco: Headquarters, Western Defense Command and Fourth Army, 30 May 1943), 20.

217 Lynn D. Smith, *Preliminary Report On Attu Landings* (Presidio of San Francisco: Headquarters, Western Defense Command and Fourth Army, 30 May 1943), 20.

218 Garfield, 201–202. Friction between the 7th Infantry Division staff and the Alaskan Defense Force staff caused logistical admonitions and advice given to go unheeded.

219 BCT 17-2, Observations made during and prior to operations on ATTU ISLAND, 13 June 1943, 3–4.

220 R.D. Orr, 'Report on Attu Operations, May 11–June 16, 1943', 30 July 1943, 84–86, 91–92.

221 R.D. Orr, 'Report on Attu Operations, May 11–June 16, 1943', dated 30 July 1943, 84–86; US Army Medical Department, Office of Medical History, Chapter V, 'The Aleutians', http://history.amedd.army.mil/booksdocs/wwii/ColdInjury/Chapter05.htm.

222 Walter Karig and Eric Purdon, 'Battle Report, Pacific War: Middle Phase', New York, Rinehart, 1977, 317; OCMH Collection World War II Pacific, File Folder – Aleutians Campaign.

223 Sewell Tyng, 'The Capture of Attu: As Told By The Men Who Fought There' (*The Infantry Journal*, Washington DC: War Department, October 1944, First Edition), Part Two: Interviews, 67–68.

224 Ibid.

225 Garfield, 201–202.

226 Ibid.

227 John Haile Cloe, *Attu: The Forgotten Battle* (Washington DC: National Park Service, 2017), 80.

228 Lynn D. Smith, *Preliminary Report On Attu Landings* (Presidio of San Francisco: Headquarters, Western Defense Command and Fourth Army, 30 May 1943), 20.

229 Garfield, 225, 232–233.

230 Charles Lynch, Frank Weed and Loy McAfee, *The Medical Department of the United States Army in the World War*, Volume 1 (Washington DC: Government Printing Office, 1923), 87.

231 McManus, *Grunts*, 120.

232 R.D. Orr, 'Report on Attu Operations, May 11–June 16, 1943', 30 July 1943, 84, 86.

233 RLG 17, Action Report (29–31 May 1943) and overlays, and Report of Operations-Attu (General Landrum's Report), 12–13.

234 Sewell Tyng, 'The Capture of Attu: As Told By The Men Who Fought There' (Washington DC: *The Infantry Journal*, United States War Department, 1944), 40.

235 Ibid., 42.

236 Wayne C. Zimmerman World War II papers, 1942–1944 (Archives and Special Collections, Consortium Library, University of Alaska Anchorage). Colonel Zimmerman describing the situation that he found on a leaders' reconnaissance on 17 May 1943.

237 General Orders Number 31: Headquarters, US Army Troops, APO 726 (Attu Landing Force), 1943; citation to accompany the Award of the Distinguished Service Cross to Lieutenant Colonel Wayne C. Zimmerman.

238 Paul Nobuo Tatsuguchi, 'Diary', captured, 2.

239 Kenneth E. Hamburger, *et al*, 'Leadership in Combat: An Historical Appraisal' (Unpublished Manuscript, Department of History, US

Military Academy, 1 January 1984; accessed from Defense Technical Information Center), 10.

240 Garfield, 245.

241 Paul Nobuo Tatsuguchi, 'Diary', captured, 2.

242 Louis J. Seaman, *The Real Triumph of Japan* (New York: D. Appleton and Co., 1909); 120–12.

243 Ibid.; Richard Gabriel and Karen Metz, *A History of Military Medicine: Volume II – From the Renaissance Through Modern Times* (New York: Greenwood Press, 1992), 225–226.

244 Sakurai, Tadayoshi, *Human Bullets, a Soldier's Story of Port Arthur*, Masajiro Honda (translator) and Alice Mabel Bacon (editor) (Boston: Houghton, Mifflin, and Company, 1907), 125, 215–226; Richard Connaughton, *Rising Sun and Tumbling Bear* (London: Cassell, 2007), 230–246; Michael Clodfelter, *Warfare and Armed Conflicts, A Statistical Reference: Volume II – 1900–91* (Jefferson, NC: McFarland and Company, 1992), 648.

245 Paul Nobuo Tatsuguchi, 'Diary', captured, 2.

246 Tyng, 'The Capture of Attu: As Told By The Men Who Fought There', 43–44.

247 Ibid., 44–45. It is unclear why there was such great fear of gas attack.

248 Ibid., 46–47.

249 Paul Nobuo Tatsuguchi, 'Diary', captured, 2. Apparently, this refers to MAJ Edward Smith and CPT Robert Edwards of 2nd Battalion, 17th Infantry Division. It is unclear how the Japanese came into possession of this document, but it demonstrates the value of exploiting combat intelligence.

250 Paul Nobuo Tatsuguchi, 'Diary', captured, 2.

251 Ibid.

252 Ibid., 50-52.

253 S.A. Stouffer, A.A. Lumsdaine, M.H. Lumsdaine, R.M. Williams Jr, M.B. Smith, I.L. Janis, S.A. Star and L.S. Cottrell Jr, *The American Soldier: Combat and its Aftermath. (Studies in Social Psychology in World War II)* (Princeton: Princeton University Press, 1949), 126.

254 McManus, *Grunts*,114.

255 Kenneth E. Hamburger, *et al*, 'Leadership in Combat: An Historical Appraisal' (Unpublished Manuscript, Department of History, US Military Academy, 1 January 1984; accessed from Defense Technical Information Center), 10.

256 'Mental Health Advisory Team 9 (MHAT 9) Report, Operation Enduring Freedom (OEF) 2013, Afghanistan', Office of The Surgeon General United States Army Medical Command and Office of the

Command Surgeon Headquarters, US Army Central Command (USCENTCOM), and Office of the Command Surgeon, US Forces Afghanistan (USFOR-A).

257 Ibid., 78–79.

258 Ibid.

259 Paul Nobuo Tatsuguchi, 'Diary', captured, 2.

260 *Action On Attu*, G2 Alaskan Defense Command, 30 July 1943, W.J. Verbeck, 20; (S-2 Journal, Headquarters RLG 17, 11 May–31 May 43).

261 Mark Rowe, 'Stickers for Nails: The Ongoing Transformation of Roles, Rites, and Symbols in Japanese Funerals' (Japanese Journal of Religious Studies, Nagoya, Japan: Nanzan Institute for Religion and Culture, 2000) 27 (3–4): 353–378, retrieved 13 September 2021.

262 Paul Nobuo Tatsuguchi, 'Diary', captured; (translators note: 1 *go*, 5 *shaku* is a measurement that equals 1.5 pounds), 2.

263 *Action on Attu*, 70.

264 Sewell Tyng, 'The Capture of Attu: As Told By The Men Who Fought There – Advancing on the Fish Hook-2', Sergeant Glenn E. Swearingen and Sergeant Earl L. Marks describe the heroism of Private First Class Joe P. Martinez, Medal of Honor recipient (Washington DC: The Infantry Journal, October 1944), 89.

265 Richard E. Matthews, *Attu Combat Diary*, personal diary written while the author was in hospital in summer 1943, updated in September 1980, published 23 April 1981, author's collection, 12.

266 Sewell Tyng, 'The Capture of Attu: As Told By The Men Who Fought There – The Attack on Buffalo Ridge', 97.

267 Ibid., 95.

268 Ibid., 96.

269 Ibid.

270 Ibid., 97.

271 Richard E. Matthews, *Attu Combat Diary*, 9, 11–12, Sergeant Matthews personally emerged successfully from a bayonet fight against two Japanese soldiers; unpublished memoir, author's collection.

272 Literal meaning: 'Ten Thousand Years for His Majesty!'

273 Paul Nobuo Tatsuguchi, 'Diary', captured, 3. The 'Edict' referred to is probably the *Senjinkun, the Imperial Rescript to Soldiers and Sailors*, etc.

274 W.H. Mapes, 'Action of BCT 17-2 on Attu Island, June 9, 1943', 6–7, Manoeuvre Center of Excellence Libraries, HQ Donovan Research Library, Fort Benning, Georgia.

275 Boyes, 9–10.

276 Ibid.

277 Private Second Class Ogawa Tamotsu, Allied Translator and Interpreter Section (ATIS), South West Pacific Area, 'ATIS Serial 545, Interrogation Report 395', 17.

278 Meiron and Susie Harries, *Soldiers of the Sun, The Rise and Fall of the Imperial Japanese Army* (New York: Random House, 1991), 324–325.

279 Paul Nobuo Tatsuguchi, 'Diary', captured, 4. If this was accurate, there would have been nobody remaining to conduct the *gyokusai*.

280 Anthony Bryant *Sekigahara 1600: The Final Struggle For Power*, Osprey Campaign Series 40. (Oxford: Osprey Publishing, 79); author's personal experience and understanding of the concept in *Judo* and *Nihon jujutsu* training.

281 Paul Nobuo Tatsuguchi, 'Diary', captured, 4. Original translators note: 'Enkist probably means Christ, since Dr Tatsuguchi returned to Japan as a Christian missionary.' *Chan* is an honourific term of endearment for children.

282 Sewell Tyng, 'The Capture of Attu: As Told By The Men Who Fought There – The Breakthrough', 102.

283 Ibid., 103.

284 Ibid., 103, 105. Garfield claims that the company received an order at 03.00 hours, 29 May 1943 to *march* (emphasis added) back to the battalion field kitchen for a hot meal, leaving only a few sentries behind. The Japanese attack subsequently blew through this undefended gap in the American lines. The eyewitness accounts in Tyng's book make no mention of why the withdrawal was ordered and do not characterise the company as marching back; they claim that they were making a tactical movement when the Japanese onslaught crashed into them.

285 Tyng, *Action on Attu*, 21.

286 George S. Blanchard, transcript of an oral history conducted by Lieutenant Colonel James Longhofer for 'Senior Officer Oral History Program', Box 1A of 9, George S. Blanchard Papers (The United States Army War College Archives, Carlisle Barracks), 78–79.

287 Sewell Tyng, 'The Capture of Attu: As Told By The Men Who Fought There – The Breakthrough', 104–107.

288 Ibid., 104. As a result of the deaths of key personnel and the loss or destruction of the official battalion headquarters records, much confusion over these events remains.

289 Ibid., 105.

290 Dean E. Galles Collection (AFC/2001/001/88536), Veterans' History Project, American Folklife Center, Library of Congress.

291 Ibid.

292 Tyng, 108–116.

293 Ibid., 108.

294 Boyes, *Short History of the Battle of Attu*, 10.

295 Mark Obmascik, *The Storm on Our Shores: One Island, Two Soldiers, and the Forgotten Battle of World War II* (New York: Simon & Schuster, 2019), 137–138.

296 Ibid., 139–151. He felt the tragedy that he had killed a man who never should have been in the fight at all.

297 Boyes, *Short History of the Battle of Attu*, 12.

298 Sewell Tyng, 'The Capture of Attu: As Told By The Men Who Fought There – The Aftermath', 139.

299 Stetson Conn, Rose C. Engelman and Byron Fairchild, *The United States Army in World War II: The Western Hemisphere, Guarding the United States and its Outposts, U.S. Army in World War II* (Washington DC: United States Army, Center of Military History, 2000), 295; George L. MacGarrigle, 'Aleutian Islands: The U.S. Army Campaigns of World War II', CMH Pub 72-6 (Washington DC: US Army Center of Military History, 1983), 24–25.

300 Garfield, 266–267.

301 Gordon H. McNeil, *History of the Medical Department in Alaska in World War II*, Chapter V, 'The Aleutians' (US Army Medical Department, Office of Medical History), 84, 401–407.

302 Brian Garfield. *The Thousand-Mile War: World War II in Alaska and the Aleutians* (Juneau: University of Alaska Press, 1995), 266.

303 Sewell Tyng, 'The Capture of Attu: As Told By The Men Who Fought There' (Washington DC: *The Infantry Journal*, United States War Department, 1944), 139.

304 Robert S. Rush, *GI: The US Infantryman in World War II* (Osceola: Osprey Publishing Ltd., 2003), 20.

305 John C. McManus, *The Deadly Brotherhood: The American Combat Soldier in World War II* (New York: Presidio Press, 1988), 4.

306 *Japanese Monograph Number 45: History of Imperial General Headquarters, Army Section (Revised Edition)*, Headquarters, United States Army, Japan, Assistant Chief of Staff, G-3, 1959, 22–23, 82–86; William J. Verbeck, 'Action on Attu: A Summary of Information of the Enemy Obtained During the Operations of the Force on Attu' (G-2 Alaska Defense Command, 30 July 1943), 45–51.

307 TM-E-30-480, 'Technical Manual: Handbook on Japanese Military Forces', War Department: Washington DC, 15 September 1944, 99–103.

308 'Combined Attu Reports on Japanese Warfare' from *Intelligence Bulletin*, Volume 2, Number 3 (Washington DC: United States War Department, 1944), 7.

309 Sewell Tyng, 'The Capture of Attu: As Told By The Men Who Fought There', *The Infantry Journal* (Washington DC: United States War Department, 1944) 165–166.

310 'Combined Attu Reports on Japanese Warfare' from *Intelligence Bulletin*, Volume 2, Number 3 (Washington DC: United States War Department, 1944), 8.

311 An excerpt from the diary of an unknown Japanese sergeant of a mountain artillery battery. The translation was done by 7th Infantry Division G-2. Throughout, it describes American air, mortar, and naval gunfire attacks but only mentions two soldiers being wounded. The diary ends on 27 May 1943, presumably due to this soldier's death (TokaiUniversitywebsite, accessed 20 March 2016), http://www.geocities.jp/torikai007/war/1943/attu.html also http://www.hlswilliwaw.com/aleutians/Attu/html/attu-japanese-nco-diary.htm.

312 William J. Verbeck, 'Action on Attu: A Summary of Information of the Enemy Obtained During the Operations of the Force on Attu' (G-2 Alaska Defense Command, 30 July 1943), 4, 16.

313 *U.S. Army Infantry Combat Pamphlet – Part Two: Attu, Tactical and Technical Trends Number 31, 12 August 1943* (Washington DC: Military Intelligence Service, War Department, 1943), 25–26.

314 *Combat Lessons Number 2, 'Rank and File in Combat: What They're Doing; How They Do It'*, Operations Division of the War Department General Staff, Washington DC, 1943, 5–8.

315 Ibid.

316 Verbeck, *Action on Attu*, 30 July 1943, 4, 11, 13; English, 16–18; M. Hamlin Cannon, *Leyte: The Return to the Philippines* (Washington DC: US Army Center of Military History, 1954), 211.

317 Matthews, 12.

318 S.A. Stouffer, A.A. Lumsdaine, M.H. Lumsdaine, R.M. Williams Jr, M.B. Smith, I.L. Janis, S.A. Star and L.S. Cottrell Jr, *The American Soldier: Combat and its Aftermath. (Studies in Social Psychology in World War II)* (Princeton: Princeton University Press, 1949), 3–4.

319 Ibid., Table 7, 126.

320 Ibid., 127, 180.

321 Ibid., 142, 156.

322 Kenneth E. Hamburger, *et al*, 'Leadership in Combat: An Historical Appraisal' (Unpublished Manuscript, Department of History, US Military Academy, 1 January 1984; accessed from Defense Technical Information Center), 1–2, 8–10.

323 Keith Ewbank, 'Observer Report on Attu Action', 14 August 1943, National Archives and Records Administration, College Park, Maryland, 7; S.L.A. Marshall, *Men Against Fire: The Problem of Battle Command in*

Future War (Washington: Infantry Journal; New York: William Morrow, 1947), 22–23, 55–57.

324 Kenneth E. Hamburger, *et al*, 'Leadership in Combat: An Historical Appraisal' (Unpublished Manuscript, Department of History, US Military Academy, 1 January 1984; accessed from Defense Technical Information Center), 8, 9.

325 Ralph Eyde, personal letter dated 28 September 1943; 'Brothers in Arms', *The Washington Post*, Dan Lamothe, 6 December 2017, accessed January 2018.

326 *Combat Lessons Number 2, 'Rank and File in Combat: What They're Doing; How They Do It'*, Operations Division of the War Department General Staff, Washington DC, 1943, 5–8; Verbeck, *Action on Attu*, 30 July 1943, 4, 11, 13; English, 16–18; M. Hamlin Cannon, *Leyte: The Return to the Philippines* (Washington DC: US Army Center of Military History, 1954), 211.

327 Keene, Donald, 'Foreword', *In The Breaking Jewel*, Oda Makoto (New York: Columbia University Press, 2003), VII–XIV. The term comes from an ancient Chinese text, *The History of North Qi*; 'A great man might as well die as a jewel shatters; he cannot be like a tile left untouched.' Accessed 6 January 2021, DOI:10.7312/oda-12612.3.

328 Drea, *Japan's Imperial Army*, 231; John W. Dower, *War Without Mercy: Race and Power in the Pacific War* (New York: Pantheon, 1986), 231.

329 John Dower, *War Without Mercy: Race & Power in the Pacific War* (New York: Pantheon Books, 1986), 184, 231.

330 Cloe, 160.

331 John Dower, *War Without Mercy: Race & Power in the Pacific War* (New York: Pantheon Books, 1986), 231–232.

332 The Imperial General Headquarters official announcement of the Attu *gyokusai*, http://www.asahi-net.or.jp/~un3k-mn/gyoku-at tu.htm, *emphasis added.*

333 Benedict, 121–125.

334 United States National Archives and Records Administration, College Park, MD, RG 165, War Department, 'P' File, Box 2313, MIS, *Tactical and Technical Trends, Number 10*, 'Japanese Prisoners of War', 22 October 1942; U. Straus, *The Anguish of Surrender: Japanese POWs of World War II* (Seattle: Washington UP, 2003), 51-52; RG 165, War Department, 'P' File, Box 321, ATIS, POW Interrogation Report Number 29, M. Yamaguchi, 1 February 1943; RG 165, War Department, 'P' File, Box 321, ATIS, POW Interrogation Report Number 54, R. Inagaki, 14 April 1943.

335 Yamakuse Yoji, *Japaneseness: A Guide to Virtues and Values* (Berkeley: Stone Bridge Press, 2016), 89–91.

336 Helen Craig McCullough, *The Tale of the Heike* (Stanford: Stanford University Press, 1988), 21.

337 RG 165, War Department, 'P' File, Box 403, Combat Intelligence Center South Pacific Area, Item Number 239, Supplement Number 1, War Diary Captured at Guadalcanal, Owner: Second Lieutenant Hiroshi Yokota (*Inouye* Unit), 18 February to 22 October 1942

338 Stouffer, *et al*, 107.

339 Otomo no Yakamochi (716–785 CE), poem 4094 in the *Man'yoshu* ('Collection of Ten Thousand Leaves'), from the eighth Century; the oldest extant anthology of Japanese poetry, quoted in Hiroaki Sato, *Legends of the* Samurai (New York: Overlook Press, 1995), 17–18.

340 Emiko Ohnuki-Tierney, *Kamikaze, Cherry Blossoms, and Nationalisms: The Militarization of Aesthetics in Japanese History* (Chicago: University of Chicago Press, 2002), plate 7.

341 Yamakuse, 90.

342 Emanuele Castano and Mark Dechesne, 'On Defeating Death: Group Reification and Social Identification as Immortality Strategies', European Review of Social Psychology, 16:1, 2005, 221–255, DOI: 10.1080/10463280500436024.

343 Algernon Bertram Freeman-Mitford, Lord Redesdale, *Tales of Old Japan* (London: University of Michigan, 1871), 5–6, 28–34.

344 Eiko Ikegami, *The Taming of the* Samurai*: Honorific Individualism and the Making of Modern Japan* (Cambridge: Harvard University, 1997), 223; James Murdoch, *A History of Japan: Volume III – The Tokugawa Epoch (1652–1868)* (New York: Greenberg, 1926), 218; Hiroaki Sato, *Legends of the* Samurai (Woodstock: Overlook, 1995), 17–18.

345 RG 165, War Department, G-2 Regional File, Box 2147, File 6675, Far Eastern Branch, MIS, *Training in the Japanese Army*, 30 September 1942; Romaji Desu: Japanese Language Dictionary and Translator, s.v. 'seishin' accessed 2 March 2021, http://www.romajidesu.com.

346 Merriam-Webster.com Dictionary, s.v. 'kami', accessed 2 March 2021, https://www.merriam-webster.com/dictionary/kami.

347 Sato Hiroaki, '*Gyokusai*' or 'Shattering like a Jewel: Reflection on the Pacific War', *The Asia-Pacific Journal*, 1 February 2008, Volume 6, Issue 2.

Chapter Three: The Battle of Kwajalein, the *Samurai* Legacy and the Myth of *Bushidō*

348 Ralph Eyde, personal letter dated 28 February 1944; 'Brothers in Arms', *The Washington Post*, Dan Lamothe, 6 December 2017, accessed January 2018.

349 Philip A. Crowl and Edmund G. Love, *Seizure of the Gilberts and Marshalls: United States Army in World War II, The War in the Pacific*, CMH Pub 5-6 (Washington DC: Office of the Chief of Military History, 1955), 210.

350 Samuel Eliot Morison, *History of United States Naval Operations in World War II: Aleutians, Gilberts and Marshalls, June 1942–April 1944* (Champaign: University of Illinois Press, 2001), 236.

351 Kent G. Budge, 'Kwajalein', http://pwencycl.kgbudge.com; The Pacific War Online Encyclopedia, retrieved 19 March 2021.

352 G. Rottman, The Marshall Islands 1944: 'Operation Flintlock, The Capture of Kwajalein and Eniwetok' (Oxford: Osprey Publishing Ltd, 2004), 7, 11; John C. McManus, *Island Infernos: The U.S. Army's Pacific War Odyssey, 1944* (New York: Dutton Caliber, 2021), 35.

353 'Where is Kwajalein?', *Global Associates Welcomes You to Kwajalein Marshall Islands* (Kwajalein: Marshall Islands, 1968), 5.

354 Love, 106.

355 Ibid.; James A. Walker, Lewis Bernstein and Sharon Lang, *The Eastern Mandates Campaign: A Staff Ride Guide for Operation Flintlock, The Seizure of Kwajalein*, US Army Space and Missile Defense Command, Huntsville, AL, 2004, 25, 34.

356 Philip A. Crowl, Edmund G. Love, *Seizure of the Gilberts and Marshalls: United States Army in World War II, The War in the Pacific*, CMH Pub 5-6 (Washington DC: Office of the Chief of Military History, 1955), 210; Walker, *Staff Ride Guide*, 37–39.

357 Ibid., 212; US Strategic Bombing Survey (USSBS), *The Campaigns of the Pacific War*, 201–202.

358 McManus, *Island Infernos*, 35.

359 Love, 106.

360 Myers, *Handbook of the League of Nations*, 378; IPS Document 6257, 13; IMTFE Defense Document 1518, 4–5.

361 Love, 106.

362 Love, 106.

363 James A. Walker, Lewis Bernstein, Sharon Lang, *The Eastern Mandates Campaign: A Staff Ride Guide for Operation Flintlock, The Seizure of Kwajalein*, US Army Space and Missile Defense Command, Huntsville, AL, 2004, 32–34.

364 McManus, *Island Infernos*, 7, 40.

365 McManus, 40–41, quoting Ernest Bears, personal account of a battalion commander, *Hourglass Newsletter*, 1993, 12, US Army Military History Institute (USAMHI).

366 Commander, Joint Expeditionary Force Report of FLINTLOCK Operation, Enclosure (B), Intelligence Report, 2; Morison, *History, vol 7: Aleutians, Gilberts, and Marshalls*, 343–351.

367 Commander, Joint Expeditionary Force Report of FLINTLOCK Operation, Enclosure (B), Intelligence Report, 15–18; Love, *Seizure of the Gilberts and Marshalls*,187–189.

368 Love, 107; Walker, *Staff Ride Guide*, 34.

369 Marshall, *Island Victory*, 138.

370 McManus, *Island Infernos*, 41, quoting from a letter, MG Charles H. Corlett to the Commandant of the Marine Corps, 14 January 1953, Record Group 319, Entry 62, Box 1, Charles Corlett Papers, Records of the Office of the Chief of Military History, 'Seizure of the Gilberts and Marshalls, 7th Infantry Division, Participation in Flintlock Operation', US Army Military History Institute (USAMHI), Carlisle PA.

371 Love, 108.

372 Ibid., 107.

373 Ibid., 108.

374 Kent Roberts Greenfield (Editor), *United States Army in World War II, Pictorial Record: The War Against Japan* (Washington DC: The US Army Center of Military History, 1952), 220–222.

375 See among others *U.S. Army Infantry Combat Pamphlet – Part Two: Attu, Tactical and Technical Trends Number 31, 12 August 1943; Number 32, 26 August 1943; No. 33, 9 September 1943.* Military Intelligence Services, War Department, Washington DC, 1943.

376 *Combat Lessons No. 2, 'Rank and File in Combat: What They're Doing; How They Do It'*, Operations Division of the War Department General Staff, Washington DC, 1943.

377 United States Army in World War II, *Pictorial Record: The War Against Japan* (Washington DC: The US Army Center of Military History, 1952), 220–222.

378 Edmund G. Love, *The Hourglass: A History of the 7th Infantry Division in World War II* (Washington DC: Infantry Journal Press, 1950), 110–112; referring to the duplex drive truck (DUKW) and the amphibious landing vehicle (LVT).

379 Dean Galles, oral history interview, August 12, 2007, AFC/2001/001/76663, Veterans' History Project, Library of Congress, Washington DC.

380 Philip A. Crowl, Edmund G. Love, *Seizure of the Gilberts and Marshalls: United States Army in World War II The War in the Pacific*, CMH Pub 5–6 (Washington DC: Office of the Chief of Military History, 1955), 219.

381 Edgar H. Schein, *Organizational Culture and Leadership* (San Francisco: Jossey-Bass, 2010), 225, 245, 291–292.

382 McManus, *Island Infernos*, 40–42; quoting Charles H. Corlett memo, 9 January 1942, Box 1, Charles Corlett Papers, Records of the Office of the Chief of Military History, 'Seizure of the Gilberts and Marshalls, 7th Infantry Division, Participation in Flintlock Operation', US Army Military History Institute (USAMHI), Carlisle PA.

383 McManus, *Island Infernos*, 36; James A. Walker, Lewis Bernstein, Sharon Lang, *The Eastern Mandates Campaign: A Staff Ride Guide for Operation*

Flintlock, The Seizure of Kwajalein, US Army Space and Missile Defense Command, Huntsville, AL, 2004, 32–34; G. Rottman, *The Marshall Islands 1944*: 'Operation Flintlock, The Capture of Kwajalein and Eniwetok' (Oxford: Osprey Publishing Ltd, 2004), 7, 9–11.

384 McManus, *Island Infernos*, 36.

385 War Department Technical Manual E 30-480, 'Handbook on Japanese Military Forces', 1 June 1945, Chapter VII, Part III, 64–68.

386 Crowl and Love, *Gilberts and Marshalls*, CMH Pub 5-6-1, 212.

387 Commander, Joint Expeditionary Force Report of FLINTLOCK Operation, 25 February 1944, Enclosure (B), Intelligence Report, 15–18.

388 Love, 107.

389 Ibid.

390 Commander, Joint Expeditionary Force Report of FLINTLOCK Operation, Enclosure (B), Intelligence Report, 16–17.

391 Crowl and Love, *Gilberts and Marshalls*, CMH Pub 5-6-1, 212, quoted in US Strategic Bombing Survey (USSBS), Naval Analysis Division, 'Interrogations of Japanese Officials, Volume I, Interrogation of Commander Nakajima Chikataka, IJN' (Washington D.C., 1946), 143–44.

392 James A. Walker, Lewis Bernstein and Sharon Lang, *The Eastern Mandates Campaign: A Staff Ride Guide for Operation Flintlock, The Seizure of Kwajalein*, US Army Space and Missile Defense Command, Huntsville, AL, 2004, 32–34.

393 Ibid., 34; Commander, Joint Expeditionary Force Report of FLINTLOCK Operation, Enclosure (B), Intelligence Report, 16.

394 Commander, Joint Expeditionary Force Report of FLINTLOCK Operation, Enclosure (B), Intelligence Report, 16.

395 Love, 112.

396 Commander, Joint Expeditionary Force Report of FLINTLOCK Operation, Enclosure (B), Intelligence Report, 15, 18.

397 Love, 113-118.

398 Commander, Joint Expeditionary Force Report of FLINTLOCK Operation, Enclosure (B), Intelligence Report, 2, 15–18.

399 James Hornfischer, *The Fleet at Flood Tide: America at Total War in the Pacific, 1944–1945* (New York: Random House, 2016), 18; Ian Toll, *The Conquering Tide: War in the Pacific Islands, 1942–1944* (New York: W.W. Norton, 2015), 413–414.

400 Morison, *History of U.S. Naval Operations in World War II: Volume VII – Aleutians, Gilberts and Marshalls*, 237.

401 Morison, *History of U.S. Naval Operations in World War II: Volume VII – Aleutians, Gilberts and Marshalls*, 238.

402 Love, *The Hourglass*, 119–120.

403 Ibid., 123.

404 Marshall, *Island Victory*, 103, 127–129; Love, *The Hourglass*, 128–131.

405 Love, *The Hourglass*, 131–136.

406 Love, *The Hourglass*, 138.

407 Love, *The Hourglass*, 138–139.

408 Love, *The Hourglass*, 139–140; Walker, Bernstein, Lang, *The Eastern Mandates Campaign: A Staff Ride Guide for Operation FLINTLOCK; The Seizure of Kwajalein Atoll*, 72.

409 Love, 141.

410 McManus, *Island Infernos*, 52; Major Clark Campbell, 'The Operations of the First Battalion (Reinforced) 184th Infantry, 7th Infantry Division in the Capture of Kwajalein Atoll, 31 January–6 February 1944 (Personal experiences of a Battalion Operations Officer), 6–8, 17–18, 26; Advanced Infantry Officers Course, 1947–1948, The Infantry School, Donovan Research Library, Fort Benning, GA.

411 Love, 141–142.

412 Marshall, 21, 140; Love, 145–149, McManus, 51.

413 Marshall, *Island Victory*, 141; Love, *The Hourglass*, 151.

414 Love, *The Hourglass*, 145–155.

415 Love, *The Hourglass*, 157–159,161–163; Marshall, *Island Victory*, 163.

416 G-2 Periodic Report 5, 4 February 1944, G-2 Report of Operations (7th Infantry Division FLINTLOCK Report, Volume IV). Detailed reports from the Japanese records on Kwajalein from 31 January–4 February 1944 are virtually nonexistent. The only information found dealing with Akiyama's death is given above. He was reported as having been killed by the bombardment on 31 January 1944.

417 Love, *The Hourglass*, 172; Marshall, *Island Victory*, 189.

418 Love, *The Hourglass*, 194; Morison, *History of U.S. Naval Operations in World War II: Volume VII – Aleutians, Gilberts and Marshalls*, 256.

419 McManus, *Island Infernos*, 54, quoting Dean Galles, oral history interview, 12 August 2007, AFC/2001/001/76663, Veterans' History Project, Library of Congress, Washington DC.

420 McManus, *Island Infernos*, 55, quoting Franklin Shermer III, Oral History, June 2, 1944, Record Group 112, Entry 302, Surgeon General, inspections Branch, Box 219, Interview 74.

421 Edgar H. Schein, *Organizational Culture and Leadership*, fourth edition (Jossey-Bass Business and Management, 2010), 18, 24.

422 Christopher Goto-Jones, 'The Way of Revering the Emperor: Imperial Philosophy and *Bushidō* in Modern Japan', *The Emperors of Modern Japan*,

Ben-Ami Shilony (editor) (Leiden and Boston: Brill, 2008), 23; quoting Itō Enkichi, *Kokutai no hongi* (Tokyo: Mombushō, 1937), 110–111.

423 *Bushidō* is frequently translated as the 'way of the warrior' or 'the way of the *samurai*'.

424 Nitobe Inazo, *Bushidō: The Soul of Japan* (Tokyo: Kenkyusha, 1939), 98.

425 Oleg Benesch, *Inventing the Way of the* Samurai*: Nationalism, Internationalism, and Bushidō in Modern Japan* (Oxford: Oxford University Press, 2014), 1–3, 5.

426 Morgan, 64; Friday, 340.

427 Friday, 340.

428 Cameron Hurst III, 'Death, Honor, and Loyalty: The *Bushidō* Ideal', in *Philosophy East & West*, 40:4 (1990), 511–527; Karl Friday, '*Bushidō* or Bull? A Medieval Historian's Perspective on the Imperial Army and the Japanese Warrior Tradition', in *The History Teacher*, 27:3 (1994), 339–349.

429 Benesch, 5.

430 Benesch, 8, 247. Basil Hall Chamberlain referred to it in 1912 as an example of the 'invention of a religion'.

431 Mark Ravina, *To Stand with the Nations of the World: Japan's Meiji Restoration in World History* (Oxford: Oxford University Press, 2018), 6–12.

432 Ronald Toby, 'Rescuing the Nation from History: The State of the State in Early Modern Japan', *Monumenta Nipponica* 56:2 (2001), 201.

433 Mark Ravina, *To Stand with the Nations of the World: Japan's Meiji Restoration in World History* (Oxford: Oxford University Press, 2018), 5–11, 13.

434 Ibid., 7–8.

435 Benesch, 12, 148.

436 Ikegami Eiko. *The Taming of the* Samurai*: Honorific Individualism and the Making of Modern Japan* (Cambridge, MA: Harvard University Press, 1995), 111.

437 Karl Friday, '*Bushidō* or Bull: A Medieval Historian's Perspective on the Imperial Army and the Japanese Warrior Tradition', Society for History Education, Volume 27, Issue 3 (May 1994): 339-349.

438 Cameron Hurst III, 'Death, Honor, and Loyalty: The *Bushidō* Ideal', in Philosophy East & West, 40:4 (1990), 511–527; Karl Friday, '*Bushidō* or Bull? A Medieval Historian's Perspective on the Imperial Army and the Japanese Warrior Tradition', in The History Teacher, 27:3 (1994), 339–349.

439 Eric J. Hobsbawm and Terence Ranger, 'Mass Producing Traditions: Europe 1870–1914', *The Invention of Tradition* (Cambridge: Cambridge University Press, 1983), 9, 263–307.

440 Bonner F. Fellers, *Psychology of the Japanese Soldier, Part 1* (Washington DC: BiblioGov Project, 2012.) Originally Published 1936, 22.

441 Morgan, 65; Robert N. Bellah, *Tokugawa Religion: The Values of Pre-Industrial Japan* (Boston: Beacon Press, 1957), 87, 155.

442 Benesch, 7; Forrest E. Morgan, *Compellence and the Strategic Culture of Imperial Japan: Implications for Coercive Diplomacy in the Twenty-First Century* (Westport and London: Praeger Publishers, 2003), 69.

443 Benesch, 87.

444 Sato Hiroaki, *Legends of the* Samurai (New York: Overlook Press, 1995), 322–325.

445 Benesch, 87.

446 Yamamoto Tsunetomo, William Scott Wilson (translator), *Hagakure* (Tokyo: Kodansha International, 1979), 30.

447 Forrest E. Morgan, *Compellence and the Strategic Culture of Imperial Japan: Implications for Coercive Diplomacy in the Twenty-First Century* (Westport and London: Praeger Publishers, 2003), 10.

448 Meirion and Susie Harries, *Soldiers of the Sun: The Rise and Fall of the Imperial Japanese Army*, 7

449 Benesch, 244–245; Ravina, *To Stand with the Nations of the World: Japan's Meiji Restoration in World History*, 13.

450 Roger H. Brown, 'Yasuoka Masahiro's "New Discourse on *Bushidō* Philosophy": Cultivating *Samurai* Spirit and Men of Character for Imperial Japan', *Social Science Japan Journal*, Volume 16, Number 1,115, 2013; Advance Access publication December 6, 2012, DOI: 10.1093/ssjj/jys021.

451 Roger H. Brown, 'Yasuoka Masahiro's "New Discourse on *Bushidō* Philosophy": Cultivating *Samurai* Spirit and Men of Character for Imperial Japan', *Social Science Japan Journal*, Volume 16, Number 1,107–129, 2013; Advance Access publication 6 December 2012, DOI: 10.1093/ssjj/jys021.

452 Brown, 116.

453 Sakurai, Tadayoshi, *Human Bullets, a Soldier's Story of Port Arthur*, Masajiro Honda (translator) and Alice Mabel Bacon (editor) (Boston: Houghton, Mifflin, and Company, 1907), 214–215.

454 Ibid., 255.

455 Morgan, 65; Benedict, 22–23.

456 Benesch, 76.

457 Sakurai, 216.

458 Sakurai, Tadayoshi, *Human Bullets, a Soldier's Story of Port Arthur*, Masajiro Honda (translator) and Alice Mabel Bacon (editor) (Boston: Houghton, Mifflin, and Company, 1907), 232.

459 Ibid., x.

460 Edward J. Drea, *Japan's Imperial Army: Its Rise and Fall, 1853–1945* (Lawrence: University Press of Kansas, 2009), 156-157.

461 Ibid.

462 Leland Ness, *Rikugun: Guide to Japanese Ground Forces, 1937–1945* (Solihull: Helion and Company, 2014), 14-15.

463 Edward J. Drea, *Japan's Imperial Army: Its Rise and Fall, 1853–1945* (Lawrence: University Press of Kansas, 2009), 156–157.

464 Drea, *In Service of the Emperor*, 73, 120.

465 Ibid., 69.

466 Ibid., 70–71.

467 Aaron William Moore, *Writing War: Soldiers Record the Japanese Empire* (Cambridge, Massachusetts and London, England: Harvard University Press, 2013), 31.

468 Arthur Swinson, *Four* Samurai*: A Quartet of Japanese Army Commanders in the Second World War* (London: Huchinson, 1968), 15.

469 Drea, *Japan's Imperial Army*, 158.

470 Edward J. Drea, *In Service of the Emperor: Essays on the Imperial Japanese Army* (Lincoln: University of Nebraska, 1998), 13.

471 *Japanese Monograph Number 45: History of Imperial General Headquarters, Army Section (Revised Edition)*, Headquarters, United States Army, Japan, Assistant Chief of Staff, G-3, 1959, 22–23.

472 Drea, *Japan's Imperial Army*, 158.

473 Kotani Ken, 'Japanese Intelligence in WWII: Successes and Failures', 10, 19, 22; 'American and British Tactics – As Viewed by the Japanese' from *Tactical and Technical Trends, Number 14, 17 December 17 1942*, US Military Intelligence Service; Edward J. Drea, *In Service of the Emperor: Essays on the Imperial Japanese Army* (Lincoln: University of Nebraska, 1998), 1, 13, 18.

474 *Tactical and Technical Trends, Number 32, 26 August 1943*, Military Intelligence Service, War Department, Washington DC 26–28.

475 *U.S. Army Infantry Combat Pamphlet – Part Two: Attu, Tactical and Technical Trends Number 31, 12 August 1943* (Washington DC: Military Intelligence Service, War Department, 1943), 25–26.

476 *Tactical and Technical Trends, Number 31, 12 Aug 1943*), 26–27.

477 G-2 Report of Operations (7th Infantry Division FLINTLOCK Report, Volume IV), 6.

478 Fred L. Borch, *Military Trials of War Criminals in the Netherlands East Indies, 1946–1949*. (Oxford: Oxford University Press, 2017), 31–32.

479 Benesch, 7.

480 Meirion and Susie Harries, *Soldiers of the Sun: The Rise and Fall of the Imperial Japanese Army*, 7.

481 Benesch, 193; John Toland, *The Rising Sun: The Decline and Fall of the Japanese Empire 1936–1945* (New York: Random House, 1970), 444.

482 Sato Hiroaki, '*Gyokusai*' or 'Shattering like a Jewel: Reflection on the Pacific War', *The Asia-Pacific Journal*, 1 February 2008, Volume 6, Issue 2, 1,5.

483 Forrest E. Morgan, *Compellence and the Strategic Culture of Imperial Japan: Implications for Coercive Diplomacy in the Twenty-First Century* (Westport and London: Praeger Publishers, 2003), 235.

484 Yamamoto Tsunetomo, *Hagakure: The Book of the* Samurai, William Scott Wilson (translator) (Tokyo: Kodansha International, 1992), 29–30.

485 Harries, *Soldiers*, 323.

486 Benesch, 107–109.

487 Nishida Kitaro, *Intelligibility, and the Philosophy of Nothingness: Three Philosophical Essays*, Robert Shinzinger (translator) (Honolulu: East-West Press, 1958), 34–36. Nishida discusses the death of the ego-self.

488 Harries, *Soldiers of the Sun, The Rise and Fall of the Imperial Japanese Army*, 336.

489 David C. Earhart, *Certain Victory: Images of World War II in the Japanese Media* (London: Routledge, 2008), 400–401; S.K. Maynard, *Japanese Communication: Language and Thought in Context* (Honolulu: University of Hawaii Press, 1997), 30, 37, 43; Morgan, 61, 63, 227–228.

490 John Dower, *War Without Mercy: Race and Power in the Pacific War* (New York: Pantheon, 1987), 68; Beatrice Trefalt, *Japanese Army Stragglers and Memories of the War in Japan, 1950–1975* (London: RoutledgeCurzon, 2003), 21.

491 Morgan, 69, 232, 235.

492 Benesch, 242–243.

493 Connable, *et al*, 'Will to Fight: Returning to the Human Fundamentals of War', RAND, 2019, xiii–xvi, 13.

494 Ibid.

495 Connable, *et al*, 'Will to Fight: Returning to the Human Fundamentals of War', RAND, 2019, xiv, xvi, 13.

496 Warren F. Kimball, 'Franklin D. Roosevelt and World War II', Presidential Studies Quarterly 34, Number 1 (2004): 83–99. http://www.jstor.org/stable/27552565; Robert Dallek, *Franklin D. Roosevelt and American Foreign Policy, 1932–1945*, second edition (New York: Oxford University Press, 1995), 259, 284–285, 541, 545.

497 Moore, *Writing War*, 207. Observation in the diary of an American officer on 11 November 1942.

498 S.A. Stouffer, A.A. Lumsdaine, M.H. Lumsdaine, R.M. Williams Jr, M.B. Smith, I.L. Janis, S.A. Star and L.S. Cottrell Jr, *The American Soldier: Combat and its Aftermath (Studies in Social Psychology in World War II)* (Princeton: Princeton University Press, 1949), 108–112.

499 See Abraham H. Maslow, *Toward a Psychology of Being* (New York: Van Nostrand Reinhold, 1968); John Ellis, *The Sharp End: The Fighting Man in World War II* (New York: Scribner's, 1980), 282, 315–316; Michael Doubler, *Closing With the Enemy*, and John McManus, *The Deadly Brotherhood*); Stephen E. Ambrose, *Citizen Soldiers: The US Army from the Normandy Battlefields to the Bulge to the Surrender of Germany, June 7, 1944–May 7, 1945* (New York: Touchstone, Simon and Schuster, 1997), 14, 473; see also on primary group cohesion theory, Primary Group Cohesion theory, Edward Shils and Morris Janowitz, 'Cohesion and Disintegration in the Wehrmacht in WWII' POQ 12 (1948), 280–315.

500 Connable, *et al*, 'Will to Fight: Returning to the Human Fundamentals of War', RAND Research Brief 10040-A (Santa Monica, CA: RAND Corporation, 2019), xvii, xiii–xvi, https://doi.org/10.7249/RB10040.

501 Morgan, 61, 63, 227–228.

502 Ikegami Eiko. *The Taming of the* Samurai: *Honorific Individualism and the Making of Modern Japan* (Cambridge, MA: Harvard University Press, 1995), 111.

503 Samuel P. Huntington, *Who Are We? The Challenges to America's National Identity* (New York: Simon and Schuster, 2004), xv, 41, 60–61, 68.

504 William Tyler Page, 'The American's Creed', accepted as a resolution by the United States House of Representatives on 3 April 1918, https://www.ushistory.org, Historic Documents, 'The Americans Creed', https://www.ushistory.org/documents/creed.htm, retrieved 18 September 2022.

505 Franklin D. Roosevelt, Annual Message to Congress (State of the Union Address), 6 January 1941.

506 Charles A. Moskos, *The American Enlisted Man: The Rank and File in Today's Military* (New York: Russell Sage Foundation, 1970), 147; Stouffer *et al*, Volume I, 437.

507 Tania M. Chacho, *Why Did They Fight? American Airborne Units in World War II*, Defence Studies, Fall 2001, 1:3, 86, DOI: 10.1080/714000045.

508 Daniel Coyle, *The Culture Code: The Secrets of Highly Successful Groups* (New York: Bantam, 2018).

509 Harold G. Moore, *We Were Soldiers Once … and Young: Ia Drang-The Battle That Changed the War in Vietnam* (New York: Random House, 1992), ii. Quoted from memory, speech to officers at the US Army Command and General Staff College, 1995.

510 Ralph Eyde, personal letter dated 24 February 1944; 'Brothers in Arms', *The Washington Post*, Dan Lamothe, 6 December 2017, accessed January 2018.

511 Schein, *Organizational Culture and Leadership*, 24, 32.

512 Schein, *Organizational Culture and Leadership*, 16–29

513 Ibid., 21.

514 Ibid., 17–18.

515 Robert S. Rush, *Hell in Hürtgen Forest: The Ordeal and Triumph of an American Infantry Regiment* (Lawrence: University Press of Kansas, 2001), 310.

Chapter Four: The Battle of Leyte and the Influence of the *Senjinkun* on Japanese Strategic Culture

516 'Come home in death' (*Shinde kaere*) paraphrased means to, 'Fight with resolve to die on the battlefield and come home only as a soul.' From 'The Song of Bivouac' (*Roei no Uta*), Shigure Otowa, *Nihon Kayoshu* (Shakai Shiso Sha, 1963), 295. Quoted by Sato Hiroaki in '*Gyokusai*' or 'Shattering like a Jewel: Reflection on the Pacific War', *The Asia-Pacific Journal*, 1 February 2008, Volume 6, Issue 2.

517 Japanese Monograph 4, Philippine Operations Record, Phase III, July–November 1944, Preparations made by the 14th Area Army for the Military Operations in the Philippine Islands, fifty pages, unpaginated, Historical Section, G2, FEC, Office of the Chief of Military History, Oct 1946; John C. McManus, *Island Infernos: The U.S. Army's Pacific War Odyssey, 1944* (New York: Dutton Caliber, 2021), 467–468, 471.

518 Nathan N. Prefer, *Leyte, 1944: The Soldier's Battle* (Havertown: CASEMATE PUBLISHERS, 2019),1-3; McManus, 470-471.

519 Edmund G. Love, *The Hourglass: A History of the 7th Infantry Division in World War II*, 204–205.

520 Ibid.

521 Love, *The Hourglass*, 200–201.

522 McManus, 471, 498; Prefer, 2, 73; 'Japanese Monograph 4, Philippine Operations Record, Phase III, July-November 1944, Preparations made by the 14th Area Army for the Military Operations in the Philippine Islands', Historical Section, G2, FEC, Office of the Chief of Military History, Oct 1946, 11-12.

523 Francis C. Steckel, 'Morale Problems in Combat: American Soldiers in Europe in World War II', *Army History*, summer 1994, Number 31 (summer 1994), US Army Center of Military History, 1–8. URL: https://www.jstor.org/stable/26304183; William J. McConnell, WWII Survey; United States Forces, European Theater, Reports of the General Board, Number 3, 'Reinforcement System and Reinforcement Procedures in the European Theater of Operations', 18.

524 Samuel E. Stouffer, *et al*, *Studies in the Social Psychology in World War II: Volume 2 – The American Soldier: Combat and Its Aftermath* (Princeton: Princeton University Press, 1949), 130–149; Steckel, 4.

525 William J. McConnell, 'WWII Survey; United States Forces, European Theater, Reports of the General Board' (Hereafter GB Report), Number 4, 'Leaves' 1–2, 7–8, 9; Steckel, 6.

526 Love, *The Hourglass*, 197–198.

527 'Sixth Army, Report of Leyte Operation, 20 October–25 December 1944', 24–25 (AAR), Record Group 407, Entry 1113, Philippines Archive Collection, Box 1478, National Archives; 'Operation Report, 7th Infantry Division, King II', MCoE HQ Donovan Research Library, Fort Benning, GA. Documents collection. Call: D793.32 .U307, 3.

528 'Operation Report, 7th Infantry Division, King II', 3; Prefer, 207.

529 'Operation Report, 7th Infantry Division, King II', MCoE HQ Donovan Research Library, Fort Benning, GA. Documents collection. Call: D793.32. U307, 1.

530 'Japanese Monograph 4, Philippine Operations Record, Phase III, July–November 1944, Preparations made by the 14th Area Army for the Military Operations in the Philippine Islands', Historical Section, G2, FEC, Office of the Chief of Military History, October 1946, 45–46.

531 Ibid.

532 Ooka Shohei, *Taken Captive: A Japanese POW's Story*, Wayne P. Lammers (editors and translators) (New York: John Wiley & Sons, 1996), 136, 149.

533 Ibid.

534 Prefer, 64, 73.

535 'Japanese Monograph 4, Philippine Operations Record, Phase III, July-November 1944, Preparations made by the 14th Area Army for the Military Operations in the Philippine Islands', Historical Section, G2, FEC, Office of the Chief of Military History, October 1946, 1–6.

536 McManus, 499; Prefer, 64, 73.

537 Japanese Monograph 4, 22.

538 Love, 213.

539 Ibid.

540 Love, 212-214.

541 Prefer, 51-52; Love, 215.

542 'King II Report'', 3.

543 Prefer, *Leyte*, 41, 54, 80–82.

544 'King II Report', 4; Love, 215. M. Hamlin Cannon, *Leyte: The Return to the Philippines, U.S. Army in World War II*, 'The War in the Pacific, Chapter VIII, Southern Leyte Valley: Part II', 128, 135; Interrogation of Private

Nakamura Isamu', attachment to 7th Infantry Division G-2 Periodic Report 5, 24 October 1944.

545 Prefer, 80; Love, 218–219.

546 'King II Report', 6; Quoted in Cannon, *Leyte: The Return to the Philippines*, 133; 'IJA *35th Army* Operations Report', 28.

547 Quoted in Cannon, *Leyte: The Return to the Philippines*, 130; '7th Infantry Division Operations Report, Leyte', App. C to Annex 2.

548 Love, 220; Cannon, 137.

549 Love, 221–222; '17th Infantry, Division Operations Report, Leyte, Annex A, The Battle for Dagami', 1–9.

550 Love, 237–238; Cannon, 135.

551 'King II Report', 7; Love, 237–241.

552 'King II Report', 7.

553 Love, 239–240.

554 Ibid., 340–241; 'King II Report', 8; Cannon, 137; '32nd Infantry, Operations Report, Leyte', 9.

555 'King Report II', 4. This appears to reflect the initial estimate. The Intelligence annex does not describe it as a withdrawal.

556 FM 7-20, The Infantry Battalion, Chapter Five: Retrograde Operations, US Army, 5–1, 5–5, 5–7, author's collection.

557 'King II Report', 9; '17th Infantry, Division Operations Report, Leyte, Annex A, The Battle for Dagami', 1–9.

558 Cannon, 141; 'Central Area Unit Operations Order 2, 27 October 1944, translated in App. C to Annex 2, 7th Infantry Division Operations Report, Leyte'.

559 Quoted in Cannon, 131; '96th Infantry Division Operations Report, Leyte, Annex C, Part III, Translated, KAKI Operational Order A-837', 22 October 1944.

560 Prefer, 73.

561 Love, 227.

562 Ibid.

563 Captain Mervin Elliott, quoted in *YANK*, The Army Weekly Magazine, Branch Office, Information and Education Division, War Department, New York, December 22, 1944, 2–3.

564 Love, 228–229.

565 Love, 230–231.

566 Private First Class Leonard C. Brostrom, War Department General Orders Number 104, 15 November 1945; Private First Class John F. Thorson, War Department General Orders Number 58, 19 July 1945.

PFC Brostrom singlehandedly destroyed a pillbox and killed six Japanese before collapsing from his wounds. PFC Thorson sacrificed his life to save his comrades by throwing himself upon an enemy grenade.

567 Ibid., 230, 232.

568 Cannon, 143.

569 Ibid.

570 Lieutenant Colonel Francis T. Pachler, interview, *YANK*, The Army Weekly Magazine, Branch Office, Information and Education Division, War Department, New York, 22 December 1944, 3–4.

571 Cannon, 144.

572 Ibid.; Prefer, 95–96.

573 Prefer, 96; Love, 235; '17th Infantry, Division Operations Report, Battle for Dagami', App., 9.

574 Prefer, 182.

575 Ibid., 185.

576 Love, 249; Prefer, 185–186.

577 King II Report, 13; Prefer, 186; Love, 251.

578 Prefer, 189, 192.

579 Prefer, 190, 192; quoted from Colonel John M. Finn, 'Shoestring Ridge', Infantry Journal, LVII, (September 1945), 47.

580 The Japanese give the number of enemy troops as two and a half battalions while the 32nd Infantry estimated it as three battalions. *IJA 35th Army*, Operations, 78; 32nd Infantry Operations Report, Leyte, 32.

581 Love, 260–261; Prefer, 194–196.

582 Love, 261.

583 Prefer, 199.

584 'Msg, 32nd Infantry to 7th Infantry Division, 1443, 27 November 1944, 32nd Infantry, Unit Journal, 27 Nov 44'.

585 Cannon, 265.

586 Cannon, 273; '32nd Infantry Operations Report Leyte, 10–26; Colonel John M. Finn, 'Shoestring Ridge', *Infantry Journal*, LVII, 3 (September-October 1945), 47.

587 'King II Report', 21, 22, 34. Cannon records 584 killed, 2,179 wounded, 1 missing.

588 Prefer, 324. The Japanese historical estimate of army ground troop strength was 70,000 men (*35th Army Opns*, 126). General Tomochika, the chief of staff of the *35th Army*, estimated that there were 61, 800 Japanese on Leyte and that 48,790 had been killed by 17 March 1945 (Tomochika, *True Facts of Leyte Opn, Interrog of Gen Tomochika*, 7).

589 Prefer, 325, quoting General Yamashita.

590 Stephen D. Biddle, *Military Power: Explaining Victory and Defeat in Modern Battle* (Princeton: Princeton University Press, 2004), ix.

591 Cannon, *Leyte: The Return to the Philippines, Chapter XIV, Measure of the Fighting*, 251–252.

592 Staff Sergeant James Madison, quoted in YANK, The Army Weekly Magazine, Branch Office, Information and Education Division, War Department, New York, December 22, 1944, 4.

593 Cannon, *Leyte: The Return to the Philippines, Chapter XIV, Measure of the Fighting*, 251–252.

594 Staff Sergeant Leland Larson, quoted in YANK, The Army Weekly Magazine, Branch Office, Information and Education Division, War Department, New York, December 22, 1944, 4.

595 Biddle, 3.

596 10th I&HS, 'Eighth Army, Staff Study of Operations of Japanese *35th Army* on Leyte, Interrogation of Gen Tomochika', 26.

597 Straus, *The Anguish of Surrender: Japanese POWs of World War II* (Seattle: University of Washington Press, 2003), 44.

598 Drea, 75.

599 Drea, 75–76; Coox, 'Japanese Army Experience', 133.

600 Drea, 82; 'Imperial Rescript to the Army and Navy', quoted from Tadayoshi Sakurai, Masujiro Honda, Alice Mabel Bacon, and Bruce Rogers, *Human Bullets: A Soldier's Story of Port Arthur* (Boston: Houghton, Mifflin & Company, 1907), 264.

601 John Toland, *The Rising Sun: The Decline and Fall of the Japanese Empire, 1936–1945* (New York: Random House, 1970), 512

602 'Imperial Precepts to Soldiers and Sailors, 1882', quoted in Ryusaku Tsunoda, William Theodore De Bary, and Donald Keene, comps., *Sources of Japanese Tradition, Volume II* (New York: Columbia University Press, 1964), 199–200; 'Imperial Precepts to Soldiers and Sailors', quoted in Paul Robinson, Nigel De Lee, and Don Carrick (editors), *Ethics Education in the Military* (Aldershot, England: Ashgate Publishing Company, 2008), 153–155.

603 Strauss, 34.

604 Thomas Kasulis, 'Japanese Philosophy', *The Stanford Encyclopedia of Philosophy* (Summer 2019 Edition), Edward N. Zalta (editor), URL: https://plato.stanford.edu/archives/sum2019/entries/japanese-philosophy/.

605 Arthur Swinson, *Four* Samurai*: A Quartet of Japanese Army Commanders in the Second World War* (London: Huchinson, 1968), 15.

606 Straus, *The Anguish of Surrender: Japanese POWs of World War II*, 34–37.

607 Straus, *The Anguish of Surrender: Japanese POWs of World War II*, 36.

608 Drea, 81–82.

609 Thomas C. Smith, *The Agrarian Origins of Modern Japan* (Stanford: Stanford University Press, 1959), 205–206.

610 Ibid.

611 James Dawes, *Evil Men* (Cambridge: Harvard University Press, 2013), 49.

612 John Toland, *The Rising Sun: The Decline and Fall of the Japanese Empire, 1936–1945* (New York: Random House, 1970), 512

613 Strauss, 38–39.

614 Also translated as 'Die rather than become a POW' or 'Do not live in shame as a prisoner. Die, and leave no ignominious crime behind you.' Part II, Article 8, *Senjinkun*; Sato Hiroaki, '*Gyokusai*' or 'Shattering like a Jewel: Reflection on the Pacific War', *The Asia-Pacific Journal*, Japan Focus, 1 February 2008, Volume 6, Issue 2, Article ID 2662; https://apjjf.org/-Hiroaki-Sato/2662/article.html.

615 Ulrich Straus, *The Anguish of Surrender: Japanese POWs of World War II* (Seattle and London: University of Washington Press, 2003), 8.

616 Strauss, 35; Edward O. Reischauer, *The Japanese* (Cambridge: Belknap, 1977), 15, 162–166.

617 Strauss, 43.

618 Daniel Coyle, *The Culture Code: The Secrets of Highly Successful Groups* (New York: Bantam, 2018), 10.

619 Forrest Morgan, 227–228.

620 Imperial Ministry of Education, 1937 (Monbusho), *Kokutai no Hongi: Cardinal Principles of the National Entity of Japan*, Robert K. Hall (editor), John Owen Gauntlett (translator) (Cambridge: Harvard University Press, 1949), 59.

621 Benedict, 117, 133, 136–137; Curtis H. Martin and Bruce Stronach, *Politics East and West: A Comparison of Japanese and British Political Culture* (Armonk, NY: M.E. Sharpe, 1992), 16

622 Yamakuse Yoji, *Nihonjin no kokoro (Heart and Soul of the Japanese)* (Tokyo: IBC Publishing, 2014) revised English text Michael A. Cooney (translator), *Japaneseness: A Guide to Values and Virtues* (Berkeley: Stone Bridge Press, 2016), 63–64.

623 Benedict, 98, 121–125.

624 Roger J. Davies, Osamu Ikeno, 'Giri: Japanese Social Obligations', *The Japanese Mind: Understanding Contemporary Japanese Culture* (Tokyo: Tuttle Publishing, 2002), 95–101.

625 Ibid., 65–66; Forrest E. Morgan, *Compellence and the Strategic Culture of Imperial Japan: Implications for Coercive Diplomacy in the Twenty-First Century* (Westport and London: Praeger Publishers, 2003), 57.

626 Benedict, 133–134, 137–138. Much of this section is based on the author's fifty years of personal experience and study of the Japanese *budo* which is deeply inculcated with this Japanese aesthetic.

627 Ibid., 121–125; Morgan, 57.

628 Roger J. Davies, Osamu Ikeno, 'Giri: Japanese Social Obligations', *The Japanese Mind: Understanding Contemporary Japanese Culture* (Boston: Tuttle Publishing, 2002), 95–101.

629 Abe, Namiko. 'Giri: Moral Obligation', ThoughtCo. https://www.thoughtco.com/giri-moral-obligation-2028017 (accessed February 7, 2021).

630 McManus, 46.

631 Morgan, 57, 74.

632 Iritani, Toshio, *Group Psychology of the Japanese in Wartime* (New York: Kegan Paul International, 1991), x.

633 Robert Lee, 'The Individuation of the Self in Japanese History', Japanese Journal of Religious Studies, Mar., 1977, Volume 4, Number 1 (March 1977), Nanzan University Stable, 5, URL: https://www.jstor.org/stable/30233128; Forrest E. Morgan, *Compellence and the Strategic Culture of Imperial Japan: Implications for Coercive Diplomacy in the Twenty-First Century* (Westport: Praeger Publishers, 2003), 61, 63, 227–229, 235.

634 Morgan, *Compellence and the Strategic Culture of Imperial Japan*, 235.

635 Robert Lee, 'The Individuation of the Self in Japanese History', 7.

636 Aaron William Moore, *Writing War: Soldiers Record the Japanese Empire* (Cambridge: Harvard University Press, 2013), 233; USMHI: 'Confidential: Statement of Prisoner of War Concerning Attitude of Japanese on Capture and Future Return Home to Japan', January 1943.

637 Benedict, 153; Doi Takeo, *The Anatomy of Dependence: Exploring an area of the Japanese psyche: feelings of indulgence* (Tokyo: Kodansha International, 1973), 35, 53.

638 Ooka Shohei, *Taken Captive: A Japanese POW's Story* (New York: John Wiley & Sons, 1996), 54.

639 Strauss, 50–51.

640 Strauss, 64–67.

641 Strauss, 77.

642 Ibid., 78.

643 Ibid., 78–79.

644 Ooka Shohei, *Taken Captive: A Japanese POW's Story* (New York: John Wiley & Sons, 1996), 5, 48.

645 Ibid., 27.

646 Ibid., 28, 31, 37.

647 Strauss, 60–61.

648 'Imperial Rescript to the Army and Navy', quoted in Tadayoshi Sakurai, Masujiro Honda, Alice Mabel Bacon, and Bruce Rogers, *Human Bullets: A Soldier's Story of Port Arthur* (Boston: Houghton, Mifflin & Company, 1907), 264.

649 James Mahoney, 'Path Dependence in Historical Sociology', Theory and Society 29, Number 4 (2000): 507–48. http://www.jstor.org/stable/3108585.

650 Sato Hiroaki, '*Gyokusai*' or 'Shattering like a Jewel: Reflection on the Pacific War', *The Asia-Pacific Journal*, Japan Focus, 1 February 2008, Volume 6, Issue 2, Article ID 2662; https://apjjf.org/-Hiroaki-Sato/2662/article.html.

651 Straus, 34.

652 Ibid., 32–33.

Chapter Five: The Battle of Okinawa, Strategic Culture and '*Yamato damashii*'

653 Richard Frank, *Downfall,* quoted from Imperial Japanese Headquarters War Journal, 1945, 89.

654 Edmund G. Love, *The Hourglass: A History of the 7th Infantry Division in World War II* (Washington D.C.: Infantry Journal Press, 1950), 283–284, 287.

655 Ibid., 288-290.

656 Joseph Wheelan, *Bloody Okinawa: The Last Great Battle of World War II* (New York: Hachette Books, 2021), 7–9; Thomas N. Huber, *Japan's Battle of Okinawa, April–June 1945,* Leavenworth Papers Number 18, Combat Studies Institute, US Army Command and General Staff College, Fort Leavenworth, Kansas, 1990, 5.

657 Huber, 5–6; Wheelan, 31; 'Japanese Monograph Number 135' (JM 135), US Army Forces Far East, Military History Section, *Okinawa Operations Record,* Number Book 1, 'Okinawa Operations Record of 32[n]d Army' (Washington DC, 1949), 11.

658 Arnold G. Fisch, *Ryukyus: 26 March-2 July 1945,* CMH Pub 72–35 (Washington DC: US Army Center of Military History, 1993.), 3–5.

659 'Japanese Monograph Number 135' (JM 135), US Army Forces Far East, Military History Section, *Okinawa Operations Record,* Book Number 1, 'Okinawa Operations Record of 32[n]d Army' (Washington DC, 1949), 1–3, 4, 9–10, 11–18.

660 Ibid., 9–10, 18–19, 45–46.

661 Roy E. Appleman, James M. Burns, Russell A. Gugeler, John Stevens, *Okinawa: The Last Battle,* United States Army in World War II, The War in the Pacific (Washington DC: War Department, Historical Division,

1947), 30; Huber, 6–8; Fisch, CMH Pub 72–35, *Ryukyus: 26 March–2 July 1945*, 11.

662 Yahara, Hiromichi, *The Battle for Okinawa*, Roger Pineau and Uehara Masatoshi (translators), with an introduction and commentary by Frank B. Gibney (New York: John Wiley & Sons, 1995), 49.

663 Huber, *Japan's Battle of Okinawa, April–June 1945*, 2, 7, 47–51.

664 Edmond G. Love, *The Hourglass: A History of the 7th Infantry Division in World War II* (Washington DC: Infantry Journal Press, 1950), 289.

665 Fisch Jr, *Ryukyus: The U.S. Army Campaigns of World War II*, CMH Pub 72–35, 6.

666 Huber, *Japan's Battle of Okinawa, April–June 1945*, 6.

667 Fisch, CMH Pub 72-35, *Ryukyus: 26 March–2 July 1945*, 6–7.

668 Fisch, CMH Pub 72-35, *Ryukyus: 26 March–2 July 1945*, 7.

669 Love, 294.

670 Fisch, CMH Pub 72-35, *Ryukyus: 26 March–2 July 1945*, 6.

671 Roy Appleman, James M. Burns, Russel A. Gugeler, John Stevens, *Okinawa: The Last Battle*, 107–109.

672 Love, 310.

673 Dean E. Galles Collection (AFC/2001/001/88536), interviewed by Christine Seifert, Veterans' History Project, American Folklife Center, Library of Congress.

674 Roy Appleman, James M. Burns, Russel A. Gugeler, John Stevens, *Okinawa: The Last Battle*, 111–113.

675 Love, 322–323.

676 Ibid., 320, 323.

677 Roy Appleman, James M. Burns, Russel A. Gugeler, John Stevens, *Okinawa: The Last Battle*, 220.

678 Ibid., 220, 224.

679 James C. McNaughton, *Nisei Linguists: Japanese Americans in the Military Intelligence Service in World War II*, Center of Military History Publication 70-99–1 (Washington DC: Department of the Army, 2006), 359-361; Appleman *et al*, *Okinawa: The Last Battle*, 184–207; Stanley L. Falk, and Warren M. Tsuneishi, *MIS in the War against Japan: Personal Experiences Related at the 1993 MIS Capital Reunion, 'The Nisei Veteran: An American Patriot'* (Vienna, VA: Japanese American Veterans' Association of Washington DC, 1995), 54–57; Ted Tsukiyama, 'The Battle of Okinawa', Hawaii Nisei Project, University of Hawaii, http://nisei.hawaii.edu; Headquarters, US Army Forces Pacific Ocean Areas, Observers Report: The Okinawa Operation, 15 June 1945, Combined Arms Research Library, Fort Leavenworth, KS, 23–24.

680 Ibid., 226, 248; Love, 351; Citation to accompany the award of the Distinguished Service Cross, Headquarters, Tenth US Army, Headquarters, Tenth US Army, General Orders Number 141 (1945).

681 Ibid., 227; Love, 352.

682 Love, 360–361.

683 Ibid., 368.

684 Appleman, et.al., *Okinawa: The Last Battle*, 64–68.

685 Huber, 13; *Japanese Memorandum Number 135*, 49–50; Appleman, *et al*, *Okinawa: The Last Battle*, 92–96.

686 Huber, 65.

687 Appleman, *et al*, *Okinawa: The Last Battle*, 255–256; Huber, 41, 66, 68, 71–74.

688 Huber, 66, 68.

689 Citation to accompany the award of the Distinguished Service Cross, Headquarters, Tenth US Army, General Orders Number 170 (1945).

690 Appleman, *et al*, 269–272; Love, 368–369, 372.

691 Appleman, *et al*, 283.

692 Appleman, *et al*, 284.

693 Appleman, *et al*, 284; Wheelan, 162.

694 James Schneider, introduction to *The Evolution of Operational Art*, by Georgii Samoilovich Isserson, trans. Bruce Menning (Fort Leavenworth, KS: Combat Studies Institute Press, 2013), XII; Thomas Bruscino, 'The Theory of Operational Art and Unified Land Operations', School of Advanced Military Studies Theoretical Paper, Command and General Staff College, Fort Leavenworth, KS, Summer 2012), 21.

Operational approach ensures that

695 Appleman, et.al., 287; From a Japanese infantryman's diary, 7th Infantry Division G-2, Periodic Report Number 38, 8 May 1945.

696 Huber, *Japan's Battle of Okinawa*, 31, 83.

697 Appleman et al., 92–96.

698 Leon Festinger, *An Introduction to the Theory of Cognitive Dissonance* (Stanford: Stanford University Press, 1957), retrieved 18 January 2022 from https://www.panarchy.org/festinger/dissonance.html.

699 Appleman, *et al*, 286, 291; 7th Infantry Division G-2, Periodic Report Number 36, 6 May 45.

700 Huber, 29–31.

701 Ibid.; Edward Drea, *In the Service of the Emperor: Essays on the Imperial Japanese Army* (Lincoln: University of Nebraska Press, 1998), 70–74.

702 Huber, 29–31, 81–83.

703 Appleman, *et al*, 289.

704 Love, 325.

705 Appleman *et al*, *Okinawa: The Last Battle*, 92–96.

706 Huber, 74–80; Love, 355.

707 Huber, 77–79.

708 Ibid.

709 Love, 355.

710 Love, 389.

711 Ibid., 388–390.

712 Ibid., 391–392.

713 Love, 393; Appleman, *et al*, 297.

714 Huber, *Japan's Battle of Okinawa, April–June 1945*, 88–90.

715 Wheelan, *Bloody Okinawa*, 165; Love, 393–396.

716 Ibid.; Huber, 88–90.

717 Love, 406–409; Appleman, *et al*, 307–309.

718 Eugene B. Sledge, *With The Old Breed: At Peleliu and Okinawa*. (Novato: Presidio Press, 2010), 278.

719 Sledge, *With The Old Breed: At Peleliu and Okinawa*, 292.

720 Appleman, *et al*, *Okinawa: The Last Battle*, Chapter XV: The Fall of Shuri, 384; Tenth Army G-2 Periodic Report Number 67, 1 June 1945; G-2 Summary, 1 Jun 45, in Tenth Army G-3 Journal, Message Number 5, 2 June 1945; Tenth Army G-3 Periodic Report Number 67, 1 June 1945.

721 Appleman, *et al*, *Okinawa: The Last Battle*, Chapter XV: The Fall of Shuri, 384–386.

722 Stouffer, *et al*, 'Psychoneurotic Symptoms in the Army', *The American Soldier: Combat and Its Aftermath* (John Wiley & Sons, 1965), 439–440, 444–445.

723 Eugene B. Sledge, *With The Old Breed: At Peleliu and Okinawa* (Novato: Presidio Press, 2010), 94, 263, 277–278.

724 Todd C. Helmus and Russell W. Glenn, 'The Lessons of War: The Causations of Battle Fatigue', *Steeling the Mind: Combat Stress Reactions and Their Implications for Urban Warfare* (Santa Monica: RAND Corporation, 2005), 26–28.

725 Ibid.

726 Robert McArthur, "Correspondence from Gerald Astor Regarding Experiences During the Fight for Okinawa", Digital Archives, US Army Heritage and Education Center (USAHEC digital archives, 2), August 20, 1994, https://emu.usahec.org/alma/multimedia/623943/20181527MNBT989106711F099341I004.pdf;

John Fitzgerald, "Correspondence from Gerald Astor Regarding Experiences During the Fight for Okinawa", Digital Archives, US Army Heritage and Education Center (USAHEC digital archives, 3–4), 24 August 1994, https://emu.usahec.org/alma/multimedia/967717/20181527MN000444.pdf.

727 Love, 410.

728 Ibid., 411.

729 Appleman, *et al*, 379, 381.

730 Ibid., 381–382.

731 Ibid., 382, 393.

732 Wheelan, *Bloody Okinawa*, 128.

733 Appleman, *et al*, 333–338.

734 Appleman, *et al*, 445.

735 Appleman, *et al*, 445–446.

736 Ibid.

737 Appleman, *et al*; 447–449.

738 PFC Roland Lea, B/1-17IN, 'Correspondence from Gerald Astor Regarding Experiences During the Fight for Okinawa', US Army Heritage and Education Center, undated (USAHEC digital archives, 5). https://emu.usahec.org/alma/multimedia/623930/20181527MNBT989106711F099340I003.pdf.

739 Appleman, *et al*; 255–256.

740 Robert Rush, *GI: The U.S. Infantryman In World War II* (Wellingborough: Osprey Publishing Limited, 2003), 86–87.

741 Huber, 109–111.

742 Huber, 112–115.

743 Yahara, Hiromichi, *The Battle for Okinawa*, Roger Pineau and Uehara Masatoshi (translators), with an introduction and commentary by Frank B. Gibney (New York: John Wiley & Sons, 1995), 137–138.

744 Thomas N. Huber, *Japan's Battle of Okinawa, April–June 1945*, Leavenworth Papers Number 18, Combat Studies Institute, US Army Command and General Staff College, Fort Leavenworth, Kansas, 1990, 112–115; Yahara, Hiromichi, *The Battle for Okinawa*, translated by Roger Pineau and Uehara Masatoshi (translators), with an introduction and commentary by Frank B. Gibney (New York: John Wiley & Sons, 1995), 191–192, 196–197.

745 Appleman, *et al*, 465; Huber, 116.

746 Wheelan, 339.

747 Alvin D. Coox, *Nomonhan: Japan Against Russia, Volume II* (Stanford: Stanford University Press, 1985), 1025.

748 David Dilworth, *Guiding Principles of Interpretation in Watsuji Tetsuro's 'History of Japanese Ethical Thought': With Particular Reference to the Tension between the Sonno and Bushidō Traditions*, 102–109, https://nirc.nanzan-u.ac.jp/nfile/2066.

749 Yonezawa Miyuki; Paul Spickard (editor), *Race and Nation: Ethnic Systems in the Modern World* (New York and London: Routledge, 2005), 126–127.

750 Forrest E. Morgan, *Compellence and the Strategic Culture of Imperial Japan: Implications for Coercive Diplomacy in the Twenty-First Century* (Westport: Praeger Publishers, 2003), 174.

751 John W. Dower, *War Without Mercy: Race and Power in the Pacific War* (New York: Pantheon Books, 1986), 263–264.

752 Dower, 266-268; Yonezawa, 126–127.

753 Robert Lee, 'The Individuation of the Self in Japanese History', *Japanese Journal of Religious Studies* 4, Number 1 (1977): 5–39. http://www.jstor.org/stable/30233128.

754 Gideon Fujiwara and Peter Nosco, 'The Kokugaku (Native Japan Studies) School', The Stanford Encyclopedia of Philosophy (Fall 2021 edition), Edward N. Zalta (editor), URL: https://plato.stanford.edu/archives/fall2021/entries/kokugaku-school/; https://plato.stanford.edu/entries/kokugaku-school/.

755 Forrest E. Morgan, *Compellence and the Strategic Culture of Imperial Japan*, 129; James B. Crowley, *Japan's Quest for Autonomy: National Security and Foreign Policy, 1930–1938* (Princeton: Princeton University Press, 1966), 202.

756 Meirion and Susie Harris, *Soldiers of the Sun: The Rise and Fall of the Imperial Japanese Army* (New York: Random House, Inc., 1991), 325.

757 Coox, 1082–1083.

758 Dower, 260; Gordon W. Prange, *At Dawn We Slept: The Untold Story of Pearl Harbor* (New York: McGraw-Hill, 1981), 517.

759 Jeffrey Record, *'Japan's Decision for War in 1941: Some Enduring Lessons'*, US Army War College, Strategic Studies Institute, Carlisle, PA February 2009, viii.

760 Love, 290–291.

761 Terry Brighton, *Patton, Montgomery, Rommel: Masters of War* (New York: Crown Publishing Group, 2009), 262–265, 'Patton's Speech to the Third Army' was a series of speeches given to the divisions of Third Army between February and June 1944.

762 Rose, Arnold. 'Bases of American Military Morale in World War II', *The Public Opinion Quarterly* 9, Number 4 (1945): 412–413, http://www.jstor.org/stable/2745554.

763 Wilfrid Owen, 'Dulce Et Decorum Est', Viking Press, 1921, https://www.poetryfoundation.org/poems/46560/dulce-et-decorum-est. The Latin phrase is from the Roman poet Horace, The Odes, III.2.13: 'It is sweet and fitting to die for one's country.'

Chapter Six: Conclusion

764 Dave Lowry, *Autumn Lightning: The Education of an American* Samurai (Boston and London: Shambhala, 1985), 201. Quoting Abe Shosaburo, a teacher of the *Yagyu Shinkage* school of swordsmanship, reflecting on the melancholy of the fate of the swordsmen who met their deaths in the Meiji Restoration.

765 Jeremy Black, *Rethinking Military History* (New York: Routledge, 2004), ix, x, xi, 4, 8–9; Jeffrey J. Clarke, Chapter 6, 'World Military History,1786–1945', 'A Guide to the Study and Use of Military History', John Jessup Jr and Robert W. Coakley (editors), Center of Military History, Washington DC, 1988, 117–138.

766 John Keegan, *The Face of Battle* (New York; The Viking Press, 1976), 78.

767 Jeremy Black, *Rethinking Military History*, 8–9, 11. Other examples include Theodore Ropp's *War in the Modern World (1962),* Michael Howard's *Studies in War and Peace* (1970) and Gordon Turner's *A History of Military Affairs in Western Society Since the Eighteenth Century* (1956).

768 Barton C. Hacker, 'Military Institutions, Weapons, and Social Change: Toward a New History of Military Technology', Technology and Culture 35.4 (1994): 768–834; Jeffrey J. Clarke, 'World Military History', 117, 129–130; Marin van Creveld, *Technology and War: From 2000 BC to the Present* (New York: Free Press, 1989), 311.

769 Hacker, 129–130; Alan L. Gropman, 'Analysis by Hyperbole', *Air University Quarterly Review*, September–October 1983, 91.

770 Hacker, 774.

771 Jeremy Black, *Rethinking Military History* (New York: Routledge,2004), ix, x, xi, 4, 8-9.

772 Ibid.

773 Jeremy Black, *Rethinking Military History* (New York: Routledge, 2004) 232-235. Jeremy Black, *War and the Cultural Turn* (Cambridge: Polity Press, 2012), 43; H. Löfstedt, 'Duels of Systems and Forces' in B. Boos-Bavnbek and J. Høyrup (eds), *Mathematics and War* (Basel: Birkhäuser, 2003), 252; J.F.C. Fuller, 1915 letter to his mother, 18 Aug. 1915, Fuller papers, IV/3/155., quoted by Jeremy Black, *Rethinking Military History*, 104.

774 Kirstin Braithwaite, 'Effective in battle: conceptualizing soldiers' combat effectiveness', *Defence Studies* (Oxfordshire: Routledge), 18 (1) 2018. 1–18; Christopher A. Lawrence, 'Measuring Human Factors in Combat: Modern Wars', *War by Numbers: Understanding Conventional Combat* (Lincoln: University of Nebraska Press, 2017), 49–59.

775 Lawrence, 22.

776 Mansoor, *The GI Offensive in Europe*, 2–3.

777 Mansoor, *The GI Offensive in Europe*, 2–3.

778 Robert B. Strassler (editor), *The Landmark Thucydides: A Comprehensive Guide to The Peloponnesian War* (New York: Free Press, 1996), 45–46, 81–82.

779 James W. Cook, Lawrence B. Glickman, *The Cultural Turn in U.S. History: Past, Present, and Future*, James W. Cook, Lawrence B. Glickman, Michael O'Malley (editors) (Chicago: University of Chicago Press, 2008), 16–21, 30–38; Jeremy Black, *War and the Cultural Turn* (Cambridge: Polity Press, 2012), vii, 53, 141).

780 Forrest E. Morgan, *Compellence and the Strategic Culture of Imperial Japan: Implications for Coercive Diplomacy in the Twenty-First Century* (Westport and London: Praeger Publishers, 2003), 28; see also Miriam Becker's definition of strategic culture: 'a nation's traditions, values, attitudes, patterns of behaviour, habits, symbols, achievements and particular ways of adapting to the environment and solving problems with respect to the threat or use of force.'

781 H. Shultz Jr, *Adapting America's Security Paradigm and Security Agenda* (Washington DC: National Strategy Information Center, 2010), 35.

782 Edward J. Drea, *Japan's Imperial Army: Its Rise and Fall, 1853–1945* (Lawrence: University Press of Kansas, 2009), 320, 593; Allison B. Gilmore, *You Can't Fight Tanks with Bayonets: Psychological Warfare against the Japanese Army in the South West Pacific* (Lincoln: University of Nebraska Press, 1998), 87.

783 Jeffrey Record, *Japan's Decision for War in 1941*, viii.

784 Morgan, *Compellence and the Strategic Culture of Imperial Japan*, 1.

785 Morgan, *Compellence and the Strategic Culture of Imperial Japan*, 38-39, 46-47; Delmer M. Brown, *Nationalism in Japan: An Introductory Historical Analysis* (Berkeley, California: University of California Press, 1955), 7-11; David A. Dilworth, 'Guiding Principles of Interpretation in Watsuji Tetsurō's History of Japanese Ethical Thought: With Particular Reference to the Tension between the Sonnō and Bushidō Traditions', in Victor Sogen Hori & Melissa Anne-Marie Curley (editors), *Frontiers of Japanese Philosophy: Neglected Themes and Hidden Variations* (Nagoya: Nanzan Institute for Religion & Culture, 2008), 104.

786 Dilworth, 39–41; Brown, 11–13; Benedict, 117.

787 Benedict, 42–44; George B. Sansom, *A History of Japan to 1334* (Stanford: Stanford University Press, 1958), 311.

788 Sansom, *A History of Japan to 1334*, 49–53; Lawrence E. Grinter, 'Cultural and Historical Influences in Sinic Asia: China, Japan, and Vietnam', in Stephen J. Blank, *et al*, Conflict, *Culture, and History: Regional Dimensions* (Maxwell, AFB AL: Air University Press, 1993), 154–155.

789 Ibid., 52–57; Peter R. Moody Jr, *Tradition and Modernization in China and Japan* (Belmont: Wadsworth Publishing Company, 1995), 92, 97; E. Herbert Norman, *Japan's Emergence as a Modern State: Political and Economic Problems of the Meiji Period* (Westport: Greenwood Press, 1940), 19–25.

790 Ness, *Rikugun*, 14.

791 R.H.P. Mason and J.G. Caiger, *A History of Japan* (Rutland: Tuttle Publishing, 1997), 264.

792 Coox, *Nomonhan: Japan Against Russia, 1939*, 1082, 1085; Edward J. Drea, *Japan's Imperial Army: Its Rise and Fall, 1853–1945* (Lawrence: University Press of Kansas, 2009), 162, 171–173.

793 Richard Tarnas, *The Passion of the Western Mind: Understanding the Ideas That Have Shaped Our World View* (New York: Ballantine Books, 1991), 282–283, 290.

794 Lewis, xvii, 34–35; Echevarria, 16, 23.

795 Adrian Lewis, *The American Culture of War: The History of U.S. Military Force from World War II to Operation Iraqi Freedom* (New York: Routledge, 2018), xvii, 34–35; Antulio J. Etchevarria II, *Reconsidering the American Way of War: U.S. Military Practice from the Revolution to Afghanistan* (Washington DC: Georgetown University Press, 2014), 16, 23; John A. Lynn, *Battle: A History of Combat and Culture* (Boulder: Westview Press, 2003), 321.

796 J.C. Wylie, *Military Strategy: A General Theory of Power Control* (New Brunswick: Rutgers University Press, 1967), 80.

797 *The Principles of Strategy for An Independent Corps or Army in a Theater of Operations* (Ft. Leavenworth, KS: Command and General Staff School Press, 1936), 19.

798 Terry Golway, *Washington's General: Nathanael Greene and the Triumph of the American Revolution* (New York: Henry Holt and Company, 2005), 238-242, 248-249.

799 Weigley, *American Way of War*, xxii, 6–7, 467–477; F.G Hoffman, *Decisive Force: The New American Way of War* (Westport: Praeger, 1996), xii.

800 Brian M. Linn, 'The American Way of War Revisited', *The Journal of Military History*, | Volume 66, Number 2, April 2002, 502.

801 Brian M. Linn, 'The American Way of War Revisited', *The Journal of Military History*, Volume 66, Number 2 (April 2002), 502–503, 530.

802 John A. Lynn, *Battle: A History of Combat and Culture* (Boulder: Westview Press, 2003), 321.

803 Jacob H. Miller, 'Strategic Culture as the Basis for Military Adaptive Capacity: Overcoming battlefield technological surprises', 1 April 2014. CUREJ: College Undergraduate Research Electronic Journal, University of Pennsylvania, https://repository.upenn.edu/curej/173.

804 Ibid.

805 Michael A. Bonura, *Under the Shadow of Napoleon: French Influence on the American Way of Warfare from Independence to the Eve of World War II* (New York: NYU Press, 2012), 3–4.

806 Edgar H. Schein, *Organizational Culture and Leadership* (San Francisco: Jossey-Bass, 2010), 7–8.

807 Thomas Mahnken, *Technology and the American Way of War Since 1945* (New York: Columbia University Press, 2008), 3, 4–6, 223–225; Schein, *Organizational Culture and Leadership* 25–35.

808 Leonard Wong and Stephen J. Gerras, 'Culture and Military Organizations', Chapter 1 in *The Culture of Military Organizations*, Peter R. Mansoor and Williamson Murray (editors) (Cambridge: Cambridge University Press, 2019), 17–20.

809 Isabel V. Hull, *Absolute Destruction: Military Culture and the Practices of War in Imperial Germany* (Ithaca: Cornell University Press, 2006), 2.

810 Ibid.

811 Edgar H. Schein, 'Coming to a New Awareness of Organizational Culture', *Sloan Management Review* 25, Number 2 (winter 1984), 3.

812 Hull, *Absolute Destruction*, 92.

813 Drea, *In the Service of the Emperor*, 73, 120.

814 David Hunter-Chester, 'Imperial Japanese Army Culture, 1918–1945: Duty Heavier than a Mountain, Death Lighter than a Feather', Chapter 9, in *The Culture of Military Organizations*, Peter R. Mansoor and Williamson Murray, 208–25 (editors). (Cambridge: Cambridge University Press, 2019), 208–225; Francis Pike, "The Development of a Death Cult in 1930s Japan and the Decision to Drop the Atom Bomb", Asian Affairs, 47:1, 1–31 (2016), DOI: 10.1080/03068374.2015.1128682.

815 William. Theodore de Bary, Donald Keene, and Ryusaku Tsunoda, eds., *The Imperial Rescript to Soldiers and Sailors, Sources of Japanese Tradition II, 1600–2000* (New York: Columbia University Press, 1958), 198–200.

816 Stephen Biddle, *Military Power: Explaining Victory and Defeat in Modern Battle* (Princeton: Princeton University Press, 2004), 190–191.

817 Drea, *Japan's Imperial Army*, 107–121.

818 David Hunter-Chester, 2019. 'Imperial Japanese Army Culture, 1918–1945: Duty Heavier than a Mountain, Death Lighter than a Feather', Chapter 9 in *The Culture of Military Organizations*, Peter R. Mansoor and Williamson Murray (editors) (Cambridge: Cambridge University Press, 2019), 222–223.

819 A.D. Coox, "The Effectiveness of the Japanese Military Establishment in the Second World War", in A.R. Millett and W. Murray (editors), *Military Effectiveness, Volume III: the Second World War* (Boston: Allen & Unwin, 1988), 1–44.

820 A.J. Barker, *Japanese Army Handbook, 1939–1945* (London: Ian Allan, 1979), 118–120; A.D. Coox, 'The Effectiveness of the Japanese Military Establishment in the Second World War', in A.R. Millett and W. Murray (editors), *Military Effectiveness, Volume III: the Second World War* (Boston: Allen & Unwin, 1988), 1–44.

821 Forrest Morgan, *Compellence and the Strategic Culture of Japan*, 66–67.

822 Op. cit.

823 Drea, *Japan's Imperial Army*, viii, 46.

824 Meirion and Susie Harris, *Soldiers of the Sun: The Rise and Fall of the Imperial Japanese Army* (New York: Random House, Inc., 1991), 325.

825 Edward J. Drea, *Japan's Imperial Army: Its Rise and Fall, 1853–1945* (Modern War Studies Series) (Lawrence: University Press of Kansas; 1st edition, 2009), 162.

826 Drea, *Japan's Imperial Army*, 119; David Hunter-Chester, 2019, 'Imperial Japanese Army Culture, 1918–1945: Duty Heavier than a Mountain, Death Lighter than a Feather', Chapter 9 in *The Culture of Military Organizations*, Peter R. Mansoor and Williamson Murray (editors) (Cambridge: Cambridge University Press, 2019), 211; Ford, *Assessments*, 329; Ivan I. Morris, *The Nobility of Failure: Tragic Heroes in the History of Japan* (New York: Holt, Rinehart, and Winston, 1975), 120.

827 Op. cit, Chapter Five from 'The Song of Bivouac' (*Roei no Uta)*, Shigure Otowa, *Nihon Kayoshu* (Shakai Shiso Sha, 1963), 295. Quoted by Sato Hiroaki, '*Gyokusai*' or 'Shattering like a Jewel: Reflection on the Pacific War', *The Asia-Pacific Journal*, 1 February 2008, Volume 6, Issue 2.

828 Ralph Eyde, op. cit.

829 Linn, 4–5.

830 Ibid., 6.

831 Linn, 6; George S. Patton, 'The Effect of Weapons on War', The Cavalry Journal, 37 (November 1930), Fort Benning, GA: 483–488, http://www.pattonhq.com/textfiles/effect.html.

832 Linn, 7–8.

833 Ibid., 8–9.

834 Antulio J. Etchevarria II, *Reconsidering the American Way of War: U.S. Military Practice from the Revolution to Afghanistan* (Washington DC: Georgetown University Press, 2014), 13, 16; Linn, 'American Way of War Revisited', 502–503, 530.

835 Williamson Murray, 'Why Did It Take the North So Long?', *Military History Quarterly*, summer 1989, 24–33.

836 S.A. Stouffer, A.A. Lumsdaine, M.H. Lumsdaine, R.M. Williams Jr, M.B. Smith, I.L. Janis, S.A. Star and L.S. Cottrell Jr, *The American Soldier: Combat and its Aftermath (Studies in Social Psychology in World War II)* (Princeton: Princeton University Press, 1949), 96–97.

837 Stephen E. Ambrose, *Citizen Soldiers: The U.S. Army from the Normandy Battlefields to the Bulge to the Surrender of Germany, June 7, 1944–May 7, 1945* (New York: Touchstone, Simon and Schuster, 1997), 14; Christopher H. Hamner, *Enduring Battle: American Soldiers in Three Wars, 1776–1945* (Lawrence: University of Kansas Press, 2011), 3.

838 Guy L. Siebold, 'The Essence of Military Group Cohesion', Armed Forces and Society, Volume 33, Number 2 (2007): 288–289, 292.

839 Samuel A. Stouffer, *et al*, *The American Soldier: Combat and Its Aftermath*, Volume II, 'Combat Incentives' (Princeton: Princeton University Press: 1949), 108.

840 Samuel P. Huntington, *The Soldier and the State: The Theory and Practice of Civil-Military Relations* (Cambridge: Belknap Press, 1957), 151–152.

841 Stouffer, *et al*, 106–111.

842 S.A. Stouffer, A.A. Lumsdaine, M.H. Lumsdaine, R.M. Williams Jr, M.B. Smith, I.L. Janis, S.A. Star and L.S. Cottrell Jr, *The American Soldier: Combat and its Aftermath (Studies in Social Psychology in World War II)* (Princeton: Princeton University Press, 1949), AMS-100, S-100D. https://catalog.archives.gov/id/7062681.

843 Ben Connable, Michael J. McNerney, William Marcellino, Aaron Frank, Henry Hargrove, Marek N. Posard, S. Rebecca Zimmerman, Natasha Lander, Jasen J. Castillo, James Sladden, Anika Binnendijk, Elizabeth M. Bartels, Abby Doll, Rachel Tecott, Benjamin J. Fernandes, Niklas Helwig, Giacomo Persi Paoli, Krystyna Marcinek and Paul Cornish, 'Will to Fight: Returning to the Human Fundamentals of War', RAND Research Brief 10040-A (Santa Monica, California: RAND Corporation, 2019), https://doi.org/10.7249/RB10040.

844 A. MacMillan, K. Booth, and R. Trood, *Strategic Cultures in the Asia-Pacific Region* (Hampshire: Palgrave, 1999), 8.

845 Rashed Uz Zaman, 'Strategic Culture: A "Cultural" Understanding of War', Comparative Strategy, 28:1, 68-88, 2009. DOI: 10.1080/01495930802679785, 81.

846 Ibid., 3, 6–7.

847 Ben Connable, Michael J. McNerney, William Marcellino, Aaron Frank, Henry Hargrove, Marek N. Posard, S. Rebecca Zimmerman, Natasha Lander, Jasen J. Castillo, and James Sladden, *Will to Fight: Analyzing, Modeling, and Simulating the Will to Fight of Military Units*, Santa Monica, California, RAND Corporation, RR-2341-A, 2018), xi.

848 Benedict, 117, 133, 136-137; Morgan, 63–64, 69, 75. Morgan, 11, 66–67, 227, 228; Thomas Cleary, *The Japanese Art of War: Understanding the Culture of Strategy* (Boston and London: Shambhala, 1991), 1–2.

849 Francis Pike, 'The Development of a Death Cult in 1930s Japan and the Decision to Drop the Atom Bomb', Asian Affairs, 47:1, 1–31 (2016), DOI: 10.1080/03068374.2015.1128682, 20.

850 Robert Lee, 'The Individuation of the Self in Japanese History', Japanese Journal of Religious Studies, March1977, Volume 4, Number 1 (March 1977), Nanzan University Stable, 7, URL: https://www.jstor.org/stable/30233128.

851 Karl Friday, '*Bushidō* or Bull: A Medieval Historian's Perspective on the Imperial Army and the Japanese Warrior Tradition', Society for History Education, Volume 27, Issue 3 (May 1994): 339–349.

852 Arthur Swinson, *Four* Samurai*: A Quartet of Japanese Army Commanders in the Second World War* (London: Huchinson, 1968), 15–18.

853 Francis Pike, 'The Development of a Death Cult in 1930s Japan and the Decision to Drop the Atom Bomb', Asian Affairs, 47:1, 1–31 (2016), DOI: 10.1080/03068374.2015.1128682, 15–16.

854 Ivan I. Morris, *The Nobility of Failure: Tragic Heroes in the History of Japan* (New York: Holt, Rinehart, and Winston, 1975), 17.

855 Japanese historian Hosaka Masakasu at the Sixth Forum (2007) of the International Forum on War History entitled 'New Perspectives on the War in the Pacific: Grand Strategies, Military Governments and POWs', Japanese National Institute for Defense Studies at the Japanese Defense Ministry. He shared the recollections of Northern Army Commander, Major General Higuchi Kiichiro about Attu, Rodney J. Szasz (translator), 2014.

856 Post war reminiscences of Corporal Asatake, a member of the Attu garrison who was wounded and captured. Brian Lane Herder, 'The Aleutians, 1942–43: Struggle for the North Pacific, Campaign 333', Marcus Cowper (series editor) (Oxford/New York: Osprey Publishing/Bloomsbury Publishing, 2019), 75, 80; originally from Sato Kazumasa, *Gyokusai No Shima (The Island of Honorable Death)* (Tokyo: Kojinsha Press, 2008); Rodney J. Szasz (translator), 2013.

857 Quoted in Emiko Ohnuki-Tierney, *Kamikaze, Cherry Blossoms, and Nationalisms: The Militarization of Aesthetics in Japanese History* (Chicago: University of Chicago Press, 2002), 197.

858 Ivan Morris, *The Nobility of Failure: Tragic Heroes in the History of Japan* (New York: Holt, Rinehart & Winston, 1975), xiii, 12, 82, 137, 196; Coox, *Nomonhan*, 1082–1083.

859 Drea, *Japan's Imperial Army*, 231.

860 Pike, 19, 24. Japanese death rates: Attu, May 1943 (99 per cent), Tarawa, November 1943 (99.4 per cent), Kwajalein, February 1944 (96.7 per cent), Roi-Namur, February 1944 (97.5 per cent), Los Negros, February 44 (98.1 per cent), Biak, May 1944 (95.7 per cent), Saipan, June 1944 (97.1 per cent), Tinian, Jul 44 (97 per cent), Peleliu, September 1944 (98.1 per cent), Iwo Jima, February 1945 (99 per cent), Okinawa, April–July 1945 (92.8 per cent).

861 Pike, 21, 24; William J. Slim, *Defeat Into Victory: Battling Japan in Burma and India, 1942–1945* (New York: Cooper Square Press, 2000), 538.

862 Wartime diaries reveal the growing disillusion, as demonstrated by Samuel Yamashita, *Leaves from an Autumn of Emergencies: Selections from the Wartime Diaries of Ordinary Japanese* (Honolulu: University of Hawai'i Press, 2009), 27; Aaron William Moore, *Writing War: Soldiers Record the Japanese Empire* (Cambridge: Harvard University Press, 2013), 216; Gregory Bateson *et al*, 'Toward a Theory of Schizophrenia', in Bateson, *Steps to an Ecology of Mind* (New York: Ballentine, 1972), 201–227; Richard Tarnas, *The Passion of the Western Mind: Understanding the Ideas That Have Shaped Our World View* (New York: Ballantine, 1991), 419–420.

863 Allan R. Millet 'The United States Armed Forces in the Second World War', Chapter Two in *Military Effectiveness*, Allan R. Millett and Williamson Murray (editors), second edition, 3:45–89. Cambridge: Cambridge University Press, 2010. DOI: 10.1017/CBO9780511762970.004.

864 Colin S. Gray, 'U.S. Strategic Culture: Implications for Defense Technology', In Defense Technology, Asa A. Clark IV and John F. Lilley (editors) (Westport: Praeger Publishers, 1989), 31–45.

865 George S. Patton Jr, *War As I Knew It* (Boston: Houghton Mifflin Company, 1947), 366.

866 Spector, *Eagle Against the Sun: The American War with Japan* (New York: Vintage Books, 1985) 560.

867 Biddle, *Military Power*, 2–4.

868 McManus, *Island Infernos*, 11; Mansoor, *The GI Offensive in Europe*, 7.

869 Phillips P. O'Brien, *How the War was Won: Air-Sea Power and Allied Victory in World War II* (Cambridge: Cambridge University Press, 2015), 17, 449–451; quoting Major General Maurice Rose in *The Papers of Dwight David Eisenhower: The War Years*, Volume IV, Eisenhower letter to Marshall, March 26, 1945, 2543–2545.

870 General Douglas MacArthur, quoted in 'Why Read Military History?', Center for Military History Journal, September 1989 (Carlisle: US Army War College), http://www.carlisle.army.mil/usawc/dnss/history/why_read.htm.

871 See Van Creveld, Hastings, O'Brien, *et al.*

872 Richard Overy, *Why the Allies Won* (New York: W.W. Norton & Co., 1995), 15.

873 Ronald Spector, *Eagle Against the Sun: The American War with Japan* (New York: Vintage Books, 1985), 560; Phillips Payson O'Brien, *How the War Was Won: Air-Sea Power and Allied Victory in World War II* (Cambridge: Cambridge University Press, 2015), 3, 5, 11, 13; Dan van der Vat, *The Pacific Campaign: World War II, the U.S.-Japanese Naval War, 1941–1945*, 121.

874 James B. Wood, *Japanese Military Strategy in the Pacific War: Was Defeat Inevitable?* (New York: Rowman and Littlefield, 2007) 79; Michael Myers,

The Pacific War and Contingent Victory: Why Japanese Defeat Was Not Inevitable (Lawrence: University Press of Kansas, 2015), 2, 3, 5.

875 Overy, *Why the Allies Won*, 33; Agawa, Hiroyuki *The Reluctant Admiral: Yamamoto and the Imperial Navy*, trans. John Bester (Tokyo; New York: Kodansha International, 1982), 219–20; Michael Myers, *The Pacific War and Contingent Victory: Why Japanese Defeat Was Not Inevitable*,40.

876 Michael Myers, *The Pacific War and Contingent Victory: Why Japanese Defeat Was Not Inevitable* (Lawrence: University Press of Kansas, 2015), 2, 3, 22–26.

877 James B. Wood, *Japanese Military Strategy in the Pacific War: Was Defeat Inevitable?* (New York: Roman & Littlefield Publishers, Inc., 2007), 7, 19; Far East Command, 'Japanese Monograph Number 45: Imperial General Headquarters Army High Command Record, Mid 41–Aug 45', 48, 50.

878 James B. Wood, *Japanese Military Strategy in the Pacific War: Was Defeat Inevitable?* (New York: Roman & Littlefield Publishers, Inc., 2007), 7, 19.

879 Stephen Biddle, *Military Power: Explaining Victory and Defeat in Modern Battle* (Princeton: Princeton University Press, 2004), ix-x, 2-3.

880 Ibid., 4–5.

881 Biddle, 4–5.

882 Ibid., 35, 44–48.

883 Editors, 'combat effectiveness', *Encyclopedia Britannica*, 12 December 2013, https://www.britannica.com/topic/combat-effectiveness, accessed 21 March 2022.

884 James M. McPherson, *For Cause and Comrade: Why Men Fought in the Civil War* (New York: Oxford University Press, 1997), x, 13, 27.

885 Trevor N. Dupuy and Gay M. Hammerman, 'Soldier Capability – Army Combat Effectiveness (SCACE)', Volume III, Historical Combat Data and Analysis, December 1980, United States Army, Training and Doctrine Command, Fort Monroe, Virginia, 6–8.

886 Coox, *Nomonhan*, 1080.

887 Ibid.

888 Ibid.; Thomas N. Huber, *Japan's Battle of Okinawa, April–June 1945*, Leavenworth Papers Number 18, Combat Studies Institute, US Army Command and General Staff College, Fort Leavenworth, Kansas, 1990, 29–31; Drea, *In the Service of the Emperor: Essays on the Imperial Japanese Army*. (Lincoln: University of Nebraska Press, 1998), 70–74.

889 Coox, *Nomonhan*,1086–1087.

890 Leland Ness, *Rikugun*, 51.

891 Peter Mansoor, *The GI Offensive in Europe: The Triumph of American Infantry Divisions, 1941–1945* (Lawrence: University of Kansas Press, 1999), 2–5.

892 *Combat Lessons Number 2, 'Rank and File in Combat: What They're Doing; How They Do It'* (Operations Division of the War Department General Staff, Washington DC, 1943), 31.

893 United States National Archives and Records Administration, College Park, MD (NARA 2): Combined Operations Headquarters, Bulletin Number Y17, 'Lessons Learned from the Guadalcanal Operations' (Summary of the Final Report by the Commanding General, 1 US Marine Division), 15 December 1943; RG 165, War Department, 'P' File, Box 1203, MIS, Intelligence Bulletin, Volume 1, Number 9, May 1943; RG 226, OSS, Research and Analysis Branch Divisions, Intelligence Reports, Box 936; War Department Technical Manual 30-480, *Handbook on Japanese Military Forces*, 21 September 1942.

894 Verbeck, *Action on Attu*, 30 July 1943, 4, 11, 13; English, 16–18; M. Hamlin Cannon, *Leyte: The Return to the Philippines* (Washington DC: US Army Center of Military History, 1954), 211.

895 Coox, 1081–1082.

896 Drea, *Japan's Imperial Army: Its Rise and Fall, 1853-1945*, 191-192; Naval Analysis Division, *United States Strategic Bombing Survey: The Campaigns of the Pacific War (*Washington DC: Government Printing Office, 1946), 1–2.

897 Kato, Masuo, *The Lost War: A Japanese Reporter's inside Story* (New York: A.A. Knopf, 1946), 107.

898 Morgan, *Compellence and the Strategic Culture of Imperial Japan*, 230–235.

899 James A. Walker, Lewis Bernstein and Sharon Lang, *The Eastern Mandates Campaign: A Staff Ride Guide for Operation Flintlock, The Seizure of Kwajalein*, US Army Space and Missile Defense Command, Huntsville, AL, 2004, 25, 32–34.

Philip A. Crowl, Edmund G. Love, *Seizure of the Gilberts and Marshalls: United States Army in World War II, The War in the Pacific*, CMH Pub 5–6 (Washington DC: Office of the Chief of Military History, 1955), 210.

900 USSBS Interrogations: Number 524: Admiral Shigeru Fukudome, IJN; Subject: War in the Pacific; Date: 12 December 1945, Tokyo; Microfilm Publication M1654, Reel 9, 10–11.

901 Coox, 1080.

902 Sharon Tosi Lacey, *Pacific Blitzkrieg: World War II in the Central Pacific* (Denton: North Texas University Press, 2013), xvi.

903 Ibid., 36.

904 Lacey, xiv.

905 Stephen Biddle, *Military Power: Explaining Victory and Defeat in Modern Battle* (Princeton: Princeton University Press, 2004), ix–x, 2–3, 4–5.

906 Trevor N. Dupuy and Gay M. Hammerman, 'Soldier Capability – Army Combat Effectiveness (SCACE)', Volume III, Historical Combat Data

and Analysis, December 1980, United States Army, Training and Doctrine Command, Fort Monroe, Virginia, 6–8.

907 Coox, *Nomonhan*, 1082; Drea, *Japan's Imperial Army*,222, 226, 230–231, 246; Richard K. Betts, *Surprise Attack: Lessons for Defense Planning* (Washington DC: Brookings Institution, 1982), 134.; Ness, *Rikugun*, 14–16; US War Department, Technical Manual, TM-E 30-480, 1 October 1944, 85.

908 Ness, *Rikugun*, 14–16; Coox, *Nomonhan: Japan against Russia, 1939* (Stanford: Stanford University Press, 1985), 1009–1032; A.J. Barker, *Japanese Army Handbook, 1939–1945* (London: Ian Allan, 1979), 7, 115.

909 Drea, 174.

910 Drea, *Japan's Imperial Army*, 171–173.

911 Douglas Ford, 'US Assessments of Japanese Ground Warfare Tactics and the Army's Campaigns in the Pacific Theatres, 1943–1945: Lessons Learned and Methods Applied', *War in History*, Volume 16, Number 3 (July 2009), 342.

912 Bonn, 221-223.

913 Coox, quoting Nishiura Susumu, a senior IJA staff officer, 1081, 1083.

914 Ibid., 1084.

915 Ford, 'US Assessments of Japanese Ground Warfare Tactics and the Army's Campaigns in the Pacific Theatres, 1943–1945: Lessons Learned and Methods Applied', 340.

916 Coox, 'Flawed Perception and Its Effect upon Operational Thinking: The Case of the Japanese Army, 1937–41', in M. Handel (editor), *Intelligence and Military Operations* (London: Routledge, 1990), 252–53; Hayashi Saburo, in collaboration with A.D. Coox, *Kogun: The Japanese Army in the Pacific War* (Quantico: The Marine Corps Association, 1959), 23–27.

917 John Dower, *War Without Mercy: Race and Power in the Pacific War* (New York: Pantheon Books, 1986), x.

918 Saburo. Ienaga, *The Pacific War: World War II and the Japanese, 1931–1945* (New York: Pantheon Books, 1978), 141.

919 United States National Archives and Records Administration, College Park, MD (NARA 2), RG 165, War Department, Security Classified Publications, box 472, JICPOA, Bulletin 12–43, 'Japanese Land Forces, Number 6', 18 February 1943, quoted by Douglas Ford, 'US Assessments of Japanese Ground Warfare Tactics and the Army's Campaigns in the Pacific Theatres, 1943–1945: Lessons Learned and Methods Applied', *War in History*, July 2009, Volume 16, Number 3, 325–358.

920 'American and British Tactics – As Viewed by the Japanese', *Tactical and Technical Trends*, Number 14, 17 December 1942, US Military Intelligence Service, 52-53, 56. Translation of a captured document, 'Land Warfare Tactics to Use Against U.S. and British Forces' (Selections from the text

compiled by the Staff of the Army in China), Part I: US Army Methods and Japanese Countermeasures', not dated.

921 Kotani Ken, 'Japanese Intelligence in WWII: Successes and Failures' (Oxford: Osprey, 2009), 11–12, 24, 26.

922 Coox, *Nomonhan*, 1086.

923 United States Strategic Bombing Survey (USSSBS) Interrogations: Number 343: General Kawabe, Masakazu, IJA; Subject: Intelligence Operations at Air General Headquarters (KOKU SOGUN SHIRIEBU); date: 13 November 1945, Tokyo; Microfilm Publication M1654, Reel 8, 343–3.

924 Kotani, 24–26; Coox, 1086; Drea, 178.

925 United States Strategic Bombing Survey (USSSBS), 'Japanese Military and Naval Intelligence', 3.

926 Coox, 1086.

927 Kotani, 'Japanese Intelligence in World War II: Successes and Failures', 108.

928 Coox, 1086–1087.

929 Edward Drea, *Nomonhan: Japanese-Soviet Tactical Combat,1939*, Combat Studies Institute: US Army Command and General Staff College, Fort Leavenworth, Kansas, January 1981, 17–19, 87, 90.

930 Louis Morton, *Strategy and Command: The First Two Years*, 232; Jeffrey Moore, *Spies for Nimitz: Joint Military Intelligence in the Pacific War*, xiii.

931 *NARA 127:* Lieutenant Colonel Warren J. Clear, 'Problems of Taking Jap Prisoners', 2–3. Considering themselves to be disgraced by capture, Japanese servicemen were willing to divulge information.

932 Douglas Ford, 'US Assessments of Japanese Ground Warfare Tactics and the Army's Campaigns in the Pacific Theatres, 1943–1945: Lessons Learned and Methods Applied', *War in History*, Volume 16, Number 3 (July 2009), 334; *National Archives and Records Administration: Record Group 337: Records of Headquarters Army Ground Forces, 1916–1956* (Hereafter *NARA 337*): Series: Intelligence Reports, compiled 1943–1946: Box 51, Folder 10. Colonel Gordon B. Rogers, 'MEMORANDUM FOR GROUND GENERAL AND SPECIAL STAFF SECTIONS, HEADQUARTERS, ARMY GROUND FORCES, Subject: Observations in Southwest and South Pacific Theaters during the period 5 April, 1943 to 14 July, 1943' (Headquarters, Army Ground Forces, 25 August 1943), 4.

933 James C. McNaughton, *Nisei Linguists: Japanese Americans in the Military Intelligence Service in World War II*, Center of Military History Publication 70-99-1 (Washington DC: Department of the Army, 2006), 72.

934 James C. McNaughton, *Nisei Linguists: Japanese Americans in the Military Intelligence Service in World War II*, Center of Military History Publication 70-99-1 (Washington DC: Department of the Army, 2006), 15–28.

935 Ichinokuchi and Aiso (editors), *John Aiso and the M.I.S*, 177.

936 McNaughton, *Nisei Linguists*,169.

937 McNaughton, *Nisei Linguists*, 263, quoting Glenn W. McDonald, letter to the editor, *San Francisco Chronicle*, 16 September 1944, reprinted in WRA, *What We're Fighting For*, 20–21.

938 Coox, *Nomonhan*, 1009–32.; Coox, 'Flawed Perception and its Effect Upon Operational Thinking: The Case of the Japanese Army, 1937–41', in M. Handel (editor), *Intelligence and Military Operations* (London: Frank Cass, 1990), 239–254.

939 Ibid.; A.D. Coox, 'The Effectiveness of the Japanese Military Establishment in the Second World War' in A.R. Millett and W. Murray (editors), *Military Effectiveness: Volume 3 – The Second World War* (New York: Cambridge University Press, 2010), 34–38; Drea, *In the Service of the Emperor: Essays on the Imperial Japanese Army* (Lincoln: University of Nebraska Press, 1998), 7; S. Hayashi, in collaboration with Alvin D. Coox, *Kogun: The Japanese Army in the Pacific War* (Quantico: Marine Corps Association, 1959), 23–27.

940 Japanese Monograph 4, Philippine Operations Record, Phase III, July-November 1944, Preparations made by the 14th Area Army for the Military Operations in the Philippine Islands, Historical Section, G2, FEC, Office of the Chief of Military History, Oct 1946, 45–46.

941 Ibid.; Ooka Shohei, *Taken Captive: A Japanese POW's Story* (New York: John Wiley & Sons, 1996), 5.

942 Coox, 1009–1011, 1023, 1078–1085; L.A. Humphreys, *The Way of the Heavenly Sword: The Japanese Army in the 1920s* (Stanford: Stanford University Press, 1995), 15.

943 Douglas Ford, 'US Assessments of Japanese Ground Warfare Tactics and the Army's Campaigns in the Pacific Theatres, 1943–1945: Lessons Learned and Methods Applied', *War in History*, Volume 16, Number 3 (July 2009), 340.

944 Mansoor, 9; Doubler, 1-9; Marshall, *Island Victory*, 201–213.

945 Operation Report, 7th Infantry Division, King II, MCoE HQ Donovan Research Library, Fort Benning, GA. Documents collection. Call: D793.32. U307, 1.; Ford, 339; John F. Shortal, *Forged by Fire: General Robert L. Eichelberger and the Pacific War* (Columbia: University of South Carolina Press, 1987), 61, 69–71; Edmund G. Love, *The Hourglass Division*, 410.

946 Floyd. W. Radike, *Across The Dark Islands: The War in the Pacific* (New York: Ballantine Books,1984, 2003), 191–192.

947 Drea, *Japan's Imperial Army*, 162.

948 Stanley Karnow, *Vietnam: A History* (New York: Penguin Books, 1983), 21, quoting Võ Nguyên Giáp, commander, People's Army of Vietnam.

949 Coox, 1091.

950 Meiron and Susie Harris, *Soldiers of the Sun, the Rise and Fall of the Imperial Japanese Army* (New York: Random House, 1991), 393–395.

951 Coox, 1085.

952 Humphreys, *The Way of the Heavenly Sword: The Japanese Army in the 1920s*, 79–83.

953 Philips P. O'Brien, *How the War Was Won: Air-Sea Power and Allied Victory in World War II* (Cambridge: Cambridge University Press, 2015), 481–483; A.J. Barker, *Japanese Army Handbook, 1939-1945* (London: Ian Allan, 1979), 7, 115.

954 John B. George, *Shots Fired in Anger: A Rifleman's View of Battle* (Plantersville: Small Arms Technical Publishing Company, 1947) (National Rifle Association, second edition, 1981), 170.

955 Williamson Murray, 'Why Did It Take the North So Long?', *Military History Quarterly*, summer 1989, 24–33.

956 Earl F. Ziemke, 'Military Effectiveness in the Second World War', Chapter Eight in *Military Effectiveness*, Allan R. Millett and Williamson Murray (editors), second edition, 3:277–319 (Cambridge: Cambridge University Press, 2010), DOI:10.1017/CBO9780511762970.010.

957 McManus, *Island Infernos*, 11.

958 Alvin D. Coox, 'The Effectiveness of the Japanese Military Establishment in the Second World War', Chapter One in *Military Effectiveness*, Allan R. Millett and Williamson Murray (editors), second edition, 3:1–44 (Cambridge: Cambridge University Press, 2010), DOI:10.1017/CBO9780511762970.003.

959 Edward J. Drea, *Japan's Imperial Army: Its Rise and Fall, 1853–1945* (Lawrence: University Press of Kansas, 2009), vii–viii.

960 Record, 'Japan's Decision for War in 1941', viii, 29–31; Dower, *War Without Mercy*, 260; Mansoor, *The GI Offensive in Europe*, 3.

961 William L. Worden, 'The 7th Made It the Hard Way', Saturday Evening Post, 22 September 1945, 18, Division Newsletter, author's collection

962 Stouffer, *et al*, soldier survey responses on their attitudes, behaviour, and ratings of combat performance. Questions were about combat stamina; are you tough enough? Combat skill; are you well trained? Can you lead others? How do you feel about going into combat? Specifically included the 7th Infantry Division, 3–5, 23, 108, 111, 124. Note: revenge and vindictiveness were noted as higher factors in will to fight for American soldiers in the Pacific.

963 Love, *The Hourglass*, 3–5; William L. Worden, 'The 7th Made It the Hard Way', *Saturday Evening Post*, 22 September 1945, 2, Division Newsletter, author's collection.

BIBLIOGRAPHY

PRIMARY SOURCES

ARCHIVES AND MANUSCRIPT COLLECTIONS

United States National Archives and Records Administration

National Archives and Records Administration: Record Group 38: Records of the Office of the Chief of Naval Operations, 1875-2006.

National Archives and Records Administration: Record Group 127: Records of the U.S. Marine Corps, 1775 - 9999.

National Archives and Records Administration: Record Group 165: Records of the War Department General and Special Staff, 1903-1947.

National Archives and Records Administration: Record Group 337: Records of Headquarters Army Ground Forces, 1916 - 1956.

National Archives and Records Administration: Record Group 338: Records of the U.S. Army Operational, Tactical, and Support Organizations (World War II and Thereafter).

National Archives and Records Administration: Record Group 496: Records of General Headquarters, Southwest Pacific Area and United States Army Forces Pacific (World War II), 1941-1947.

National Archives and Records Administration: Record Group 550: Records of the U.S. Army, Pacific, 1945 - 1985.

National Archives and Records Administration, NARA 127: Lt. Col. Warren J. Clear, "Problems of Taking Jap Prisoners,".

National Archives and Records Administration: Record Group 337*: Records of Headquarters Army Ground Forces, 1916 - 1956* (Hereafter *NARA 337*): Series: Intelligence Reports, compiled 1943 – 1946: Box 51, Folder 10. Colonel Gordon B. Rogers, "MEMORANDUM FOR GROUND GENERAL AND SPECIAL STAFF SECTIONS, HEADQUARTERS, ARMY GROUND FORCES, Subject: Observations in Southwest and South Pacific Theaters during the period 5 April, 1943 to 14 July, 1943," (Headquarters, Army Ground Forces, 25 August 1943).

National Archives and Records Administration: *U.S. Army. "Sixth Army, Report of Leyte Operation, 20 October-25 December 1944, (AAR)"*. Record Group 407, Entry 1113, Philippines Archive Collection, Box 1478, National Archives.

Japan Center for Asian Historical Records (JACAR). National Archives of Japan.

Ministry of Justice, Research Group in the Secretariat of the Ministry of Justice. *Instruction to Japanese Soldiers at the Front* (English) (No. 107). Microfilm Reel 2200. Records of International Military Tribunal for the Far East on Class A War Crimes. Records of War Crime Tribunals. Records of War Crimes. Ministry of Justice. National Archives of Japan, Tokyo.

Ministry of Education. *Kokutai no Hongi: Cardinal Principles of the National Entity of Japan*. Edited by Robert K. Hall. Translated by John Owen Gauntlett. Cambridge: Harvard University Press, 1949.

U.S. Army Heritage and Education Center, U.S. Army War College

Commanding General, Army Ground Forces. "Report on Okinawa Operation, 1 May 1945". Army War College, Carlisle, Pennsylvania.

Combined Arms Research Library (Archives), U.S. Army Command and General Staff College

Addlestone, A.B., Commander, 707th Ordnance Company Report, 15 Jun 1943. Ordnance Company, to Commanding General, Landing Force, Subject: Operation Land Crab. Combined Arms Research Library (Archives), U.S. Army Command and General Staff College, Ft. Leavenworth, Kansas.

Commander, Fifth Amphibious Force, "Report of Flintlock Operation, 19 April 1944". Combined Arms Research Library (Archives), U.S. Army Command and General Staff College, Ft. Leavenworth, Kansas.

____________ G-2 Periodic Report 5, 4 Feb 44, G-2 Report of Operations (7th Inf Div FLINTLOCK Report, Vol IV). Combined Arms Research Library (Archives), U.S. Army Command and General Staff College, Ft. Leavenworth, Kansas.

Commander in Chief Pacific Fleet-Commander in Chief Pacific Ocean Area (CINCPAC-CINCPOA) Translation 9614, Summary of the Reorganization of the Third, Fifth, and Thirteenth Divisions, the Independent Mixed Brigades, the Amphibious Brigades, and the South Seas Detachments, and of the 250th Return Demobilization, War Ministry Order, 16 Nov 43. Combined Arms Research Library (Archives), U.S. Army Command and General Staff College, Ft. Leavenworth, Kansas.

Commander in Chief Pacific Fleet-Commander in Chief Pacific Ocean Area (CINCPAC-CINCPOA) Translation 9499A. Combined Arms Research Library (Archives), U.S. Army Command and General Staff College, Ft. Leavenworth, Kansas.

Commander in Chief Pacific Fleet-Commander in Chief Pacific Ocean Area (CINCPAC-CINCPOA) Translation 9536, Excerpts Taken from the 31st Army Monthly Reports for March and April 1944, dated 30 Apr 44. Combined Arms Research Library (Archives), U.S. Army Command and General Staff College, Ft. Leavenworth, Kansas.

Ewbank, Keith H. Amphibious Branch, G-3 Section, Army Ground Forces, Lecture, given 17 Jun 1943 to Quartermaster School Students, Camp Lee, Virginia. Subject: Action on Attu. Combined Arms Research Library (Archives), U.S. Army Command and General Staff College, Ft. Leavenworth, Kansas.

U.S. Army Combat Lessons No. 2, "Rank and File in Combat: What They're Doing; How They Do It.", Operations Division of the War Department General Staff, Washington D.C., 1943. Combined Arms Research Library (Archives), U.S. Army Command and General Staff College, Ft. Leavenworth, Kansas.

U.S. Army Infantry Combat Pamphlet – Part Two: Attu, Tactical and Technical Trends No. 31, 12 August 1943. Military Intelligence Services, War Department, Washington D.C., 1943. Combined Arms Research Library (Archives), U.S. Army Command and General Staff College, Ft. Leavenworth, Kansas.

U.S. Army Infantry Combat Pamphlet –Tactical and Technical Trends No. 32, 26 August 1943. Military Intelligence Services, War Department, Washington D.C., 1943. Combined Arms Research Library (Archives), U.S. Army Command and General Staff College, Ft. Leavenworth, Kansas.

U.S. Army Infantry Combat Pamphlet –Tactical and Technical Trends No. 33, 9 September 1943. Military Intelligence Services, War Department, Washington D.C., 1943. Combined Arms Research Library (Archives), U.S. Army Command and General Staff College, Ft. Leavenworth, Kansas.

U.S. Army. "Army Battle Casualties and Non-battle Deaths In World War II, Final Report 7 December-31 December 1946". Office of the Adjutant General, Statistical and Accounting Branch, 31 December 1946. Combined Arms Research Library (Archives), U.S. Army Command and General Staff College, Ft. Leavenworth, Kansas.

U.S. Army. "Army Ground Forces Observers Report". War Department, October-November 1942. Combined Arms Research Library (Archives), U.S. Army Command and General Staff College, Ft. Leavenworth, Kansas.

U.S. Army. "Army Ground Forces Observers Report". War Department, Washington D.C., 14 January 1943. Combined Arms Research Library (Archives), U.S. Army Command and General Staff College, Ft. Leavenworth, Kansas.

U.S. Army." Intelligence Memorandum #8, Japanese Occupation of Attu." Western Defense Command and 4th Army, 20 October 1942-31 May 1943. Combined Arms Research Library (Archives), U.S. Army Command and General Staff College, Ft. Leavenworth, Kansas.

U.S. Army. "Alaska Area Defense and Japanese Invasion of the Aleutians". War Department, Washington D.C., Combined Arms Research Library (Archives), U.S. Army Command and General Staff College, Ft. Leavenworth, Kansas.

U.S. Army. "Battle Casualties of the Army, 7 December 1941-30 January 1946". United States Army, January 1946. Combined Arms Research

Library (Archives), U.S. Army Command and General Staff College, Ft. Leavenworth, Kansas.

U.S. Army. "Battle Group in Northern Operations". War Department, Washington D.C., 24 March 1958. Combined Arms Research Library (Archives), U.S. Army Command and General Staff College, Ft. Leavenworth, Kansas.

U.S. Army. 'Clothing Almanac for Army". War Department, Washington D.C., 18 April 1949. Combined Arms Research Library (Archives), U.S. Army Command and General Staff College, Ft. Leavenworth, Kansas.

U.S. Army Command and General Staff College, Letter, Subject: "Report of Combined-Joint Committee on Arctic Operations," 26 March 1951, with 1st Indorsement, 26 March 1951. Combined Arms Research Library (Archives), U.S. Army Command and General Staff College, Ft. Leavenworth, Kansas.

U.S. Army Command and General Staff College, Manual, "The Principles of Strategy for An Independent Corps or Army in a Theater of Operations". Ft. Leavenworth, KS: Command and General Staff School Press, 1936.

U.S. Army. "General Order #12, Organization of Troops". Western Defense Command, War Department, 22 January 1943. Combined Arms Research Library (Archives), U.S. Army Command and General Staff College, Ft. Leavenworth, Kansas.

U.S. Army. "G-1 Conference on World War II Replacements and Personnel". United States Army, 1944. Combined Arms Research Library (Archives), U.S. Army Command and General Staff College, Ft. Leavenworth, Kansas.

U.S. Army. "G-2 Reports". Western Defense Command, Alaska Sector, United States Army, 14 May 1942-1 April 1943. Combined Arms Research Library (Archives), U.S. Army Command and General Staff College, Ft. Leavenworth, Kansas.

U.S. Navy. Commander, Joint Expeditionary Force (TF 51) "Report of Amphibious Operations for the Capture of the Marshall Islands (FLINTLOCK and CATCHPOLE), February 25, 1944.". Combined Arms Research Library (Archives), U.S. Army Command and General Staff College, Ft. Leavenworth, Kansas.

Maneuver Center of Excellence (MCoE), Donovan Research Library

After Action Report, 1st Battalion, 32nd Infantry Regiment less A and B Companies, "Battle of Attu," undated, Maneuver Center of Excellence (MCoE), Donovan Research Library, Fort Benning, Georgia.

Arnold, Archibald V. "Operation Report, 7th Infantry Division, King II, 21 August - 20 October 1944". Maneuver Center of Excellence Headquarters (MCoE), Donovan Research Library, Fort Benning, Georgia.

Campbell, Clark. "The Operations of the First Battalion (Reinforced) 184th Infantry, 7th Infantry Division in the Capture of Kwajalein Atoll, 31 January-6 February 1944 (Personal experiences of a Battalion Operations Officer). Advanced Infantry Officers Course, 1947-1948, The Infantry School, Donovan Research Library, Fort Benning, GA.

English, R.O. "The Operations of the 3rd Battalion, 17th Infantry (7th Infantry Division) In the Attack of a Ridge Nose, Attu Island, 21-22 May 1943 (Aleutian Campaign)". Advanced Infantry Officers Course, 1950, The Infantry School, Donovan Research Library, Fort Benning, Georgia.

Mapes, W.H, Action of BCT 17-2 on Attu Island, June 9, 1943, Maneuver Center of Excellence (MCoE), Donovan Research Library, Fort Benning, Georgia.

U.S. Army. *"Attu Campaign, 11-31 May 43, 17th Infantry Regiment, Initial Landing, Massacre Bay, Holtz Bay Pass"*. Microfilm Box 356, Item 1556. Maneuver Center of Excellence (MCoE), HQ Donovan Research Library, Fort Benning, Georgia.

U.S. Army. *"Report of Action at Attu Campaign, 11 May – 10 June 43, 17th Infantry Regiment"*. Items 1557A, 1557B, 1557C, 1557D, 1557E, 1557F. Maneuver Center of Excellence (MCoE), HQ Donovan Research Library, Fort Benning, Georgia.

U.S. Army. *"17th Infantry Regiment, S-2 Journal, Attu"*. Microfilm Box 356, Item 1558, Maneuver Center of Excellence (MCoE), Donovan Research Library, Fort Benning, Georgia.

U.S. Army. *"Memorandum from COL Wayne C. Zimmerman, Attu, 14 June 1943, 17th Infantry Regiment"*. Item 1559. Maneuver Center of Excellence (MCoE), Donovan Research Library, Fort Benning, Georgia.

U.S. Army. *"Field Order #1, Plan E, 2 May 43, 17th Infantry Regiment"*. Item 1560. Maneuver Center of Excellence (MCoE), Donovan Research Library, Fort Benning, Georgia.

U.S. Army. *"Battle Report of Company B, 11 May – 6 June 43, 17th Infantry Regiment"*. Item 1561. Maneuver Center of Excellence (MCoE), Donovan Research Library, Fort Benning, Georgia.

U.S. Army. *"32nd Infantry Regiment, Report of Action on Island of Attu."* Microfilm Box 356, Item 1562, Maneuver Center of Excellence (MCoE), Donovan Research Library, Fort Benning, Georgia.

U.S. Army. *"32nd Infantry Regiment, Journal and Journal File, Northern Landing Force, Attu"*. Microfilm Box 356, Item 1563, Maneuver Center of Excellence (MCoE), Donovan Research Library, Fort Benning, Georgia.

U.S. Army. *"32nd Infantry Regiment, Report of Action on Island of Attu."* Microfilm Box, Item 1562, Maneuver Center of Excellence (MCoE), Donovan Research Library, Fort Benning, Georgia.

U.S. Army. *"Operation Report, 7th Infantry Division, King II"*. Maneuver Center of Excellence (MCoE), Donovan Research Library, Fort Benning, Georgia. Documents collection. Call #: D793.32.U307

US Air Force Historical Research Agency

USAAF Historical Narratives. *Army Air Forces In the War Against Japan, 1941-1942*. Washington, D.C., Headquarters, Army Air Forces, 1945. US Air Force Historical Research Agency, Maxwell Air Force Base, Alabama.

U.S. Army Air Forces. *"AAF Study #34, AAF in the War Against Japan, 1941-42"*. Headquarters, U.S. Army Air Forces, 1946. US Air Force Historical Research Agency, Maxwell Air Force Base, Alabama.

United States Strategic Bombing Survey (USSBS), Naval Analysis Division, "Interrogations of Japanese Officials, Vol. I, Interrogation of Commander Nakajima Chikataka, IJN". Washington, D.C., 1946. U.S. Air Force Historical Research Agency. Maxwell Air Force Base, Alabama.

United States Strategic Bombing Survey, Military Analysis Division. *Japanese Air Power*. Washington, D.C.: United States Strategic Bombing Survey (Pacific) Military Analysis Division, 1946.

United States Strategic Bombing Survey, Naval Analysis Division. *The Campaigns of the Pacific War*. Washington, D.C. : U.S. Strategic Bombing Survey (Pacific) Naval Analysis Division, 1946.

United States Strategic Bombing Survey. *Japanese Military and Naval Intelligence Division. Japanese Intelligence Section, G-2. Dates of Survey: 1 November 1945 through 1 February 1946*, Its [Reports. Pacific War, 97]. Washington: U.S. Govt. Print. Off., 1946.

The Pacific War Archive

Japanese Monograph No.4, Philippine Operations Record, Phase III, July-November 1944, Preparations made by the 14th Area Army for the Military Operations in the Philippine Islands, 50 pages, unpaginated, Historical Section, G2, Far East Command, Office of the Chief of Military History, October 1946. Japanese Monographs, The Pacific War Archive.

Japanese Monograph No.5, Philippine Operations Record, Phase III, July-December 1944, Preparations made by the 14th Area Army Command in Leyte, Historical Section, G2, Far East Command, Office of the Chief of Military History, October 1946. Japanese Monographs, The Pacific War Archive.

Japanese Monograph No.6, Philippine Operations Record, Phase III, July-December 1944, Defense of Leyte by 35th Army, 204 pages, unpaginated, Historical Section, G2, Far East Command, Office of the Chief of Military History, October 1946. Japanese Monographs, The Pacific War Archive.

Japanese Monograph No. 45: History of Imperial General Headquarters, Army Section (Revised Edition). Headquarters, United States Army, Japan, Assistant Chief of Staff, G-3, 1959. Japanese Monographs, The Pacific War Archive.

Japanese Monograph No. 46. The Aleutian Islands Campaign, June 1942-July 1943. Japanese Studies in World War II. Headquarters, United States Army, Japan, Assistant Chief of Staff, G-3, 1959. Japanese Monographs, The Pacific War Archive.

Japanese Monograph No. 88. Aleutian Naval Operation, March 1942-February 1943. Headquarters, United States Army, Japan, Assistant Chief of Staff, G-3, 1959. Translated by the Office of Military History. n.d. Japanese Monographs, The Pacific War Archive.

Japanese Monograph No. 135. Okinawa Operations Record, March 1944-June 1945, Book 1, "Okinawa Operations Record of 32d Army,". Headquarters, United States Army, Japan, Assistant Chief of Staff, G-3, 1949. Translated by the Office of Military History. n.d. Japanese Monographs, The Pacific War Archive.

BOOKS AND MEMOIRS

Ito, Hirobumi. *Commentaries on the Constitution of the Empire of Japan.* Translated by Miyoji Ito. Tokyo: Insetsu Kyoku [Government Printing Office], 1889.

George, John B. *Shots Fired in Anger: A Rifleman's View of Battle.* Plantersville: Small Arms Technical Publishing Company, 1947; National Rifle Association, 2d Edition, 1981.

Matthews, Richard E. *Attu Combat Diary.* Maneuver Center of Excellence (MCoE), Donovan Research Library, Fort Benning, Georgia, July 1943; updated September 1980.

Ooka, Shohei. *Taken Captive: A Japanese POW's Story.* Translated and edited by Wayne P. Lammers. New York: John Wiley & Sons, 1996.

Radike, Floyd W. *Across The Dark Islands: The War in the Pacific.* New York: Ballantine Books,1984, 2003.

Sakurai, Tadayoshi, *Human bullets, a soldier's story of Port Arthur,* translated by Masajiro Honda and edited by Alice Mabel Bacon. Boston: Houghton, Mifflin, and Company, 1907.

Sledge, Eugene B. *With The Old Breed: At Peleliu and Okinawa.* Novato: Presidio Press, 2010.

Yahara, Hiromichi, *The Battle for Okinawa,* translated by Roger Pineau and Uehara Masatoshi, with an introduction and commentary by Frank B. Gibney. New York: John Wiley and Sons, 1995.

OFFICIAL HISTORIES

Appleman, Roy E., Burns, James M., Gugeler, Russel A., and Stevens, John. *The U.S. Army in World War II: The War in the Pacific, Okinawa: The Last Battle.* Washington D.C.: Center of Military History, 1993.

Cannon, M. Hanlon, *The U.S. Army in World War II: The War in the Pacific, Leyte: The Return to the Philippines,* "Chapter VIII, Southern Leyte Valley: Part Two". Washington D.C.: Office of the Chief of Military History, 1964, 2000.

Cate, James Lea and Craven, Wesley Frank. *The Army Air Forces in World War II, Volume IV; The Pacific-Guadalcanal to Saipan, August 1942 to July 1944.* Air Force Historical Division. Chicago: University of Chicago Press, 1950.

Conn, Stetson, Engelman, Rose and Fairchild, Byron. *The United States Army in World War II: The Western Hemisphere: Guarding the United States and its Outposts.* "Chapters IX/X/XI". Washington D.C.: Office of the Chief of Military History, 1964, 2000.

Crowl, Phillip L. and Love, Edmund G. *Seizure of the Gilberts and Marshalls: United States Army in World War II, The War in the Pacific,* Center of Military History Publication 5-6. Washington, D.C.: Office of the Chief of Military History, 1955.

Fisch, Arnold G. *Ryukyus: The U.S. Army Campaigns of World War II.* Center of Military History Publication 72-35. Washington D.C.: U.S. Army Center of Military History, 1993.

Kent, Roberts Greenfield (Editor), *United States Army in World War II, Pictorial Record: The War Against Japan.* Washington, D.C.: The U.S. Army Center of Military History, 1952/2001.

MacGarrigle, George L. "Aleutian Islands: The U.S. Army Campaigns of World War II". Center of Military History Publication 72-6, Washington D.C.: U.S. Army Center of Military History, 2001.

Morison, Samuel Eliot. *Aleutians, Gilberts and Marshalls, June 1942 – April 1944.* Volume 7 of the History of United States Naval Operations in World War II. Champaign: University of Illinois Press, 2002.

Morton, Louis. *Strategy and Command: The First Two Years,* United States Army in World War II: The War in the Pacific. Washington, D.C.: Office of the Chief of Military History, Dept. of the Army, 1962.

Palmer, Robert R. *The United States Army in World War II, The Army Ground Forces: The Procurement and Training of Ground Combat Troops.* Washington D.C.: U.S. Army Center of Military History, 1993.

Wright, Burton. *Eastern Mandates: The U.S. Army Campaigns of World War II.* Washington D.C.: U.S. Army Center of Military History, 1993.

ARTICLES AND ONLINE PAPERS

Abe, Namiko. "Giri: Moral Obligation." ThoughtCo. https://www.thoughtco.com/giri-moral-obligation-2028017.

Miller, Jacob H. "Strategic Culture as the Basis for Military Adaptive Capacity: Overcoming battlefield technological surprises" 01 April 2014. CUREJ: College Undergraduate Research Electronic Journal, University of Pennsylvania, https://repository.upenn.edu/curej/173.

INTERVIEWS

Blanchard, George S. transcript of an oral history conducted by Lieutenant Colonel James Longhofer for "Senior Officer Oral History Program," Box 1A of 9, George S. Blanchard Papers, The United States Army War College Archives, Carlisle Barracks.

Galles, Dean E. Collection, (AFC/2001/001/88536), Veterans History Project, American Folklife Center, Library of Congress.

REPORTS AND STUDIES

Drea, Edward. *Nomonhan: Japanese-Soviet Tactical Combat,1939.* Combat Studies Institute: U.S. Army Command and General Staff College, Fort Leavenworth, Kansas, January 1981.

Dupuy, Trevor N., and Hammerman, Gay M. "Soldier Capability – Army Combat Effectiveness (SCACE)", Volume III, Historical Combat Data and Analysis. United States Army, Training and Doctrine Command, Fort Monroe, Virginia, December 1980.

Huber, Thomas M. *Japan's Battle of Okinawa, April–June 1945, Japan's Battle of Okinawa, April-June 1945,* Leavenworth Papers Number 18, Combat Studies Institute, U.S. Army Command and General Staff College, Fort Leavenworth, Kansas, 1990.

Kamish, Robert J. Commander, 7th Medical Battalion. Subject: Report of Medical Evacuation on Attu, not dated. Combined Arms Research Library (Archives), U.S. Army Command and General Staff College, Ft. Leavenworth, Kansas.

Landrum, Edward M. Commanding Landing Force to Commanding General, Western Defense Command, Subject: Report of Operations, Attu, 22 Jun 1943. Combined Arms Research Library (Archives), U.S. Army Command and General Staff College, Ft. Leavenworth, Kansas.

McConnell, William J. WWII Survey; United States Forces, European Theater, Reports of the General Board, no. 3, "Reinforcement System and Reinforcement Procedures in the European Theater of Operations".

______________ WWII Survey; United States Forces, European Theater, Reports of the General Board, no. 4, "Leaves".

Orr, Robert. D. "Report on Attu Operations, May 11-June 16, 1943", dated 30 July 1943. Washington D.C.: U.S. Army Medical Department, Office of Medical History.

Record, Jeffrey. *Japan's Decision for War in 1941: Some Enduring Lessons.* U.S. Army War College, Strategic Studies Institute, Carlisle, Pennsylvania, February 2009.

Smith, Davis. Assistant Chief of Staff G-3, Western Defense Command. Subject: Preliminary Report on Attu Landing, 30 May 1943. Combined Arms Research Library (Archives), U.S. Army Command and General Staff College, Ft. Leavenworth, Kansas.

Smith, Maj Gen Holland M. USMC, U.S. Pacific Fleet Amphibious Force, Subject: Operations Against Attu-May 1943, 8 Jul 1943. Combined Arms Research Library (Archives), U.S. Army Command and General Staff College, Ft. Leavenworth, Kansas.

Steckel, Francis C. "Morale Problems in Combat: American Soldiers in Europe in World War II *Army History*, Summer 1994, No. 31 (Summer 1994). U.S. Army Center of Military History.

Stouffer, S. A., Lumsdaine, A. A., Lumsdaine, M. H., Williams, R. M., Jr., Smith, M. B., Janis, I. L., Star, S. A., & Cottrell, L. S., Jr., *The American Soldier: Combat and its Aftermath,* (Studies in Social Psychology in World War II). Princeton: Princeton University Press, 1949.

Weckerling, John. Assistant Chief of Staff G-2, Western Defense Command. Subj: Intelligence Memorandum No. 8, Final Report of Reduction and Occupation of Attu from the Combat Intelligence Point of View, 9 Aug 1943. Combined Arms Research Library (Archives), U.S. Army Command and General Staff College, Ft. Leavenworth, Kansas.

Japanese Studies in World War II, No. 50, Southeast Area Naval Operations, Vol. III, Office of the Chief of Military History, Washington, D.C. (OCMH)

Japanese Studies in World War II, No. 55, Operations in the Central Pacific. Office of the Chief of Military History, Washington, D.C. (OCMH).

Japanese Studies in World War II. Japanese Studies in World War II, No. 73, Marshall Islands Operations, Office of the Chief of Military History, Washington, D.C. (OCMH).

Joint Intelligence Center, Pacific Operations Area (JICPOA) Bulletin 48-44, Japanese Defenses, Kwajalein Atoll, 10 Apr 44. Combined Arms Research Library (Archives), U.S. Army Command and General Staff College, Ft. Leavenworth, Kansas.

Joint Intelligence Center, Pacific Ocean Area (JICPOA) Translation 6234, Distribution of Forces and Dispositions of the 1st South Seas Detachment. Combined Arms Research Library (Archives), U.S. Army Command and General Staff College, Ft. Leavenworth, Kansas.

Joint Intelligence Center, Pacific Ocean Area (JICPOA) Bulletin 88-44, 1st Amphibious Brigade, Japanese Army, 13 Jun 44. Combined Arms Research Library (Archives), U.S. Army Command and General Staff College, Ft. Leavenworth, Kansas.

Joint Intelligence Center, Pacific Ocean Area (JICPOA) Bulletin 89-44, Japanese Defense of Eniwetok Atoll, 12 Jun 44. Combined Arms Research Library (Archives), U.S. Army Command and General Staff College, Ft. Leavenworth, Kansas.

Joint Intelligence Center, Pacific Ocean Area JICPOA Translation 5545, Inner South Seas Force Secret Operations Order 26-43. Combined Arms Research Library (Archives), U.S. Army Command and General Staff College, Ft. Leavenworth, Kansas.

Report, Alaska Defense Command, with comments by Lt. Gen Simon B. Buckner, "Action on Attu," not dated. Intelligence report on the Japanese on Attu following the battle to retake the island. Combined Arms Research Library (Archives), U.S. Army Command and General Staff College, Ft. Leavenworth, Kansas.

Report, AC/AS Intelligence Evaluation Report, Provides Account of Japanese Bomber Attack 22 May with description and approach chart, 10 Jun 1943. Combined Arms Research Library (Archives), U.S. Army Command and General Staff College, Ft. Leavenworth, Kansas.

Report, AC/AS Intelligence Evaluation Report 11425, Provides Account of William Gilman's Observations of Battle of Attu, 6 Dec 1943. Combined Arms Research Library (Archives), U.S. Army Command and General Staff College, Ft. Leavenworth, Kansas.

Report, Assistant Chief of Staff A-2, 11th Air Force. Subj: Special Intelligence Report on Observations Made by Col. B.B. Talley, USA Corps of Engineers in Beach Purple Area, Attu Island, the Aleutians D Plus 1 to D Plus 5 Inclusive, 18 May 1943. Combined Arms Research Library (Archives), U.S. Army Command and General Staff College, Ft. Leavenworth, Kansas.

Report, Comdr, USS *Nassau* (CVE-16) to Commander-in-Chief, U.S. Pacific Fleet. Subject: Action Report, Attu Island, May 11 to May 20, 1943, 5 Jun

1943. Combined Arms Research Library (Archives), U.S. Army Command and General Staff College, Ft. Leavenworth, Kansas.

Report on the Okinawa Operation, Headquarters Army Ground Forces, Army War College, Washington D.C., 1 May 1945. Combined Arms Research Library (Archives), U.S. Army Command and General Staff College, Ft. Leavenworth, Kansas.

PERIODICALS, JOURNALS, REFERENCES

Bears, Ernest, personal account of a battalion commander, *Hourglass Newsletter*, 1993.

Commander, US Army Combined Arms Center, FM 101-5-1, Operational Terms and Graphics, Headquarters, Department of the Army Washington, DC, 1997/2004. Author's collection.

Lamothe, Dan. "Brothers in Arms: Letters from War". Washington Post, December 6, 2017. https://www.washingtonpost.com/podcasts/letters-from-war/

Patton, George S. "The Effect of Weapons on War" Cavalry Journal, #37, (November 1930), Commander, U.S. Army Cavalry School. "The Infantry Journal". Fort Benning, Georgia. http://www.pattonhq.com/textfiles/effect.html

Worden, William, L. "The 7th Made It the Hard Way", Saturday Evening Post, September 22, 1945, 2, Division Newsletter. Author's collection.

YANK, The Army Weekly Magazine, Branch Office, Information and Education Division, War Department, New York. Author's collection.

AUTHOR'S COLLECTION

Boyes, B.W. *Short History of the Battle of Attu*. Post Executive Officer and Intelligence and Operations Sections, Post Headquarters, Camp Earle, Attu, Alaska. Third Edition July 1945. Author's collection.

Eyde, Ralph personal letters dated, 1943-1944; "Brothers in Arms" The Washington Post, Dan Lamothe, Dec. 6, 2017. Author's collection.

Tatsuguchi, Paul Nobuo. *The Diary of Paul Nobuo Tatsuguchi.* Translated by the U.S. Army. Washington D.C.: The War Department. May 1943. Author's collection.

Tyng, Sewell. "The Capture Of Attu: As Told By The Men Who Fought There". United States War Department. Washington DC: The Infantry Journal, October 1944. Author's collection.

Verbeck, William. *"Action on Attu: A Summary of Information of the Enemy Obtained During the Operations of the Force on Attu"*. G-2 Alaska Defense Command, 30 July 1943. Author's collection.

U.S. Army. "Handbook on Japanese Military Forces". War Department Technical Manual: TM-E 30-480, United States Army, 1 October 1944. Hyperwar: A Hypertext History of the Second World War. Author's collection.

SECONDARY SOURCES

Agawa, Hiroyaki. *The Reluctant Admiral: Yamamoto and the Imperial Navy*, trans. John Bester. Tokyo; New York: Kodansha International, 1982.

Ambrose, Stephen E. *Citizen Soldiers: The US Army from the Normandy Battlefields to the Bulge to the Surrender of Germany, June 7, 1944-May 7, 1945.* New York: Touchstone, Simon, and Schuster, 1997.

Astor, Gerald. *Crisis in the Pacific: The Battles for the Philippine Islands by the Men Who Fought Them.* New York: Dell Publishing, 1996.

______________ *Operation Iceberg: The Invasion and Conquest of Okinawa in World War II – An Oral History*. New York: Dutton, 1995. New York: Harper and Rowe, 1970.

Bacon, Alice Mabel, and Rogers, Bruce. *In the Land of the Gods: Some Stories of Japan*. Boston: Houghton, Mifflin, and Company, 1905.

Barker, A.J. *Japanese Army Handbook, 1939-1945.* London: Ian Allan, 1979.

Bateson, Gregory et. al., "Toward a Theory of Schizophrenia," in Bateson, *Steps to an Ecology of Mind.* New York: Ballentine, 1972.

Bellah, Robert N. *Tokugawa Religion: The Values of Pre-Industrial Japan*. Boston: Beacon Press, 1957.

______________ "Japan's Cultural Identity: Some Reflections on the Work of Watsuji Tetsuro." *The Journal of Asian Studies* 24, no. 4 (1965): 573–94. doi:10.2307/2051106.

Belote, James H., and Belote, William M. *Typhoon of Steel: The Battle of Okinawa.* New York: Harper and Rowe, 1970.

Benesch, Oleg. *Inventing the Way of the Samurai: Nationalism, Internationalism, and Bushido in Modern Japan*. Oxford: Oxford University Press, 2014.

Betts, Richard K. *Surprise Attack: Lessons for Defense Planning.* Washington D.C.: Brookings Institution, 1982.

Biddle, Stephen. *Military Power: Explaining Victory and Defeat in Modern Battle.* Princeton: Princeton University Press, 2004.

Black, Jeremy. *War and the Cultural Turn.* Cambridge: Polity Press, 2012.

Bonn, Keith. *When the Odds Were Even: The Vosges Mountains Campaign, October1944 - January 1945.* Novato: Presidio Press, 1994.

Bonura, Michael A. *Under the Shadow of Napoleon: French Influence on the American Way of Warfare from Independence to the Eve of World War II.* New York: NYU Press, 2012

Borch, Fred L. *Military Trials of War Criminals in the Netherlands East Indies, 1946–1949.* Oxford: Oxford University Press, 2017.

Braithwaite, Kirstin. "Effective in battle: conceptualizing soldiers' combat effectiveness". *Defence Studies.* Oxfordshire: Routledge, 2018.

Brown, Delmer M. *Nationalism in Japan: An Introductory Historical Analysis.* Berkeley, CA: University of California Press, 1955.

Brown, Roger H. "Yasuoka Masahiro's 'New Discourse on Bushidō Philosophy': Cultivating Samurai Spirit and Men of Character for Imperial Japan", Social Science Japan Journal Vol. 16, No. 1, 2013.

Bruscino, Thomas. "The Theory of Operational Art and Unified Land Operations,". School of Advanced Military Studies Theoretical Paper, Command and General Staff College, Fort Leavenworth, KS, Summer 2012.

Bryant, Anthony. *Sekigahara 1600: The Final Struggle for Power*. Osprey Campaign Series #40. Oxford: Osprey Publishing.

Chacho, Tania M. *Why Did They Fight? American Airborne Units in World War II*, Defence Studies, Fall 2001, 1:3.

Chandonnet, Fern editor. *Alaska at War, 1941-1945, The Forgotten War Remembered.* Juneau: University of Alaska Press, 2008.

Citino, Robert M. *The German Way of War.* Lawrence: University Press of Kansas, 2005.

Clausen, Walter B. *Blood for the Emperor. A Narrative History of the Human Side of the War in the Pacific.* New York: D. Appleton-Century Company, Inc., 1943.

Clausewitz, Carl von. *On War.* Edited and translated by Michael Howard and Peter Paret. Princeton: Princeton University Press, 1976.

Clarke, Jeffrey C. Chapter 6, "World Military History,1786-1945", "A Guide to the Study and Use of Military History". John Jessup, Jr. and Robert W. Coakley, editors. Center of Military History, Washington D.C., 1988.

Clayton, James D. "American and Japanese Strategies in the Pacific War." *Makers of Modern Strategy from Machiavelli to the Nuclear Age*, edited by Peter Paret. Princeton: Princeton University Press, 1986.

Cleary, Thomas. *The Japanese Art of War: Understanding the Culture of Strategy.* Boston and London: Shambhala, 1991.

Cloe, John Haile. *Attu: The Forgotten Battle,* National Park Service. Washington, D.C.: Department of the Interior, 2017.

Cohen, Stan. *The Forgotten War: A Pictorial History of World War II in Alaska and Northwestern Canada.* Missoula: Pictorial Histories Publishing Co., 1988.

Connable Ben, et.al., *Will to Fight: Analyzing, Modeling, and Simulating the Will to Fight of Military Units.* Santa Monica, Calif.: RAND Corporation, RR-2341-A, 2018.

Cook, Haruko and Theodore. *Japan at War, An Oral History.* New York: The Free Press, 1992.

Cook James W., and Glickman, Lawrence B. *The Cultural Turn in U.S. History: Past, Present, and Future,* edited by: James W. Cook, Lawrence B. Glickman, Michael O'Malley. Chicago: University of Chicago Press, 2008.

Coox, Alvin D. *Nomonhan: Japan against Russia, 1939.* Stanford: Stanford University Press, 1985.

______________ "Flawed Perception and Its Effect upon Operational Thinking: The Case of the Japanese Army, 1937-41", in M. Handel, ed., *Intelligence and Military Operations.* London: Routledge, 1990.

______________ "The Effectiveness of the Japanese Military Establishment in the Second World War." Chapter One. In *Military Effectiveness,* edited by Allan R. Millett and Williamson Murray, 2nd edition. Cambridge: Cambridge University Press, 2010.

Corum, James S. *The Roots of Blitzkrieg: Hans von Seeckt and German Military Reform.* Lawrence: University of Kansas Press, 1992.

Costello, John. *The Pacific War, 1941-1945.* New York: William Morrow, 1981.

Coyle, Daniel. *The Culture Code: The Secrets of Highly Successful Groups*. New York: Bantam, 2018.

Crowley, James B. *Japan's Quest for Autonomy: National Security and Foreign Policy, 1930-1938,* Princeton: Princeton University Press, 1966.

Dallek, Robert, *Franklin D. Roosevelt, and American Foreign Policy, 1932-1945,* Second Edition. New York: Oxford University Press, 1995.

Davies, Roger J. and Ikeno, Osamu. "Giri: Japanese Social Obligations", *The Japanese Mind: Understanding Contemporary Japanese Culture.* Tokyo: Tuttle Publishing, 2002.

Dawes, James. *Evil Men.* Cambridge: Harvard University Press, 2013.

de Bary, William, Carol Gluck, and Arthur E. Tiedemann, *Sources of Japanese Tradition, Volume Two: 1600–2000.* 2nd ed. New York: Columbia University Press, 2005.

de Bary, William, Keene, Donald, and Tsunoda Ryusaku, eds., *The Imperial Rescript to Soldiers and Sailors, Sources of Japanese Tradition II, 1600-2000.* New York: Columbia University Press, 1958.

Dilworth, David A. Guiding Principles of Interpretation in Watsuji Tetsurō's History of Japanese Ethical Thought: With Particular Reference to the Tension between the Sonnō and Bushidō Traditions. In Victor Skagen Hori & Melissa Anne-Marie Curley (eds.), *Frontiers of Japanese Philosophy: Neglected Themes and Hidden Variations.* Nagoya: Nanzan Institute for Religion & Culture, 2008.

Doi, Takeo. *The Anatomy of Dependence: Exploring an area of the Japanese psyche: feelings of indulgence.* Tokyo: Kodansha International, 1973.

Doubler, Michael. *Closing With the Enemy: How GIs Fought the War in Europe, 1944-1945.* Lawrence: University Press of Kansas, 1994.

Dower, John. *War Without Mercy: Race & Power in the Pacific War.* New York: Pantheon Books, 1986.

Drea, Edward. *In the Service of the Emperor: Essays on the Imperial Japanese Army.* Lincoln: University of Nebraska Press, 1998.

______________ *Japan's Imperial Army: Its Rise and Fall, 1853-1945,* Lawrence: University of Kansas Press, 2009.

Dull, Paul S. *A Battle History of the Imperial Japanese Navy (1941-1945).* Annapolis: Naval Institute Press, 1978.

Earhart, David C. *Certain Victory: Images of World War II in the Japanese Media.* London: Routledge, 2008.

Earle, Edward Mead. *Makers of Modern Strategy: Military Thought from Machiavelli to Hitler.* Princeton: Princeton University Press, 1943.

Echevarria, Antulio J. *Reconsidering the American Way of War: U.S. Military Practice from the Revolution to Afghanistan.* Washington D.C.: Georgetown University Press, 2014.

Ellis, John. *The Sharp End: The Fighting Man in World War II.* New York: Scribner's, 1980.

Falk, Stanley L., and Tsuneishi, Warren M. *MIS in the War against Japan: Personal Experiences Related at the 1993 MIS Capital Reunion, "The Nisei Veteran: An American Patriot".* Vienna, VA: Japanese American Veterans Association of Washington, D.C., 1995.

Fellers, Bonner F. *Psychology of the Japanese Soldier, Part 1.* Washington D.C.: BiblioGov Project, 2012. Originally Published 1936.

Festinger, Leon. *An Introduction to the Theory of Cognitive Dissonance.* Stanford, CA: Stanford University Press, 1957.

Ford, Douglas. *Dismantling the 'Lesser Men' and 'Supermen' Myths: US Intelligence on the Imperial Japanese Army after the fall of the Philippines, Winter 1942 to Spring 1943.* Taylor and Francis Online, Intelligence and National Security, Vol. 24, No. 4, August 2009. DOI:10.1080/02684520903069496

______________. *U.S. Assessments of Japanese Ground Warfare Tactics and the Army's Campaigns in the Pacific Theatres, 1943-1945: Lessons Learned and Methods Applied. War in History,* Sage Publications, Vol. 16, No. 3. July 2009.

Frank, Richard, B. *Downfall: The End of the Imperial Japanese Empire.* New York: Penguin Books, 1999.

______________ *Guadalcanal: The Definitive Account of the Landmark Battle.* New York: Random House, 1990.

Friday, Karl. "Bushidō or Bull? A Medieval Historian's Perspective on the Imperial Army and the Japanese Warrior Tradition", Society for History Education Vol. 27 Issue. 3 (May 1994) 27:3, 1994.

Fussell, Paul. *Wartime: Understanding and Behavior in the Second World War.* Oxford University Press, 1989.

Gardner, Bruce, and Stahura, Barbara. *The Seventh Infantry Division, Serving America for 75 Years.* Paducah: Turner Publishing, 1997.

Garfield, Brian. *The Thousand-Mile War: World War II in Alaska and the Aleutians.* Juneau: University of Alaska Press, 1995.

Geuss, Raymond. *The Idea of a Critical Theory: Habermas and the Frankfurt School.* Cambridge: Cambridge University Press, 1981.

Gilmore, Allison B. *You Can't Fight Tanks with Bayonets: Psychological Warfare against the Japanese Army in the South West Pacific.* Lincoln: University of Nebraska Press, 1998.

Golway, Terry. *Washington's General: Nathanael Greene and the Triumph of the American* Revolution. New York: Henry Holt and Company, 2005.

Goto-Jones, Christopher. "The Way of Revering the Emperor: Imperial Philosophy in Modern Japan". The Emperors of Modern Japan, edited by Ben-Ami Shilony. Leiden & Boston: Brill, 2008.

Gray, Colin. *Modern Strategy.* Oxford: Oxford University Press, 1999.

______________ "Strategic Culture as Context: The First Generation Strikes Back," Review of International Studies, vol. 25, no. 1, January 1999.

____________ "U.S. Strategic Culture: Implications for Defense Technology," In Defense Technology. Eds. Asa A. Clark IV and John F. Lilley, (Westport, CT: Praeger Publishers, 1989), 31-45.

Griffis, William Elliot. *The Japanese Nation in Evolution; Steps in the Progress of a Great People*. New York: T. Y. Crowell, 1907.

Grinter, Lawrence E. "Cultural and Historical Influences in Sinic Asia: China, Japan, and Vietnam", in Stephen J. Blank, et. al. *Conflict, Culture, and History: Regional Dimensions*. Maxwell, AFB AL: Air University Press, 1993.

Gropman, Alan L. "Analysis by Hyperbole," *Air University Quarterly Review*, September-October 1983, 91.

Hacker, Barton C. "Military Institutions, Weapons, and Social Change: Toward a New History of Military Technology." *Technology and Culture*, 35, (4). 1994.

____________ "The Machines of War: European Military Technology in the Twentieth Century." *Technology and History*. In press.

Hall, Wayne M. *The Power of Will in International Conflict: How to Think Critically in Complex Environments*. Santa Barbara: Praeger, 2018.

Hamner, Christopher H. *Enduring Battle: American Soldiers in Three Wars, 1776-1945*. Lawrence: University of Kansas Press, 2011.

Harries, Meirion and Susie. *Soldiers of the Sun: The Rise and Fall of the Imperial Japanese Army*. New York: Random House, 1991.

Harrington, Joseph D. *Yankee Samurai: The Secret Role of Nisei in America's Pacific Victory*. Detroit, Michigan: Pettigrew Enterprises, 1979.

Hart, Russell. *Clash of Arms: How the Allies Won in Normandy*. Boulder: Lynne Rienner Publishers Inc., 2001.

Hayashi Saburo, in collaboration with A.D. Coox, *Kogun: The Japanese Army in the Pacific War*. Quantico: The Marine Corps Association, 1959.

Helmus, Todd C. and Glenn, Russell W. *Steeling the Mind: Combat Stress Reactions and Their Implications for Urban Warfare*. Santa Monica: RAND Corporation, 2005.

Henderson, William. Darryl. *Cohesion: The Human Element in Combat*. Washington DC: National Defense University Press, 1985.

Hobsbawm, Eric J. and Ranger, Terence. "Mass Producing Traditions: Europe 1870-1914", *The Invention of Tradition*. Cambridge: Cambridge University Press, 1983.

Hoffman, F. G. *Decisive Force: The New American Way of War*. Westport: Praeger, 1996.

Hornfischer, James. *The Fleet at Flood Tide: America at Total War in the Pacific, 1944–1945*. New York: Random House, 2016.

Howard, Michael. *Studies in War and Peace*. Viking Press, 1971.

Hull, Isabel V. *Absolute Destruction: Military Culture and the Practices of War in Imperial Germany*. Ithaca: Cornell University Press, 2006.

Humphreys, L.A., *The Way of the Heavenly Sword: The Japanese Army in the 1920s*. Stanford: Stanford University Press, 1995.

Hunter-Chester, David. "Imperial Japanese Army Culture, 1918-1945: "Duty Heavier than a Mountain, Death Lighter than a Feather." Chapter 9, in *The Culture of Military Organizations,* edited by Peter R. Mansoor and Williamson Murray. Cambridge: Cambridge University Press, 2019.

Huntington, Samuel P. *The Soldier and the State: The Theory and Practice of Civil-Military Relations.* Cambridge: Belknap Press, 1957.

____________ *Who Are We? The Challenges to America's National Identity.* New York: Simon and Schuster, 2004.

Hurst III, Cameron. "Death, Honor, and Loyalty: The Bushidō Ideal", in Philosophy East & West, 40:4, 1990.

Ichinokuchi, Tad and Aiso, Daniel eds. *John Aiso and the M.I.S.: Japanese-American Soldiers in the Military Intelligence Service, World War II.* Los Angeles: The Club, 1988.

Ikegami, Eiko. *The Taming of the Samurai: Honorific Individualism and the Making of Modern Japan.* Cambridge, MA: Harvard University Press, 1995.

Iritani, Toshio. *Group Psychology of the Japanese in Wartime.* New York: Kegan Paul International, 1991.

Iriye, Akira. *Power and Culture: The Japanese-American War, 1941-1945.* Cambridge: Harvard University Press, 1981.

____________. *The Origins of the Second World War in Asia and the Pacific.* New York: Longman, 1987.

____________. *Across the Pacific: An Inner History of American-East Asian Relations.* Introduction by John K. Fairbank. New York: Harcourt, 1967.

Johnson, Alasdair. 'Thinking About Strategic Culture' in International Security, 19 (4) 1995.

Karnow, Stanley. *Vietnam: A History.* New York: Penguin Books, 1983.

Kato, Masuo. *The Lost War: A Japanese Reporter's Inside Story.* New York: A. A. Knopf, 1946.

Keegan, John. *The Face of Battle.* Penguin Books, 1976.

____________ *The Second World War.* New York: Penguin Books, 1990.

Kotani, Ken. "Japanese Intelligence in WWII: Successes and Failures". Oxford: Osprey, 2009.

Lacey, Sharon Tosi. *Pacific Blitzkrieg: World War II in the Central Pacific.* Denton: North Texas University Press, 2013.

Lawrence, Christopher A. "Measuring Human Factors in Combat: Modern Wars." *War by Numbers: Understanding Conventional Combat.* Lincoln: University of Nebraska Press, 2017.

Liddell Hart, B.H. *Strategy.* New York: New American Library, 1974.

Lee, Robert. "The Individuation of the Self in Japanese History." *Japanese Journal of Religious Studies* 4, no. 1 (1977).

Lewis, Adrian. *The American Culture of War: The History of U.S. Military Force from World War II to Operation Iraqi Freedom.* New York: Routledge, 2018.

Linn, Brian. *The Echo of Battle: The Army's Way of War.* Cambridge: Harvard University Press, 2007.

Löfstedt, H. 'Duels of Systems and Forces' in B. Boos-Bavnbek and J. Høyrup (eds), *Mathematics and War*. Basel: Birkhäuser, 2003.

Love, Edmond G. *The Hourglass: A History of the 7th Infantry Division in World War II*. Washington D.C.: Infantry Journal Press, 1950.

Lowry, Dave. *Autumn Lightning: The Education of an American Samurai*. Boston and London: Shambhala, 1985.

Lynn, John A. *Battle: A History of Combat and Culture*. Boulder: Westview Press, 2003.

MacMillan, A., Booth, K., and Trood, R, *Strategic Cultures in the Asia-Pacific Region*. Hampshire: Palgrave, 1999.

Mahoney, James. "Path Dependence in Historical Sociology." *Theory and Society* 29, no. 4 (2000): 507–48. http://www.jstor.org/stable/3108585.

Mahnken, Thomas. *Technology and the American Way of War since 1945*. New York: Columbia University Press, 2008.

______________ *United States Strategic Culture*. Defense Threat Reduction Agency, Advanced Systems and Concepts Office, 1996.

Mansoor, Peter. *The GI Offensive in Europe: The Triumph of American Infantry Divisions, 1941-1945*.

Mason, R.H.P. and Caiger, J.G. *A History of Japan*. Rutland, Vermont: Tuttle Publishing, 1997.

Marshall, George C. *The Papers of George Catlett Marshall*, volume. 2, *"We Cannot Delay," July 1, 1939-December 6, 1941*. Edited by Larry I. Bland, Sharon Ritenour Stevens, and Clarence E. Wunderlin, Jr. Lexington: The George C. Marshall Foundation, 1981.

______________ *Selected Speeches and Statements of General of the Army George C. Marshall*, edited by Harvey Arthur de Weerd, (Washington, D.C.: The Infantry Journal, 1945), 121-125.

Marshall, S.L.A. *Island Victory: The Battle of Kwajalein Atoll*. Washington D.C.: The Infantry Journal, 1945.

Maslow, Abraham H. *Toward a Psychology of Being*. New York: Van Nostrand Reinhold, 1968.

Matloff, Maurice. *Strategic Planning for Coalition Warfare, 1943-1944*. The United States Army in World War II. Washington D.C.: Center of Military History, 1959.

____________ *Command Decisions*. Washington, D.C.: Center of Military History, 1984.

Maynard, S. K., *Japanese Communication: Language and Thought in Context*. Honolulu: University of Hawaii Press, 1997.

McClain, James L. *Japan: A Modern History*. New York: W. W. Norton and Company, 2002.

McGinnis, George. *Radio Intelligence in Japanese and American North Pacific Naval and Air Operations, Cryptologic Quarterly*. Cryptologic Documents Collection in the Library of the U.S. Army Military History Institute, Carlisle Barracks, Pennsylvania.

McManus, John C. *The Deadly Brotherhood: The American Combat Soldier in World War II.* New York: Presidio Press, 1988.

_____________ *Fire and Fortitude: The U.S. Army in the Pacific War, 1941-1943.* New York: DUTTON CALIBER, 2019.

_____________ *Island Infernos: The U.S. Army's Pacific War Odyssey, 1944.* New York: Dutton Caliber, 2021.

McNaughton, James C. *Nisei Linguists: Japanese Americans in the Military Intelligence Service in World War II,* Center of Military History Publication 70-99-1. Washington, D.C.: Department of the Army, 2006.

McPherson, James M. *For Cause and Comrades: Why Men Fought in the Civil War.* New York: Oxford University Press, 1997.

Millett, Allan R. "The United States Armed Forces in the Second World War." Chapter Two. In *Military Effectiveness,* edited by Allan R. Millett and Williamson Murray, 2nd edition. Cambridge: Cambridge University Press, 2010.

Moody, Peter R. Jr., *Tradition and Modernization in China and Japan.* Belmont: Wadsworth Publishing Company, 1995.

Moore, Aaron William. *Writing War: Soldiers Record the Japanese Empire.* Cambridge and London: Harvard University Press, 2013.

Moore, Harold G. *We Were Soldiers Once . . . and Young: Ia Drang-The Battle That Changed the War in Vietnam.* New York: Random House, 1992.

Moore, Jeffrey M. *Spies for Nimitz: Joint Military Intelligence in the Pacific War.* Annapolis, MD: Naval Institute Press, 2004.

Morris, Ivan I. *The Nobility of Failure: Tragic Heroes in the History of Japan. New* York: Holt, Rinehart, and Winston, 1975.

Moteki, Hiromichi. *Japan's Master Plan for Victory: What Could Have Been,* translated by Connie Prener. Tokyo: Society for the Dissemination of Historical Fact, 2020.

Moskos, Charles C. Introduction to *Cohesion: The Human Element in Combat.* Washington D.C.: National Defense University Press, 1985.

_____________ *The American Enlisted Man: The Rank and File in Today's Military.* New York: Russell Sage Foundation, 1970.

Murray, Williamson "Why Did It Take the North So Long?", *Military History Quarterly,* Summer 1989, 24-33.

Myers, Michael. *The Pacific War and Contingent Victory: Why Japanese Defeat Was Not Inevitable.* Lawrence: Univ. Press of Kansas, 2015.

Ness, Leland. *Rikugun: Guide to the Japanese Ground Forces, 1937 – 1945, Volume 1: Tactical Organization of Imperial Japanese Army and Navy Ground Forces.* Solihull: Helion and Company, 2014.

Nishida, Kitaro. *Intelligibility and the Philosophy of Nothingness: Three Philosophical Essays,* translated by Robert Shinzinger. Honolulu: East-West Press, 1958.

Nitobe, Inazo. *Bushido: The Soul of Japan.* Tokyo: Teibi Publishing Company, 1907.

Norman, E. Herbert. *Japan's Emergence as a Modern State: Political and Economic Problems of the Meiji Period*. Westport: Greenwood Press, 1940.

Obmascik, Mark. *The Storm on Our Shores: One Island, Two Soldiers, and the Forgotten Battle of World War II*. New York: Simon & Schuster, 2019.

O'Brien, Philips P. *How the War Was Won: Air-Sea Power and Allied Victory in World War II*. Cambridge: Cambridge University Press, 2015.

Ohnuki-Tierney, Emiko, *Kamikaze, Cherry Blossoms, and Nationalisms: The Militarization of Aesthetics in Japanese History*. Chicago: University of Chicago Press, 2002.

Ota, Masahide. *This Was the Battle of Okinawa*. Naha: Naha Publishing, 1981.

Overy, Richard. *Why the Allies Won*. New York: W. W. Norton & Co., 1995.

Palmer, Robert R. and Colton, Joel. *A History of the Modern World*. New York: Alfred A. Knopf. 1991.

Patton, George S. *War As I Knew It*. Boston: Houghton Mifflin Company, 1947.

Pierson, Paul. "Increasing Returns, Path Dependence, and the Study of Politics." *The American Political Science Review* 94, no. 2, June 2000.

Pike, Francis. *Hirohito's War: The Pacific War, 1941-1945*. New York: Bloomsbury, 2016.

______________"The Development of a Death Cult in 1930s Japan and the Decision to Drop the Atom Bomb", Asian Affairs, 47:1, 1-31, (2016).

Possony, S.T. and Pournelle, J.E. *The Strategy of Technology: Winning the Decisive War*. New York: Dunellen, 1970.

Prange, Gordon W. *At Dawn We Slept: The Untold Story of Pearl Harbor*. New York: McGraw-Hill, 1981.

Prefer, Nathan N. *Leyte 1944: The Soldiers' Battle*. Philadelphia and Oxford: CASEMATE, 2012.

Ravina, Mark. *To Stand with the Nations of the World: Japan's Meiji Restoration in World History*. Oxford: Oxford University Press, 2018.

Reischauer, Edwin O. *The Japanese*. Cambridge: Belknap, 1977.

Robinson, Paul, De Lee, Nigel, and Carrick, Don eds., *Ethics Education in the Military*. Aldershot: Ashgate Publishing Company, 2008.

Roland, Alex. 'Technology and War: The Historiographical Revolution of the 1980s', Technology and Culture, 34. 1993.

Ropp, Theodore, A. *War in the Modern World*. Baltimore: Johns Hopkins University Press, 2000.

Rottman, G. *The Marshall Islands 1944: "Operation Flintlock, The Capture of Kwajalein and Eniwetok"*. Oxford: Osprey Publishing Ltd, 2004.

Rose, Arnold. "Bases of American Military Morale in World War II." *The Public Opinion Quarterly* 9, no. 4 (1945).

Sakurai, Tadayoshi. *Human bullets, a soldier's story of Port Arthur*. translated by Masajiro Honda and edited by Alice Mabel Bacon. Boston: Houghton, Mifflin, and Company, 1907.

Sansom, George B. *A History of Japan to 1334*. Stanford: Stanford University Press, 1958.

Sato Hiroaki. *Legends of the Samurai*. New York: Overlook Press, 1995.

______________ "Gyokusai or "Shattering like a Jewel": Reflection on the Pacific War", The Asia-Pacific Journal, February 1, 2008, Volume 6, Issue 2.

Schein, Edgar H. *Organizational Culture and Leadership*. San Francisco: Jossey-Bass, 2010.

______________ "Coming to a New Awareness of Organizational Culture," *Sloan Management Review* 25, no. 2 (Winter 1984).

Schneider, James. Introduction to *The Evolution of Operational Art*, by Georgii Samoilovich Isserson, trans. Bruce Menning. Fort Leavenworth, KS: Combat Studies Institute Press, 2013.

Siebold, Guy L. "The Essence of Military Group Cohesion," Armed Forces and Society, Vol. 33, No. 2, 2007.

Shortal, John F. *Forged by Fire: General Robert L. Eichelberger and the Pacific War*. Columbia: University of South Carolina Press. 1987.

Shils, Edward A. "Primary Groups in the American Army," in *Studies in the Scope and Method of "The American Soldier."* Ed. Robert K. Merton and Paul F. Lazarsfeld. Glencoe: The Free Press, 1950.

Showalter, Denis. "Storm Over the Pacific: Japan's Road to Empire and War, in Daniel Marston, ed. *The Pacific War Companion: From Pearl Harbor to Hiroshima*. New York: Osprey, 2005.

Shultz, H. Jr., *Adapting America's Security Paradigm and Security Agenda*. Washington, DC: National Strategy Information Center, 2010.

Smith, Thomas C. *The Agrarian Origins of Modern Japan*, Stanford: Stanford University Press, 1959.

Spector, Ronald H. *Eagle Against the Sun: The American War with Japan*. New York: Vintage Books, 1985.

Sterling, George. *The History of the Radio Intelligence Division Before and During World War II, 1940 – 1945*.

Strassler, Robert B. Ed., *The Landmark Thucydides: A Comprehensive Guide to The Peloponnesian War*, (New York: Free Press, 1996

Strauss, Ulrich. *The Anguish of Surrender: Japanese POWs of World War II*. Seattle and London: University of Washington Press, 2003.

Swinson, Arthur. *Four Samurai: A Quartet of Japanese Army Commanders in the Second World War*. London: Huchinson, 1968.

Tanaka, Yuki. *Hidden Horrors: Japanese War Crimes in World War II*. Oxford: Westview Press, 1996.

Tarnas, Richard. *The Passion of the Western Mind: Understanding the Ideas That Have Shaped Our World View*. New York: Ballantine, 1991.

______________ *Cosmos and Psyche: Intimations of a New World View*. New York: Viking, 2006.

Toby, Ronald. "Rescuing the Nation from History: The State of the State in Early Modern Japan." *Monumenta Nipponica* 56:2. 2001.

Toland, John. *The Rising Sun: The Decline and Fall of the Japanese Empire, 1936-1945*. New York: Random House, 1970.

Toll, Ian. *The Conquering Tide: War in the Pacific Islands, 1942–1944*. New York: W. W. Norton, 2015.

Trefalt, Beatrice. *Japanese Army Stragglers and Memories of the War in Japan, 1950-1975*. London: RoutledgeCurzon, 2003.

Turner, Gordon B. *A History of Military Affairs in Western Society Since the Eighteenth Century*. New York: Harcourt Brace, 1956.

Ulio, James A. "Military Morale,". *American Journal of Sociology*, vol. 47, no. 3. 1941.

Uz Zaman, Rashed. "Strategic Culture: A "Cultural" Understanding of War". Comparative Strategy, 28:1, 2009.

Van Creveld, Martin. *Fighting Power: German and U.S. Army Performance, 1939-1945*. Westport: Greenwood Press, 1982.

______________ *Technology and War: From 2000 BC to the Present*. New York: Touchstone Books, 1991.

van der Vat, Dan. *The Pacific Campaign: World War II, the U.S.-Japanese Naval War, 1941-1945*. New York: Simon & Schuster, 1991.

Walker, James A., Bernstein, Lewis, Lang, Sharon. "The Eastern Mandates Campaign: Staff Ride Guide for Operation Flintlock, the Seizure of Kwajalein Atoll", Colorado Springs: U.S. Army Space and Missile Defense Command, Historical Office, 2004.

Wheelan, Joseph. *Bloody Okinawa: The Last Great Battle of World War II*. New York: Hatchette Books, 2020.

Winton, John, *Ultra in the Pacific: How Breaking Japanese Codes & Cyphers Affected Naval Operations against Japan 1941-45*. Annapolis: Naval Institute Press, 1993.

Wong, Leonard and Gerras, Stephen J. "Culture and Military Organizations", Chapter 1 in *The Culture of Military Organizations*. edited by Peter R. Mansoor and Williamson Murray. Cambridge: Cambridge University Press, 2019.

Wood, James B. *Japanese Military Strategy in the Pacific War: Was Defeat Inevitable?* New York: Roman & Littlefield Publishers, Inc., 2007.

Wylie, J.C. *Military Strategy: A General Theory of Power Control*. New Brunswick: Rutgers University Press, 1967.

Yamakuse, Yoji. *Japaneseness: A Guide to Virtues and Values*. Berkeley: Stone Bridge Press, 2016.

Yamamoto Tsunetomo. *Hagakure: The Book of the Samurai*, translated by William Scott Wilson. Tokyo: Kodansha International, 1992.

Yamashita, Samuel. *Leaves from an Autumn of Emergencies: Selections from the Wartime Diaries of Ordinary Japanese*. Honolulu: University of Hawai'i Press, 2009

Yonezawa Miyuki; edited by Paul Spickard, *Race and Nation: Ethnic Systems in the Modern World*, New York, and London: Routledge, 2005.

Ziemke, Earl F. "Military Effectiveness in the Second World War." Chapter Eight. In *Military Effectiveness*, edited by Allan R. Millett and Williamson Murray, 2nd edition. Cambridge: Cambridge University Press, 2010.

UNPUBLISHED MANUSCRIPTS

Burklund, Richard A. "Hell in the Mist: The Seventh Infantry Division and the Battle of Attu". Master's thesis, Southern New Hampshire University, 2015.

Cronin, Monica. "U.S. Combat Morale in the World Wars: The European Theater of Operations" (2017). Undergraduate Honors Thesis Paper, College of William and Mary. https://scholarworks.wm.edu/honorstheses/1104.

Johnson, Robert J. "Aleutian Campaign, World War II: Historical Study and Current Perspective." Master's thesis, Army Command and General Staff College, Fort Leavenworth, Kansas, 1992.

Metcalf, Matthew. "The Battle for Attu and the Aleutian Island Campaign". Master's thesis, Army Command and General Staff College, Fort Leavenworth, Kansas, 2014.

Polhamus, John A. "The Aleutian Islands Campaign in World War II: A Strategic Perspective". Master's thesis, Army Command and General Staff College, Fort Leavenworth, Kansas, 2005.

Tooke, Lamar. "Infantry Operations in the Aleutians: The Battle for Attu". Research paper, U.S. Army War College, Carlisle Barracks, Pennsylvania, 1990.

DIGITAL ARCHIVES AND WEBSITES

The Aleutians. "The Japanese in the Aleutians". Web page.

http://aleutians.hlswilliwaw.com/Attu/html/attu-tsukiji-diary-translation.htm.

http://aleutians.hlswilliwaw.com/Attu/html/attu-japanese-nco-diary.htm.

Chronicling America: Historic American Newspapers. The Library of Congress. Websitehttp://chroniclingamerica.loc.gov.

Foreign Correspondents Club of Japan. https://www.fccj.or.jp/number-1-shimbun.html.

Fusou Note. Web page. http://aki-akiaki.blogspot.com/2008/08/diary-of-nobuo-tatsuguchi.html.

Hyperwar: A Hypertext History of the Second World War. Website.

https://www.ibiblio.org/hyperwar/.

Japan Center for Asian Historical Records (JACAR). National Archives of Japan. Website. http://www.jacar.go.jp/english/index.html.

Japan Institute of International Affairs. Website. https://www.jiia-jic.jp/en/.

Japan National Institute for Defense Studies (NIDS). Ministry of Defense. Website. http://www.nids.mod.go.jp/english/.

"Japanese Soldiers of World War II: A Collection of Primary Documents". Website. https://sites.google.com/site/collectionprimarydocuments/home/gyokusai.

Japanese Monographs, The Pacific War Archive. Website.

https://pacificwararchive.wordpress.com/2019/01/27/japanese-monographs/.

Kokuritsu Kobun Shokan [National Archives of Japan]. Website. https://www.digital.archives.go.jp/index_e.html.

Japan National Diet Library Digital Collections. Website. https://dl.ndl.go.jp/?__lang=en

Library of Congress, "Experiencing War: Stories from the Veterans History Project". Website. https://www.loc.gov/vets/stories/ex-war-aleutians.html.

MacArthur Memorial Library and Archive, Norfolk, VA. Website. https://www.macarthurmemorial.org/31/Library-Archives.

The Pacific War Archive. Web page. https://pacificwararchive.wordpress.com

The Stanford Encyclopedia of Philosophy (Summer 2019 Edition), Website. https://plato.stanford.edu/archives/sum2019/entries/japanese-philosophy/.

Shattered Jewels, "Gyokusai" web site. https://shatteredjewels.wordpress.com.

Tokai University, Peace and War On Line, Torikai Lab Network. Web page. http://torikai.starfree.jp/1943/attu.html.

US Air Force Historical Research Agency. Website. https://www.afhra.af.mil/Site_Map.aspx.

US Army Center of Military History, US Army Training and Doctrine Command. Website. https://www.history.army.mil/html/bookshelves/collect/usaww2.html.

US Army Maneuver Center of Excellence Libraries, (MCoE) HQ Donovan Research Library. Website. https://www.benning.army.mil/library/.

US Army Military History Institute, Carlisle, PA, (MHI). Website. https://history.army.mil/html/bookshelves/collect/collect.html.

US Army Heritage and Education Center, US Army War College. Web site. https://arena.usahec.org/?fbclid=IwAR3d4ZkSmfwNxSmqELQ8z5ummq0pfAixBJ39MAyeDyWaUKGCJSbA2l5vCCE.

US Army Combined Arms Research Library, US Army Command and General Staff College. Web site. https://cgsc.contentdm.oclc.org.

US National Archives and Records Administration. Website. https://www.archives.gov/research.

MAPS AND PHOTOGRAPHS

Imperial Japanese Army. *Japanese troops on Attu* [photograph]. Captured by U.S. Army, 1943. Accessed March 19, 2016. https://upload.wikimedia.org/wikipedia/commons/f/f3/AttuJapaneseTroops.jpg

U.S. Army. Tactical Situation, *7th Infantry Division on Attu, 28 May 1943.* [map]. Library of Congress. http://hdl.loc.gov/loc.pnp/fsa.8e01339.

U.S. Amy Signal Corps. *Fighting in the Jarmin Pass.* 26-27 May 1943. [photograph]. Accessed March 19, 2016. http://vilda.alaska.edu/cdm/search/searchterm/Battle%20of%20Attu/order/nosort).

U.S. Army Signal Corps. *7th Division troops after taking a Japanese trench.* [photograph]. May 1943'. Accessed March 19, 2016. http://vilda.alaska.edu/cdm/search/searchterm/Battle%20of%20Attu/order/nosort).

U.S. Army Signal Corps. *American troops hauling supplies forward.* [photograph]. Accessed March 19, 2016. http://vilda.alaska.edu/cdm/search/searchterm/Battle%20of%20Attu/order/nosort). National Archives.

U.S. Army Signal Corps. *Evacuating an American casualty.* May 1943. [photograph]. Accessed March 19, 2016. http://www.nps.gov/places/attu-battlefield-and-us-army-and-naval-airfields.htm) Hanna-Call Collection, University of Alaska, Fairbanks, and National Park Service.

U.S. Army Signal Corps. *Colonel Zimmerman and Captain Mapes.* May 1943. [photograph]. http://vilda.alaska.edu/cdm/search/searchterm/Battle%20of%20Attu/order/nosort National Archives 2, Record Group 111-156-174146. Accessed March 19, 2016.

U.S. Amy Signal Corps. *American 60mm mortar firing in support of riflemen.* May 1943. [photograph]. http://vilda.alaska.edu/cdm/search/searchterm/Battle%20of%20Attu/order/nosort).

National Archives 2, Record Group 111-157-174502. Accessed March 19, 2016.

U.S. Navy. *Massacre Bay, Attu, 11 May 1943.* [photograph]. Accessed March 19, 2016. http://www.theatlantic.com/photo/2011/08/world-war-ii-battle-of-midway-and-the-aleutian-campaign/100137/).

U.S. Navy. *Fish Hook Ridge.* May 1943. [photograph]. http://vilda.alaska.edu/cdm/search/searchterm/Battle%20of%20Attu/order/nosort

National Archives 2, Record Group 208). Accessed March 19, 2016.

United States Army in World War II, Pictorial Record: The War Against Japan, The U.S. Army Center of Military History. *Training at the Jungle Training Center.* [photograph]. 1943.

United States Army in World War II, Pictorial Record: The War Against Japan, The U.S. Army Center of Military History. *The effects of the bombardment of Japanese defenses on Kwajalein atoll.* [photograph]. 1944.

United States Army in World War II, Pictorial Record: The War Against Japan, The U.S. Army Center of Military History.*7th Infantry Division fighting on Kwajalein Island.* [photograph]. January 1944.

United States Army in World War II, Pictorial Record: The War Against Japan, The U.S. Army Center of Military History. *7th Infantry Division soldiers use flamethrowers to drive Japanese soldiers from a blockhouse on Kwajalein atoll.* [photograph]. January 1944.

United States Army in World War II, Pictorial Record: The War Against Japan, The U.S. Army Center of Military History. *The Victors on Kwajalein Island.* [photograph].

United States Army in World War II, Pictorial Record, The War Against Japan. [photograph]. *A 7th Infantry Division rifleman examines a firing position on the Pinnacle.* U.S. Army Center of Military History.

United States Army in World War II, Pictorial Record, The War Against Japan. *A typical Japanese defensive position on Okinawa.* [photograph]. U.S. Army Center of Military History.

United States Army in World War II, Pictorial Record: The War Against Japan. [photograph]. *Attacking the Rocky Crags.* The U.S. Army Center of Military History.

United States Army in World War II, Pictorial Record: The War Against Japan. [photograph]. *A tank-infantry team breach a minefield as the approach enemy defenses.* The U.S. Army Center of Military History.

United States Army in World War II, Pictorial Record, The War Against Japan. [photograph]. *Japanese soldiers emerge from a cave to surrender to the 7th Infantry Division.* U.S. Army Center of Military History.

The U.S. Army Campaigns of World War II: Eastern Mandates, CMH Pub 72-23. *Operation Flintlock Scheme of Maneuver.* [map]. https://commons.wikimedia.org/w/index.php?curid=47139000

The U.S. Army Campaigns of World War II: Eastern Mandates. *Assault Landings, Kwajalein 1944.* [map]. https://commons.wikimedia.org/w/index.php?curid=47139000).

The U.S. Army Campaigns of World War II: Eastern Mandates. *Third Day, Kwajalein, February 1944.* [map]. https://commons.wikimedia.org/w/index.php?curid=47139000).

US Army Campaigns of World War II. *Invasion of Leyte.* [map]. http://www.ibiblio.org/hyperwar/USA/USA-C-Leyte/maps/USA-C-Leyte-3.jpg Accessed 19 Nov 2021.

U.S. Army Campaigns of World War II: Leyte. *Invasion of Leyte, 20 October 1944.* [photograph]. National Archives.

U.S. Army Campaigns of World War II: Eastern Mandates. *Last Day of the battle of Kwajalein.* February 1944. [map]. https://commons.wikimedia.org/w/index.php?curid=47139000).

The Return to the Philippines, U.S. Army in World War II, The War in the Pacific. *XXIV Corps Landings, 20 October 1944.* [map]. https://www.ibiblio.org/hyperwar/USA/USA-P-Return/maps/USA-P-Return-6.jpg Accessed 19 Nov 2021.

Leyte: The Return to the Philippines, U.S. Army in World War II, The War in the Pacific. *The 7th Infantry Division's Advance to Dagami.* [map]. https://www.ibiblio.org/hyperwar/USA/USA-P-Return/maps/USA-P-Return-6.jpg Accessed 19 Nov 2021.

U.S. Army Campaigns of World War II: Leyte. *American infantrymen in cautious advance against enemy machine gun nest, Leyte, 21 Oct 1944.* [photograph]. National Archives. https://history.army.mil/brochures/leyte/leyte.htm

U.S. Army Campaigns of World War II: Leyte. *Mortarmen fire 81mm mortar in attack, Leyte, 1944.* [photograph]. National Archives. https://www.army.mil/article/252972/christmas_day_1944_7id_u_s_forces_secure_leyte_philippines)

Appleman, Roy E., Burns, James M., Gugeler, Russel A., and Stevens, John. *The U.S. Army in World War II: The War in the Pacific, Okinawa: The Last Battle.* Washington D.C.: Center of Military History, 1993. [map]. *Tenth Army Invasion Plan, Okinawa, April 1945.* Washington DC: Center of Military History, 1948, 2000.

Appleman, Roy E., Burns, James M., Gugeler, Russel A., and Stevens, John. *The U.S. Army in World War II: The War in the Pacific, Okinawa: The Last Battle.* Washington D.C.: Center of Military History, 1993. [map]. *At the Pinnacle: Fighting through the outposts to the Shuri Line, 4-6 April 1945.* Washington DC: Center of Military History, 1948/2000. United States Army Center of Military History.

U.S. Army Space and Missile Defense Command Historical Office, 'The Eastern Mandates Campaign: A Staff Ride Guide for Operation FLINTLOCK; The Seizure of Kwajalein Atoll'. *Typical Japanese Beach Defensive Fortification.* [photograph]. 2004. National Archives.

U.S. Army Space and Missile Defense Command Historical Office, 'The Eastern Mandates Campaign: A Staff Ride Guide for Operation FLINTLOCK; The Seizure of Kwajalein Atoll'. *Attacking a Japanese bunker.* [photograph]. 2004, National Archives.

U.S. Army Space and Missile Defense Command Historical Office, 'The Eastern Mandates Campaign: A Staff Ride Guide for Operation FLINTLOCK; The Seizure of Kwajalein Atoll'. *7th Infantry Division soldier eating lunch behind a destroyed Japanese pillbox.* [photograph]. 2004, National Archives.

Appleman, Roy E., Burns, James M., Gugeler, Russel A., and Stevens, John. *The U.S. Army in World War II: The War in the Pacific, Okinawa: The Last Battle.* Washington D.C.: Center of Military History, 1993. [photograph]. *The Pinnacle, 5-6 April 1945.* Washington DC: Center of Military History, 1948/2000.

Appleman, Roy E., Burns, James M., Gugeler, Russel A., and Stevens, John. *The U.S. Army in World War II: The War in the Pacific, Okinawa: The Last Battle.* Washington D.C.: Center of Military History, 1993. [map]. *Stalemate at Kochi Ridge, 25 April – 3 May 45.* The U.S. Army in World War II, Washington DC: Center of Military History, 1948/2000.

Appleman, Roy E., Burns, James M., Gugeler, Russel A., and Stevens, John. *The U.S. Army in World War II: The War in the Pacific, Okinawa: The Last*

Battle. Washington D.C.: Center of Military History, 1993. [map]. *The Japanese Counteroffensive.* The U.S. Army in World War II, Washington DC: Center of Military History, 1948/2000. Accessed 27 May 2022. http://www.ibiblio.org/hyperwar/USA/USA-P-Okinawa/maps/USA-P-Okinawa-37.jpg.

Appleman, Roy E., Burns, James M., Gugeler, Russel A., and Stevens, John. *The U.S. Army in World War II: The War in the Pacific, Okinawa: The Last Battle.* Washington D.C.: Center of Military History, 1993. [photograph]. *Japanese rocket fire in support of the 4-5 May 45 counteroffensive.* The U.S. Army in World War II, Washington DC: Center of Military History, 1948/2000.

Appleman, Roy E., Burns, James M., Gugeler, Russel A., and Stevens, John. *The U.S. Army in World War II: The War in the Pacific, Okinawa: The Last Battle.* Washington D.C.: Center of Military History, 1993 [photograph]. *Night attack on Yaeju Dake.* The U.S. Army in World War II, Washington DC: Center of Military History, 1948/2000.

Cannon, M. Hanlon, *The U.S. Army in World War II: The War in the Pacific, Leyte: The Return to the Philippines,* 'Chapter XV, Battle of the Ridges. *Battle of Shoestring Ridge.'* U.S. Army in World War II, The War in the Pacific. [map]. Office of the Chief of Military History, 1964, 2000. (https://www.ibiblio.org/hyperwar/USA/USA-P-Return/maps/USA-P-Return-13.jpg).

Conn, Stetson, Engelman, Rose and Fairchild, Byron. *The United States Army in World War II: The Western Hemisphere: Guarding the United States and its Outposts.* "Chapters IX/X/XI". *The Capture of Attu.* [map]. Washington D.C.: Office of the Chief of Military History, 1964, 2000. https://commons.wikimedia.org/w/index.php?curid=259311.

Huber, Thomas, *Japan's Battle of Okinawa, April-June 1945,* Leavenworth Papers Number 18, Combat Studies Institute, U.S. Army Command and General Staff College. [map]. *The Japanese 32d Army Defensive Plan.* Fort Leavenworth, Kansas, 1990.

INDEX